A JOURNEY TRAVELLED

A JOURNEY TRAVELLED

Aboriginal-European relations at Albany and the surrounding region from first contact to 1926

Murray Arnold

UWA PUBLISHING

First published in 2015 by
UWA Publishing
Crawley, Western Australia 6009
www.uwap.uwa.edu.au

THE UNIVERSITY OF
WESTERN AUSTRALIA

Copyright © Murray Arnold 2015

ISBN: 978-1-74258-663-2
A full CIP data entry is available from the National Library of Australia

Typeset in Bembo by Lasertype
Printed by Lightning Source

The Charles and Joy Staples South West region publications fund was established in 1984 on the basis of a generous donation to The University of Western Australia by Charles and Joy Staples.

The purpose of the Fund was to make the results of research on the South West region of Western Australia widely available so as to assist the people of the South West region and those in government and private organisations concerned with South West projects to appreciate the needs and possibilities of the region in the widest possible historical perspective.

The Fund is administered by a committee whose aims are to make possible the publication (either by full or part funding), by UWA Publishing, of research in any discipline relevant to the South West region.

CONTENTS

ACKNOWLEDGEMENTS

This book began as a PhD thesis completed in 2012 under the supervision of Associate Professor Charlie Fox of the History Department of the University of Western Australia.

Many people have willingly assisted with specialised knowledge, suggestions and practical support. I wish to acknowledge in particular, Charlie Fox, Robert Reynolds, Bob Reece, Barbara Black, Holly Ruscoe, Jane and Brian Taylor, Harvey Arnold, Vernice Gillies, Mark Chambers, David Bird, Joan Fox, Neville Green, Averil Dean, John Dowson, Malcolm Trail, Glenda Williams, Arly Egerton-Warburton, Bob Howard, Eugene Eades, Ray Garstone, Douglas Selleck, Tiffany Shellam, Maxine Laurie, Ian Conochie, Bill Hassell, Harley Coyne, Tim Rowse, Albert Knapp, John Clapin, Sim Clapin, Lyndal Ryan, Carol Pettersen, David and Nan Anderson, Roger Arnold, Andrew Knight, Sue Smith, and the staff at the Western Australian Public Records Office.

Lynette Knapp has been particularly helpful in passing on to me some of her extensive knowledge about her family's history, and I am greatly indebted to her for her cooperation.

Finally, I thank my family and friends for their sustained interest and encouragement, and express gratitude to my wife, Val, for her unwavering support and assistance over many years.

AUTHOR'S NOTE

This book necessarily includes some statistical information, principally about numbers of Aboriginal and European people who inhabited various towns and rural areas in the wider Albany region at differing times during the period of one hundred years it covers. Readers may periodically find it useful to refer to Appendix 3, where much of the information is presented in tabular form.

The book contains images of Aboriginal people now deceased.

LIST OF MAPS AND ILLUSTRATIONS

Introduction

A glance at the Australian history section of any major bookshop shows that the story of human habitation of the Australian continent is rich and varied, yet one will find almost nothing on the shelves dealing with either of the two topics that arguably far outweigh all others in importance – the arrival of the first humans to our shores about 50,000 years ago, and the story of how the Aboriginal people and European settlers interacted with each other during the extended period following the invasion that took place in the eighteenth and nineteenth centuries. Although details of the first event remain sketchy and open to conjecture, there has always been a wealth of documentary and oral information available about the second. What has been lacking until quite recently is the sense among historians and the general Australian public that the history of Aboriginal–European relations, not only for the first few years of contact but for a period of many decades, is absolutely central to our nation's story.

N

100km

Moore River

New Norcia

Northam

Bruce Rock

Perth

York

Beverley

GREAT SOUTHERN
RAILWAY

Bunbury

Carrolup

Katanning

Kojonup

Eticup

Broomehill

Gnowangerup

Tambellup

Jerramungup

Gordon River

Cranbrook

Bremer Bay

Tenterden

Stirling Ranges

Kendenup

Cape Leeuwin

Frankland River

Kalgan River

Hay River

Mt Barker

Warriup

Walpole

Denmark

Albany

Torbay

South-west Western Australia

2

King River

Kalgan River

N↑

Oyster
Harbour

1. Government Farm
2. Railways Football
   Ground
3. Parade St Site –
   site of garrison
4. Mt Melville
5. Mt Adelaide
6. Mt Clarence

2.

4.   1.

3. ALBANY   Middleton
     6.   Bay
          5.

Michaelmas
Island

Princess
Royal
Harbour

King George
Sound

Breaksea Island

Southern Ocean

5km

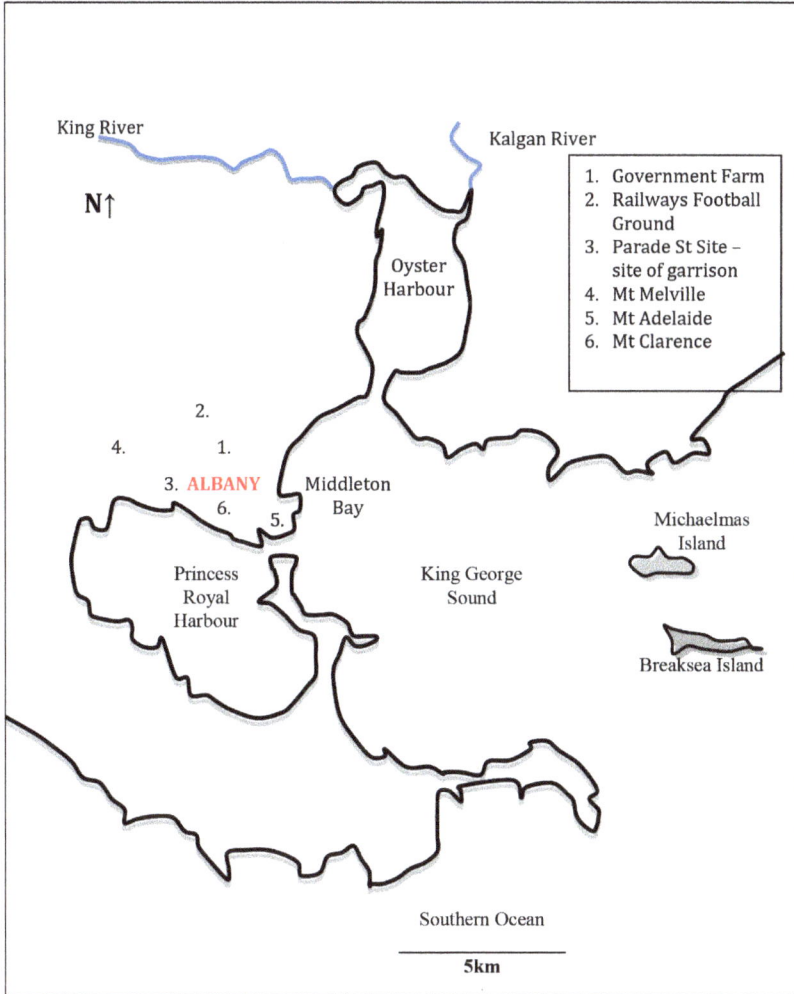

King George Sound; the Town of Albany and its environs

Following the introduction of the pivotally important White Australia Policy soon after Federation in 1901, there was an almost universal tendency for Australians to treat the history of Aboriginal dispossession with an embarrassed silence. It was widely felt that Australians needed to feel pride in their newly formed nation and its place in the British Empire – a pride that historians generally believe was not to take root fully until the events at Gallipoli in 1915 – and any criticism of those who had settled the land was therefore not welcomed. Popular national narratives portrayed early settlers as worthy pioneers who had braved drought, bushfire, flood and isolation, and had from time to time been forced to put up with briefly mentioned and largely unspecified difficulties caused by a small Aboriginal population that somehow faded away as the frontier expanded under the 'civilising' influence of the British. During the early to mid twentieth century Australian historians concentrated almost exclusively on economic and political history, and virtually ignored any serious study of Aboriginal–European relations on the Australian frontier.

This extraordinary situation persisted with very few exceptions until the intense cultural and political foment that occurred throughout the Western world in the decade of the 1960s inevitably impacted upon the history departments of Australian universities. Asian and African decolonisation movements, the struggle for African-American Civil Rights in the USA, the Vietnam War and the rise of the New Left were all influential in a trend towards radicalisation in Australian academic circles. The 1965 Yirrkala bark petition, the 1967 Referendum, the Gurinji people's strike for equal wages and land rights, and the rise of new, radical, articulate and effective spokespersons from among the Aboriginal community focused this trend upon Aboriginal issues. Historians began to show how Aboriginal people, the prior owners of the continent, had been brutally dispossessed of their heritage by the process of colonisation, indeed that colonisation explicitly *demanded* dispossession. For the first time, Australians were confronted by the reality of their past as the old reluctance to write about the history of Aboriginal–European relations came to an abrupt end.

Although pressures outside and within Australia had been building towards a fundamental shift in the way that historians treated Aboriginal–European relations, observers are over-whelmingly of the opinion that the 1968 ABC Boyer Lectures delivered by the noted anthropologist W. E. H. Stanner were instrumental in making the critical breakthrough. There were five lectures in the series, but it was the second, 'The Great Australian Silence', that had the greatest impact. Stanner challenged historians to begin to take Aboriginal history seriously. Charles Rowley and Henry Reynolds were two of the first to rise to this challenge with the publication of a number of very influential books in the 1970s demonstrating for the first time the level and nature of the violence that had accompanied European settlement throughout the Australian continent.

In time, a reaction set in against published histories that some historians regarded as focusing unduly on European atrocities and Aboriginal maltreatment. In 1987 Perth-based historian Bob Reece wrote:

> In their enthusiasm to document the bloodiness of the process of colonisation, Reynolds and others have not been so interested in documenting and highlighting that other major characteristic of Aboriginal–European interaction: accommodation.[1]

Reece also contended that while the new historians had correctly noted the inaccuracy of the old idea that Aborigines simply 'faded away' as Europeans settled on their traditional lands, they were wrong in asserting that Aboriginal resistance to invasion had been the standard response throughout the continent. He and others showed how some Aboriginal people had chosen not to oppose white settlement, and had instead made attempts to adapt their traditional way of life to accommodate the new realities.

Although the new wave of historians principally centred their attention on the national scene, some began to take up the challenge of writing histories that focused upon Aboriginal–European interaction at the level of individual colonies or states. However, vital as these histories are – not least because it is at the national and state levels that Aboriginal policies are formulated and implemented – they can lack the immediacy, intimacy and gritty relevance of works that focus in on the story at the *local* level. My own experience has convinced me that there are many Australians interested in the history of Aboriginal–European interaction in their town and district who find it frustrating that the only information they are able to access relates to a national or very broad regional level. In most cases, they have no alternative to decades-old shire-based histories written by people with no specific interest in Aboriginal history, almost all of whom treat the story of Aboriginal–European relations briefly as a side issue to the main story of settler pioneers and their achievements.

This study adopts a fresh and fundamentally different approach by focusing on Aboriginal–European relations in one major town and its hinterland over a period of one hundred years. Instead of this relationship being treated as one small part of the greater story of the town and region's progress from small beginnings to the present, it forms the central core around which events and changes take place.

Albany is the port and principal centre of Western Australia's Great Southern region, and is today a thriving and beautiful city with 33,000 inhabitants. Situated on the shore of Princess Royal Harbour, a large body of sheltered water connected by a narrow channel to the wide expanse of King George Sound, Albany has one of the few safe anchorages along the continent's rugged south coast. European settlement of Albany began two-and-a-half years prior to the arrival of the *Parmelia* at the Swan River, the event that is officially regarded as marking the beginning of British settlement of Western Australia. For much of the nineteenth century it was only Albany's extensive natural harbour and her situation on the route between Britain and eastern Australia that allowed the settlement to remain viable. The economic development and population growth that occurred in other areas of south-western Australia largely bypassed Albany and the surrounding region because the natural extreme infertility of most of the area's soils prevented the establishment of profitable farms in all but a few favoured pockets. The slow rate of development for the first hundred years of settlement allowed Aboriginal people to retain elements of their traditional way of life for an extended period in a way that was not possible in many of the other settled areas of the colony and state.

After commencing research, it soon became apparent that there was a need to cover a considerably wider area than the townsite and immediate surrounds of Albany. The region's Menang people had always moved throughout an extensive area, and this did not cease with the arrival of European invaders. As pastoralists and others began taking up holdings away from the initial settlement at Albany, the story of contact and interaction spread ever wider from the town. The geographical boundaries set for this history – from Denmark to Frankland River, Kojonup, Katanning, Jerramungup to Bremer Bay – are necessarily somewhat arbitrary, but reflect research-based evidence showing that most Aboriginal people and settlers living within them had significant ties to Albany. This area is somewhat larger than that usually regarded as comprising the traditional land of the Menang group from the King George Sound region. However, the extension of the boundaries to include what is more or less the Great Southern region is justified by evidence indicating that from about the mid nineteenth century their members moved relatively freely throughout the extended area. This is a local history, but one that recognises that the concept of 'local' can sometimes best be defined by people's movements, rather than by strict geographical constraints.

Historians such as Neville Green and Tiffany Shellam have written extensively about the first five years of the settlement when Albany was a military garrison, before land became available for purchase by free settlers. This very early period of Albany's history is fascinating because of the unusual opportunity it provides to study relations between Europeans and Aborigines during their first few years together in a context of co-operation rather than exploitation – a very different context to that which typified the nineteenth-century Australian frontier. However, almost nothing has been written about how the relationship between the two groups at Albany developed once unrestricted settlement began and the inevitable European usurpation of Aboriginal land took hold.

Albany is not the only place in Western Australia where historians have tended to concentrate upon the early contact period when writing about Aboriginal–European interaction. Extraordinarily, no comprehensive study has been published of Aboriginal–European relations anywhere in the state's south-west between 1840 and 1900. This study breaks this pattern by looking at the relationship prior to the establishment of Western Australia's first British settlement in late 1826, and then tracing the story through to Albany's Centenary celebrations in late 1927. The book has been written from a social history perspective, and shows how decisions made by Europeans at all levels affected the lives of Aboriginal people living in the region.

Not all of the Aboriginal people who lived in the region permanently or temporarily prior to 1927 had ancestral links to Albany; indeed some had no such ties to *any* part of the area covered by this book. However, as this is a study of Aboriginal–European relations in general, rather than a history purely concerned with those Aboriginal people originally from Albany and its hinterland, all Aborigines who lived part or all of their lives in the region are of interest to the story.

The shape of the book has been determined partly by the availability of documents. There is a wealth of relevant official letters, police records, court transcripts, and Protectors' reports held at the State Records Office at Perth, and the Battye Library holds many other semi-official and unofficial documents such as newspapers, church records, and diaries. The Local History Section of the Albany Public Library holds published local histories, newspapers, and unpublished letters and diaries from the region. The works of other historians have also proved an invaluable resource. In making use of both official and unofficial documents, I have been acutely aware that they were all written by men and (much less frequently) women for their own reasons. I have therefore read them critically in an attempt to see what may have been actually happening without being specifically spelt out. Wherever the sources allow, I have discussed how Aboriginal people reacted to European presence and European decisions, and acted in ways that reflected their own perceived best interests.

Local history was once disdained by academic historians, but is now widely appreciated for its ability to bring together at an intimate level many different aspects of the life of a community, such as land use, social structure and religion. This increasing interest in local history is a reaction against globalisation, and reflects a growing desire to make a claim for the role of place and space in understanding ourselves. Gender, race, ethnicity, class and other distinctions are important, but none of these confer the ability to locate oneself in the space in which we spend our lives. This does not mean that we should abandon national and international perspectives for a purely local outlook, but that historians should keep in mind the importance of all three perspectives. To focus on the shared Australian experience to the detriment of diversified Australian experiences is to do injustice to history. Albany represents a classic opportunity to demonstrate the power of local history to illustrate this diversity.

Albany and its hinterland, perhaps uniquely in the Australian experience, deserves the label of the 'friendly frontier' because of the amicable relationship that developed following the arrival of the first Europeans to settle there. However, we will see how the initial era of friendship gradually but surely gave way to a relationship that differed very little from other regions of south-west Western Australia. The Albany region had its own unique set of geographical, political and human circumstances, all of which helped determine how its Aboriginal and European people related to each other during the first hundred years after the British established their settlement. Aboriginal people were not simply manipulated by Europeans – they made choices that varied between resistance and accommodation, and I have sought to give these choices due attention and respect.

Once the British Government decided to establish a settlement on the west coast of the Australian continent, the die was cast. No one has yet been able to devise any realistic combination of enlightened official policy and benevolent intent on the part of those Europeans who entered the Aboriginal world, either through choice or compulsion, that could have led to a long-term situation devoid of injustice. As we today look back on earlier philosophies, perspectives and decisions, we are able to see that many things ought to have been approached in a different manner. However, this should not preclude us from acknowledging that the men and women from both the Aboriginal and European communities at Albany negotiated the complex circumstances and relationships of colonial invasion in a way that has few, if any, parallels in Australian history.

Chapter One

The Original Inhabitants of the Albany Region

Until the late eighteenth century, the Aboriginal inhabitants of the region around King George Sound had no reason to doubt that their way of life and their uncontested possession of the land would ever be challenged. Their religion provided a holistic explanation for both the creation of their country, of which they were an integral part, and their role in nurturing it. The land gave them a reliable and wholly sustainable source of all of their physical needs, and their culture ensured spiritual and social well-being. What is known of their existence prior to the arrival of strangers from another world, who would bring about profound and permanent disruption?

Archaeologists have yet to reach a consensus about an approximate date for the first arrival of humans to the Australian continent, although significant advances in the last thirty years in the field of radiometric dating have allowed known ancient sites of

Aboriginal occupation to be dated more accurately. Writing in the December 2003 edition of the journal *Australian Archaeology*, Allen and O'Connell noted that the difficulty is not one of dating technologies; rather it is an archaeological debate about artefact context and the rate of deposition and decay of organisms, and until these issues receive sufficient attention, the problem of establishing a definitive date will remain unresolved. The oldest site yet excavated and dated in Western Australia is at Devil's Lair, a large limestone cave in the Margaret River region in the state's south-west. Radiocarbon dating from a series of ancient hearths gives evidence for human occupation dating beyond 40,000 years BP (before present), and possibly as early as 46,000 years BP. It is unlikely that the antiquity of human colonisation of Australia will ever be precisely resolved, but the consensus view of archaeologists is that the most likely date lies between 45,000 years BP and 60,000 years BP.[1]

Not all Aboriginal people fully accept such archaeological evidence. Writing in 1979, Aboriginal historian Jack Davis expressed his belief that the whole concept of human migration to Australia was flawed:

> There is a strong possibility that when the archaeologists dig a little deeper they will find that the indigenes never migrated here, but are the spawn from an Australian cradle of mankind.[2]

When the *Historical Encyclopedia of Western Australia* was published in 2009, Jill Milroy's contribution, 'Aboriginal culture and society', made the same claim, stating that 'many' Aboriginal people hold to the view.[3]

The oldest identified site of human occupation in the Albany region is an area around the Upper Kalgan Hall, approximately 20 kilometres north of the Albany CBD. A nearby rocky bar stretches across the Kalgan River providing a convenient fording place where Aboriginal people could cross except in times of exceptionally high water levels. It also marks where the river ceases to be tidal, with salt water on the southern side and fresh water on the northern side as far as the Stirling Ranges. These two features made the area a significant camping location where a wide variety of food could be obtained. The site was first identified and excavated by the archaeologist W. Ferguson in 1978, and is surrounded by extensive artefact scatters where the ground has been disturbed by road-making machinery. Ferguson obtained a date of 19,000 years BP for the site; however, artefactual material extended 50 centimetres below the dated layers of ancient hearth material and it is considered likely that future carbon dating of this will provide evidence for an even earlier date of human habitation in the Albany region.[4] There is evidence that the coastline near Albany was 30 kilometres south of its present position 6,000 years ago and, since Aboriginal people favoured coastal areas because of their rich food resources, it is reasonable to assume that many even earlier sites of human habitation lie submerged inaccessibly under the Southern Ocean.[5]

It is obviously an impossible task to compile a complete and accurate description of the lifestyle and beliefs of the Aboriginal people of the Albany region prior to the arrival of the first Europeans. It is now more than 200 years since first contacts were made between the two groups, and although a number of local Aboriginal people have significant cultural knowledge of bush foods and other aspects of their deep past, none would claim to be able to reconstruct completely their ancestral mode of living and systems of belief. We have to rely upon archaeological traces, as well as information obtained and recorded by a few untrained observers among the first European visitors and settlers, and this reliance must always produce difficulties. In the absence of a written Aboriginal language, Europeans could gain information only through conversations with co-operative Aboriginal informants, and their own observations. The accurate transferral of complex information about the subtleties of a culture requires experienced observers possessing a comprehensive understanding of the group's spoken language, and given that these conditions did not exist at Albany, it is certain that an incomplete and in places inaccurate account was recorded. It is also possible that some Aboriginal spokespeople seeking to protect secret and sacred aspects of their culture purposely conveyed misleading information, and there may have been an unwillingness on the part of others to co-operate with what they saw as an invasive and pointless activity.

When they arrived at King George Sound on the *Amity* in 1826 as part of a group sent to establish a British military garrison commanded by Major Edmund Lockyer, those who observed and attempted to record aspects of the culture of the local Aboriginal people faced the major barrier of language. Since there were approximately 500 languages spoken in Australia in 1788, it would have been a futile exercise for the British to have brought with them an interpreter from one of the Aboriginal groups near Sydney.[6] The communication barriers facing the new arrivals at Albany must have been formidable.

However, as the next chapter illustrates, the British who arrived and set up the military garrison were not the first of their countrymen to have spent time at King George Sound, and those who came with Lockyer found that some of the local Aboriginal people had some capacity, however basic, to speak and understand the English language. Fortunately, some of the new arrivals were greatly interested in learning about and recording details of the Aboriginal people and their way of life, and took the time to build on this prior knowledge of English and form a new language that enabled some verbal communication to take place. Communication between Aborigines and Europeans at Albany prior to and during the first few years of European settlement was not at a sophisticated level, yet a surprising amount of information could be passed on and recorded.

By far the most valuable information comes from four remarkable men who lived at the Sound for varying periods during the first twelve years of the settlement's existence, and their observations form the major part of the primary source material used in this chapter. Isaac Scott Nind arrived on the *Amity* in late 1826, and remained in the post of Assistant Surgeon until his departure in October 1829. Captain Collet Barker arrived in late November 1829, and soon took up the post of commandant, a position he held until he left the Sound in early March 1831 when the military settlement ceased being governed by New South Wales and became administratively a part of the Colony of Western Australia. He kept a comprehensive and fascinating daily journal which was transcribed by John Mulvaney and Neville Green and published as *Commandant of Solitude* in 1992. Dr Alexander Collie spent from September 1830 to January 1831 as Naval Surgeon at the Sound, returning as Albany's first Resident Magistrate in March of that year. He remained there until late 1832, when he returned to Perth to take up the post of Colonial Surgeon.[7] James Browne arrived in 1836 with his parents – his father held the position of Commissary General at King George Sound – and left two years later. Although he was aged only fifteen when he moved to Albany, his writings show that he was a keen observer of Albany's Aboriginal people.

Almost all of the recorded discussions that occurred between Europeans seeking to understand the local Aboriginal society, and informants from within that society, were carried out by these four European men and their male Aboriginal acquaintances – men speaking with men. Thus, any impressions we have of the position of Aboriginal women are incomplete, and suffer from a lack of balance that could only have been redressed by female recorders discussing their observations directly with the women themselves. Anthropologist Diane Bell noted that this problem was still very much in evidence in Australia in the 1980s, when her assertion that models of culture that did not take into account women's views of that culture were skewed was not universally accepted by her fellows. She points out that all ethnography is gender inflected, and her work with Aboriginal women in Central Australia showed that descriptions of culture where neither the interviewer nor any of the interviewees were women are less than satisfactory.[8] Obviously, this presents a dilemma for historians basing their assumptions about the role of Aboriginal women at Albany purely on Nind, Barker, Collie and Browne's findings.

Influential Australian anthropologist Catherine Berndt spent her lifetime interviewing Aboriginal women across the continent; in the eulogy he delivered at her funeral in 1994, Dr John Stanton said 'no other Westerner has had the privilege…of working with so many Aboriginal women across the continent'.[9] Berndt wrote:

> Aboriginal women, on the whole, in Western Australia as in other parts of the continent, probably had a greater measure of independence – economically, domestically and personally – than their European–Australian counterparts did (and do?)…they have a *positive* image to draw on.[10]

She described the maintenance of Aboriginal society across Australia as a collective, co-operative endeavour in which women played a significant, and at times crucial, role. She rejected the notion that women were little more than suppliers of babies and regarded as intellectual inferiors whose role was confined to providing food and physical comfort to the rest of the Aboriginal population.

Berndt's views command deep respect given her experience and eminence in this field. The dilemma arises when one examines the accounts written by early observers at Albany, who uniformly give a picture of Aboriginal women that appears strongly at odds with the tone of Berndt's views. It is therefore my intention to present their observations for what they are: eyewitness accounts certainly, but accounts written by anthropologically untrained males who had little opportunity or ability to discuss their impressions with the Aboriginal women about whom they were writing. It is instructive to note that Nind was aware of his inadequacy when dealing with this subject:

> Their customs, however, as regards their women are not only very curious, but also so intricate, and involved in so many apparent contradictions and singularities, that it is probable we have been mistaken in some of them.[11]

Collie observed:

> The female…seems to be esteemed rather as a precious article of possession, a valuable slave, than entitled to all the rights, human and divine, of the other sex, – far less receiving the support, protection and devonement [devotion?] which their fair sex demands…[12]

He described how an Aboriginal man prepared an animal for food, taking the best parts for himself and throwing a lesser part to his wife 'not to a dog, but in the same way'.[13] Nind noted: 'but their treatment of women is not always gentle, and many of them have spear wounds in the legs or thighs inflicted by their husbands'.[14] Marital infidelity could result in a woman receiving wounds, or even being killed.[15] Browne found them to be in a state 'of wretchedness which beggars description'.[16]

There is no doubt that the British during the early settlement period, whether accurately or mistakenly, felt that Aboriginal women were often badly mistreated and valued by their husbands as possessions rather than as companions.

From the written records left by Nind, Barker, Collie and others it is possible to ascertain that a form of language described by linguists as 'Pidgin' was progressively developed and used as a means of communication between members of both groups at the Sound. Although such languages may eventually evolve into completely functional means of communication, the evidence suggests this had not fully occurred at the new settlement at the time the principal British recorders were researching and writing their material. Several written examples of conversations that took place there at the time give some idea of the difficulties faced, and illustrate the high degree of uncertainty often felt about the subject matter under discussion. Those seeking to understand Aboriginal culture via such conversations were obviously aware of the problem. Barker wrote in his journal: 'If one could understand their language thoroughly, they would be very manageable'.[17]

The European observers at Albany were amateurs in the field of ethnography, but they had the priceless benefit of very close contact with the people whose lives they were studying. To have had present in such a tiny settlement three educated men with the ability and interest to form close friendships with several of the original inhabitants, together with an inquisitive and observant young man, is quite remarkably fortunate. That there were also a number of Aboriginal men who were sufficiently interested and generous to spend long periods discussing details of their way of life with the new arrivals is also extraordinarily fortuitous.

The original Aboriginal inhabitants of King George Sound were part of the larger Noongar group which occupied the south-west of Western Australia, and whose territory broadly corresponds with the area west of the 175 millimetre rainfall line that extends 1200 kilometres from the west coast to the south coast.[18] Australian anthropologist Norman Tindale identified thirteen 'tribal groups' based upon socio-linguistic boundaries.[19] His map is reproduced as Appendix 4 and details a large and well-defined area centred on Albany as the territory of the Menang group. Recently, however, doubt has been cast on the validity of the names and the boundaries set by Tindale. Prominent Western Australian historian Neville Green presented a paper at the Biennial Conference of the Australian Historical Association held at the University of Western Australia in July 2010 which strongly questioned the Tindale map. He concluded 'the majority of Tindale's sources do not support or even justify his southwest territories either by name or locality or in extent'.[20] The map has been very influential for a number of decades and it will be interesting to see whether Green's criticisms are borne out by future research.

There is no agreement as to the spelling of *Minang, Mineng,* or *Menang.* It is not possible to make a definitive judgement on the matter for the obvious reason that Aboriginal words were recorded phonetically by English speakers whose ideas varied about how best to spell words of a very different-sounding language. For the purpose of consistency, except when quoting sources that have used a different form, 'Menang' is used as this is the spelling favoured by the authors of *Kinjarling,* a report written in 2004 after considerable consultation with the Aboriginal people of Albany.[21]

There is also a degree of confusion apparent in the literature with respect to exactly who should be referred to as the Menang. The authors of *Kinjarling* agree with Tindale in using it to describe the four Aboriginal groups – the Murray, the Weal, the Cockatoo and the Kincannup – who occupied the region identified by Tindale's map.[22] Others, however, have followed Nind in using this term in a narrower sense to apply only to a smaller group who enjoyed the principal property rights over the land in the immediate proximity of Albany. Nind was the first to note: 'The inhabitants of the Sound and its immediate vicinity are called Meananger, probably derived from mearn, the red root...and anger to eat'.[23] It is not possible to be certain whether the word was simply another form of the word 'Menang'. From this, it is apparent that Nind believed the Meananger was the name of the group living in and around Albany, and that it was inappropriate to use the term to describe the totality of the four groups making up Tindale's wider region. Browne details the area occupied by each of the four groups without using any single term to cover all four.[24]

Tiffany Shellam's book *Shaking Hands on the Fringe*, which ends with the conversion of the garrison to a free settlement within the colony of Western Australia in early 1831, uses *King Ya-nup* to describe 'any Aboriginal person who contributed to life around the settlement from 1826 to the early 1830s'.[25] The explorer and surgeon Thomas Braidwood Wilson recorded this name as being the Aboriginal name for the area around the British settlement.[26] Shellam is somewhat dubious about the use of 'Menang', pointing out that the term was not recorded as being in use by Aboriginal people from the area in the early years of the settlement.[27] In his 1842 wordlist, prominent Swan River settler George Fletcher Moore recorded that 'Menang' meant 'south, or southerners'.[28] Certainly, today the Aboriginal and non-Aboriginal people of Albany have widely embraced the term to include Aboriginal people from the Albany region.

I have followed James Browne in using the word 'Kincannup' to describe those Aboriginal people who lived for the greater part of each year in the immediate vicinity of Albany. Browne took a keen interest in the Aboriginal people he associated with at Albany and it is reasonable to assume that he was recording information he received directly from them.[29] Ken Macintyre and Barbara Dobson, in their book reproducing Browne's articles about his time at Albany, have speculated that 'Kincannup' is actually a Pidgin word derived from 'King George Sound', and was adopted by those Aboriginal people living in the vicinity of the settlement in order to make it clear that any benefits to be obtained from the British would be theirs alone.[30]

After the mid nineteenth century, migration from other areas and the decline in the Kincannup population led to a situation where 'Noongar' seems more appropriate to describe those Aboriginal people living near Albany. 'Menang' will be used to describe the wider group, comprised of the Kincannups and the three other neighbouring groups whose members seasonally or intermittently visited the area around King George Sound. It is frequently ambiguous whether the Aboriginal people referred to in incidents recorded in contemporary journals and other documents were from the local Kincannup population, or were (or included) people from more outlying areas who should be more accurately referred to as 'Menang'. Historians Michael Powell and Rex Hesline have argued that it is extraordinarily difficult to be certain about a range of topics concerned with Aboriginal naming practices. They have also pointed out that the concept of 'tribe' was a product of eighteenth- and nineteenth-century European nationalism coupled with an Enlightenment obsession with naming and classifying. It was an assumed aspect of colonial populations rather than one revealed from indigenous sources.[31]

The other neighbouring groups who comprised the Menang were connected to the Kincannups by intricate ties of kinship through marriage, and formed with them a social and cultural network that was based on shared use of land and resources. European observers found the complexities in the relationship between the Kincannups and their immediate neighbours impossible to comprehend fully. As will be discussed in detail in Chapter Three, even close observers such as Nind and Barker were never able to understand why periods of evident close friendship and harmony should quickly deteriorate into intense fear and actual violence.

Europeans recorded the group living to the west of the Kincannups in the early nineteenth century as the 'Murrum', 'Murram', 'Murray', 'Murray-men' or 'Murrymin'.[32] Eyre wrote that they were the proprietors of Wilson Inlet east of Denmark, but did not define their boundaries.[33] Browne held that:

The Murray tribe, the most numerous of all, occupies a territory exceeding in extent that of any of the rest: that is, the whole of the coast running some 300 miles from King George Sound westward and to the Murray River in the Swan River Colony.[34]

To the north of Albany were the people recorded variously as the 'Wills', the 'Weal', or the 'Weill'. Europeans noted that they were the most significant neighbours of the Kincannups, and the most common source of their fears. To the north-east lived the White Cockatoo, or Cockatoo people. The Kincannups saw each of these neighbouring groups as distinct from themselves and each other. Mokare, a prominent young Kincannup man who forged deep friendships with several British men in the early years of the settlement, informed Barker:

Wills people gay and volatile like the French. Very early risers, up at cock crow, sleeping little. White Cockatoo tribe great sleepers & of a grave disposition. To the westward [Murrum] of a medium cast between the two. He has heard of people far off to the East or NE, all life and spirit, fond of laugh & joke from morning to night.[35]

Because contemporary observers disagreed over details, it is impractical to attempt precise boundary definitions for the territories occupied by the various Aboriginal groups who lived at or visited Albany and its hinterland, or to grasp fully the complex relationships that each group had with its neighbours.

Each socio-linguistic Noongar group, such as the Menang, consisted of a number of smaller groups. Anthropologists commonly refer to the larger socio-linguistic group as the 'tribe', while the smaller group comprising related men and their wives and children is usually variously described by anthropologists as a 'family', a 'band' or a 'horde'.[36] The Kincannups comprised one such kin group. Browne stated that in 1838 they comprised about twenty to thirty people.[37] Nind stated that the size of their encampment 'rarely exceeded 50 people residing together and usually about 20' and because of his close observation over a relatively long period, this would appear to be as accurate a figure as we are ever likely to possess.[38] Allowing for the likelihood that Nind had recorded the upper figure of fifty during periods when visiting Aborigines from other groups were present, his observations agree with French explorer Dumont d'Urville's 1826 observation that the Aborigines at the Sound lived in 'little tribes' of about twenty people.[39]

The basic unit in local Aboriginal society was the family. This included a man, his wife or wives, and their children. Several of these families would form a kin group living in small 'villages' of approximately twenty people.[40] These villages consisted of about seven huts, described by contemporary European observers as being 'like a beehive with a radius of three to four feet sliced in two by a vertical separation'.[41] Collie gave his eyewitness account of an Aboriginal woman building one of these shelters:

> Dinner over, the lady immediately began the erection of her hut, by getting a few slender and leafy twigs, sticking the large ends forcibly into the ground and intertwining the smaller branches with one another; and, with others, the tops of which she inclined obliquely downwards. The form it assumed was that of half a hay cock made by a vertical section and excavated, so small as to scarcely admit one or two persons in an inflected and laterally incumbent position. Here, however, the family of father, mother, and two children reposed or took shelter for the night.[42]

Favoured locations were sheltered areas near the coastline, rivers, estuaries and lakes.[43] The huts each had a fire kept continually burning outside an open front, and were built with their backs facing the prevailing wind. Nind noted: 'dogs are also admitted to a share of the bed'.[44] Huts were located in such a way that the entrances did not overlook each other.[45] The evidence appears to point to single men living in huts by themselves, while married men, perhaps with a favourite wife, occupied others. The remainder were occupied by other wives and their children.[46] Barker noted that some families made other arrangements for their shelter:

> Saw Wannewar & family in Deane's Harbour as I passed. They have taken a snug berth & made their fire under a large rock by a bush near the water side. There was no hut. Huts pretty general, I believe, even for the single men.[47]

He also noted: 'The blacks however do not talk of such a one's hut but, to express his home or resting place, they say such a one's fire'.[48]

Europeans occasionally found evidence of Aboriginal villages at King George Sound numbering considerably more huts than the usual six to nine. In 1791, the British explorer, George

Aboriginal shelters at Albany. *Panoramic view of King George's Sound, part of the colony of Swan River* (detail), by Lt Robert Dale, 1834.
Courtesy National Library of Australia, an7404363-6.

24

Vancouver found a village on the shore of Princess Royal Harbour comprising about two dozen recently abandoned huts. It is difficult to account for the unusually large number seen at this site, but Nind gave a clue by stating that an encampment *rarely* exceeded seven or eight huts, and perhaps his observation that visitors from the interior came to the coast during the fishing season provides an explanation.[49]

The original inhabitants of King George Sound enjoyed a richly varied diet characterised by strongly seasonal patterns of availability. Their range was geographically and botanically highly diverse, and this necessitated a lifestyle based upon family group movement as various food sources became available at particular places at different times of the year. South-west Western Australia is recognised by Conservation International as one of only twenty-five biodiversity hotspots in the world and is home to more than 1500 plant species.[50] The Menang made further divisions than the four seasons into which Europeans traditionally divide the year, although a degree of uncertainty exists over the exact division of the Aboriginal year, and over the names used to describe them. Sue le Souef has compiled a table of known information, and I have included this as Appendix 1, acknowledging that minor differences in seasonal divisions and terminology were identified by some contemporary observers.

Although the Menang used all areas of their range, certain zones were preferred because of the richness of the resources they provided. Areas that were particularly favoured included the coastline, estuaries, rivers, streams, lakes, wetlands and the more open areas of woodland. They visited these locations more frequently, and set up their principal campsites there. Areas of denser forest were also used, but only intermittently because of difficulties associated with access and the spearing of animals.[51] Menang society was highly mobile, with *bidis* or well-worn tracks following corridors of easy movement such as the banks of the King and Kalgan rivers, and linking campsites with regions of plentiful resources. These tracks received constant use, for although there was definite seasonal migration, small groups and individuals moved throughout their range at all times of the year.[52] Interestingly, five years after the British settlement was established, Collie found a man 20 miles inland from the settlement who had never seen a European, further demonstrating that no simple assumptions about patterns of Menang travel are adequate to describe the situation conclusively.[53]

Fish represented a major part of the Menang diet during spring and early summer. Large groups from throughout their range moved camp to King George Sound and Oyster Harbour, where they made use of the plentiful supply of a wide variety of species taken by spearing in shallow water, and by the use of stone and brushwood fish traps (some of which are still in evidence, although not in their original condition). Unlike many Aboriginal groups, the Menang did not eat shellfish and made no use of fishhooks, nets or watercraft. Being unable to swim, they were prepared to venture into the ocean only to waist depth in order to spear fish.[54]

In common with other Noongar groups, the Kincannups did not remain at the same campsite throughout the year, hence the 'abandoned' huts seen by Vancouver. Ferguson noted:

> Even on their own estates they often shifted their camp. They might move only a short distance, occasionally not more than a few hundred metres, but they rarely stayed longer than two or three days in one place, almost never more than a week and usually only a day.[55]

As well as this local movement, Noongars throughout their territory moved inland during the peak winter period and this movement was noted by all observers at Albany. They reported that the Kincannups' visits to the settlement became infrequent during June and July, with most moving inland in family units in order to hunt, and to escape the worst of the coastal winter storms.[56] Collie wrote:

> During the winter (Mokkar of the Natives), scarcely any of them came into the Settlement. They appeared for some reasons already adduced to obtain their food more easily in the interior.[57]

Browne observed that kangaroos migrated inland during the winter months and believed this to be a major reason why the Kincannups largely abandoned coastal areas at this time.[58]

Other European observers have generally followed Collie in assuming that this annual migration was mainly a response to Albany's renowned cool winter climate. Because Albany is indeed cooler than the inland region for much of the year, it appears logical to assume that this would also be the case in the winter months. However, an analysis of the Australian Government Bureau of Meteorology's long-term climate information for Albany and Mount Barker (a site representative of the region to which migration took place) shows that June and July maximum and minimum temperatures are actually *higher* at Albany, while the number of rainy days are the same.[59] Certainly, wind strengths are higher at Albany, but an analysis of the two sites for the months of June and July using the Bureau's Apparent Temperature Indices shows that, even taking this into account, Albany *feels* the warmer place during these months.[60] Mount Barker is also prone to winter frosts, which only rarely occur at Albany. Given that wind speeds at the height above ground that humans occupy are substantially lessened by trees and shrubs and that Albany is well timbered, it seems questionable that the great majority of the Kincannups left the Albany coast each winter simply because of the weather. It appears much more likely that Browne was correct in his observation that these annual movements were actually primarily connected with changes in the availability of food resources.

The Kincannups also had important social and ritual obligations to the other groups of the Menang from inland areas, and these obligations sometimes led young men to travel 70 or 80 kilometres to visit the area adjacent to Albany for a short period of rejoicing and feasting in conjunction with ceremonies denoting peace.[61] The warmer seasons were a favourite time for these ceremonial and social gatherings, because the assured and plentiful supply of fish allowed large numbers of people to take time from the hunting and gathering normally essential for their survival. Important corroborees (one recorded as having lasted for seven days), when law ceremonies and initiations occurred, were held at the King River and at other areas close to Albany.[62] Browne described how old grievances occasionally turned these 'jovial' gatherings into a general quarrel involving all present: 'spears begin to fly about; pierced legs and broken heads are the consequence, and the parties separate vowing vengeance against each other'.[63]

Freshwater lakes and wetlands also provided a seasonal abundance of a variety of food, including tortoises and their eggs, koonacs, frogs and water birds. Nind noted that various roots and tubers formed the staple food source for much of the year. The roots of fern, sedge and other plants were eaten, as were at least two types of mushroom and another species of fungus. Some of this vegetable material was cooked, while other types were eaten raw. When the different species of banksia trees were flowering, large amounts of nectar were taken by sucking the flowers following heavy dews.[64]

Wallabies and grey and brush kangaroos formed a considerable part of the Menang diet. Nind described how Aboriginal hunters, either singly or in small parties, favoured hunting during days of heavy rain or strong wind since such weather prevented kangaroos from hearing their stealthy approach. They lit fires in summer and autumn to drive kangaroos and other small game onto a line of waiting hunters who used spears to bring down game for despatch by stone hammers. Nind observed how 'poorly trained' dingoes were used to catch smaller animals such as brush kangaroos, possums, and bandicoots as they fled the fires.[65] Hunters built pit-falls to trap kangaroos and emus, the latter being highly regarded as a source of food but difficult to hunt by methods other than trapping. Snakes and lizards provided a considerable proportion of the food consumed at certain times of the year, as well as the eggs of one of the larger lizard species.[66] During spring, the principal sources of food were the eggs and young of birds, especially parrots, but also those of other species such as hawks, ducks, swans and pigeons. Hunters were expert tree climbers and used this skill to take birds' eggs, as well as possums from hollows in older trees.[67]

Because most food resources were seasonal, they could be reliably obtained only through the intricate knowledge that the Menang possessed about their extensive territory. There were times when some types of food were in abundance, but this does not imply that the Aboriginal people always enjoyed an easy, idyllic lifestyle characterised by high levels of nutrition won through a minimum of effort. Nind found the opposite to be the case at certain times of the year when the food supply was 'poor in quality and often scanty'.[68] During periods of shortage, it required an almost continuous effort skilfully applied by all members of the family to assure an adequate level of nutrition.

It is not known how many hours in each day the Menang needed to devote at differing times of the year to hunting and foraging. Referring to Aboriginal people in the south-west, explorer and colonial administrator George Grey wrote that they were frequently able to obtain their food for the day with two or three hours' effort.[69] Given that the Albany area was richer in food resources than much of the south-western region, it would appear reasonable to speculate that for much of the year it may have taken the Menang no longer than this.

It is interesting to note that the great majority of Nind's descriptions of food gathering relate to descriptions of hunting rather than foraging, although it is probable that the latter provided the bulk of the food obtained on a typical day. The ratio of calorific value between food obtained by hunting or foraging would have altered quite dramatically at times of the year when various resources were either scarce or abundant, and it is not possible to make a categorical statement about which strategy was the more important overall at Albany. International studies have shown that gathering, an occupation almost universally the responsibility of women and older children in hunter-gatherer societies, usually provides between 60 and 80 per cent by weight of food consumed. This proportion has been found to hold good for the Aborigines of the Central and Western desert regions of Western Australia,[70] and, although Albany is a very different area to these, it may be assumed that gathering or foraging was a very productive strategy for the Menang. In Central Australia, women's access to food, and their right to control its distribution according to kin obligations, made them the economic mainstay and gave them a degree of independence. It was women who determined camp locations, and the time when the group moved on to a new site where food was more plentiful.[71]

Anthropologists note that it is common in hunter-gatherer societies for men to forgo the more efficient technique of foraging because good hunters tend to enjoy a higher social status and more reproductive success, and this was probably the case at Albany.[72] Nind certainly focused heavily on the hunting side of food provision, but this was quite possibly because the Menang were reluctant to allow the British to converse with their women and children, thus making it more difficult for him to arrive at a balanced picture.

In discussing how various groups of Aboriginal people from the Albany region were observed to own and use their land, it is interesting to note Australian anthropologist W. E. H. Stanner's Australia-wide model of estate, range and domain. He stated that each family had a tract of land with which they most closely identified, referring to it as their *kalla* or fireplace. It was where they normally lived, although they might temporarily leave this 'estate' for cultural or foraging reasons.[73] Each estate was precisely marked out using trees or other objects, and it was clearly understood by all that the land belonged to that particular family.[74] Nind gave the clearest information with respect to Albany:

> Those families who have locations on the seacoast quit it during the winter for the interior; and the natives of the interior, in like manner, pay visits to the coast during the fishing season. Excepting at these times, those natives who live together have the exclusive right of fishing or hunting on the neighbouring grounds, which are, in fact, divided into individual properties; the quantity of land owned by each individual being very considerable. Yet it is not so exclusively his, but others of his family have certain rights over it; so that it may be considered as partly belonging to the tribe. Thus all of them have the right to break down grass trees, kill bandicoots, lizards and other animals, and dig up roots; but the presence of the owner of the ground is considered necessary when they fire the country for game.[75]

The association that a group had with this area was primarily as its spiritual custodians, although they also held special hunting rights over its extent. As long as permission was sought (especially for burning in order to flush out animals) other groups were permitted to forage over the estate during periods when food resources were plentiful. At Albany, hunting without permission was spoken of as *quippel* and, especially if burning was involved, could lead to serious consequences including the non-fatal spearing of the offender.[76]

The estate was the normal home of the family group and is sometimes referred to as its 'Dreaming place'. Ownership passed from fathers to sons.[77] The group knew and kept alive the myths and rituals associated with their land and its sacred places, and these were considered vital elements in their ownership claims and responsibilities.[78]

As well as having ownership over an estate, a family group held rights to a larger area of land – a necessity imposed upon Aboriginal society by the impermanent and intermittent nature of many of the items of food available to them, and the consequent necessity to access places where alternative sources of food were seasonally available. These rights were not as comprehensive as those held by a family over its estate, but were sufficient to allow them to travel over its extent in search of seasonally plentiful food, and for social and ceremonial purposes. Ferguson produced a map showing the extent of one such 'range': that of Mokare whose family estate included the Albany settlement and land on the Torndirrup peninsula to its south. Barker and the others who showed an interest in the movements of the Aboriginal people noted that Mokare, one of the members of the Kincannup group and an almost constant resident with the British when at Albany, was often away travelling for periods that sometimes exceeded a month at a time. The map shows boundaries deduced from Mokare's statements at the settlement, as well as the observations of English explorers who went on journeys of exploration with Mokare or his brother Nakinah as their guide.

When Surgeon T. B. Wilson travelled westward to the approximate site of today's town of Denmark, Mokare began to show considerable unease, and was only happy when the party turned back towards his Albany territory.[79] Ferguson used this incident to prove that Mokare was at the extent of his range, and others have followed his lead without always acknowledging that there is another possible interpretation of what occurred. Wilson actually recorded that Mokare was uneasy because of the length of the trip and the shortage of their rations, and it is possible that this *was* the true cause. Similarly, when Mokare expressed reluctance to proceed north-east of the Stirling Ranges during an expedition when acting as a guide for Collie in April 1831, Ferguson assumed this indicated he had reached the limit of his range. Again, the actual reason Mokare gave was quite possibly the real one: that water would not be available in what is a relatively harsh and dry area.[80]

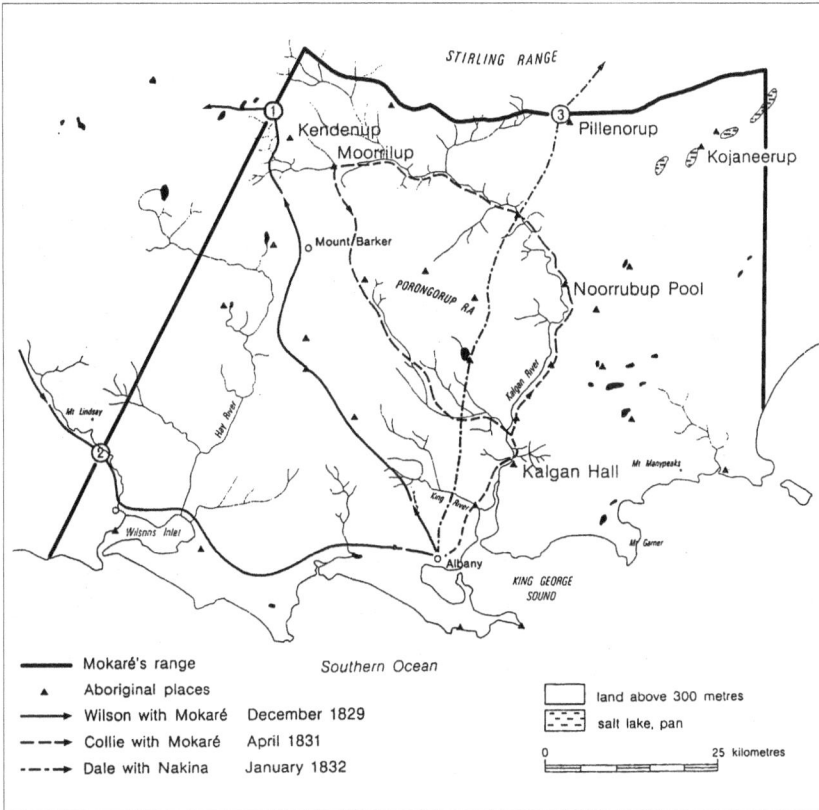

Ferguson's map showing explorations that appeared to indicate the area of Mokare's range. W. Ferguson, 'Mokarés Domain', p. 135.

Ferguson was on surer ground in fixing the Stirling Range as the northern limit of the Kincannups' range, since Nakinah spoke of a special plant that only grew north of the Stirlings, one which he had never seen for himself.[81] That the place where Mokare wished Collie to turn back was also at the foot of the Stirlings gives support for Ferguson's map showing this as the northern extent of the Kincannups' range. Ferguson found that there was even less information to allow an eastern boundary to their range to be fixed with any precision.

Assuming that the map is broadly accurate, the Kincannups' range extended over an area of about 6,000 square kilometres, covering a wide variety of climatic and vegetative zones from karri forest near Wilson Inlet where the annual rainfall averages 1,250 mm to the open low mallee heathlands at Kojaneerup where only 500 mm falls in an average year. The region includes two rivers and a considerable number of smaller streams, as well as numerous lakes and swamps.

Le Souef used the fact that Barker noted the names of seventy-four adult males with whom the British came into contact in the region frequented by the Menang to extrapolate a number of about 200 for their total population.[82] This is a bold assumption to make, but it is interesting to note that Perth newspaper proprietor William Nairne Clark, during a visit to Albany in 1842, estimated there were 100 Aboriginal people living within 20 miles of King George Sound, and this gives a similar population density of between nine and ten people per 100 square miles.[83] The region around Albany is relatively drought free. This fact, together with the reliability of food resources provided by the ocean and the two major rivers, almost certainly would have allowed population levels to remain fairly consistent from year to year.

Of all the contemporary reporters, Nind gave the most com-prehensive description of the Menang's physical appearance. He described the men and women as being of medium stature with slender limbs, differing little from the Aborigines of Sydney. Their only article of clothing was a kangaroo skin cloak, or *buka*, fastened at the right shoulder and reaching almost to the knee. These were usually worn with the fur inwards but could be reversed in rainy weather. A waistband, or *noodle-bul*, spun from possum fur and wrapped around the waist several times was sometimes worn by men around the upper arm and head, while some girls wore a similar item around their neck.

Single men sometimes wore dog tails and feathers in their hair which they wore long and wound around their head. Women wore their hair quite short. Nind described both sexes as having a disagreeable odour from the custom of smearing their faces and upper bodies with a mixture of red pigment, or *paloil*, and fat taken from fish or seals. The Menang informed Nind that this was done both as a protection from the sun and in order to keep themselves clean. They rubbed the same mixture into their hair, which became matted as a result. This custom of applying pigment mixed with oil gave freshly painted individuals a brick-dust colour, which Nind described as 'most singular'. When preparing to dance or to visit neighbouring groups, the Menang were particular to paint their bodies, although some individuals were never observed by Nind to do so. The men's shoulders and chests were lacerated, with clay rubbed into the wounds in order to cause permanent raised scarring, which was regarded as both a mark of distinction and an identifying mark for different groups.[84] Nind failed to mention whether this practice of scarification was confined solely to men.

The Menang had few material possessions. Barker noted: 'Property they do not value beyond the spear, Wanera [spear-thrower], knife, tomahawk and kangaroo skin'.[85] Nind described how the men each carried two to five spears of different types depending upon whether they intended to hunt animals, spear fish or go to war. They also carried a throwing stick (*meara*) which could be used as a close-quarters weapon, and a hammer (*koit*) made by fixing a stone to a short stick using gum and used for climbing trees, breaking down grass trees and as a hunting weapon. As well as these items, some carried a knife (*taap*), similar to the koit, but with sharpened edges, a short stick (*towk*) for throwing at or striking small animals, and a *curl*, or boomerang.[86] Nind focused on men's possessions, but noted that women carried a needle made from the claw of a kangaroo, and also carried a bark drinking vessel.[87]

Young children were included in family journeys soon after birth, and became a part of foraging parties with women and older girls once they became able to walk. When young boys were old enough to keep up with their father and older brothers, they were included in the male group and accompanied them when hunting. Learning was usually more by imitation than instruction.[88] Nind observed that the Menang were very fond of their children, rarely chastising them.[89] He also noted their practice of infanticide in the case of the birth of twins, only the female being kept alive if a boy and a girl had been born. Nind's Aboriginal informants stated that this was done because a mother would not have sufficient milk for both babies, and that looking after two babies at once would prevent her from foraging for food. Children were not weaned until four or five years of age, by which time much of their nutrition came from other sources.[90]

At the age of about fourteen or fifteen, girls left the family unit to live with their husband, while boys underwent initiation. Initiation for boys involved more than a single, short ceremony and had as one of its main purposes the imparting of detailed knowledge about the group's range and its inhabitants. The process began with a ceremony attended by the young boys and their fathers, when a senior *mulgarradock* (doctor) pressed a sharpened kangaroo bone through each boy's nasal septum. Following this, boys would sometimes leave their family for an extended period that could last several years. One or two older men from his family would take a boy to a distant part of their range where he would be supervised by a senior male member of another family who would take on the task of educating him.[91] Barker's journal shows clearly that the process of initiation was complex, and it is evident that his searching enquiries failed to satisfy him that he understood all that was involved.[92]

The first Europeans to live at Albany showed a keen interest in the betrothal and marriage customs of the Menang and clearly were aware of the broad picture, although they could not fully understand all that was taking place:

> There appear to be some peculiar regulations here, but what they are we could not ascertain. In some instances it happens that the exchange is mutual. The persons to whom the girls are betrothed are not infrequently men of the middle or an advanced age, and possessing already several wives. They are, however, often more equally matched.[93]

Nind noted that fathers appeared to be responsible for the selection of marriage partners for their daughters, who were betrothed at an early age, sometimes even before their birth.[94] He also ascertained that it was considered desirable for a father to arrange the marriage with a man who lived at a considerable distance from the daughter's home area. Presumably, apart from its value as a precaution against marriage to a close relative, this practice also had the benefit of allowing any subsequent children to hunt in the mother's old home territory.[95] Although there did not appear to be any type of marriage ceremony, Nind described how the father would be presented with gifts of food and artefacts such as spears when his daughter reached puberty and was delivered by him to her new husband.[96] Barker noted:

> The blacks have sometimes four wives, but who do not live together. When a man has even two, they are kept in different

directions. It is the older men who have so many wives, the younger men are generally single & consequently sometimes carry off those of the old men.[97]

In the likely event that the normal age disparity resulted in the husband predeceasing his wife, she would marry one or more of his brothers.[98]

In a society where men remained single until past thirty years of age and older men had several wives, it is scarcely surprising that marital infidelity was common. Collie believed it a common occurrence for a young woman to desert her old and infirm husband for a younger man, even though this brought general ignominy to the woman concerned. Should the wronged husband retain sufficient strength, the woman and her new husband could be subjected to wounding, or even death.[99]

Strict rules were in place as to who was eligible to become lawfully married to whom, with the Menang adhering to the complex regulations common throughout the south-west whereby two primary moiety divisions existed. Daisy Bates, who spent a significant period of time at Katanning in the early twentieth century becoming very familiar with Aboriginal people from the region, divided these into two further subsets and believed this system under various names pertained throughout 'every tribe in Western Australia'. She named the principal divisions as 'Manichmat' (white cockatoo) and 'Wordungmat' (crow), further dividing the former into 'Tondarup' and 'Didarruk', and the latter into 'Ballaruk' and 'Nagarnook'.[100] Interestingly, Nind used 'Erniung' and 'Tem' or 'Taaman' for the two major divisions, stating: 'The children always follow the denomination of the mother'.[101] Bates on the other hand observed that Aboriginal people: 'below Augusta and the Donnelly River' followed a system based on patrilineal descent, and noted:

> All along the borderline where the two lines of descent met, the tribes were friendly with each other, intermarrying and adjusting their 'in-law' relationships to suit the form of descent obtaining.[102]

She described the only lawful marriages as: 'the cross–cousin marriage of paternal aunts' children to the maternal uncles' children'.[103] Nind saw that some marriages did not comply with these laws: 'Those who infringe this rule are called *Yuredangers*, and are subject to very severe punishment'.[104]

There were occasions when large gatherings took place in order to bring to an end a chain of spearings resulting from an individual's death, and to restore the fragile harmony that months of the ensuing low-grade conflict had destroyed. Nind explained how the always fragile peace could be broken by conflict over women (he identified this as the most common cause) or by broken territorial hunting protocols. However, more serious problems arose when a man was killed because of a deliberate act, or by accident. Such premature deaths were believed to be the result of malevolence shown to the deceased by a *mulgarradock* possessing supernatural powers, and belonging to another group. The men of the victim's group would immediately plan revenge upon an individual belonging to the group of the particular *mulgarradock* identified by an involved process of enquiry as being responsible. The custom whereby a seriously ill man would sometimes attempt to kill someone in the hope that this would prevent his own illness from proving fatal was another reason the peace could be broken at any time.[105]

In the case of relatively minor offences to do with women or inappropriate hunting of animals on another's property, the resulting spearing would be in the leg or thigh and designed to wound rather than kill. For a more serious offence adjudged to merit fatal retaliation, the revenge attack would be made by stealth and usually at night while the victim slept.[106] Spearing was a way of settling scores and restoring harmony within Aboriginal society after its strict rules had been infringed. It was considered necessary to avenge a man's death before his spirit could properly rest, and pressure was brought to bear by his family upon those charged with taking revenge.[107] The rules governing retaliation were complex and imperfectly understood by European observers who nevertheless saw the frequent fear and insecurity they caused. The disruption to Aboriginal society caused by invasion was later to cause an increase in these acts of violence as traditions began to be less rigorously followed, but it would be wrong to assume that pre-European Menang society was idyllically peaceful. When Barker suggested in June 1830 that the British had been the cause of the violence within the local Aboriginal group, his friend Mokare informed him that the Aboriginal people of the area were actually less ferocious and inclined to murder than had been the case in the past.[108]

The Menang had no chiefs in the European sense of the word. However, there were individuals who held considerable influence over the rest of Menang society. These *mulgarradocks* were described by Nind:

> Of these they have several grades, differing very materially in the nature and extent of their power, which, like other savages, they attribute to supernatural agency. A *mulgarradock* is considered to possess the power of driving away wind or rain, as well as bringing down lightning or disease upon any object of their or others' hatred.[109]

Nind also described how they treated snakebite and administered herbal remedies to those who were ill or had been wounded by spearing.[110] Browne gave a detailed description of their methods:

> The Cockatoo-man [Browne believed *mulgarradocks* to be generally members of that group] approaches, and, gravely gazing on the

sick man, begins to probe with his knuckles, to find the exact spot where lies the pain. Having determined this, he commences to rub down or shampoo the body, from the part affected, towards one of the extremities, either the feet, the hands, the head, or the ears – the object being to force Jahnac [a spirit] out at one of these points. During the operation, he frequently blows on his fingers with great solemnity, as if to disperse the infection of the evil one. Suddenly ceasing his rubbing and seizing the patient by the hair of his head, or back of the neck, he treats him to a most energetic shaking; and thus he proceeds, with alternate rubbing, and blowing and shaking until Jahnac is forced out of the afflicted one, and appears in the hand of the operator, in the shape of a small piece of wood or quartz. The cure being thus satisfactorily performed, this bit of wood or stone is handed to the individual from whom it was extracted, and by whom it is cherished ever afterward as an object of particular value.[111]

Barker's description of Aboriginal methods of treating snakebite is intriguing. When Taragon, a man who spent a considerable amount of time at the British settlement at Albany and was well known to Barker, was bitten on the hand, the settlement's surgeon Dr Davis found that the victim's companions had bound the hand and wrist tightly – a treatment that accords with modern methods of treatment. The surgeon immediately removed the binding and in an action that was perhaps the worst possible in the circumstances, vigorously rubbed the hand; the patient lingered but eventually died.

Water sources had special mythological significance throughout the south-west. All Aboriginal groups in the region shared a belief in a water-creating serpent and its association with rivers, lakes and soaks. The Menang were unique among south-west Aboriginal groups in that this spirit serpent was not referred to as the *Waugal* – a name reserved by them for the carpet snake. Instead, the serpent was named the *Marchant*.[112]

The Menang were a deeply religious people, possessed of a rich mythology about the creation and sustenance of their land.[113] This all-encompassing view of the land, and the place of the people within it, is usually referred to as the Dreaming. It provided an ideological and philosophical basis for the close connection Aboriginal people felt for their land, and also referred to a time in the distant past when mythic beings inhabited the Earth, creating animal and plant species and shaping the landscape through their struggles with each other. The Menang knew the sites of these struggles and regarded them as sacred. Each of these sites belonged to one or more groups, and the ancient rights to these sites created the hunting rights that each group possessed over their land. In his chapter 'The Murrum and their country', in *Contested Country*, the anthropologist Ian Crawford wrote:

> The Nyungar believed that their world had been created by Ancestral Beings known as Demma Goomber (Great Grandparent), or Mammangurra. These Ancestral Beings lived on Earth in the creation period called Nyitting (translated by Bates as the 'Cold Time'). They acted both in human ways (hunting, marrying, trading, fighting) and also in ways characteristic of the animal they were to become (burrowing, flying, making typical sounds). The Ancestral Beings pushed the land around, created mountains, flats, rivers, lakes, trees and tracks. The environment was therefore an inheritance from the Ancestral Beings and embodied what they had done in the creation period...
>
> Every human was linked to an Ancestral Being who was also the progenitor of a species of living thing which included some natural phenomena such as cloud, rain and fire. Thus each human was linked spiritually with a species of living thing...Each species was represented by an Ancestral Being whose actions were recorded in songs and verse. Where an Ancestral Being did something significant, that place manifested life spirits which

grew into people...A person whose life spirit came from such a location was seen as the descendant of the Ancestor and custodian of the species...It must have contributed to the Nyungar sense of unity that together, the people cared for the well-being of every living thing in their well-ordered universe.[114]

Barker showed a keen interest in understanding Aboriginal spirituality, and he and Mokare frequently discussed their respective religious beliefs. Barker's journal entries provide a fascinating picture of two insightful men attempting to come to some sort of understanding of each other's religious beliefs. Mokare told Barker several stories which are recorded in the journal. Barker noted that the Kincannups had no belief in either a supreme being or superior beings, although he noted that Mokare addressed 'someone' at times of fear, such as in a severe thunderstorm or when seriously ill. The Kincannups were aware of invisible beings Barker called 'ghosts'. These were deceased Aborigines who wandered around at night, and would only be seen prior to a death.[115] Some ghosts were 'great thieves', and carried off useful items such as spears and kangaroo skins. Mokare stated that his people believed that theft by humans would be punished by sickness.[116] As an example of their discussions Barker wrote:

> Wanting to know the ideas of the blacks on the origin of mankind, I got him [Mokare] this evening after some difficulty to understand my questions, when he told me that a very long time ago the only person living was an old woman named Arregain who had a beard as long as the garden. She was delivered of a daughter & then died. The daughter called Moenang grew up in course of time to be a woman, when she had several children (boys and girls), who were the fathers & mothers of all black people.[117]

Ethel Hassell also showed an uncommon respect for the religion of the Aboriginal people with whom she enjoyed close contact over a long period on her isolated station at Jerramungup in the late nineteenth century. She listened to many of their stories and wrote them in a diary that was published in 1975 as *My Dusky Friends*.[118] These stories are too detailed to quote here, but give a highly valuable insight into Aboriginal beliefs, and illustrate how they accounted for the creation of many features of the region's landscape and flora and fauna.

Interestingly, Hassell recorded how some Aboriginal girls were terrified by what appeared to be puffs of wind disturbing leaves and dust: '*Jannocks* they breathlessly whispered...the *Jannocks* [evil spirits] were out playing, and woe betide anyone who watched them, or crossed their path'.[119] The girls explained that the supreme evil one was named *Noitch*, who was concerned with departed spirits, while the numerous *Jannocks* concentrated on the living. To placate them, the girls said that Aboriginal people sometimes made a separate fire and placed food next to it for the spirits to take.[120] Possibly the *Jannocks* were Mokare's 'ghosts'. Several local Noongar authors with strong ties to the region have recently had books and sound recordings published telling some of the stories that were handed down to them many years ago by their older family members.[121] Their religion was the primary integrating force that brought together the material and spiritual aspects of life into one coherent whole, joining the Menang to their land and to the mythic beings who had created it. This belief system led to a society based on co-operation rather than individuality, whose members felt a part of the environment and of the spirit world that nurtured it. Because of geographical isolation, confidence in their way of life was never challenged by exposure to any other systems of belief until the end of what Europeans knew as the eighteenth century, when the forerunners of the eventual European invasion that would shake the very foundations of Aboriginal society began to visit their world.

Chapter Two

First Contact

European–Aboriginal interaction at King George Sound prior to British settlement

A bust of Captain Nicholas Thomas Baudin overlooking King George Sound by Peter Gelencser, 2005

In 2001, the French and Australian governments erected a large bronze bust of French naval captain Nicolas Baudin on the boardwalk connecting Middleton Beach to the Albany City waterfront precinct. From this vantage point on the eastern slope of Mount Adelaide stretches a breathtaking 180-degree vista of King George Sound that has remained virtually unaltered since the Menang, completely unaware that on the other side of the globe existed a very different group of people from themselves, caught sight of the first Europeans to enter their world.

Walkers commonly pause to read the inscription on the accompanying plaque, frequently giving up after finding the raised lettering frustratingly difficult to read. They move on, aware that the Frenchman with his enigmatic expression must hold some significance for the history of Albany, but remaining unsure of who he was, or what he did. The few who persevere with the task of reading the complete text and relate it to the accompanying map of the voyage may wonder why the map shows Baudin's vessel apparently vanishing at a point approximating the ocean boundary of Victoria and South Australia, when the text clearly states that the expedition included an extended stay at Sydney.

The enigmatic Baudin bust and plaque serve admirably as metaphors for our incomplete knowledge of the extended period from the first contacts between the Menang and a number of visiting European seafarers, and the commencement of British settlement at the Sound in late 1826. We know that explorers, whalers and sealers, as well as those sailing between the colony of New South Wales and the port of Cape Town, called at King George Sound during this period to refill their ships' water containers, take on board firewood for their stoves and repair storm damage to their vessels. From some of the few remaining ships' logbooks from this period we know that contact was made with the local Aboriginal inhabitants. We even have some detailed accounts of the interaction that occurred between these visitors and some members of the Menang who chose to assist or trade with them. What must, however, always remain imperfectly understood is the effect that these early contacts had upon subsequent relationships between Albany's Aboriginal people and those who arrived on their shores, firstly as generally friendly visitors, but then as invaders and supplanters of Aboriginal traditional rights as owners of the land.

It is most unlikely that any Europeans were aware of the existence of the sheltered waters of King George Sound prior to the year 1600. However, in 1610, a voyage took place that had profound implications for the region's future. The young Dutch captain Hendrick Brouwer proved the validity of his theory that his fellow Dutch East Indies mariners could save time and company money by utilising the strong westerly winds that consistently blow at southern latitudes, rather than continuing to sail the traditional route up the east coast of Africa before heading east to the islands of the East Indies (Indonesia). He showed that as much as six months could be cut from a voyage that commonly took a year to complete. In 1617, the company formally instructed its captains to sail directly eastwards from the Cape of Good Hope for a distance of 1,000 Dutch miles (about 4,000 statute miles), before turning northwards to the East Indies. The policy was sound in theory, but in practice the inaccuracy of longitude measurements and the impossibility of making completely accurate dead-reckoning calculations meant that some ships inevitably sailed too far east and made contact, either visually, or at times violently, with the west coast of the Australian continent – the then uncharted Terra Australis.

In 1616 Dirk Hartog became the first Dutch master to make this mistake and live to return with a record of the nature of the coast. His unfavourable reports on the barren nature of the country tallied with those of later Dutch observers and resulted in a lack of commercial interest in the area. For the next 170 years the region received no dedicated voyages of discovery, although the fact that updated Dutch maps showed a harbour named Monkbeelven in the approximate position of King George Sound indicates that Dutch mariners continued to sail occasionally along its shores and probably were well aware of the existence of the harbour.[1] If any of these ships sailed into the uncharted waters of the Sound, no record has yet been found, and if any contact took place between these mariners and the Menang, it has to date been lost to history.[2]

France and Britain had long been maritime rivals, and as their power increased relative to the Dutch during the eighteenth century they sought to increase their knowledge of the southern continent from both a scientific and a strategic viewpoint.[3] François de St Alouärn reached Cape Leeuwin in 1792 but was unable to land. He then sailed north to Dirk Hartog Island, taking possession for France of 'the land to the north-west' of his anchorage, an action that was not taken seriously in Paris.[4] Bruny d'Entrecasteaux led a voyage in 1792 of two more French vessels, *Recherche* and *Esperance*, to explore the largely uncharted south coast east of Cape Leeuwin, but the ships were unable to enter King George Sound. Britain and France were each acutely aware of the strategic ambitions of the other, and a voyage of discovery in the southern seas by one nation resulted in the almost simultaneous despatch of an expedition by the other; as a counter to the French expedition, the British sent George Vancouver to explore and chart the southern coast of New Holland.

On 28 September 1791, Vancouver sailed into King George Sound in the *Discovery*, accompanied by the *Chatham*. This visit of a little over two weeks' duration was a turning point in the lives of the Menang, even though no contact took place with the British. For the first time, the commodious and sheltered harbour was explored by Europeans, assessed for its value to maritime travel, and located accurately on maps that would be keenly studied by those who would seek to pursue their varied purposes in its shelter. Whatever the future held for the area's Aboriginal people, Vancouver's entry into their world ensured that it would be shared with others.

Vancouver was immediately aware of the strategic and economic importance to the British Government of such a vast natural harbour, not least because it would afford shelter and fresh water to ships sailing to and from the new penal settlement at Sydney. Vessels on this route usually sailed well to the south of the area on their way to rounding the southern tip of Van Diemen's Land, but the knowledge of a safe place to replenish water stocks or to seek a sheltered anchorage to effect repairs could be of great value to mariners. At this time, the dramatic events of the 1789 French Revolution caused concern in Britain about French political instability and the potential threat this presented to British interests at home and abroad. Fearing that this fundamental shift in French affairs could lead to an expansionary phase which might see the region come under French domination, Vancouver claimed all of the land from 'Cape' Chatham (later found to be an island south-east of Cape Leeuwin) to as far east as he may later sail. Perhaps because the authorities in London had no plans to form a settlement in the area, there is no evidence that Vancouver's pre-emptive annexation was ever officially recognised by the British Colonial Office.[5]

Vancouver was of course aware of the presence of Aborigines in the area around the newly discovered Sound. He made some efforts, including leaving some gift items 'as tokens of our friendly disposition, and to induce any of the natives, who might, unperceived by us, have been in the neighbourhood, to favour us with a visit'.[6] He came across:

the most miserable human habitation my eyes ever beheld... The reflections which normally arose on seeing so miserable a contrivance for shelter against the inclemency of seasons, were humiliating in the highest degree; as they suggested in the strongest manner, the lowly condition of some of our fellow creatures...[7]

Surprisingly, given the experience of subsequent European visitors, his crew made no contact with those who dwelt in the 'deserted village' of about two dozen huts. Atypically for British ships of the period fitted out for voyages of exploration, *Discovery* carried only one person (Menzies, a surgeon–naturalist) who would today be regarded as a scientist. Vancouver had no one aboard with the specific responsibility to make contact with Aboriginal people. It would appear that London believed the Aboriginal inhabitants of New Holland were unlikely to be of scientific interest, perhaps because the British assumed there would be little difference between them and the Aborigines of the region of the Port Jackson settlement with whom they were by then familiar.

Once King George Sound had been charted and noted as a safe harbour, French and American whaling ships began to call in for shelter and to take on fresh water from the several springs at Frenchman Bay and along the shores of Princess Royal Harbour. It is highly likely that some contacts were made by the crews of these vessels with the Menang, although it appears that any records of such encounters have not survived. There is, however, one piece of indirect evidence that points to the probability that whalers treated Aboriginal people at least reasonably well. Dr T. B. Wilson, surgeon appointed to the British settlement at Albany in late 1829, wrote:

It is quite notorious on many parts of the coast, that if a small vessel makes her appearance, the natives get out of the way as fast as possible, while, if the ship be large, they come down to the beach without mistrust or fear.[8]

Whaling ships were much larger than the small boats used by sealers, and according to Wilson's observation, which he presumably checked with other British members of the settlement who had been there longer than he, those sailing in them were not feared by the Aboriginal coastal people. The men who entered the harbour in smaller vessels were another story altogether.

Vancouver's account of his voyage made the southern coast of New Holland a magnet for those who read his observations of numerous whales and seals in the area. Already, gangs of sealers were operating in the waters around Van Diemen's Land and as far west as Kangaroo Island; Vancouver's sightings of seals, together with his charts of the western coastline, gave the incentive for the more venturesome of these men to try their luck in the new and unexploited seas far to the west. While not under the type of stern discipline enforced by the Royal Navy, whaling crews were nevertheless under a form of control by their masters. Sealers were under no such restraints. Commonly a gang would be hired at Hobart and brought to the area between King George Sound and the Recherche Archipelago where they were left for months at a time to hunt and skin seals. Until the ships returned, the men lived on islands or at temporary camps on the coast where they were loathed and feared by Aborigines unable to prevent their women being taken as concubines and virtual slaves.

Albany author Sarah Drummond's research for her PhD thesis about the history of the sealers and Aboriginal women who lived on the south coast islands between Albany and Esperance around the beginning of the nineteenth century has shown that while some of the women were abducted from Bass Strait islands, others were sold to sealers by Tasmanian Aboriginal groups that had forcefully taken the women from neighbouring groups. Her examination of Tasmanian Protector G. A. Robinson's biographies of sealers shows that as few as two from a total of thirty had ever been convicts, effectively challenging the common assertion that the sealers were almost all men of that class.[9]

Wilson's comment about Aborigines fleeing sealers' boats accords with the fact that during 1825 and early 1826 there was a campaign by churches and the press in Sydney and Hobart to have the 'nests of sealers wallowing in beastly sensuality' removed from the Australian south coast, including the western areas around King George Sound. This strong and widespread feeling of revulsion towards the sealing gangs because of their reported cruelties to Aboriginal people caused pressure to be exerted on the authorities to send an armed naval vessel to wipe out these 'criminal outposts'. It was suggested that military settlements be established at Western Port and King George Sound to put a permanent end to the sealers' 'debasing' activities.[10]

The trade in sealskins was substantial and lucrative. Between 1800 and 1806, more than 100,000 sold at Sydney for prices as high as two guineas each, although it is not known how many of these came from vicinity of King George Sound.[11] Fortunately, Vancouver's estimate of the number of seals in the area was highly exaggerated – had it proven accurate, the numbers of sealers would have been much larger and the scale of cruelty and exploitation of the Aboriginal people would have been even greater.

Although Aboriginal people were cruelly victimised by sealing gangs during the pre-settlement era, there is one clear indication that they were not always prepared to accept ill treatment passively.[12] Shortly after the establishment of the settlement, Aborigines attacked a group of British officers and convicts who believed that they had been mistaken as sealers, and a convict was speared, almost fatally. This incident is revisited in Chapter Three. Shellam, who examines the event in detail, indicates that revenge was not the sole motive for the incident – 'It is hard to know what the spearing signified for the King Ya-nups' – but does not conclusively show that the British were wrong in assuming that the Menang were retaliating for injuries received at the sealers' hands.[13]

The first settlers believed that Aboriginal children from the King George Sound region who were not of full descent were the result of liaisons between sealers and Aboriginal women. William Nairn Clark wrote in 1842 that the first sealers to visit the area were from Van Diemen's Land, and had called in at Port Phillip Bay where they kidnapped several Aboriginal women and took them to the islands to the east of King George Sound. It was the children that these women bore to the sealers who could be seen at the settlement.[14] Not surprisingly, given the lack of formal recording procedures and the sensitivities then involved, it is not possible to verify these assumptions. However, there is little doubt that the sealers bear the responsibility for being the first to introduce three scourges of European civilisation that were to prove so devastating to the Menang – alcohol, tobacco and venereal disease.

In 1801, Commander Matthew Flinders became the next recorded visitor. His ship, the *Investigator*, was equipped in England for a voyage intended to make landfall at Cape Leeuwin from whence he was to sail to a point near Ceduna reached by the Dutch navigator Thyssen in 1626. Flinders was ordered to continue to chart the coast as far as the already mapped Bass Strait. On the evening of 8 December his vessel sailed into what was then named King George Third's Sound, before entering the inner harbour and establishing a shore camp near the site of what was to become the city of Albany. Unlike Vancouver, Flinders' party made contact with a group of the Menang soon after arrival. As we have seen, this was possibly not the first meeting between European and Aboriginal people at Albany – it is likely that sealers or whalers had previously called at the Sound – but it is the first encounter of which a written record has survived.

When reading accounts of meetings between two very different groups of people, it is critical to attempt to understand the writers' attitudes and cultural assumptions about those from the other group. Around the beginning of the nineteenth century, a number of important schools of thought existed in Britain and France about inhabitants of newly 'discovered' lands. Since it was French and British sailors who visited King George Sound prior to European settlement, it is the attitudes of the people of these two nations that are relevant to this story. It would clearly be simplistic to assume that every visitor to the Sound held firmly and exclusively to any one theory. It would be even more unrealistic to make the assumption that as the educated elites in Britain and France moved from older schools of philosophy to ones more in tune with emerging scientific and cultural ideas, those from the less educated sections of those societies always moved with them. Those who journeyed to visit the Sound inevitably held preconceptions about the Aboriginal people they fully expected to encounter on arrival. Although we can never know what these preconceptions were in detail, an examination of some commonly accepted viewpoints of the time provides a framework for looking at the records through the eyes of contemporary writers.

At the end of the eighteenth century, the dominant Western philosophy concerning the structure of the universe was still the medieval *scala naturae* or 'The Great Chain of Being', although the idea was coming under increasing challenge in Great Britain where it had never been as strongly held as in Continental Europe.[15] This theory provided an explanation of how every substance or creature in the universe had a place on a 'chain of being', with God at the top of the chain and beneath him angels, stars, kings, nobles, various lesser grades of men, the lion as king of the beasts, then lesser animals and so on. An essential understanding of the concept was that all places on the chain were fixed – it was not a ladder that could be climbed by personal effort or merit. It gave a philosophical and logical basis to the doctrine of the divine right of kings, and to those who supported and enforced a socially immobile stratified society.[16] Laird wrote:

> Next to the word 'Nature', 'The Great Chain of Being' was the sacred phrase of the eighteenth century, playing a part somewhat analogous to that of the blessed word 'evolution' in the late nineteenth.[17]

The relevance of this worldview to events at King George Sound lies in the position it assigned to various levels of humanity, and the relationship that it held to exist between humans and the so-called higher forms of the animal kingdom. The division between the two was believed to be very indistinct.[18] Some people were ordained by God's plan to be superior to others, while close observation of newly discovered peoples might well show that it was they who occupied the mysterious position on the chain between men and the higher placed animal species. Obviously, those who held to the theory, and had grown up in the rigidly enforced hierarchic social structure engendered by its application, had the preconditioning to regard indigenous peoples throughout the world as their racial and social inferiors.

By the time the first British and French ships called at King George Sound, the influence of this philosophy was still significant, although in decline in both Britain and France. A frightened British middle class saw the writings of Voltaire, Erasmus Darwin, and especially Thomas Paine, as a major cause of the revolutionary turmoil that swept over France in the 1790s.[19] This fear gave impetus to Evangelicalism, with its fundamental antagonism towards the static continuity advocated and enforced by those holding to the Chain of Being as their guiding philosophy.[20] Evangelicalism was a powerful and politically influential movement within the Church of England at this time that aimed at rejuvenating the Church and promoting social and humanitarian projects, such as the William

Wilberforce–led campaign to abolish the Atlantic slave trade. In France, the old idea of the Chain of Being was swept away by the Revolution as a relic of absolute monarchism and the perceived tyranny of the Ancien Régime.

Another influential contemporary theory held that people are essentially virtuous unless corrupted by civilisation. This concept, generally referred to as the idea of the 'Noble Savage', is at least as old as ancient Greece and Rome, and is found in writings of classical scholars from both of these societies. Barbaric acts committed by 'civilised' Europeans, such as the St Bartholomew's Day Massacre of 1572 in France, and the treatment of indigenous peoples by the Spanish Conquistadors, led to a revival of the theme. The Spanish Dominican priest Bartolomé de las Casas witnessed and wrote about incredible acts of cruelty in sixteenth-century Spanish America and attacked those who held to the widely accepted view that 'Indians' were essentially inferior beings to the Spanish. His criticisms of the colonial system powerfully influenced many throughout Europe to embrace the concept of the Noble Savage in reaction to such cruelty.[21]

It is possible to see the concept in the writings of Captain James Cook following his 1770 voyage in the *Endeavour*:

> From what I have said of the Natives of New-Holland they may appear to some to be the most wretched people on Earth, but in reality they are far more happier than we Europeans; being wholly unacquainted not only with the superfluous but the necessary Conveniences so much sought after in Europe they are happy in not knowing the use of them. They live in a Tranquillity, which is not disturb'd by the inequality of Condition: The Earth and sea of their own accord furnishes them with all the things necessary for life, they covet not Magnificent Houses, Household stuff etc, they live in a warm and fine Climate and enjoy a very fine and wholesome Air, so that they have very little need of

Clothing and this they seem to be fully sensible of, for many to whome we gave Cloth etc to left it carelessly upon the Sea beach and in the woods as a thing they had no manner of use for. In short they seem'd to set no Value.[22]

The Noble Savage point of view was essentially theoretical, and was commonly held by intellectuals rather than by the less educated members of society. As increasing contact led to an increase in observed (as distinct from purely theoretical) knowledge about the indigenous inhabitants of Australia and North America, the unreality that had always characterised much of the ideal of the Noble Savage became apparent and its influence waned. However, it proved to be an idea that refused to die completely, and as late as 1893 when Cook's journal was finally published the editor felt it necessary to point out in a footnote that the explorer's views about the Australian Aborigines were in error. Indeed some modern commentators see evidence that it is still alive in some quarters. Australian academic and writer Larissa Behrendt has attacked what she refers to as 'the romanticism of the "noble savage" pervasive in texts and cinema' still being used for political ends today.[23]

The French reacted against the old ideas because they saw them as inconsistent with their new, modern, scientific republic. The British reaction against Primitivism, a term that embraces the concept of the Noble Savage, came from two different quarters. Clearly, when one considers the extent to which the British Empire was then expanding by taking land from 'primitive' peoples, it was not a useful model around which the Colonial Office in London might form policy. Secondly, and crucially, Evangelical Anglican Christianity and the rise of the influence of Enlightenment thinkers in the late eighteenth century combined in a powerful new philosophical movement that swept away the older paradigms of thought among the elite stratum that largely controlled decisions in what was still an oligarchic society.

This new philosophical viewpoint held that all humans were descended from common ancestors. Any variety in peoples was due to a form of evolutionary development, the ultimate goal of which was a society not unlike that advocated by Enlightenment theorists.[24] Man had passed from hunter to shepherd to farmer to merchant, with a corresponding shift in social organisation from tribe to modern state. The fundamental difference between this point of view and those held by previous generations of the elite of British and European society was that the human race was now seen to be one, with the evident variations caused by culture, rather than by biology or an unchangeable decision of God.[25] Alexander Maconochie, who later held the position of commandant at Norfolk Island, demonstrated the sincerity with which educated men of the period held to the idea by giving lectures speculating that the ancestors of British and Europeans were black, before 'the effect of civilisation' turned them white.[26]

This philosophy allowed for the possibility of 'improvement' for all peoples, even if the desired improvement was seen as being necessarily along the lines of moving towards the model of British society at the turn of the eighteenth and nineteenth centuries. Since racial differences were believed to be only skin deep, indigenous peoples deserved full respect as fellow humans. However, the influence of Evangelical Anglicanism upon the British elite ensured that this respect did not extend to Aboriginal religion or culture. Aboriginal society, with its emphasis on community rather than the individual and on its own non-Christian spirituality, was something to be superseded, rather than valued and encouraged.

The contrast between this new and relatively enlightened view, and those positing 'savage' people as occupying an indeterminate position between mankind and the animal kingdom, is crucial to any understanding of the philosophies underlying the first contacts at King George Sound, and the subsequent history of Aboriginal and European interaction in the area. Many settlers in early nineteenth-century Australia still held the older view. Stanner observed:

> In the early years of settlement [in eastern Australia] insensibility towards the Aborigines' human status hardened into contempt, derision and indifference. The romantic idealism, unable to stand the shock of experience, drifted through dismay into pessimism about the natives' capacity for civilisation.[27]

This view was being expressed as late as 1965, when the Western Australian author Alexandra Hasluck wrote that the land around Mandurah when she was a child 'had hardly been seen by human eyes, save those of black men, if they could be called human'.[28]

The attitudes and assumptions of the Menang towards the first Europeans with whom they came into contact are obviously of equal importance in understanding the significance of the interaction that took place prior to permanent British settlement at the Sound. Unfortunately we don't have access to any documents from this period written by an Aboriginal person, and only very little was written by Europeans at Albany that touched on the subject.

The most comprehensive source of information about how Australian Aboriginal groups in general rationalised the existence of Europeans is the influential Australian historian Henry Reynolds' book *The Other Side of the Frontier*, written in 1981. Reynolds noted that their arrival caused Aboriginal groups to indulge in prolonged and intense debate about the true nature and intent of these newcomers. Numerous contemporary European observers, as well as castaways who had spent considerable time living with Aborigines, believed that the pale-skinned visitors were initially seen as Aboriginal individuals returning from the dead. This idea was held in widely geographically separated areas of the Australian continent. Reynolds stated that the various words used by Aboriginal groups to describe Europeans could be translated as 'ghost', 'spirit', 'eternal departed' and 'the dead', and that throughout much of Australia the Aboriginal people who first came into contact with settlers withheld the use of their word for 'person' as a descriptor of the newcomers.[29]

To a society with no knowledge of people from across the ocean, this was a logical assumption to make. The cosmos was a very limited place and most, if not all, of the human race were kin, or potentially so. The known number of people was small, but the number of inhabitants of the spirit world was vast. The spirit world was just as tangible as the world inhabited by the living, and it is little wonder that Aboriginal groups across the continent separately reached the conclusion that the visitors were a form of returning spirits. In a world where the existence of other countries was neither known nor suspected, there was no other logical alternative.

We have information from several sources about the way the Aboriginal people of the south-west of Western Australia fitted the pale-skinned men into their cosmology. Francis Armstrong, who arrived at Perth in 1829 and maintained a deep and lifelong interest in Aboriginal people, is probably the best and most accurate source of information about the subject, despite criticism of him by several of his contemporaries. He wrote that Perth Noongars rationalised the existence and presence of Europeans as Djanga, a Noongar word meaning the ghosts of their dead ancestors who had returned from the spirit island of Kurannup.[30] Similar beliefs also existed among coastal groups in many other parts of the continent.[31] Aboriginal people at Perth frequently identified individual Europeans as one of their deceased relatives, and it is interesting to note that this initial belief was still adhered to at least as late as 1838, when Captain George Grey described how an elderly Noongar woman near Perth assured him that he was the ghost of her dead son.[32] Grey believed that the concept of anyone voluntarily leaving their homeland was so alien to Noongar people that they thought Europeans must be Noongar spirits returning to their old campsites.[33]

None of the observers at Albany recorded detailed information on the subject. This is surprising given the frequency of reports from Perth; Armstrong wrote that the belief was so common there that several hundred people were regarded as Aborigines returned from the dead.[34] Nind, Barker and Collie all took a keen interest in Aboriginal beliefs and it is inconceivable that they would not have raised the subject in their enquiries and discussions. However, they wrote almost nothing about the issue. The most comprehensive record that we have concerning the topic is one account in Barker's journal. The settlement's commandant broached the subject on a day when there was 'much hail and rain', presumably a good opportunity to sit together in the house and have an extended conversation with Mokare, who was his close companion and frequent informant on Aboriginal matters. Barker wrote: 'Conversation with Mokarè about 1st arrival of White People here. He said black fellows knew nothing about them or their reasons for coming...'[35] It is probable that Mokare was not born when the first encounters at King George Sound occurred, but it is reasonable to assume that he would have been aware of any knowledge possessed by his immediate ancestors about European visitors to Australia before the first arrivals at their area.

Nind regarded the custom of interring personal implements in a deceased Aboriginal person's grave as evidence for a belief in the afterlife, and noted their belief that their fathers went to the westward after death.[36] There is, however, one piece of later information which indicates that the beliefs held by the Menang were similar to those of other Noongar groups. In 1908, Nebinyan, an elderly Aboriginal man who had worked in the whaling industry at Albany from 1862 to 1877, told how his ancestors at Albany had seen and touched the Djanga.[37]

There is a further piece of indirect evidence that supports the idea that the Aboriginal people at Albany held some version of the reincarnation belief. Reynolds noted that in some areas of Australia where European settlement occurred later than at places some distance away, the 'secular' view of Europeans was taken from the outset. This was because Aboriginal people from the earlier settled areas had abandoned the reincarnation idea and informed their neighbours of the actual nature of white men.[38] By the time Perth was settled by Europeans, a considerable number of ships had called in at King George Sound over a long period, and some information about the Europeans aboard them must have reached the Swan River Aborigines. The well-attested fact that the Aborigines at Perth held strongly to the reincarnation belief would appear to be evidence that the Menang had not come to any differing conclusion by the late 1820s.

Matthew Flinders' arrival at King George Sound on 8 December 1801 meant that the officers and crew of the *Investigator* were much more likely to meet the Menang than was Vancouver, who visited at a time when many of the Aboriginal people would still have been inland before returning for the summer. Six days later, the first recorded contact between Aborigines and European people at Albany took place. Flinders' journal described how during the ensuing four-week period 'frequent and amicable communication with the natives of this country' occurred.[39]

It is interesting to note that no meeting took place until the sixth day after the British arrived, even though parties had gone ashore on each of the intervening days – and that it was the British who initiated the contact. Flinders' journal entry for 14 December records that various parties were assigned tasks, including the naturalists, who: 'ranged the country in all directions, being landed at such places as they desired; while my [Flinders] own time was divided betwixt the observatory and the survey of the Sound'.[40] One of these parties, headed by the chief naturalist

Robert Brown, decided to investigate some smoke that was visible at the entrance to Princess Royal Harbour. There they met with 'several of the natives who were shy but not afraid'. Having given the Menang men a handkerchief and a bird that they had shot, the men found that:

> like the generality of people hitherto seen in this country, these men did not seem to be desirous of communication with strangers; and they made very early signs to our gentlemen to return from whence they came.[41]

The next morning, a cautious group of Aboriginal men approached the British tents with what the new arrivals felt was a very mixed message. One walked up to the British with a raised spear and, with the others in the group, made what were taken to be threatening words and gestures. The British found it perplexing that the purpose of the 'vociferous parleying' that followed seemed to fluctuate between the issuing of threats if they remained on Aboriginal land, and the granting of permission to stay. Eventually an exchange of goods took place and the two groups parted, 'apparently on very good terms'.[42] During the remainder of the stay, other peaceful contact occurred and Flinders referred in his journal to the Aboriginal people of the area as: 'Our friends the natives...'[43] For reasons not made clear in his journal, Flinders decided to exercise his marines in the presence of the Aboriginal people who had frequently visited the British camp. The brightly coloured uniforms, together with the music of the fifes and drums, made a deep impression on the audience, and it is most interesting to note that the marines' drill movements were carefully memorised and subsequently incorporated into a corroboree performed at Katanning in 1908.[44]

Flinders' visit influenced the future direction of Aboriginal–European relations at Albany in several ways. Firstly, comments in his journal clearly indicated his belief that the Aborigines of King George Sound were fundamentally the same as those at Port Jackson. This meant that the British could plan any future settlement at this strategically interesting natural harbour with the knowledge that the local Aboriginal people could be managed as 'easily' as had been the case at Sydney over the past thirteen years. From an Aboriginal perspective, the significance of Flinders' visit for the future was that they had met Europeans and had found them to be friendly and non-threatening. Following Flinders' visit, those who sailed into King George Sound would find people who had incorporated the presence of Europeans into their own view of the world, and were generally prepared to meet them on a basis of mutual, if guarded, friendship.

In 1803, two French ships called at the Sound as part of a scientific expedition given the task of thoroughly investigating the north, west and south coasts of the still partly unknown Australian continent. Nicolas Baudin, already an experienced leader of scientific missions, was in command. The scientists on board *Géographe* and *Casuarina* had been given most comprehensive instructions about how to carry out a study of the physical and moral conditions of the Aboriginal people who were reported to be living in the western part of Australia. Historian Leslie Marchant has proposed that it was these instructions that marked the turning point in the study of humans, and led to the beginning of scientific anthropology.[45]

The expedition spent eleven days at King George Sound and, as Flinders had experienced two years earlier, the Aboriginal inhabitants were found to be peaceable and friendly. The pattern of Aboriginal men approaching the visitors, while ensuring that their women and children remained out of sight, was again noted. Baudin was impressed with the construction of fish traps, but noted little else about the Aborigines. The French officers and crew were under strict naval discipline and motivated by high scientific ideals, and their visit would have reinforced the idea among the Aboriginal inhabitants that Europeans were both friendly and short-term visitors.

In 1818, Phillip Parker King sailed into King George Sound in the *Mermaid*, anchoring at the entrance to Oyster Harbour where Flinders had anchored seventeen years earlier. Despite seeing their fires each night, King and his men made no contact with the Menang during their eleven-day stay. This is curious since Allan Cunningham, the expedition botanist, explored extensively around the area looking for new specimens for his collection, and John Septimus Roe walked a very considerable distance alone around the perimeter of Oyster Harbour. Given the friendly relations that had developed during Flinders' visit in 1801, it is surprising that the Aboriginal people chose not to make contact with King and his crew.

It is possible that the visit of the *Emu*, a British transport vessel that called in to take on firewood in 1816, may have been significant in this regard. While the ship was anchored, the 'gentlemen' on board (including W. C. Wentworth) made frequent visits ashore where they were received in a 'most friendly manner' by the local Aboriginal people who came unarmed. On several days Aborigines happily came aboard, but on the last day of the visit the boat's crew were attacked without any warning by a group of men who threw a volley of spears. Although Mrs Napper's bonnet was grazed, no one was injured. The crew immediately discharged their muskets in the general direction and fled to the ship without knowing whether they had hit any of their attackers.[46] When King called at the Sound again in late 1821, he recorded that the local Aborigines were well acquainted with the use of muskets. King would have been aware of the *Emu* incident, but the actions of the members of his expedition in walking around the area, in Roe's case by himself, would indicate that they did not expect the affair to be repeated.

There are two grounds to dismiss the possibility that King was either not interested in making contact during his first visit, or that he actively avoided it. Firstly, his instructions from the Colonial Office in London specifically stated that he was to observe in detail the appearance, language, occupation and preparedness to trade of all of the Aboriginal people along the Australian coast. Secondly, King's behaviour on his next voyage clearly indicated that he was diligent in fulfilling his task of meeting Aboriginal people. He welcomed the contact that occurred at King George Sound during his second visit three years later, even after his journal indicated his crewmen had recently been attacked at several locations on the northern Australian coastline. If King had been reluctant to meet Aboriginal people on his first visit, he would have had every reason to be even more reluctant on his second. It would therefore appear likely that it was the Menang who chose not to make contact during his first visit.

King circumnavigated the Australian continent on three occasions, calling at King George Sound on each voyage. It was during his second visit of two weeks between December 1821 and January 1822 that he and his crew enjoyed extensive contact with considerable numbers of the local Aboriginal people. In direct contrast with their policy of keeping away from all contact with the British that had characterised their approach to King's first visit three years earlier, the Menang showed a desire for close and continuing contact.

The *Bathurst* arrived late on the afternoon of 23 December and anchored in the Sound. Early next morning, members of the crew heard 'Indians' calling from the rocky northern side of the entrance to Princess Royal Harbour and returned their calls. As the ship's whaleboat entered the harbour, the Aboriginal men walked along the shore inviting the British to land, wading out to greet them. King was not prepared to risk the 'quarrel' that a refusal to share whatever was in the boat might cause and pulled off into deeper water, much to the 'disappointment and mortification at our want of confidence' that this action caused.[47] The British crew, not unnaturally cautious following their recent clashes with Aboriginal groups in northern Australia, carefully ascertained that the men on the shore were unarmed. However, they decided to return to the ship and move to the entrance to Oyster Harbour where they 'could anchor near enough to the shore to carry on our different operations without being impeded by the natives, even though they should be amicably disposed'.[48]

At their new anchorage in deep water close to shore, King felt secure enough to welcome on board small parties of Aboriginal men. Soon, he was referring to them in his journal as 'our friends', noting that they were 'totally free from timidity or distrust'. Menang men assisted the British in the work of gathering stores of firewood and fresh water, and permitted them to carry out botanical research over an extensive area bordering the harbour. The crew became particularly attached to a young man to whom they gave the name 'Jack'. They allowed him to visit and leave the ship whenever he wished, and he became so attached to the British that he accepted their offer to sail with them on the remainder of their journey, only to decline after experiencing seasickness during a period of rising swell that preceded the *Bathurst*'s departure. The Menang eagerly traded weapons for ship's biscuit, and the British took a considerable quantity of Aboriginal artefacts on board.[49]

King generally treated the Menang with a degree of respect, and it appears from his journal that he welcomed their friendship. There was, however, a jarring note: on the day after the *Bathurst* arrived, King had Jack dressed in sailors' clothing and plied him with alcohol in the form of watered-down rum, the 'grog' traditionally rationed to sailors aboard vessels of the Royal Navy.[50]

Ten months later, King returned to King George Sound for a brief visit during which he noted the presence of the American sealing schooner the *San Antonio*. King's journal mentioned meeting with 'our old friend Coolbun', but apart from noting

Jack's absence he wrote almost nothing about any interaction the crew may have had with the local Aboriginal population.

In 1825, the French Government gave Jules Dumont d'Urville command of a voyage of scientific discovery to the Pacific region. Western Australia was not part of his official itinerary, but the requirement to repair storm damage to his ship, the *Astrolabe*, made necessary a stay of eighteen days at King George Sound in October 1826.[51] As King had done earlier, Dumont d'Urville took Aboriginal men aboard his vessel, dressing one in European clothing before putting him ashore. Like King, the French Captain gave alcohol to at least one Aboriginal man, the first to go aboard the ship. Dumont d'Urville stated that the man had suffered greatly from the 'evil effects', and it is interesting to read that when eight local men later made their acquaintance with Dumont d'Urville and some members of his crew, the Aborigines refused to take any of the brandy that was offered to them.[52]

It is difficult at this remove to state confidently why both King and Dumont d'Urville resorted to plying Aboriginal men with alcohol aboard their vessels. One possible explanation is that it had become common for Europeans to react against what they saw as the unrealistic concept of the Noble Savage by casting indigenous people in a comic role. So common was the practice that it had its own conventions. Artists depicted Aboriginal men and women as grotesque caricatures of Europeans, complete with inappropriate forms of European clothing, a clay pipe, and 'comical' nicknames.[53] The widespread view that in many ways the antipodes represented the inversion of things in the northern hemisphere reinforced the idea, allowing even those with some residual sympathy with the Noble Savage theory to rationalise that it was an inappropriate concept to apply to indigenous people from the southern hemisphere.[54] A painting by the *Astrolabe*'s official artist, Louis Auguste de Sainson, shows clear signs that it was not only the British who were influenced by this attitude towards

Aboriginal people. Three Europeans are portrayed as meticulously dressed, while an Aboriginal man is depicted as wearing shabby and ill-fitting European clothing. His Aboriginal companions are depicted as barely human. The artist was obviously intent on producing this painting in the comic savage genre – his other paintings of the King George Sound area show Aboriginal people with realistic physiques and possessing an obvious dignity.

Apart from this incident, the journals of Dumont d'Urville, de Sainson and the two naturalists Joseph Gaimard and Jean Constant Quoy present a picture of respect for the people with whom they came into contact at King George Sound. Given the different experience of British visitors prior to settlement, it is interesting to note that the Menang almost immediately brought their children to meet the French visitors. However, like the British, they were not permitted to see or meet with the women.[55] Only three days after their arrival, the relationship between the visitors and the residents was such that three French men spent most of the night at the camp where the Aboriginal people were living at the time. The picture of the evening presented in de Sainson's journal is that of two very differing groups of people, each intent upon learning as much as possible about the other, and each feeling safe in the other's company.[56] Apart from confirming that men who arrived in large ships were likely to be friendly, interesting and useful trading partners, a lasting consequence of the enforced stay of the *Astrolabe* was the opportunity it provided for de Sainson to paint a number of carefully detailed scenes which have survived to the present.[57]

Albany's early history was very different from that of almost every other area of the Australian continent – by the time the first contingent of British men and women arrived on the scene with intentions of staying on a long-term basis, the Aboriginal residents of the region had known of the existence of Europeans for well over thirty years, and had had time to consider how they fitted into the Aboriginal spiritual world. The experience of European contact had been generally positive, and where problems had arisen, the Menang were well able to differentiate between the exploitative sealers and the much more amicable and interested men who visited for short periods in the big white-sailed ships. Aboriginal people welcomed these ships and the people who lived in them, because they brought different opportunities for trade than did visitors from other Aboriginal groups who travelled across country.[58] Initially there appeared no reason to suspect that the *Amity*, which arrived only a few weeks after the departure of the *Astrolabe*, represented any change in the already well-established pattern. Had the Menang been aware that this ship was actually the forerunner of countless others that would bring men, women and children who would ultimately dispossess them of their sacred land, the events recounted in the next chapter may well have played out in a very different fashion.

Chapter Three

From Visitors to Invaders – The Garrison Era, 1826–1831

The early years of a permanent British presence at King George Sound, and the relationship that developed between the Menang and the new arrivals in their midst

Early nineteenth-century Britain was not alone in possessing a criminal code that provided for felons to be sentenced to transportation; French law also specified transportation for certain classes of offenders but the sentences could not be carried out since France had no overseas territory considered suitable for the establishment of a penal settlement. In order to alleviate what was a growing problem, the French Minister of the Interior set up a committee to report on potential sites that could provide a solution. In 1819 he was advised that three places in south-western Australia would serve the purpose: Flinders Bay near Cape Leeuwin; the Swan River; and King George Sound.[1] This recommendation resulted in the despatch of a series of French naval expeditions with orders to thoroughly investigate the region.

Information indicating the success of the British penal colony at Sydney was brought back to Paris and in early 1826 two reports from Jules de Blosseville, a French intellectual and navigator, recommended that the area between Esperance and the Tropic of Capricorn be claimed as French territory. King George Sound was identified as the most suitable site for the capital.[2] Given the centuries-long tradition of hostility between Britain and France, it is not surprising that the former maintained an extensive intelligence network in Paris, and that information about French ambitions in New Holland quickly reached London. In early 1826, the British Colonial Secretary, Lord Bathurst, sent a despatch to Governor Darling at Sydney apprising him of the threat posed by the French scheme and advising him of actions to take to forestall it. Marchant's assiduous search of French archives uncovered conclusive evidence that the French in early 1826 did have intentions for King George Sound, but that by late 1826 they had diverted their attention to New Zealand. The British fear of French settlement on the western coast of the Australian continent was soundly based, but their action to forestall this was based on intelligence that was several months out of date.[3]

However, fear of French expansion was not the only factor influencing Darling's thoughts on the advisability of establishing a British presence on the western coast. By the mid 1820s, officials in both London and Sydney believed that the Port Macquarie penal settlement established for convicts who had committed crimes after arriving at New South Wales was unsuited to the task and should be closed. In March 1826, Bathurst instructed Darling to send an expedition to Shark Bay on the western coast of the continent to survey its suitability as the site of a replacement for Port Macquarie.[4] Ten days later he wrote to Darling ordering him to instruct the captain of the ship to call at King George Sound before proceeding to Shark Bay. The officer was to assess the soil quality and other aspects of the area around the Sound that would indicate its suitability and, should his report prove favourable, Darling was instructed to establish a settlement there.[5] Darling responded in October giving his strong opinion that both places were barren and unfit, even for a penal settlement. He believed distance and unfavourable winds would make governance from Sydney unworkable, and it was with great reluctance that he complied with Bathurst's orders.[6] Before the ship, the *Amity*, sailed, Darling decided to omit Shark Bay from its itinerary and make King George Sound the site of the new settlement.

Those aboard the *Amity* who were to remain at King George Sound included Major Edmund Lockyer, his deputy Captain Joseph Wakefield, a sergeant and eighteen rank-and-file soldiers of the 39th Regiment of the British Army, a surgeon, a gardener, twenty-three convicts and a storekeeper. There were also three soldiers' wives, together with two of their children.[7]

After arriving from Britain in 1825, the 39th Regiment was stationed in Van Diemen's Land where it had become embroiled in what was a virtual state of war with the colony's Aboriginal population.[8] The regiment was not specifically chosen to garrison King George Sound because of this recent experience in controlling resistance to British invasion – its members had been given the task of providing a military force at each outpost on the continent and the new posting was routine. However, it is reasonable to assume that the recent bitter campaign in the island colony would have instilled attitudes into the soldiers that were scarcely calculated to assist in the establishment and maintenance of good relations with the original inhabitants of King George Sound and its surrounding area.

Immediately upon entering the Sound, Lockyer was confronted with the undeniable reality that the land over which he had been instructed to raise the Union Jack was already occupied – and that from that time forward the destinies of the British and the local Aboriginal people would become inextricably linked. As the *Amity* sailed past Michaelmas Island, the crew saw a large fire burning, 'as if by persons requiring assistance'.[9] In an act that prefigured ongoing British priorities Lockyer chose to sail into Princess Royal Harbour, leaving what he believed to be Aboriginal problems to a more convenient time. This is not necessarily a criticism of Lockyer. His official orders from Alexander Macleay, the Colonial Secretary at Sydney, made clear that Lockyer was to 'use every exertion to conciliate the Natives, and with this end in view a supply of Tomahawks and Blankets is sent as presents for them'.[10] However, the fact that this single sentence comprised the *only* written instructions about Aboriginal matters must have provided Lockyer with a clear indication of where official priorities lay. The paucity of his instructions reflected the fact that by 1826 the British already had thirty-eight years' experience of settling areas populated by Australian Aboriginal people, but had discovered no formula that guaranteed the establishment of good relations.[11] Once his vessel and crew were safely anchored in harbour and had attended to more urgent matters, he would investigate the matter further.

The *Amity* sailed through the narrow entrance to Princess Royal Harbour at 5 pm on 26 December 1826. Lockyer noted that no signs of any Aboriginal presence on the mainland were visible from the ship's anchorage close to shore. However, any questions he may have had as to how he was to make contact with them were resolved the next day when he and Lieutenant Colson Festing, the *Amity*'s Captain, went on shore at 4 am and were met by two Aboriginal men and a small boy who approached the new arrivals 'without the slightest hesitation'.[12] Lockyer assented to the younger man's wish to go aboard the *Amity*, where he remained until the crew had eaten breakfast and fitted him with a pair of white trousers. The British soon concluded that he was the man King had named 'Jack', and were pleased to reciprocate his obvious wish for friendship.

Lockyer and the others of his shore party spent the day exploring the area between Princess Royal and Oyster harbours, climbing Mount Clarence to obtain a panoramic view of the area. During this extensive excursion they saw no Aboriginal people. At dawn on the following day Lockyer finally decided to send a small boat to investigate the signal fires on Michaelmas Island, thereby inadvertently setting in motion a train of events that could very easily have ended in the existence of a state of open warfare between the British and the Menang.

The convict overseer found four Aboriginal men marooned on the island by a sealing gang, and returned them to the mainland near the *Amity*'s anchorage. It is an interesting insight into Lockyer's expectations of Aboriginal reaction to the arrival of European visitors to find that he sent the overseer on this mission alone and unarmed. The four marooned men rejoined their compatriots at the foot of Mount Melville where Lockyer, Festing and several others were in the process of walking to the water's edge to check on the progress of a team of ten convicts and an overseer who had been given the task of refilling the ship's water containers. The complicated and confused chain of events that followed is vividly described by Tiffany Shellam in her book *Shaking Hands on the Fringe*.[13] In summary, Dennis Dineen, a member of the convict watering party who had decided to go off by himself to swim, was suddenly aware of a number of painted Aboriginal men who were obviously preparing to ambush the party by attacking them with spears. As he called out a warning, he was speared three times: through the thigh; the lower back; and the arm. Lockyer believed that it was only Dineen's shouted warning that saved the others in the party, himself included.

Most surprisingly, neither Lockyer nor any of his companions retaliated although at least five of them were carrying firearms. The Aborigines ran away into the sand hills while the British returned quickly to the *Amity* where Nind, the expedition's surgeon, removed the spears and narrowly managed to save Dineen's life. One can imagine the extent of British anger at what they felt to have been a betrayal of their trust and friendship – just before the attack Lockyer's small party had met with a group of Aboriginal men in what he felt was a 'friendly encounter'. He had shot a cockatoo for them and they returned the favour by pointing out where the British could find kangaroos. The spearing seemed to the British to have been arbitrary, and explicable only by assuming that the attack had resulted from a misunderstanding; the Aboriginal men had believed the newcomers were in some way responsible for marooning the four men on Michaelmas Island and mistreating their women. Lockyer accepted the misdirected revenge attack:

> on reflecting that the people had made this attack in consequence of the injuries they had received, I gave positive orders that no retaliation should take place on our side except in absolute self defence, and I am certain with proper precaution nothing further will occur.[14]

This was a powerful statement coming from an officer who had personally seen the whitened bones of a British detachment wiped out by indigenous Ceylonese in 1803.[15] What the rank-and-file soldiers from a regiment that had so recently handled armed Aboriginal attacks in a very different fashion thought of Lockyer's response was not recorded.

Lockyer's statement was generous in the circumstances of that day, and it highlights the profound effect on history that can be exerted by men and women of unusual goodwill. Over the course of the ensuing years at Albany, the relationship that developed between the British and the Menang would be affected repeatedly by such men from both sides of a vast cultural divide that could very easily have led to bloodshed. Sporadic acts of violence did occur, but Albany was largely free of the hostility and virtual warfare that characterised Australian contact history elsewhere.

Much of the credit for this was due to the great good fortune that Albany enjoyed in the choice of the four commandants, but the wise nature of some other individuals, both British and Aboriginal, involved in the vital first few years following the arrival of the *Amity* also played an important part.[16]

With Lockyer's departure in April 1827, the settlement came under the command of Joseph Wakefield, a captain in the 39th Regiment. Wakefield held the position until early December 1828, concentrating on the construction of buildings to replace the very crude structures that were 'so exceedingly temporary that they are quite unfit to be occupied'.[17] Wakefield had the benefit of serving an apprenticeship under the older and more experienced Lockyer, and continued his policies with respect to the Aboriginal inhabitants. His reports to Macleay were less comprehensive and reflective than those of Lockyer, and only a few entries mention Aboriginal people. This is not to diminish the vital part that Wakefield played in keeping the relationship at King George Sound on a friendly basis; the potential for a worsening of relations once the battle-experienced 39th had one of their own officers in charge clearly existed, and it is greatly to Wakefield's credit that the relationship remained generally amicable during his tenure.

Within a few weeks of the new commandant taking over, a potentially major problem arose. In his report dated 21 May 1827 Wakefield wrote: 'The Natives continue to visit us daily, and do not appear at all hostile, but, from the strong disposition they show for thieving, are become rather troublesome...'[18] Two Aboriginal men had been allowed to sleep beside the settlement's cooking fire and it was found early next morning that they had taken two axes with them as they left the camp. In the early nineteenth century, even such a relatively minor theft was treated with great severity by the British justice system. Wakefield was presented with a most awkward situation – one where a more bureaucratic officer might have acted so harshly that the developing relationship would have come to a sudden end. In the event, it was the Kincannups who solved the problem in their own way.

By this time, several Aboriginal men had taken up almost constant residence at the settlement, and they expressed their anger to Wakefield at the behaviour of the two newcomers who had disappeared with the axes. They promised to restore the stolen property, and a few days later returned with the news that they had speared one of the offenders. Soon afterwards the other man returned his axe and, although the British attempted to interfere with the process by allowing his escape, a severe spear wound was inflicted in his leg.[19] Typically, Wakefield made no further comment on the issue in his report. Presumably this incident resolved the potentially serious problem of theft from the settlement during the remainder of Wakefield's time as commandant, for he made no further written references to it. Although Lockyer instructed Wakefield to keep an official journal, there is no evidence that he either complied with the order or wrote an unofficial account of his experience at the settlement for his own private purposes. In the absence of such documents, one presumes that Wakefield was satisfied to have the Aboriginal people handle such a troublesome situation according to their own laws.

It is unclear why Wakefield included this story in his report while failing to mention a much more serious incident. If an overseer who was present at the settlement at the time had not related the story to a later commandant, Captain Collet Barker, who recorded it in his journal in January 1830, it would have remained untold. A small Aboriginal boy named Yallepolle came into the settlement suffering from the effects of some illness, lay down on a convict's bed and subsequently died. The Kincannups were furious, and large numbers of them threatened to retaliate in their traditional fashion by spearing a member of the British garrison, whom they held jointly responsible for the death. Wakefield was singled out as the subject of the revenge attack but the spear providentially failed to strike home, from either inaccuracy or a lack of willingness to shed British blood and thereby bring to an end a potentially useful alliance with the powerful newcomers. It was three weeks before the British felt safe once more. The boy was the younger brother of the man who was the main link between the British and the Kincannups, and his death must have sorely tried the always tentative and fragile peace that existed at the settlement.[20]

Wakefield's 'Despatch no. 9' to Colonial Secretary Macleay, written in late October 1827, mentioned another problem that arose between the British and the Kincannups. 'Native dogs' were driving the settlement's sheep and pigs away from their feeding grounds close to the settlement. This threatened to become a major source of conflict, and to avoid the soldiers having to kill the dogs, the British planted maize in the hope that this would provide food for the stock, thereby allowing them to be penned away from the marauding animals. Unfortunately the maize failed to thrive and the problem remained. The number of livestock held at this time was not recorded, but would not have been large (in the previous July the settlement had only five sheep and eighteen pigs) but they were highly prized as sources of fresh meat for those who were ill.[21] Dingoes had taken several sheep from the sheepfold adjacent to the storekeeper's hut, and had also eaten some pigs. Given the value to the British of these animals and the small numbers of them that were at the settlement, it is not surprising to read that they used firearms to drive the dingoes away. Dogs were valuable aids to the Aboriginal men in hunting, and considerable diplomacy must have taken place to avoid serious problems arising from the use of firearms in this way. The same despatch included, 'We continue on the same friendly terms with the Natives', indicating that neither side was prepared to allow a potentially explosive situation to develop beyond a certain mutually tolerable level.[22]

In December 1828, Wakefield handed over command to Lieutenant George Sleeman, his fellow officer in the 39th Regiment. Sleeman had previously served at the Raffles Bay settlement near modern Darwin, so had recent experience with the management of a small, isolated garrison on Aboriginal land. At this time, the *Challenger* under Captain Fremantle was sailing from England as the forerunner of the party to establish the settlement at the Swan River. This was intended to be a substantial settlement, one that would ultimately greatly lessen the importance of King George Sound to the British Colonial Office.

The fact that Sleeman's first bundle of despatches from Sydney included letters dated from 6 May to 26 November 1828 provides an indication of the administrative difficulties caused by distance.[23] In his letter dated 25 March 1829, Sleeman showed that he took seriously the maintenance of good relations with the local Aboriginal people:

> The Natives continue to frequent the Settlement in the most friendly manner, and although they occasionally bring small presents, yet they are generally very importunate for Biscuit, of which they are extremely fond. Where fish are so very plentiful, it is to be regretted we are without the Means of catching them, as with the aid of a Seine [net] we could not only abundantly supply our Own wants but satisfy those of our black friends. Should His Excellency be pleased to permit One of the Seines at Raffles Bay [recently closed] to be brought here by the next vessel, it will be of most essential Service.[24]

The only other occasion that Sleeman's reports mentioned anything to do with Aboriginal issues was a request that Macleay endorse his decision to give the garrison's surgeon, Isaac Scott Nind, an extra twenty pounds of flour a month to provide rations for a Kincannup man who had been residing with Nind for 'many months'. Sleeman pointed out that:

> the Native in question is almost always on the Settlement (although by no Means wholly dependent on Mr. Nind for

support), and as he has proved himself useful in many instances in communicating with his fellow Natives and restoring things that have been taken away.[25]

Nind's formal letter to Sleeman requesting the flour contained the first definite written reference in any British document to a young Kincannup man who was destined to play a crucial role in ensuring that the history of Aboriginal–European relations at King George Sound followed a very different path from that taken by the vast majority of other Australian regions. Nind spelled his name as 'Mawcarrie', but although Nind was the first Englishman to attempt to transcribe the name, he was not the first European to do so.[26] Louis de Sainson, a member of Dumont d'Urville's expedition of 1826, wrote the name as 'Mokoré', using an acute accent on the final letter.[27] Captain Collet Barker, who replaced Sleeman as commandant on 3 December 1829 and had very close contact with the young Kincannup man over an extended period of time, consistently spelt the name 'Mokarè', indicating that the final syllable should be pronounced as in *care*. Throughout his remarkable journal, Barker always used a grave accent on the final letter, although since he incorrectly used the same accent when writing *naivetè* it is probable that he intended the pronunciation to be that indicated by the use of an acute accent, with the last syllable pronounced as in *ray*.[28]

Given Barker's confusion, and since the use of accents is an integral part of the French language, it is almost certain that the form used by de Sainson reflects more accurately the pronunciation used by contemporary local Aboriginal people. There are at least five other forms of spelling that exist, and the Noongar people living at Albany today are not unanimous as to how the name ought to be pronounced. I have followed the spelling favoured by Barker, but with the omission of any accent.

It is possible that Mokare was the same friendly and confident young man who spent time with King and the rest of the crew during the *Bathurst's* stay in late 1821 and early 1822. Certainly he made a strong and favourable impression upon the French officers of the *Astrolabe* just prior to Lockyer's arrival, in a way that is reminiscent of the description of 'Jack' by King a few years earlier. Mokare so impressed the French that his portrait, together with that of three other named Kincannup men, was painted by their official artist, Louis de Sainson.

Mokare had four brothers and a sister, and his family holds particular significance for the story of Aboriginal–European interaction at Albany, for it was their land that was chosen by Lockyer as the site of the British settlement.[29] The intricacies of Aboriginal land ownership were far from clear to the British, who initially misinterpreted the respect shown by the Kincannups and other groups to the family's oldest male member, Nakinah, as indicating his status as the 'chief' of the entire region. In fact, the Aboriginal people were simply acknowledging Nakinah as head of the family on whose land they were living whenever they visited the settlement. By camping on the family's estate, the British were not necessarily unwelcome intruders according to Aboriginal law: provided permission was obtained from the family and certain rules of behaviour were followed, other groups commonly shared the area's resources for short periods. The British, probably through a mix of arrogance and ignorance, failed to seek such permission. In this situation of mutual cultural incomprehension, in the absence of a natural peacemaker the understandably indignant Nakinah might well have chosen to react to this rude intrusion violently and thereby stymied any chance of an amicable relationship developing. Fortunately, his younger brother managed to act as a cultural go-between during the potentially dangerous period following the arrival of the *Amity*, and it is entirely appropriate that Mokare's dignified figure in statue form today occupies a place of honour in Albany's main street. Green has described him as 'certainly one of the most remarkable personalities in Australian frontier history'.[30]

Mokare, 'a man of peace'

From at least the time of the arrival of the *Astrolabe* in late 1826 (and well before then if he was indeed 'Jack') Mokare showed a confident and intelligent interest in the Europeans who entered his world, an interest that his bright, open nature ensured was generally reciprocated. Mokare had an extraordinary ability to form close cross-cultural friendships, and during the four-and-a-half-year period from the arrival of the *Amity* until his death in August 1831, he frequently shared living quarters in turn with Nind, Sleeman, Barker and Collie. It is obvious that each of these men saw the situation as involving more than a simple exploitative relationship based on placating and humouring an important local personage in order to facilitate the official business of the garrison. The houses occupied by the British officers and officials at King George Sound were very small, and although contemporary standards of privacy – especially those of naval officers used to cramped cabins aboard ship – differed greatly from those of today, it is unlikely that anyone other than a close and respected friend would have been permitted to share accommodation in this way.[31]

Nind found his time at the Sound very difficult. He must have felt socially and professionally isolated in an era when rigid social barriers meant that his position as surgeon necessitated an aloofness from the great majority of the other members of the garrison who were either beneath him socially, or were military officers who associated socially only with each other. He became deeply depressed and suicidal.[32] Fortunately, Nind was still able to maintain a friendship and close association with Mokare and write an extensive ethnography, despite his evident mental illness. He was sufficiently perceptive to note that the arrival of the British quickly altered some customs that had almost certainly been in existence at the Sound for countless generations. He observed how the Aboriginal people saw that the British were eating shellfish with no ill effects, and began to add these previously forbidden food items to their diet.[33] Nind also described how the custom of dancing naked was modified to allow the wearing of kangaroo skin cloaks around the lower part of their body when the British were present.[34] These two observations are interesting for the evidence they present that the Aboriginal people were not necessarily rigid in the application of their customs, but were sometimes prepared to modify them in both their own direct interests and in the interests of maintaining harmony with the British.

Nind left the Sound in October 1829, and so had no opportunity to introduce Mokare to Sleeman's successor, Captain Collet Barker, who arrived on the *Governor Phillip* in late November. Sleeman remained in command until 3 December, leaving the Sound nine days later. There can be no doubt that Mokare would have been discussed by the two officers – on the departure of Nind, the gregarious young man had transferred his lodgings to Sleeman's house and the question of whether this arrangement was to continue after the latter returned to Sydney must have arisen.

Sleeman was concerned at the poor state of housing at the settlement, and ordered the construction of a brick dwelling with stone gabled ends for his own use.[35] The house was small, comprising a kitchen, living room, office and one bedroom, so privacy must have been at a premium with two people sharing the accommodation. From the very limited records left by Sleeman it appears that he achieved little at either King George Sound, or earlier at Raffles Bay; Mulvaney and Green noted that isolated command might have been a burden he was unable to bear comfortably.[36]

Barker took command at a time when the future existence of the settlement was in serious doubt due to the recent commencement of the Swan River Settlement approximately 400 kilometres to the north-west. In the event, the original settlement was never abandoned, but Barker was to be its last commandant before it was handed over to be administered as a part of the new Swan River Colony.[37] The settlement was officially known as Frederick's Town but usually referred to in contemporary despatches and journals as King George's Sound. Some early writers referred to the area as King George Third's Sound, following the usage of Vancouver, but this was never a common practice. James Stirling changed the official name to Albany in 1831 (both names honoured Frederick George Augustus, the Duke of Albany) but King George's Sound, and particularly the later King George Sound, remained in common use, along with Albany, for the remainder of the century.

At the beginning of 1830, the settlement had not altered greatly from the time of Lockyer's departure approximately three years earlier, a fact that is not surprising considering its limited purpose as a military outpost and as a scoping operation for a possible penal settlement for reoffending convicts from eastern Australia. A small farm had been established about 2 kilometres from the encampment at the foot of Mount Melville to complement the often unsuccessful attempts to grow vegetables and other food items at the camp, and at various other sites in a region where fertile soils are rare and patchy in nature.[38] A few small and rudimentary buildings were in existence to house the British population, which

Detail of a panorama painted by Lt Robert Dale showing the early settlement at King George Sound, 1832. The complete intaglio sheet is 18 cm × 274.5 cm, engraved at London by Robert Havell. nla.pic-an7404363-6-v

had risen to only fifty-nine. At this point, the British tread upon Kincannup land had been light indeed.

Although both Western Australia and South Australia have towns named Mount Barker in his honour, Collet Barker eminently deserves to be better known and celebrated, and this undoubtedly would have been the case had his handwriting been even reasonably legible. During his sixteen months at the Sound he kept an almost daily journal that represents one of the most remarkable documents in the history of Aboriginal–European frontier relations in Australia.[39] It is probable that this most erudite and sensitive man would have used his journal as the basis of a unique cross-cultural work of historical literature had he not met his death at the hands of a group of Aboriginal men who mistook him for a rapacious sealer during a survey expedition near the mouth of the Murray River in South Australia only a few weeks after leaving Albany.[40] Instead, the journal was stored at the office of the Colonial Secretary until its transfer to the Mitchell Library. In 1934 it was transferred to the Archives Office of New South Wales[41] where its virtual illegibility ensured it was almost totally neglected by historians until Western Australian historian Dr Neville Green began to decipher it in 1973. In 1982, Green and Professor Bob Reece of Murdoch University obtained a grant to further this work. The prominent archaeologist Professor John Mulvaney then agreed to do more work on the text and co-operated with Green to publish the journal, together with the journal written by Barker while at Raffles Bay, as the book *Commandant of Solitude* in 1992.[42]

Barker arrived at his new post as a single man in his mid forties, experienced in the administration of a remote outpost precariously established on Aboriginal land and well aware of the necessity and desirability of maintaining good relations with the local indigenous population. His previous posting at Raffles Bay had been difficult because of the problems involved in supplying provisions to the settlement and the resulting illnesses that dogged its inhabitants.[43] Dumont d'Urville visited the site in 1839, ten years after it had been abandoned, and wrote: 'I doubt that there exists anywhere in the world a more unpromising spot for founding a colony'.[44]

While at Raffles Bay, Barker had made the most of an impossible situation and had shown that he was not only interested in promoting trade with the region to the north, the reason for the settlement's establishment, but was also interested in the welfare of the Aboriginal inhabitants of the area. The journal that he kept at Raffles Bay showed a deep concern for their welfare and a frustration at the attitude of his compatriots towards the Aboriginal people. The settlement's surgeon, T. B. Wilson (also later to serve at King George Sound) concluded that Barker:

> had a great deal of difficulty to contend with, in his method of treating the natives; as no other individual in the settlement could be brought to consider these poor beings in any other light than wild beasts.[45]

Barker had the benefit upon arrival at King George Sound of an existing relationship built upon the amicable nature of the pre-settlement contacts between British and French exploratory expeditions, and the work of his predecessors. During his tenure the relative peace continued, and no deaths or bloodshed appear to have occurred from the actions of either group against the other. His good work at King George Sound did not go unnoticed: Governor Ralph Darling adjudged him as meriting appointment as Resident in New Zealand, where the establishment of racial harmony was seen as paramount following major unrest between the Maori people of the North Island and the newly resident British.[46]

The edited version of Barker's journal published in *Commandant of Solitude* is an impressively comprehensive document that runs to approximately 100,000 words. Mulvaney and Green list 132 Aboriginal people who were named by Barker in the journal, a strong indication that he saw the Kincannups and other Menang people as individuals in their own right, rather than 'the aborigines' that feature in so many accounts of the contact era in Australia. Tellingly, only eighteen of Barker's recorded names are female. Flinders, Dumont d'Urville and Lockyer all noted that it was Aboriginal males who were prepared to approach Europeans (virtually all of whom at King George Sound at this time were of course themselves men) while the women and children usually remained well out of sight. It was some years before this pattern, common to other areas in south-west Western Australia, began to alter.

A striking feature briefly mentioned by some earlier observers, but expanded upon at some length in Barker's journal, is the very close contact that a number of Kincannups sought with some of the British at the settlement. For example, Barker noted how an Aboriginal man and his wife entered his house very early one morning out of curiosity, and insisted on watching him shave and dress. He allowed them to stay, as it was 'vain to try to get her away without a greater effort than it was worth'. On the same day he entertained another family group before sharing breakfast with Talwyn, a young man who had an aptitude for learning English and who sometimes used Mokare's room in Barker's house while Mokare was away from the settlement. Later that day Barker spoke with Mokare about an issue involving an Aboriginal group's theft of young parrots from Mokare's land.[47] This was not an unusual day for Barker, who regularly involved himself in the daily happenings of the Kincannup community.

There are several reasons why some members of the Kincannup group sought this close contact, and why the British permitted it to occur. It appears that Aboriginal people believed that a range of benefits could be derived from making friends with the British and, when it suited both parties, sharing their living accommodation.

Firstly, as Alexander Collie noted, some simply preferred 'a good house to the cold bush', and on a more or less regular basis slept on the floors of the rough buildings occupied by the British.[48] Secondly, some Aboriginal people valued their close ties with the British as a guarantee of continued access to biscuit, flour and the other European supplies that were highly prized for the variety they presented to traditional food sources. From the beginning of the settlement, the British used food to gain the friendship of the Kincannups and to reward those, such as Mokare, whose services were often required.

Numerous references in Barker's journal show that the British also dispensed food to encourage behaviour they deemed desirable, and that they were prepared to withhold it as a form of punishment. For example, Barker gave biscuit to Wannewar, whose mother and brother's family were sleeping at the settlement in May 1829, as a reward for promising to postpone spearing another Aboriginal man until the summer.[49] Barker's journal shows how the British put a high priority on the prevention of revenge spearings within the Menang community because of a persistent fear that the violence would spill over and involve themselves in ways which they would find unable to control. In various ways, each group involved in the relationship at King George Sound was using the other for its own ends.

There were other less tangible, but no less important, reasons why the Kincannups chose to set up porous boundaries between their world and that of the settlement. Their engagement with the British enabled the local Aboriginal people largely to control the relationship to their own diplomatic as well as material advantage. Gifts of food and clothing were valued,[50] but what was more important to the Kincannups was the status they gained throughout the region through their association with the newcomers. Alexander Collie described in a letter to Stirling how the Kincannups would boast to travellers from distant groups of their knowledge gained, and would take great delight in recollecting the astonishment, wonder and envy that this would invariably cause. Alexander Collie wrote in an 1832 report to Stirling:

> They make a boast of the learning obtained from the white people among the more distant tribes; and if I have deduced a correct inference from the details which some of them, Nakinah especially, have given me, this ostentation not only affords them delight at the time, but the bare recollection of the astonishment, wonder and envy it excited, gives them an ecstasy of pleasure.[51]

Even more significant was the protection this close association gave them from the ever present threat of attack from the Wills people to the north. Barker recorded how a group of 'King George's men' met with him in the settlement garden and proposed that he should accompany them with a party of soldiers to attack the Wills.[52] Ongoing fear of the Wills, the continuing intrigue associated with revenge spearings within their own community, and the ever present need to find food and perform ceremonies remained crucial priorities. The British presence was a significant factor in the Kincannup world, but during the first few years of coexistence at the Sound, it was not necessarily the most important thing in their lives.

The British also saw an advantage in cultivating friendships with the local Aboriginal people, and in encouraging their visits to the settlement. From the beginning, the officers realised they were in a precarious position should a concerted and skilful attack be made by a large number of Aboriginal men. Friendship was the only tenable solution to this ominous possibility. It was also official British policy that good relations be maintained, and the successive commandants would have been aware of the possibly detrimental effect on their future careers if their superiors in Sydney felt that they had failed to make at least a reasonable effort in this direction.

These were compelling imperatives, but a reading of Barker's journal shows that his simple wish to make friends on an unofficial level with some of the Kincannups was another important factor in allowing close contact to occur. The routine nature of life at King George Sound enabled Barker to spend many hours with Mokare in particular, but also at times with others, discussing matters in a way that showed a genuine interest in Kincannup spirituality and mythology. The conversations clearly show that there were times when there was a depth to the relationship that transcended self-interest by either side.

A striking feature of life at the settlement during this period was the degree of respect that grew between the Kincannups and the British – respect that was neither automatic nor easy, as can be seen from its frequent absence in contact situations in other areas of Australia. The British 'settlement' at King George Sound was, in fact, an invasion of Kincannup country. The British then proceeded to compound the act of invasion by acting in numerous ways that would have shown gross disrespect according to Aboriginal culture. The evidence shows that Lockyer and Barker in particular were sensitive to the difficulties posed by their position as intruders and attempted to tread lightly on local sensitivities, but the complexities involved ran so deep that it was inevitable there would be many occasions when British actions offended the Kincannups' ideas of what was acceptable and appropriate behaviour. Yet it is apparent that the Aboriginal people of the area did not see these failures as placing the British beneath their respect.

Similarly, there were cultural reasons why the British at the Sound could very easily have followed the lead shown by so many of their compatriots, and placed the Aboriginal people in the category of a group to be grudgingly tolerated, rather than one to be awarded genuine respect. Some of these were so profound that one can only marvel that the British, like the Kincannups, were able to transcend the barriers to respect that they presented.

Firstly and fundamentally, Britons in the early nineteenth century brought with them to any contact with 'native' people a deep sense of the superiority of their own race, the concept of the Noble Savage having been almost completely abandoned by this time.[53] They were proud of their industrial technology, and of the strong work ethic underlying the conviction that material possessions were the principal indicators of success for an individual and for a society as a whole. They had an innate belief in the complete superiority of their own culture and form of religion. It is often forgotten that there was virtual unanimity among people from a Christian background at this time that all of humanity had descended from Adam and Eve only a few thousand years earlier. As archaeologists began to show that highly developed civilisations had flourished soon after this time in the Middle Eastern region considered to have been the site of the Garden of Eden, and thus the birthplace of all mankind, it was widely assumed that 'primitive' peoples must have deliberately turned their backs on civilisation and regressed to a 'lower' level.

It is important to remember that the Albany commandants and officers were not immune from these ideas. Barker, despite his friendship with Mokare, could still say, 'If one could understand their language thoroughly, they would be very manageable'.[54] Clearly, the British intended to *manage* the Aboriginal population, not to adapt their own behaviour to form some sort of amalgamated society based on cultural equivalence. Yet, despite their obvious assumption of the superiority of their own British culture, these men were still able to form relationships based on friendship.

The position of Aboriginal women at King George Sound presented another potential barrier to the formation of respect by the British. Scottish Enlightenment theorists had placed a strong emphasis on the status of women as a prime index of social development,[55] and the newcomers at Albany perceived that the status of Menang women was well below a level that would indicate a highly developed society. The basic methods used to prepare, cook and eat kangaroos and other smaller animals also presented a cultural problem for the British, who found these practices difficult to accept. The *Perth Gazette and Western Australian Journal* of 12 August 1834 carried an account (generally accepted as being written by Alexander Collie) describing in detail how an Aboriginal couple at Albany – 'Mr and Mrs Botup' – prepared several small animals for cooking. The writer noted how 'Mr Botup' disembowelled each animal and then proceeded to clean the interior by licking vigorously.

The British also frequently commented upon the Menang practice of anointing themselves with strong-smelling oil and grease from dead seals and fish, and clearly found it an example of their own superiority. Yet, despite these very considerable barriers to the development of respect on both sides, the evidence indicates that respect did exist at King George Sound, and it was on the foundation of this respect that a perhaps unique degree of amicability, fragile as it always remained, was able to be constructed and maintained.

Important as the qualities of some of the leading personalities at King George Sound were to the prevention of the violence that characterised so much of Australian contact history, other factors were also at work. Of fundamental importance to this is the unique set of circumstances surrounding its establishment. Firstly, when the *Amity* sailed into Princess Royal Harbour in 1826, the Aboriginal people of the area had already enjoyed a generally positive acquaintance with Europeans that had extended over a considerable period of time. Certainly, their traumatic experiences at the hands of sealers in the latter years had taught them that not all European men were well intentioned, but the evidence indicates that the local people were prepared to differentiate between sealers and those visitors who arrived in large ships. This extended, if superficial, relationship had allowed time for an incorporation of the existence of Europeans into the Menang worldview.

Prior to 1826, some Aboriginal people had acquired the ability to converse in a form of English, a skill that was crucial to Barker's ability to converse in some depth with Mokare and others four years after the initial settlement.[56] The *Amity* was no doubt initially seen as simply the latest in a series of ships that brought trade opportunities, as well as food, clothes and other gifts. The expectation that this new vessel would soon depart in the same way as all previous ships was eventually replaced by the realisation that this group of Europeans was intent upon a permanent settlement. By the time this occurred the British had built upon the credit established by previous visitors and had begun to establish an amicable relationship.

Secondly, and crucially, the settlement at King George Sound differed from the great majority of other British incursions upon Aboriginal land in Australia in that it was initially established purely as a military garrison. Its occupants had no interest in taking land beyond a hectare or so at the foot of Mount Melville and a small area at the nearby government farm. The British took fish and native animals, but the evidence shows that this was in the context of a sharing relationship, rather than one which exploited the Aboriginal inhabitants' economic resources as commonly occurred elsewhere. From the beginning, the British shared the large quantities of fish they caught and were generous with their supplies of biscuit and flour. They gave firearms to several Kincannup men to assist them in the hunt for birds and animals. It is probable that the arrival of the British actually initially increased the amount and reliability of food supplies at the Sound for its Aboriginal inhabitants – a reversal of the situation at almost every other settlement, where the speedy annexation of land and food resources soon resulted in shortages and consequent disharmony.

The small number of British present at the Sound during the four-and-one-quarter years between the arrival of the *Amity* and the opening of the region for free settlement was a further positive factor. Supplies of most necessities came by sea, and the surrounding land did not come under the economic pressure that the arrival of large numbers usually involved with new settlements would have necessitated. The self-sufficient and insular nature of the settlement had a further benefit upon social relations. Very few Europeans ventured far from the foot of Mount Melville, thus preventing the inadvertent or deliberate destruction of sacred sites and objects that eventually occurred as significant numbers of later arrivals spread into the hinterland. The British were focused upon the sea, while the Aboriginal people's prime focus was upon the land, and this helped prevent the violence that so often accompanied economic competition on the Australian frontier.

It is also significant that the few convicts, overseers, soldiers and others at King George Sound were all under very close supervision. No doubt this was a major reason why during the garrison period there is only one obscure written reference to the topic of sexual contact between the British and the Aboriginal people of the area. Barker noted in his journal that a private soldier came under suspicion: 'Information respecting [Private] Quin & Numal's wife, could not recollect authority'.[57] Whatever occurred, Barker treated it seriously, investigating the evident allegation immediately and noting the following day that it was 'without foundation'.[58] There is nothing in Barker's journal that sheds any further light upon the affair. He frequently wrote in such cryptic fashion; presumably he intended to reconstruct the details from memory at a later date.

In a footnote to this episode Mulvaney and Green stated that sexual relations between Europeans and Aboriginal women 'surely occurred', but gave no reasons for making such a strong statement beyond the implied judgement that no form of discipline could have been strong enough to prevent the generally young men of the settlement from offending in this regard. Given the sometimes severe problems caused by sexual liaisons between European men and Aboriginal women at Albany in later years, and the evident lack of such problems during the garrison era, it appears safe to assume that at worst only a few such cases occurred.

A further reason why a relatively harmonious situation developed during the pre–free settlement era was the presence of a dedicated European labour supply in the form of convicts. The British commanders did occasionally employ local Aboriginal people as labourers, but it appears that this was done mainly in order to accustom them to the European concept that there was moral value in the concept of work. When they did work, they were paid. Lockyer saw such employment as mutually beneficial, writing:

> I am in hopes that the good understanding which now exists will continue. I am very sanguine that in a short time they may be made very useful in a variety of ways in making roads, as they can handle a spade as well as any of our people and are very strong, making them a small remuneration for what they can do will induce them to work as it will also help towards their becoming civilized.[59]

It is also possible that the Kincannups felt culturally obliged to co-operate with the British as a result of the seriousness with which Lockyer and his successors treated the offences committed by sealers against them. James Browne certainly believed this to be so. Since he arrived at Albany only in 1836, he must have heard this being discussed at the settlement, and this is a strong indication that those living there at that time were convinced that Lockyer's actions had been pivotal.[60]

A close reading of the various texts written by Barker and other Europeans residing at the settlement gives at least some indication of how the relationship was viewed by the Kincannups and other Aboriginal people who frequented the British enclave on either a regular or an intermittent basis during the first few years of its existence. Barker's journal in particular makes it clear that the

Aboriginal people were not a completely homogenous group possessing a single attitude towards the newcomers. Individual personality played a crucial role in determining how each person saw the British: were they desirable friends and interesting companions? An easy and reliable source of attractive new food sources with the technology also to provide supplies of traditional food such as fish? Potentially valuable allies against their Aboriginal enemies? Or simply largely irrelevant to their continuance in a fully traditional lifestyle? Some, such as Mokare, had their lives greatly altered by their relationship with the British, others passed in and out of the British world on an infrequent basis, while an unknown number evidently chose to ignore their presence altogether. The fact that the settlement was so small numerically, and self-contained, allowed for these choices to be made.

Given the fact that individual Aboriginal people acted in differing ways, it is perhaps surprising to find that none during this period were recorded as offering serious acts of resistance to the British, apart from the initial problems during the early part of Lockyer's tenure as commandant. Green's 'friendly frontier' label for the first years of the settlement appears fully justified, both by the absence of resistance, and by the evidence of genuine cross-cultural friendships. As it slowly became clear that the British incursion in late 1826 was going to be permanent, the Kincannups and other members of the Menang accepted the new reality and incorporated it into their world. During this period, the British were few in number, fixed in locality, and generally benign in outlook.

On 7 March 1831, King George Sound and its region administratively became a part of the Swan River Colony,[61] and the name of the settlement was changed to Albany, with the surrounding district becoming Plantagenet County.[62] The decision to alter the status of the settlement and open the land to free settlers was to have profound implications for the future of Aboriginal–European relations at King George Sound.

Two brief vignettes from the latter part of Barker's journal foreshadow the gravity of these changes: the day after the first European party to walk from Perth to the Sound arrived at the settlement in a dangerously weak state from hunger and exhaustion, its abrasive leader insisted on inspecting the land on the opposite side of the harbour with a view to making an immediate application to purchase. The tone of Barker's entry for the day showed that he was offended by Thomas Bannister's haste and his very evident lack of respect – this was, after all, Mokare's land.[63] Three weeks later, Barker's journal entry for 26 February indicated that the Kincannups were also aware their future was about to undergo a radical transformation. A number of them came into the settlement anxiously to enquire of Barker whether they would be employed and fed by the new settlers. Barker wrote:

> Mokarè speaking of settlers coming & black fellows working, said several were now talking of settling with the whites, but they must have shirt & trowsers, or they would be obliged to go to the bush to spear Kangaroo…Mokarè again told me again in the evening that they talked of coming to stop constantly about King Geo[rge Sound]…On Asking M if his people would make good shepherds…he said 'yes', that just at first they might not but in a little time.[64]

Already, the Aboriginal people around Albany were aware that there were other ways of interpreting the world than through the eyes of their traditional culture – they had been exposed to European attitudes, knowledge, and religion – and some must have been troubled by the subtle challenge this knowledge within their community presented to the continuance of their ordered world.

Mokare and Barker were also acutely aware that momentous and forced changes were about to occur for the original inhabitants of King George Sound as settlers, small in numbers at first but with their eyes fixed determinedly on taking ownership of Menang land, replaced members of the British garrison. The sharing of land that had characterised the first era of European settlement was drawing to a close, and the mutual appreciation and respect that had evolved at Albany would become subject to increasing challenge on the uncharted path ahead.

Chapter Four

The Beginning of Free Settlement and Aboriginal Dispossession at Albany, 1831–1850

The transition from a garrison of the British Army to an outpost of free settlement of the Colony of Western Australia, and the beginning of European dispossession of Aboriginal land

It was inevitable that free settlement would eventually prove profoundly disruptive to the Menang. Crucially, however, the extraordinarily poor quality of the vast majority of the region's soil types caused the disruption to occur at a much slower pace than in most other regions of the continent. The fact that almost no land was cleared for agriculture in the Albany region prior to 1850 allowed many Aboriginal traditional practices to continue. This was in stark contrast to the region around Perth where a much quicker expansion of European settlement rapidly began to change Aboriginal people's dress, tools, accommodation and means of food gathering.[1] Certainly pastoralism (the practice of running sheep or cattle over extensive areas of unfenced natural bushland), the only large-scale European land use between 1831 and 1850, had a significant effect upon the resources required by Aboriginal people. However, unlike much of Australia, the

Albany region contained few extensive areas of grassed plains where pastoralists could run stock easily and profitably. Large areas of timbered country and sand-plain scrub were virtually useless in their natural state, and contained numerous plants that were highly poisonous to both sheep and cattle.[2] Albany resident Bill Hassell remembers that when the family property at the Warriups east of Albany was a purely pastoral holding with none of its area cleared of vegetation, the only areas suitable for grazing stock were relatively small pockets of natural open grassland.

Because of these impediments, pastoralism was limited in extent. Even in those areas where it did occur, its nature was far less immediately disruptive to Aboriginal–European relations than the close agricultural development that took place in most other medium to high rainfall areas in Australia.

On 20 March 1831, the *Isabella* arrived at Albany carrying Lieutenant William Carew and the twenty men of the 63rd Regiment of the British Army who had been sent to serve as replacements for Captain Collet Barker and the other members of the garrison. Significantly, the authorities failed to order any key personnel to remain at the Sound for a time sufficient to allow the Aboriginal population to have become accustomed to the new reality of free settlement while still in the presence of some familiar and friendly British faces. Instead after only six days Barker, together with the men of the 39th Regiment and all of the convicts except for one who chose to remain, sailed away in the *Isabella* leaving the new arrivals to form their own relationships with the Kincannups and other Menang groups in the region. The most likely explanation for this apparently thoughtless decision is that of administrative simplicity: the 39th was part of the command of Governor Darling at Sydney, while the 63rd came under Governor Stirling at Perth, and to have left some members of the Sydney-based regiment behind at Albany would not have been normal military practice. Evidently British officialdom regarded administrative simplicity as more important than the maintenance of the excellent Aboriginal–European relations so carefully nurtured at King George Sound over the previous four-and-a-half years.

The behaviour of the members of the British army at the settlement during the six-day changeover period did nothing to improve matters. Barker's journal entries for the period present a strong indictment of British military discipline, and provide a clear indication that few members of either regiment shared his view that the maintenance of good Aboriginal relations was important. Stirling had written to the commanding officer of the 63rd Regiment instructing him to ensure that Carew should continue to cultivate the friendship of the King George Sound Aborigines and maintain any customary distribution of food.[3] Given the poor behaviour of the troops and the lack of any subsequent disciplinary action taken against the officers in command, it appears that Stirling issued the orders primarily to satisfy the Colonial Office in London, rather than from any deeply felt obligation to the colony's original inhabitants.

Widespread drunkenness was evident to Barker even before Carew's men disembarked from the *Isabella*, and continued to present him with problems until he sailed from the settlement six days later. On their first evening ashore the new arrivals were treated to a corroborree, but rather than showing respect for what was obviously an act of friendship and welcome to the Kincannups' homeland, the non-commissioned officers and enlisted men went on a drunken, riotous spree. Barker stated that the 'whole detachment [was] unhinged'.[4] The men were so out of control that Marignan, an Aboriginal man who sometimes slept in Barker's house, felt it necessary to place his wife under the commandant's personal protection.[5]

Barker found the heavy drinking and consequent collapse of discipline abhorrent, but neither he nor Carew was able to do anything to prevent its extended continuation. It is perhaps surprising to find that Barker wrote about this period so frankly in his journal. Had he lived long enough to publish a book about his time at King George Sound, it would have been interesting to see whether he modified his account of those six days, or erased them altogether from public view. Barker described in some detail the breakdown in military discipline, but unfortunately wrote nothing about the effect it had upon the Aboriginal people who witnessed the all too evident results.

In March 1831, the new Colony of Western Australia was proclaimed officially, and James Stirling received confirmation of his long-awaited promotion from Lieutenant Governor to Governor. At the same time, it was decided that the larger settlements remote from Perth were to be administered by government residents – civil officers who would be responsible for local government matters as well as fulfilling the role of Resident Magistrate. Stirling offered the position at King George Sound to Thomas Bannister, a choice that Barker, had he known, may have found difficult to accept given Bannister's insensitive behaviour towards the Aboriginal people of the area during his visit in the previous month. However, Bannister set too many conditions upon his acceptance and Stirling decided instead to offer it to Dr Alexander Collie, a naval surgeon who had arrived at Fremantle on the *Sulphur* in June 1829. Collie had visited the Sound in September 1830 and looked forward to accepting the position, believing that it would prove both congenial and career enhancing.[6]

Collie's arrival in April 1831 ended the era of military governance and ushered in civilian rule at the settlement. From this date forward, the soldiers were there solely to provide armed protection, should it be required. As well as his work as Resident Magistrate, Collie's duties included the provision of medical care to both Europeans and Aboriginal people, supervision of the government farm, and the carrying out of further exploration in the region. He found the position less interesting than he had hoped, and returned to Perth in November 1832 to take up a position as Colonial Surgeon. During his nineteen months at Albany, Collie formed a particularly strong friendship with Mokare, and used the information obtained from him and from other sources to write a valuable ethnography of approximately 16,000 words.[7] Collie obviously had extensive dealings with Aboriginal people at Albany, but his writings lack reflection upon any changes in the Aboriginal–European relationship that he observed during the period of transition to free settlement.

This omission may seem surprising given Collie's obvious interest in the Aboriginal people of Albany, but an examination of the history of the progress of free settlement in the region during his period of office provides a simple explanation. For a variety of reasons the number of settlers who chose to move to Albany in the first few years after land became available was extraordinarily small, and the resulting changes in the Aboriginal–European relationship were initially much smaller than had been expected. Rather than the anticipated large influx of European settlers and their families, as late as ten years after land became available, only one man was commercially farming in the region. Lamentable as this lack of progress was from a European point of view, it had the inestimable benefit of allowing a slow introduction to the new reality that all Menang land was now available to any British settler who chose to buy a portion of it from the Colonial Government. The slow pace of settlement stood in stark contrast to that at Perth, York and the vast majority of other settlements throughout Australia.[8] Instead of an initial flood of settlers, barely a trickle disturbed the life of those Aboriginal people who chose to continue living away from the town of Albany.[9]

Collie expressed his frustration with his predecessors' failure to leave an official record of their interaction with the local Aboriginal people:

It is also unnecessary for me to state, that in order to preserve the uniformity of treatment, a public record should be left with the chief authorities of the district by their predecessors, in addition to the more essential personal information to be obtained, wherever it is possible, of the customs and manners, and as far as may be known, of the individual disposition of such natives as frequent the settlement.[10]

Barker had, of course, written exactly such a document in the form of his private journal, but had taken it with him when he left King George Sound.

There are several reasons why, despite initial enthusiasm and official encouragement, the take-up of land at Albany proceeded at such an extraordinarily slow pace. Firstly, a large area of relatively good quality land had recently been made available for selection in the Avon Valley, and this region's proximity to the capital at Perth made it seem a far better prospect than the very remote area centred on Albany. The British Colonial Office provided an even greater disincentive with its decision in early 1831 to cease granting land in Australia. Instead, land was to be offered for sale at a standard price of five shillings per acre, the price of a labourer's hire for a day.[11] It is therefore not surprising that settlers believed this to be an exorbitant price for unimproved uncleared land of generally poor quality.[12] This edict had a marked dampening effect on Western Australian agricultural progress, as much better land was available for the same price at the older settlements in New South Wales and Van Diemen's Land, where farming communities and townships were already established.

A few settlers did however choose to buy land in the town of Albany, and by August 1831, four had bought blocks laid out in the town-site survey undertaken by Raphael Clint.[13] Most prospective rural landowners took a quick look at the sandy soils that characterise most of the hinterland of Albany and returned to

Perth without buying, while others bought land with the intention of farming but subsequently failed to occupy their holdings. The judgement of those early potential agriculturalists was later to be proven sound. When parts of the extensive areas of sandy soil were eventually cleared and farmed much later in the nineteenth and twentieth centuries, they were found to be almost totally unproductive without heavy applications of fertilisers, especially superphosphate.

The photograph reproduced below graphically illustrates the extent of the problem. It was taken in the early 1960s on a newly cleared property just south of the Stirling Ranges when the statewide campaign to increase the area of farmland – as many as 1,000,000 acres were cleared *per year* – was at its peak. Even the notoriously infertile soils north of Albany benefited from scientific research designed to make farming possible and profitable, and almost the whole area was at last brought under production. The availability of economical supplies of superphosphate, coupled

First cereal crop grown on farmland north of Albany, displaying the natural infertility of much of the region's soils

with the mid twentieth century discovery that minute amounts of zinc, copper and other trace elements were essential for cereal and pasture growth on these soil types, created a local green revolution.

The photograph shows an oat crop, most of which is chest-high and obviously healthy and productive. The small section of the crop in the bottom right of the photo is only a few centimetres high and virtually non-existent – the only difference between the two areas being that the farmer failed to notice that the seed drill had run out of fertiliser and had continued to plant the oat seed by itself. Little wonder then that farming in much of the Albany region would only be possible once adequate and appropriate fertilisers became available more than one hundred years after the events described in this chapter, and that pastoralism was for so long to remain the only profitable land use undertaken in the region.

For the first three years of free settlement there was only minimal change or economic development at Albany. The total European population did not exceed sixty during this period, and all but about thirty of these were troops and their dependants.[14] The only land actively farmed was the 10 acres or so at the settlement and the small government farm near Middleton Bay, while the only land actually occupied away from the town was a block of 300 acres at the mouth of the King River selected by the Henty family, who owned property in Van Diemen's Land and subsequently founded Portland in Victoria. Their Albany enterprise proved unsatisfactory and was soon abandoned.

The fact that eighteen-year-old John Henty felt sufficiently secure from Aboriginal attack to live by himself on a holding several kilometres from military protection gives a strong indication that relations continued to be peaceful during this early period. Collie did however issue one instruction indicating that some tensions existed which were perhaps more serious than he admitted in his later writings. Following a section of his monograph in which he extolled the Aboriginal peoples' honesty, stating that any thefts of food that did occur were the work of 'young boys and lads', Collie described a more serious robbery that took place at night. Some adult Aboriginal men were suspected of taking vegetables from the settlement garden:

> A musket was supplied to the head gardener, and I gave it out that he would in future shoot any black whom he should see in the garden, and this seemed to have the desired effect, as no more attempts at similar depredations were made for some time.[15]

Unless Collie was bluffing, this effectively amounted to a shoot-to-kill policy, since a musket was a very inaccurate weapon and could not be reliably used in a situation where the person using the firearm intended only to wound. It is possible to speculate that Collie's orders were to use less-lethal shot rather than solid ball ammunition (Captain Cook, for example, recorded that he had used shot for such a purpose at Botany Bay) but one would expect him to have pre-empted any official criticism by emphasising this in his writings, had this been the case.

Collie's order appears to be at complete variance with the tenor of the rest of his monograph. It could simply have been a slip on his part that revealed that the real state of affairs at Albany was worse than he was prepared to admit, but it is unlikely that Collie would have made such an obvious blunder. It is considerably more probable that the incident highlighted the truth that however important the British believed their relationship with the Menang to be, it would always be subservient to their own reasons for being at Albany. The British had no intention of leaving, and given that fact, the security of their food supply was of paramount importance.

The Aboriginal inhabitants of the Albany region found their lives little altered during this initial period of free settlement. Collie's *Anecdotes and Remarks Relative to the Aborigines of King George's Sound* presents a picture of a settlement virtually unchanged since Barker's departure. Few Europeans made Albany their home and only a very few ships called at the port, although some sealing continued on a small scale.[16] Even Mokare's practice of befriending the head of the British settlement continued, and he remained living in the same house which was now occupied by Collie. This friendship developed into one that Donald Garden, the author of an informative history of Albany published in 1977, described as possibly unique in Australian colonial history.[17] Collie was fascinated by the insights into Aboriginal culture that Mokare gave him, and evidently enjoyed becoming involved in some of the very complex negotiations that occurred within Menang society. Collie found their unpredictable habit of leaving the settlement for extended periods very difficult to understand or accept. He was distressed to find that Mokare, who had been ill and was taking a mercury preparation which he had prescribed, 'unaccountably' left the settlement during a day of heavy rainfall and wind.[18]

Mokare and his brother Nakinah remained in the bush for five weeks in mid winter. When they returned to the settlement, Mokare was in a physically weak condition and near death. Collie nursed his friend in the kitchen of his house until Mokare died nine days later. He ensured that the burial took place precisely as Menang rites required, writing about the process at some length in his *Anecdotes*.[19] He then followed Barker's example by persuading the Kincannup men that it would be wrong for them to avenge Mokare's death by the traditional method of spearing an individual held to be responsible. Perhaps this persuasion was intended to spare Aboriginal life; perhaps it had more to do with an official desire to bring a halt to a disturbing practice that the British could neither fully understand nor control.

Three years later, Collie (who was then living at Perth) realised that his own death was imminent, and he decided to return to England to spend his last days with his family. The ship on which he took passage called at Albany, where it became clear that his illness was so advanced that further travel was impossible. He died in 1835, and at his request was buried next to Mokare's grave. This story highlights the complexities inherent in Aboriginal–European relations at Albany at this time. Mokare and Collie's friendship was obviously sincere and a model for others to emulate if the two groups were to coexist peaceably into the future. However, Collie carried a disease (probably tuberculosis) against which the Menang had no resistance, and the closeness of their friendship ultimately proved fatal for Mokare.

The precise sites of Mokare and Collie's graves have not been definitively established, although they are almost certainly under the car park at the rear of Albany's Town Hall. Only a few years after Collie's death, some of his friends (including the surveyor John Septimus Roe) came to the conclusion that building work that could be carried out at some future time might disturb the grave-site, and Collie's remains were moved to the newly established cemetery. In 2009, an attempt was made to locate the original site using ground-probing radar, but the results were inconclusive owing to the considerable depth of soil that had been placed over the area during construction of the car park.

When Collie had returned to Perth in November 1832, he was temporarily replaced as Resident Magistrate by Lieutenant Donald Macleod who was then the military commandant at Albany. Stirling appointed a retired British naval officer, Sir Richard Spencer, to fill the position and he arrived from England with his family in September 1833, taking up the position the following month. Spencer bought the government farm and turned its small house into a comfortable home for his large family. He held the Resident Magistrate's position until his death in mid 1839, and played a major role as administrator and leading agriculturalist of Albany's hinterland during the difficult early years of free settlement.

Although this period at Albany was characterised by economic stagnation, some limited business activity did take place in the town. Digory Geake arrived at Albany with his wife and daughter and rented one of the former soldiers' houses. He saw an opportunity to cater for the influx of settlers he obviously expected, and built the town's first hotel on a block east of the present Old Gaol Museum. The population failed to increase in line with his expectations and he was unable to afford the £20 licence fee in 1833, but was nevertheless permitted to continue to trade.[20] The opening of a hotel at Albany was significant because it increased the opportunity for unscrupulous Europeans to supply Aboriginal people with alcohol. Previously, all alcohol at the settlement had been under the strict control of the military authorities, and the written evidence indicates that Collie, at least, had been aware of the problems increased access to alcohol could cause. In an official report to Stirling in early 1832, Collie wrote:

> There is one precaution which is generally the foremost to demand attention, and the excess soonest to be evaded in the communications of civilized with barbarous nations; that against the introduction among the latter of the custom and habit of indulging in ardent spirits, and which, I sincerely hope, will continue to be as successful in succeeding years as it has been since the formation of the settlement. The Beveridge which the natives have been happily taught to prefer, is the agreeable and innocuous tea, and few of them will drink spirits when offered and none to excess.[21]

Collie's hopes were not to be realised, and dependency upon alcohol and tobacco later played a socially corrosive role in the continuing relationship between the town and region's European and Aboriginal inhabitants.[22]

Following the initially slow progress of free settlement at Albany, from late 1833 a three-year period began when optimism rose as increasing numbers of British settlers decided to make the area their home. The publication of favourable reports of the district by Isaac Nind, Thomas Wilson and John Septimus Roe, and the private letters of Alexander Collie, enhanced Albany's reputation at a time when British demand for Australian wool rose strongly.[23] Stirling's advocacy of Albany's agricultural and pastoral potential during his temporary return to England played a role in leading a number of people to migrate to the town. The *James Pattison* arrived at Albany from London in 1834, carrying James Stirling and a number of new settlers including ten men with some capital, and fourteen boys whom Stirling had sourced from the Society for Promoting Juvenile Emigration. This influx appeared to bode well for Albany's future, but many of the new arrivals moved away to Perth or elsewhere after spending only a short time at the town.[24]

This period was marked by two events that changed the dynamic of Aboriginal–European relations. Firstly, and most importantly, the death of Mokare deprived Albany's settlers of their chief translator and friend within the Kincannup community. Secondly, Sir Richard Spencer's decision to make his new home at the government farm his official as well as his personal address marked the end of the period when European authority was centred on the site of the original settlement. These changes, which occurred in quick succession, marked the end of an era. Although Spencer showed sympathy for the Aboriginal inhabitants of his new domain, never again would there be the degree of intimacy between the leaders of the two communities that had been such a marked, and possibly unique, feature of Albany's history. The relationship altered subtly, but much of the goodwill remained.

By 1833, Aboriginal–European relations at the Swan River and its outlying settlements had deteriorated alarmingly. Initially, as at King George Sound, explorers and settlers found the Noongar inhabitants to be friendly, and Stirling believed that the harmonious relationship could be maintained into the future. The relatively rapid pace of European settlement at Perth and surrounding districts soon presented the Aboriginal people of that region with a very different set of problems to those experienced by the Menang.[25] Green identified three major reasons for the deterioration that quickly set in at the Swan River: the exploitation of Aboriginal labour; the overriding European imperative to increase material wealth; and the enclosure of land to exclude its resources from traditional Aboriginal uses.[26] These factors had been absent at the southern settlement in its early years, initially because of its military nature, and post-1831 because of the extremely slow rate of development and land alienation. The situation at Perth continued to worsen and by late 1834 Stirling regarded the threat to colonists as completely unacceptable. He led a punitive expedition to Pinjarra, where at least fifteen Aboriginal people were shot and killed.[27]

Earlier, Stirling and his family had spent the summer of 1831–32 at Albany, living in a small four-roomed house specially constructed at the government farm for the visit. During his stay, Stirling received his much-awaited commission as Governor of the Colony of Western Australia.[28] He was so impressed with Albany and its surrounding district that he decided to exchange some land he had earlier selected at Leschenault for three sections totalling 45,000 acres in what he believed to be the better areas of land north of the town.

Stirling became deeply concerned with what he perceived as the undesirable, even treacherous, behaviour of the Noongars living near Perth. Following a worrying increase in conflict during 1831, Stirling found it necessary to establish military detachments at Perth, Augusta, Mandurah, Upper Swan, Clarence and Kelmscott, besides maintaining the small pre-existing garrison at Albany. The situation had deteriorated so markedly at Perth that a citizen force was organised to assist the military, and a system of bugle calls was put in place in order that the citizenry might respond in case the feared mass Aboriginal attack materialised.[29]

During 1832, the situation steadily worsened. In June, the spearing of Mr Walcott's bullock on his Swan River farming property brought matters to a head, with armed settlers carrying out a massed dawn attack on the camp of the Noongars believed to be responsible. In the confusion, an Aborigine was wounded and Walcott's servant was caught in crossfire and killed. The fifty Noongar people who made up the camp had their weapons confiscated and were warned to keep completely away from the settlers' farms on pain of being shot on sight.[30] The situation further deteriorated, and Stirling sought to lessen the potential for violence by setting up food stores at Mongers Lake and the Upper Swan so that Aborigines would not be continually seeking food from settlers. John Morgan, a settler who felt strongly that any signs of weakness would only lead to an Aboriginal attack, publicly announced:

> There are always in my office, sixty stands of arms, with a full supply of ammunition, for those who may require it, ready to inflict a prompt and heavy punishment on the natives should their conduct at any time be considered to deserve it.[31]

So bad had the situation become at the settlements near Perth and at York that by the end of April 1833, the military and settlers had killed at least twenty-one Aborigines and had wounded at least ten more. The violence was not all one-sided; during the same period, nine Europeans had been speared to death and thirteen were wounded.[32] In strong contrast, apart from the violence perpetrated by sealing gangs and the spearing of Dineen soon after the *Amity* arrived, Green found no evidence for any deaths or injuries caused by inter-racial violence at Albany during the early years, although deaths and injuries continued from spearings within the Menang community.[33]

The difference between Aboriginal–European relations at the two settlements of Albany and Perth must have struck Stirling forcibly, for his later actions showed that his mind had turned to how lessons learned at the older settlement might be transferred to the colony's new capital. Shortly after arriving back at Perth Stirling wrote:

> At King George's Sound where I found a good understanding established, I have caused it to be preserved and cultivated, and the natives confide in and in fact live very much with the Europeans. In the Swan River District they sometimes meet us in amity and perhaps on the following day they commit a robbery or murder.[34]

It is therefore not surprising to find that when two Aboriginal men from King George Sound in late 1832 volunteered their services as peacemakers at the troubled settlements to their north, the authorities at Perth gladly accepted their offer. Stirling had sailed from Fremantle in early August that year on a voyage to London, not returning until mid 1834, and was therefore not directly involved in planning the visit.

Although Manyat and Gyallipert had approached Donald Macleod, who was at that time Government Resident at Albany, the idea of an Aboriginal delegation to Perth initially came from another source. Robert Lyon, a religious man deeply concerned with the deterioration in the relationship between settlers and Aborigines at the Swan River, had proposed to the Executive Council at Perth and the British Colonial Secretary that he be permitted to live with Yagan and the other Aboriginal prisoners exiled on Carnac Island off the coast near Fremantle. To assist him with learning the language spoken by Perth Noongars, Lyon proposed inviting some Kincannup men to live on Carnac for a period. This idea did not meet with official favour, and the whole enterprise came to an end when the Aboriginal prisoners abandoned both Lyon and Carnac Island, rowing ashore in a captured boat.

While developing his plan, Lyon had travelled to Albany and probably discussed the idea with some Kincannup people. This would explain how Manyat and Gyallipert heard of the difficulties at the Swan River and became interested in visiting Perth to help alleviate them. Macleod arranged for the two men to travel by ship to Fremantle, but only after receiving consent from the Kincannup people as a whole.[35] Certainly, the author of the news item in the issue of the *Perth Gazette* describing their arrival at Fremantle had no doubt that relations were better at King George Sound, and that this was due to:

> the uniformly humane and kind treatment pursued since the earliest settlement of King George's Sound, by every rank of inhabitant towards the Natives...' which had instilled a 'beneficial confidence...not only into these individuals, but into the whole of their tribe...'[36]

Alexander Collie met the two Kincannup men at Perth and held several meetings with the local Noongars led by Yagan. Ironically, during the month they spent at Perth they lived for part of the time with John Morgan, presumably in close proximity to his sixty stands of arms and full supply of ammunition. Perth colonists expected great things of the visit but Shellam points out that there is every reason to believe that the several meetings between the King George Sound men and the local Noongars were actually more about intricacies of Aboriginal diplomacy than about attempting to achieve harmony between colonists and Aborigines. The evidence she presents in her comprehensive account of the affair indicates that Manyat and Gyallipert had their own complex reasons for wishing to travel to Perth, reasons that probably had little to do with their publicly avowed purpose.[37] Shellam describes their behaviour as 'enigmatic', acknowledging that the records are too scant to enable a historian to identify with certainty the reasons why the two Kincannup men were so keen to undertake the journey.[38]

The prominent Perth settler George Fletcher Moore held high hopes for the future as a result of the visit, but these were dashed when violence actually increased.[39] Before the year was out, Yagan had been shot, and his father executed, as punishment for spearing colonists.

Manyat and Gyallipert, accompanied by Lieutenant Governor Irwin, Moore and Ensign Robert Dale, returned to Albany to an enthusiastic welcome from their Aboriginal friends. No doubt one of the purposes of the European visitors from Perth was to see for themselves what could be learned from the amicable situation at Albany. When it was time to return to the Swan River after two weeks at Albany, Moore described how many Kincannup people lined up to volunteer to go to the northern settlement.[40] John Morley, who had been at Albany for less than two years but had evidently acquired a degree of fluency in the Kincannup pidgin, took the opportunity to address the local Aboriginal people on behalf of Irwin:

> Now now twonk, Gubbernor wonka me wonka black fellow, black fellow pear white man white man poot. Black fellow queeple no good. Black fellow pear black fellow no good. Black fellow plenty shake hand black fellow, no black fellow no queeple, black fellow give him white man's wallabies, wood come here, water come here, white man plenty shake hand black man, plenty give it him bikket, plenty ehtah, plenty blanket, arrack, tomahawk. Now Gubbernor wonka me give it him one guy black fellow one guy knaif.

Moore wrote an English translation of this remarkable speech:

> Now attend, the Governor desires me to tell the black man if the black man spear the white man the white men will shoot

them. If a black man steal it is not good. If the black man be friendly with the black man, if the black man do not steal, if the black man gives the white man wallabies, bring wood, and bring water, white man will befriend the black man, and give him plenty of biscuits, plenty to eat, and give him blankets, rice, tomahawk. Now the Governor desires me to give each black man one knife.[41]

One can only guess why Irwin chose to ask Morley to make this speech. Given the deteriorating situation at Perth, it would appear to have been an appropriate speech to make there, but why at Albany? Was this Irwin's standard address to Aboriginal groups at Perth, and he simply had it repeated at Albany despite its evident unsuitability for the local audience? One might have expected him to take the opportunity to thank publicly the two emissaries of peace, and to thank the rest of the Kincannup people for their consistent co-operation with the European settlers at Albany. However, the *Australian Dictionary of Biography* describes Irwin as stern and fond of moralising, and the contrast between his approach and that taken by men such as Barker and Collie is one reason why the relationship at Albany was so much better than at Perth.[42] George Fletcher Moore's memoirs reveal that he found the speech most amusing; it is likely that Barker and Collie would have found it tragic.

The official Perth party sailed from Albany soon afterwards, taking Gyallipert, Manyat and four other Kincannup men with them to meet again with the Swan River Aborigines. Irwin wrote to Goderich, the Colonial Secretary in Grey's Cabinet, informing him of 'the most perceptibly beneficial results' of the meetings, and the progress both Aboriginal groups were making in understanding each other's language. Irwin's letter also indicated that he had other reasons for encouraging the two Aboriginal groups to engage with each other:

> I feel warranted in saying, that we can obtain, by means of the King George's Sound Natives, earlier and clearer information of the existing feelings and intended movements of the local tribes, than from the most friendly and familiar of the latter.[43]

Irwin's words appear to indicate that he was more concerned with the gathering of tactically useful information by the King George Sound men than in the possibility of them being able to persuade the local Aborigines to adopt a more peaceable attitude towards the Perth settlers. Relations at Perth and York continued to deteriorate, and there is no evidence that the Kincannup emissaries achieved any of the high hopes held by Perth officials and settlers.

While in England, Stirling found an acquaintance who was willing to fill the position of Government Resident at Albany. Sir Richard Spencer left England in April 1833 as a fifty-three-year-old naval captain on half pay with a pregnant wife and nine children. He believed that his family would never achieve the degree of success and social respectability he sought if they remained in England, and he determined to make Albany his permanent home where the Spencers would form 'the groundwork for a respectable society'.[44] He intended taking up a large area of land at Albany for himself and his sons, and later wrote, 'I thought to make farmers of them all'.[45]

Spencer was the first administrator to establish himself and his family permanently at Albany with the intention of making economic use of its hinterland. It would be reasonable to assume that this fundamental shift in the nature of administration would have marked a major turning point in European–Aboriginal relations as economic exploitation of Menang land became virtually the sole reason for the settlement's existence. However, due to the extremely slow rate of agricultural and pastoral development during Spencer's six years in office, this did not prove to be the case.

In her biography of Spencer, Gwen Chessell describes him as forceful and far-sighted, but also intemperate and irascible.[46] His autocratic style of administration resulted in heated clashes with several other settlers, leading Stirling to carry out an enquiry into his administration which concluded that there was fault on both sides. Inevitably there were some changes in the European–Aboriginal relationship during Spencer's tenure, but he was able to maintain a level of amicability. Although the relationship was not perfect during the time Spencer was in office, the contrast between the absence of any recorded deaths on either side at Albany and the situation at Perth and the Avon Valley during this six-year period, when fourteen Europeans and at least fifty-three Aborigines were killed, is remarkable.[47] Spencer wrote in 1837:

> The natives here are more numerous than in any other part of Australia and I believe better disposed towards the Europeans. In four years that I have been here there has been no quarrel…[48]

It is impossible to be certain from where he gained the idea that Albany had a uniquely large number of Aboriginal people, or that the relationship between them and the settlers was so much better at Albany than in other areas of the continent, but the letter does give a valuable insight into how Spencer perceived that Albany fitted into the broader Australian picture.

At this point it is appropriate to examine the motives behind the Spencer family's aims with respect to Aboriginal people, since in broad outline they typify those of British settlers at Albany and its hinterland during the years covered in this chapter. The first and fundamental motive was the need to ensure their personal safety. The Spencer home was in close proximity to a traditional Aboriginal campsite, ensuring that the question of how best to coexist with the region's original inhabitants became very much a personal, as well as official, concern for the Government Resident and his family. Spencer had fought bravely in hand-to-hand combat against the French and Spanish while serving in the Royal

Navy, receiving several serious wounds; he was a man accustomed to facing danger and his training and experiences would have taught him the necessity of making prudent preparations to assess and deal with risk. It is in this light that one should read those of his letters which at first sight appear to express contradictory assessments of the situation in which Spencer and his family found themselves at Albany. For example, in January 1834, he wrote to the authorities at Perth:

> The great number of natives who frequently Bivouack close to my House, renders it in consequence of its distance from the settlement an unsafe residence without some Military Protection... although the natives are at present on the most friendly terms with us, the only way to remain so is never to let them feel that you are entirely within their power.[49]

In this letter, Spencer summed up the settlers' dilemma: the Aborigines might be friendly, but it was only prudent to acknowledge that the great imbalance in numbers meant that the potential for trouble was always present. In this letter, which included a request for a large number of muskets and ammunition to be kept ready at Spencer's house, can be seen what long remained the underlying fear of settlers at Albany as well as in other isolated areas – how would a few poorly armed Europeans be able to fight off a determined attack by a large number of Aboriginal men skilled in the use of their traditional weapons? No amount of amity could ever erase this primal fear while the number of Europeans was so small, and while military protection was weak and concentrated at only a few points.[50]

In an era when Great Britain was frequently involved in exploring and 'settling' areas of the world inhabited by indigenous people, it is not surprising to find that the topic of fear was a matter of some interest for those personally involved in such enterprises. James

Stirling, for example, had acquired some experience of how men exposed to frontier contact situations developed a set of practices they believed would result in the least danger to themselves. His first involvement with such a situation occurred in 1813, when as a newly promoted naval captain he sailed his vessel, the *Brazen*, to Churchill on the shores of Hudson Bay as escort to a convoy of ships taking settlers and supplies to the small trading post. Upon arrival, Stirling was briefed by company representatives experienced in interacting with the different indigenous groups who lived in the area. He would have been told that it was dangerous to show fear, and that he should neither initiate nor refuse contact with them. [51] Stirling later spent part of 1826 and 1827 in New South Wales, and he must have been well aware of the violence still occurring on the frontiers of that colony.

Even given the unrealistic assumption of total goodwill on both sides, the inability of the British and Aboriginal people to fully understand each other's culture prevented the settlers, especially those living with their families in areas remote from the availability of immediate military assistance, from ever feeling completely safe. Settlers sometimes gave inadvertent offence by acting in ways that were inappropriate in Aboriginal cultural terms, and such transgressions could quickly lead to a dangerous confrontation. They took this as providing evidence to support Stirling's accusation that even apparently friendly Aborigines could not be trusted to behave in a consistently non-violent fashion. Europeans were aware that Aboriginal men were known to spear their fellows while the victims were sleeping, and this knowledge tended to heighten the fear that only constant alertness could guarantee their own safety. The fact that these spearings were reserved for Aboriginal transgressors of their own customary law was well understood by the settlers. However, the practice was so at variance with contemporary British ideals of fair play that it was inevitably seen as indicating that Aboriginal people were capable of treachery and it was therefore only prudent to maintain a degree of caution when away from immediate military protection. Some Perth settlers were so aware of Native American attacks on British settlers that they repudiated friendly gestures made by local Aborigines out of a sense of fear.[52]

It is inconceivable that Stirling would not have discussed his experience and expressed his opinions when he visited Spencer at his home at Lyme Regis in England in order to offer him the position of Government Resident at Albany. The Spencer family must have seriously considered the subject of their physical security before deciding to accept, and they would have arrived at Albany with a certain amount of trepidation.

Once Spencer arrived at Albany, he found that there were actual grounds for some apprehension. He wrote to Peter Brown, the Colonial Secretary at Perth about an incident that occurred only three months after taking up residence:

> Last week a numerous body of natives of the Wiel Man and Cockatoo tribes, about 90 stout men, assembled here with a hostile intention towards the King George Tribe. All our native men and women came crying to me for protection and the men assembled, armed and went forwards to meet them, when, after a long parley, peace was made and they all returned together, bivouacked near my house and in the morning as they had nothing to eat, I found it necessary to give them half a pound of biscuit each and to boil them a quantity of tea. On the third day, they went away.[53]

The letter, which also noted that Spencer was employing Aboriginal men and providing rations for an elderly widow and three young children described as 'starving', was written in a matter-of-fact tone that belied the concern for his family's safety that he must surely have felt at the time. It was not written to request further military protection, but to ask that the Lieutenant Governor would send twelve frying pans and the same number of cooking pots to assist the Aboriginal people for whom Spencer clearly felt some responsibility. Unfortunately, Spencer failed to note or speculate upon the reasons why the widow and children were starving, or why the large assemblage of both local and visiting Aboriginal men was without food. James Browne wrote that the over-hunting of kangaroos around Albany had already adversely affected the amount of food available; it is also possible that temporary food shortages had always been a part of such large movements of people away from their usual hunting grounds.[54]

Spencer wrote very little about the relationship that grew up between his family and the Aboriginal people who continued to use what had almost certainly been a traditional campsite from time immemorial. His letters show that from the outset there was a considerable degree of peaceful and close interaction, but they shed little light on the subject. A close reading presents a picture of a family that felt itself under no immediate threat, but was understandably determined to maintain the personal safety of its members. Although Spencer did not specifically address the point in his correspondence, it would appear that he believed it was better to achieve this aim through co-operation rather than confrontation. Europeans continued to be apprehensive about Aborigines for years into the future as settlement spread in the region, but never allowed their fears to dominate the relationship or curtail their activities.

Settlers believed that while their own numbers, and those of the military detachment remained so low, their only certain protection lay in their capacity to so Christianise and 'civilise' the Aboriginal inhabitants that they would abandon what the settlers believed to be their propensity for unpredictable violence. Settlers generally believed that no one could ever be truly secure until this was achieved. The word 'civilise' was frequently used throughout colonial Australia and it is important to realise how European settlers understood its meaning. The idea of civilisation, as distinct from the opposite – barbarism, or (at best) a society that was primitive in its religious beliefs and social organisation – had its origins in Renaissance Europe. Most Europeans believed civilised societies were those that had sophisticated political and social systems, laws and culture. Such societies were seen as having a moral superiority over others which appeared to lack these institutions. China, Japan and some Middle Eastern countries obviously had institutions that were very different from those of European nations, yet Europeans considered them civilised. The indigenous societies of Africa and the Americas were not so considered.[55]

Beyond the imperative of personal security, there were further motives for Spencer and the other settlers at Albany to attempt to co-operate with the Menang. Labour was in extremely short supply for any farmer or pastoralist with ambitions to establish his family on the land, and it would obviously be to their economic advantage if Aborigines could be persuaded to take up employment on their properties. Within three months of his arrival, Spencer recorded having employed:

> six or eight natives daily the last fortnight as Agricultural labourers, cutting down trees, clearing the land and paying them a lb. of flour and two ounces of suet for a forenoon's work or a job equal to that for which they are all very grateful.[56]

This represented a progression from the more informal pattern established by Barker whereby Aborigines carried out occasional specified tasks, such as catching swans, in return for biscuit.[57] The practice of paying both Aboriginal and non-Aboriginal workers in kind had become common throughout the colony by this time, and was quite legal until the passage of the Truck Act in 1900.[58]

The topic of Aboriginal employment and its impact is very relevant to any history of Aboriginal–European interaction in Western Australia since employment was the most important single factor in breaking down much of the traditional way of life of Aboriginal people in the colony.[59] It was recognised from the beginning of European settlement in Western Australia that this would be an inevitable outcome of Aboriginal employment and, since at that time this was seen by the authorities as a highly desirable development, policies were put in place to encourage settlers to employ Aboriginal people. In 1841 Governor John Hutt introduced incentives for settlers to train and employ Aboriginal men and women; the men as farm labourers, and the women as 'house servant, sempstress or dress maker, laundress or bonnet maker...'[60] Should the employer comply with the conditions for a period of two years, he or she would be eligible for a remission of £18 from the purchase price of farmland for training and employing a farm labourer or domestic servant, and double that amount if the Aboriginal employee was trained to a journeyman standard in a trade. It was specifically stated that the scheme was designed to promote 'civilisation and improvement' among the colony's Aboriginal population.[61] Should that not be a sufficiently clear statement of official intent, a subsequent announcement stated that:

> any native on whose account the remission was claimed is expected to be not only weaned from the habits of savage life, but also voluntarily seeking and likely to continue to seek a livelihood by some of the occupations of civilised life of the nature specified therein.[62]

Obviously, employment was considered a powerful weapon in the battle to change the Aboriginal lifestyle to one that Europeans thought more desirable. That Hutt's scheme failed miserably to achieve its objectives is shown by a report in 1847 noting that only ten applicants in the colony had been granted the bounty, and that only one of these had actually claimed the remission.[63] The scheme was ended in 1848. This particular scheme was a failure, but the fact that more than 500 Aboriginal people were employed in Western Australia by 1850 meant that a considerable number were in continuous and close contact with Europeans. This must have had a weakening effect upon Aboriginal social organisation, irrespective of whether the motive in providing employment was one of social engineering, or solely to improve the economic situation of those settlers involved.[64]

Spencer wrote briefly about his Aboriginal employees in several of his letters, generally in the context of their economic value to him as an employer. In June 1834, he mentioned that they were becoming more useful, one learning carpentry, while another was employed as a pit sawyer.[65] Three years later he wrote to the Church of England Bishop of Australia, mentioning that he was employing about eight men and boys on general labouring work on his property.[66] Naturally, the letter turned to the subject of religion and its application to the Aboriginal people who were by then such a part of the Spencer family's life at Albany. This letter, together with other documents from the early period of free settlement, provides an insight into Spencer's third motive in his dealings with Albany's Aborigines.

As mentioned previously, most figures in authority in colonial Western Australia at that time and later believed that ultimately the only way forward in achieving a desirable outcome in European–Aboriginal relations lay in the settlers' ability to both Christianise and civilise the indigenous population as quickly as possible. Only when this had occurred would settler safety be assured and a significant supply of cheap labour become available. According to this Eurocentric view, Albany was now a colony of the British Empire and the sooner its Aboriginal inhabitants gave up their old heathen and economically unproductive ways, the better it would be for everybody. In some respects, this is an oversimplification of an idea that was devastating in its implications for the continuation of traditional Aboriginal culture, but a study of contemporary letters, official reports and the recorded actions of many settlers, shows that it was widely held, especially by those in positions of power and authority.

In seeking to understand the settlers' attitudes and actions towards the Aboriginal people they encountered at Albany and its hinterland, it is crucial to understand and acknowledge the pivotal role played by the Christian religion in the lives of the great majority of British people in the early nineteenth century. British historian G. Kitson Clark stated that in England at this time:

> Christianity and the Bible supplied the only comprehensive system of thought of which many people were aware. They supplied the only philosophy or ethics easily available, the only cosmology or ancient history.[67]

However, the increased interest in science, and the concomitant emphasis upon rational thinking brought by the Enlightenment, had begun to offer an alternative to this monolithic approach.[68]

Perth-based historian and Anglican priest Rowan Strong has made a powerful case for a reappraisal of the role of religion in Australian colonial history, noting that Australian historians have been predominantly content to reduce religion to a position of marginal importance in Australian history.[69]

When the Anglican clergyman John Wollaston arrived at Fremantle in early 1841, he commenced keeping a comprehensive diary which has since been published in three volumes. These are invaluable as a primary source of information about the role nineteenth-century Anglican Christianity played in shaping the thoughts and actions of influential colonists towards Aboriginal people in the south-west of Western Australia as a whole, and at Albany in particular, following Wollaston's appointment there in July 1848. Strong has taken issue with the idea that poor church attendance by settlers in the new colony indicates that religion played a relatively insignificant part in their worldview. Although Wollaston was often despondent about the numbers at his services in the area of his responsibility (he was also Archdeacon for the colony as a whole) he noted that 'people are jealous of the *name* of Churchman'.[70] Attendance at worship might have been irregular, but the Church, particularly the Church of England, continued to set much of the ethical and social agenda in colonial Western Australia.

Wollaston's views about the position that indigenous peoples throughout the British Empire ought to occupy typified British establishment thought of the first half of the nineteenth century.[71] Firstly and critically, although Aboriginal people had a right to humane treatment, they had no right to either land, culture or a religion of their own:

> Notwithstanding the natives are often troublesome, the only feeling in the breast of a really humane and religious settler on viewing their condition is one of pity; a feeling painfully increased when he reflects that God has given their lands to Christian Englishmen in possession with the imperative duty annexed to the gift that they should both by precept and example teach them the good and right way.[72]

In this understanding of the will of God, the proper response of the Menang was to acquiesce peacefully in the agenda of both Church and State – to be re-cultured as reliable agricultural labourers or domestic servants occupying a socially inferior position in a transplanted British society. The settler was to be humane, and should welcome Aborigines as Christians through baptism, but the land was now his as a reward from God for bringing it under cultivation. The culture was to be British, and the nature of this culture meant that no prospect of social equality could be entertained.[73]

Wollaston was quite prepared for Aboriginal culture to be destroyed, should it stand in the way of Christian conversion. If God had given Australia to the British Empire, it was because of the opportunity this presented for men like himself to preach the gospel of Christ – from a contemporary Evangelical viewpoint this was the very *reason* God had brought the Empire into being.[74] At the heart of Evangelicalism were Jesus' words: 'I am the way, the truth and the life: no man cometh unto the Father, but by me'.[75] The commonly accepted interpretation in the early 1800s of this pivotal statement was that all those who failed to heed Christ's words and become Christians were inevitably condemned to an eternal punishment in Hell. The power of this doctrine in shaping the attitudes of so many of the people who interacted with the Aboriginal people of Albany and its hinterland during the 1830s and 1840s should not be underestimated. Unless its influence is appreciated fully, many of the recorded settler attitudes and actions are today incomprehensible.

Evangelical Anglicanism was a powerful force in both religious and secular Britain.[76] People such as William Wilberforce exerted both moral and Parliamentary authority to influence the nation to end practices such as slavery that they believed to be contrary to the teachings of Christ. Others such as Sir James Stephen, who held the position of Assistant Under Secretary of the Colonial Office from 1834 until 1836 when he became Permanent Under Secretary, took their beliefs so seriously that they deliberately sought positions of power and authority in order to bring Evangelical influence to the centres of power in their nation. Stephen held the post until his retirement in 1847, and exerted a powerful Evangelical influence over worldwide British colonial policy during that period.[77] Claire

McLisky has shown that Australian historians have frequently erred in describing such men as humanitarians, equating them with modern advocates for Aboriginal land rights and reconciliation.[78] In reality, they were men who took for granted the idea that post-Enlightenment Western civilisation was the natural peak of human achievement, and therefore saw no place for the continuance of Aboriginal culture or religion.[79]

Supporters of the Anglican Evangelical movement founded the Aborigines' Protection Society in 1837, the same year the House of Commons released its Select Committee Report. This report provides perhaps the clearest statement ever written about contemporary British colonial policy and practice. The committee's general opinion has been summed up as a 'conviction that there is but one effectual means of staying the evils we have occasioned, and of imparting the blessings of civilisation, and that is the propagation of Christianity...'[80] The Society continued in existence until 1909, when it merged with the Anti-Slavery Society.

Naturally, not all Australian settlers were sympathetic to the relatively liberal policies advocated by the Aborigines' Protection Society, believing that they were out of touch with 'colonial realities'. Henry Reynolds lists some of the epithets given to its adherents by unsympathetic contemporaries:

> The 'friends of the blacks' were seen to gratuitously assume an air of moral superiority, to consider themselves as more virtuous than the rest. Their contemporaries called them Exeter Hall [after the London building where the Evangelicals held many of their meetings] enthusiasts, maudlin philanthropists, meddling pseudo-philanthropists, do-gooders, bleeding hearts, nigger-lovers and many more abusive epithets...[81]

During the nineteenth century, the Exeter Hall school of thought had its supporters at Albany, while others opposed all that it stood for. Much of the subsequent history of Aboriginal–European relations in the region was affected by the playing out of these very different approaches.

Inextricably intertwined with the British idea that Christianity provided the only way forward for Aboriginal–European relations at Albany was the belief that this could only satisfactorily occur once the local indigenous people had abandoned their tribal ways and accepted their new roles as labourers and domestic servants. However, throughout Australia there had been a persistent and almost total resistance to European society and its Christian religion by Aboriginal adults. George Grey, who spent three years in Western Australia including a brief period in 1839 as Government Resident at Albany, had identified some of the causes of the problem in 1841. He found settlers reluctant to accept Aboriginal people socially, even those who had followed the officially sanctioned approach by converting to Christianity and attempting to integrate into European society. Although many settlers believed employment to be the path through which civilisation would take root, in fact they offered only very poorly paid jobs that were usually intermittent in nature, effectively economically precluding an Aboriginal person from abandoning completely his or her traditional way of life.[82]

Grey identified a further problem. He believed that experience proved that unless an Aboriginal person, especially a child, underwent total separation from those remaining in a traditional cultural environment there could be no chance of success in European terms.[83] Although the problems involved in implementing British colonial policy with respect to Aboriginal people were self-evident, the solutions proved perplexingly and frustratingly difficult to discover and implement.

A theory developed that the only real hope of achieving the missionary agenda of re-acculturation and evangelisation lay in educating and otherwise influencing the children before they had undergone the rites of initiation. With this aim in mind, a school for Aboriginal pupils began at Albany 1843. In the previous year, new regulations had been introduced throughout the colony to regulate Aboriginal behaviour in towns as settlers increasingly came to the view that the initial era of contact had passed, and the time had arrived for British culture and sensibilities to be respected by 'wild' Aborigines. Spears were no longer permitted to be carried into towns, 'decent' clothing had to be worn, and the practice of settlers giving food, without any expectation of work in return, had to cease.[84]

Inherent in this endeavour to create conditions in the colony more in line with British social expectations was the need to so educate and civilise Aboriginal children that they would readily accept the new realities. If the adults were too difficult to influence, a properly designed school program would ensure that Aboriginal children passing into adulthood would have an understanding of what was required of them as British citizens. Under this colony-wide policy, children were to be taken from their parents and sent to live with settler families who would employ them as servants. They would learn European habits and manners in the home, and would learn the three Rs and scripture during each afternoon, when they would be educated at school.

The scheme failed throughout the colony when insufficient families were found willing to employ Aboriginal children. The only way children could be persuaded to attend school was by bribing their parents with gifts of flour. The teacher at Albany, John McKail, found the children quick at rote learning but uncomprehending with respect to Christian doctrine. After three years of struggle, his school was pronounced a failure and closed by the Government Resident, John Randall Phillips.[85]

A further attempt at integrating Albany's Aboriginal inhabitants into some aspects of European society came from a completely different quarter. The same month that Phillips closed the Aboriginal school, he received a request from five French Catholic priests from the order of the Immaculate Heart of Mary. They applied for a loan of 4 acres near Albany to establish a farm where Aboriginal people could be taught the benefits of growing vegetables. The venture was not successful and the priests moved to land near Kendenup where they struggled for a few months before near starvation forced them to abandon the project completely.[86] The Menang were clearly not prepared to co-operate with any plan that would see them abandon their traditional lifestyle.

Although whaling began off the south coast of Australia in the very early years of the nineteenth century with the irregular voyages of a few whaling ships from the United States of America, the Menang were not greatly affected because the ships usually stayed at sea. However, during the mid 1830s, and through to the 1840s, several shore-based whaling ventures were set up near Albany and large supplies of whale meat, an unwanted by-product of an industry based on the extraction of oil from blubber, became available at the time of the year when the Menang customarily left the coast for the interior. To this point European settlement had probably not extensively altered the traditional patterns of life of many Menang people. They had always consumed whale meat on an opportunistic basis as whales beached themselves and died. However, the more regular supply of whale meat, together with the opportunity to supplement their diet occasionally with European food, presented a challenge to ancient traditions of migration and culture associated with the annual winter movement.[87]

James Browne observed that during the winter months of 1836, 1837 and 1838 many Aborigines were seriously ill from starvation because of the over-hunting of kangaroos by settlers.[88] It is likely that the hunting of kangaroos and wildfowl by settlers for both food and sport had dramatically reduced the food supply in the immediate vicinity of the town, and had helped bring about an increasing and debilitating reliance on European food by those Aboriginal people who had chosen to forgo a fully traditional lifestyle. The decision to abandon the annual winter migration inland where food was still plentiful caused serious hardship among those who made this choice. As shore-based whaling declined after 1840, there was a return to the old pattern of winter migration.

The Menang had clearly been seeking to make use of the new opportunities presented by European settlement and the whaling vessels that hunted in the seas around King George Sound. When the first bay whaling venture began in 1836, no settler had yet taken sheep or cattle into the old inland winter hunting lands, and kangaroos and other traditional food resources must therefore still have been plentiful there. The initial decision to cease annual migration therefore demonstrated a deliberate choice to adapt to and exploit change. It would be erroneous to assume that such modifications represented an abandonment of Aboriginal traditional life. As conditions changed, the Menang made opportune adjustments to their old way of life to accommodate the new realities, while continuing to pursue their own priorities.

A few French and American whaling ships returned to the area in the late 1830s, and by 1840 their numbers had increased dramatically. Between April 1840 and March 1841, twenty-five American and three French whaling vessels called at the port of Albany, as well as nineteen other ships. This effectively marked the end of the era when Aboriginal–European interaction was confined to those more or less permanently living at Albany and its hinterland. From this time forward, other European elements, often brutal, uncaring, uncontrolled and exceedingly disruptive, would play an increasing role in the relationship.

When ashore at Albany's still tiny settlement, ships' crews were virtually a law unto themselves. Whalers were generally rough men used to a cruel existence aboard ship, and the sudden descent of large numbers of them in the late 1830s upon the town's four hotels presented problems that local law enforcement officers found impossible to control.[89] At times as many as 300 foreign seamen, all more or less under the influence of alcohol, were in the town at the one time.[90] Alcohol, together with equally addictive tobacco, was commonly used to pay both local labourers and Aboriginal people at Albany at this time.[91] Although his statement is uncorroborated, Patrick Taylor, a local settler from the Kalgan River, wrote in 1844:

> they gather in the hope of obtaining money, biscuits, tobacco and ardent spirits from the seamen who they may encounter... In this way they are more and more corrupted; acquiring the vicious habits of the most abandoned seamen; encouraged by idleness; and tempted when disappointed in their expectations to commit crime in order to satisfy their cravings of nature.[92]

Taylor also stated that whalers had 'extensively communicated' venereal disease to Aborigines at Albany with devastating results upon their health.[93]

Government Resident Phillips wrote in 1840 that seamen (nationality unspecified) were giving Albany Aborigines spirits 'thereby causing constant disturbances amongst themselves when drunk'. He appointed an Aboriginal man as a constable in an attempt to control his fellows' behaviour.[94]

Perhaps surprisingly, given Lockyer's crackdown on the sealers he found at King George Sound in 1826, Aboriginal people were still being adversely affected by their actions as late as 1839. Government Resident Captain George Grey wrote to the Colonial Secretary at Perth that year roundly condemning sealers for abandoning Aboriginal women and their part-descent children. He claimed that sealers were perpetrating acts of great cruelty, but he was unable to bring them before the courts because Aboriginal people at that time were not permitted to give sworn evidence. Grey described Albany's Aboriginal people as well conducted, and his letter shows frustration at the position he found himself in.[95]

When Spencer died in July 1839, he was succeeded in his post by Grey, who spent less than a year in office before being replaced briefly by Captain Peter Belches in an acting capacity. In September 1840, the position was filled by John Randall Phillips, an early settler on the Canning River who had subsequently been appointed Government Resident at Williams River. While at the Canning River in mid 1833, he personally witnessed Yagan, Midgegooroo, Munday and Migo spear to death two Velvick brothers who were his employees at the time. Six years later, a boy who was working for him was also speared fatally.

However, Phillips was able to adapt to the different situation at Albany and became a respected, competent and successful administrator.[96] He ended Spencer's practice of distributing flour to Aborigines every second month because these regular gatherings had begun to degenerate into violence. He believed this was caused by groups of Aboriginal people coming together at times and in ways that were culturally inappropriate. The distribution was originally planned to reward good behaviour, but Phillips believed it had come to be seen as a right. His action in reducing the frequency of flour distributions to two or three times per year was seen by some residents of Albany as constituting a major cause of the partial breakdown in Aboriginal–European relations that occurred during the 1840s, and which is discussed later in this chapter, and in more detail in Chapter Five.[97]

One practical outcome of the 1837 House of Commons Report on Aboriginal Tribes was the establishment of Protectors of Natives in the Australian colonies.[98] In early 1839 John Hutt, a supporter of the Exeter Hall approach, was sworn in as Governor of Western Australia. He evinced a strong interest in Aboriginal affairs before leaving England, and wrote soon after his arrival:

Are they to be swept off by aggression and disease, or will they pine away under a feeling of their immeasurable inferiority to the white men; or if they survive, will it be to sink into a state little better than the slave, or gradually to be absorbed into and become one people with their intruders? The last, however apparently unobtainable, is the result which in our conduct towards them we should ever keep in view.[99]

Hutt's succinct and direct views provided the framework under which colonial policy towards Aboriginal people would operate in Western Australia during his seven years in office, a time that coincided with a temporary increase in problems at Albany.

In January 1840, two men appointed by the Colonial Office in London as Protectors of Natives arrived at Perth from England to take up their postings. Charles Symmons was given responsibility for the Perth region and the coast as far as Augusta, while Peter Barrow was stationed at York with responsibility for that area, as well as that of Albany. Because of the isolation of Albany from York, it was decided to add to the duties of whoever held the position of Government Resident at Albany by making him a Sub-Protector of Aborigines, responsible to the Protector at York. When Phillips, who had resigned as Government Resident in 1847 to take up the role of Sub-Guardian of Natives at Albany, died in late 1852, the position was given to a local man, Arthur Trimmer.[100] This position had been created under the authority of the local Sub-Protector of Aborigines (sometimes referred to as Sub-Protector of Natives) who had many other responsibilities in his major role as Government Resident. The line of authority ran from the Governor at Perth, through the Protector at York, to the Resident Magistrate at Albany as Sub-Protector, and finally to the Sub-Guardian whose role it was to actually do the majority of the work in the town and the wider Albany region.

From 1842 each Protector or Sub-Guardian in the colony was assigned one or two mounted police to:

> put an effectual stop to settlers taking the law into their own
> hands by leaving no excuse for those who may have suffered and
> are still suffering from the depredations of the natives going out
> in pursuit of them.[101]

In 1853, these specially qualified police officers were placed on normal duties, and the Protectors and Sub-Guardians lost their valuable auxiliaries.[102]

Protectors (or their delegated Sub-Guardians) were given a range of responsibilities by the British Colonial Office: they were to attach themselves to Aboriginal groups; induce them to accept a more settled existence; protect their interests from oppression and injustice; present their wants to the government; teach them how to cultivate the land and build houses; see to the education of their children; attend to religious education; learn their language; obtain information about them; and distribute food and clothing.[103] Little wonder that successive officials, sympathetic though they were, found themselves unable to fulfil adequately such an unrealistic range of roles – and little wonder that Exeter Hall became a byword in some sections of the community because of the evident lack of an appreciation of reality by its supporters in the home country. Regardless of how effective their work turned out to be, giving Protectors and Sub-Guardians such breathtakingly broad duties in a colony with vast distances and poor communications can at least partly be seen as designed to placate British consciences, since the tasks set were clearly beyond the realms of what was possible to achieve.

Trimmer is one of the more interesting and controversial figures from this period of Albany's history. He arrived in the colony in 1831, taking up farmland at York where he narrowly survived an attack by twelve Aborigines in 1835. Two years later, a young farmhand employed by Trimmer killed an Aboriginal man at York, and Trimmer was accused of nailing the dead man's ears to his kitchen wall.[104] Perth-based Anglican priest Louis Giustiniani accused Trimmer of having set a trap by placing the farmhand in a shed and ordering him to shoot at any Aborigine who came to take wheat. Violence escalated, and a European resident of the property was killed by the brothers of the Aboriginal man murdered in the shed. An Aboriginal woman was shot during the police search for the brothers, one of whom was later shot while escaping custody. An official enquiry exonerated Trimmer and his business partner, Revett Henry Bland, who was later appointed Protector of Aborigines at York in 1841.[105]

Trimmer visited Albany in 1835 as a member of an expedition led by Stirling, and subsequently married one of Sir Richard Spencer's daughters in 1836. He later moved to the Spencer farm on the Hay River where, according to Spencer, he was involved in 'foolishly' provoking the local Aboriginal people, forcing Spencer to remove his son-in-law and family back to Albany. In 1860 he leased land near present-day Tambellup, later moving to Eticup. By the time of his death at the age of seventy-one in 1877 he also held extensive pastoral leases east and north-east of the Stirling Ranges.[106]

Trimmer combined his pastoral activities with his role as Sub-Guardian. His geographical area of responsibility was vast. Every four months he travelled through the bush with an Aboriginal assistant checking on what was occurring. Unfortunately, however, insufficient information remains on file at the State Records Office to allow for a full assessment of how Trimmer performed his duties.[107] He wrote a considerable number of letters and several non-detailed brief reports to the Colonial Secretary at Perth, and these show that he was prepared to criticise those he believed were ill-treating Aborigines or wrongly accusing them of stock theft.

For example, in 1859 he wrote that shepherds were neglecting their duties by deserting their stations and leaving Aborigines in charge, 'for the sake of obtaining their women'.[108] Some of his letters show that he was frequently engaged in what might generally be considered police work. An example of this occurred in 1859, when he pursued an Aboriginal man named Mournong for a period of six weeks without being able to find him.[109]

The very survival of Albany's Aborigines, both individually and as a group, was threatened by their exposure to introduced diseases. Experience must have told those responsible for colonial settlement throughout the British Empire that British settlers would bring catastrophic levels of disease to indigenous peoples, yet this was ignored in the over-riding program of expanding the Empire. Disease was rife in early nineteenth-century Britain, as well as in the other countries from where ships sailed to the port of Albany; at Spencer's home town of Lyme Regis, 40 per cent of children died before their fifteenth birthday.[110] As late as 1848, between June and October of that year more than 72,000 people in England and Wales died of cholera.[111] It is not possible to be certain of the disease status of the Menang prior to their first contact with Europeans, but it is tragically evident that the new arrivals brought with them a range of diseases such as whooping cough, influenza, measles and scarlet fever (scarlatina), to which the Aboriginal people had never been exposed and therefore had no resistance.[112] Browne observed that:

> During our stay [at Albany between 1836 and 1838] there were many cases of sickness, and some of the abjects were taken into the houses of the families, attended by the Doctor, supplied with nourishing food and in fact treated like one of themselves. The present surgeon, Dr Harrison, shews the greatest attention to any case of sickness, and his liberality and humanity to the natives deserves the highest praise.[113]

From an Aboriginal perspective these new diseases were not only physically devastating; they presented a challenge to traditional Aboriginal culture as it became apparent that their own doctors were powerless to treat them effectively. This challenge did not completely spell the end of Aboriginal people's confidence in their own doctors' ability to treat the type of ailments and injuries that had existed prior to the arrival of Europeans. In 1980, historian Anna Haebich interviewed Lilly Hayward (born in 1914 or 1915) and was told that Hayward's parents' generation living around Kojonup had their own Noongar doctors.[114]

There is no evidence to show that any of the new diseases were deliberately introduced at Albany – a practice that was not unknown elsewhere in British colonial history. For example, Lord Jeffery Amherst, General of the British Army in North America, wrote in 1763: 'You will do well to try to inoculate the Indians [with smallpox] by means of blankets, as well as to try every other method that can serve to extirpate this execrable race'.[115] Tuberculosis passed into the Aboriginal community via milk from infected cows being given to nursing mothers, and the well-intentioned practice of giving blankets to replace kangaroo skin cloaks led to respiratory problems caused by wool not remaining dry during periods of frequent rainfall.[116] Both of these actions, misguided as they certainly proved to be, represented sincere attempts to ameliorate Aboriginal suffering.

When the Irish Anglican Priest the Reverend George King visited Albany in June 1847 he stated:

> The native population is yearly disappearing and I feel convinced, from my personal observation, that the fine tribe which, twelve years ago, could muster 300 fighting men in an hour's notice, will not be able in the next generation to furnish hewers of wood and drawers of water for the few European families who remain in the settlement.[117]

Certainly, much of this observed decline was due to people moving into the hinterland in search of employment, but disease also played a major role. Until John Host with Chris Owen issued a strong challenge in 2009, Western Australian historians were united in their assertion that disease in the south-west had had a devastating effect on both Aboriginal numbers and the ability of those who remained to maintain their traditional Noongar society. Jesse Hammond, who spent much of his life with Aboriginal people in the latter nineteenth century, certainly believed this to be so and Green wrote that his recollections 'suggest that the measles epidemic [of 1883] all but obliterated the traditional Nyungar of the South-West'.[118] Green has written more on the topic of disease in the Noongar population than any other historian, and is a leading advocate of the view that it proved disastrous. He notes that it is possible to trace 'fairly accurately' the impacts of various epidemics through a close study of settlers' letters, explorer's journals and government records, and gives a brief description of several of the most important.[119] Prominent historian Geoffrey Bolton states in support of Green:

> In the settled South-West, the fabric of Nyungar society was shattered by the measles epidemic of 1860, which swept ferociously through a population whose earlier isolation left them vulnerable to exotic diseases. Many years later, Ralph Ashworth remembered how as a boy coming into York he saw 'fifteen or sixteen blacks lying dead and their mates too weak to bury them…There were hundreds of blacks before then, but that was the end of them.[120]

Certainly, disease played a terrible role in the lives of Albany's Aboriginal inhabitants. The town's role as a coaling port brought large numbers of visitors from many parts of the world – a most dangerous situation given the lack of adequate quarantine regulations or facilities. In 1860, the *Salsette* sailed from England, calling at Suez and Ceylon, and docked at Albany in late June, where her Captain stated that none of her passengers or crew was ill. In fact, measles was on board the vessel and was soon carried ashore. Trimmer's two reports to Perth about the ensuing epidemic contain some of the most disturbing information of any of the century's official records pertaining to Albany. His first report stated:

> every native to the amount of sixty-four has suffered, and out of that number twenty-nine have died, and several more are now at the point of death. Those that have died are chiefly the best & strongest men. The old have generally escaped. I cannot at present give a full number of the deaths in the countryside. I am aware from good information they exceed those in the town. I will as soon as I can be spared, proceed to the country. The medical officer has lent every assistance in his power, but has found it dangerous to apply remedies to the natives that have no other coverings than bush huts. I have paid for the burial of several natives, their families being unable to perform the duty.[121]

Two months later Trimmer sent another report stating that it was his opinion that the epidemic had by then killed more than 200 Aboriginal people in the district.[122] He initially identified the disease as scarlet fever, presumably on local medical advice, but the census of 1870 recorded it as measles and this is now the accepted belief.

Given the lack of detailed official reports and statistics from the period there is no method of definitively resolving the issue of exactly how Albany's Aboriginal people were affected by disease during the nineteenth century.[123] It is, however, quite clear from Trimmer's two reports that a single epidemic reduced the Aboriginal population of the town and surrounding district by as much as 50 per cent – a figure comparable to the death toll caused by the Black Death in many areas of medieval Europe.

Host's book questions the convention that introduced diseases devastated the Aboriginal community in south-west Western Australia, stating 'the available evidence simply does not support it'.[124] It considerably weakens his case, however, that he fails to note or comment upon the very large number of deaths of Aboriginal people in the Albany region in the 1860 epidemic. In fairness, it should be noted that Host disowned the published book version of his report and it is possible that the Albany epidemic was discussed in his original report (unavailable for review). As Sub-Guardian of natives for the region, it was Trimmer's responsibility to observe the Aboriginal population closely, and his claim that more than 200 had died cannot be ignored. The epidemic certainly spread much further afield than the town of Albany, as shown by Ashworth's observations at York and by a statement in the Perth *Inquirer & Commercial News* of 28 November 1860 that 'The measles are very prevalent in Perth and Fremantle, there being scarcely a family without one of its members prostrate...' Medical historian Judy Campbell states that measles requires a population of more than 200,000 to become endemic, and this is why the colony had a series of epidemics in the nineteenth century, rather than a consistent pattern of infection.[125]

There is also the relevant evidence that numerous Aboriginal women contracted venereal diseases through contact with whalers and others who either visited or lived at the port of Albany. Dr Baesjou, medical officer at Albany, noted in 1861 that more than 90 per cent of the Aboriginal people he treated suffered from syphilis and associated venereal diseases.[126] Widespread venereal disease coupled with respiratory and other infectious diseases caused low birth rates and high infant mortality in Aboriginal communities across Australia in the early and mid nineteenth century, and the evidence supports the view that Albany and its region were not exceptions to this pattern.[127] Relatively few Noongar families today claim direct descent from Aboriginal people who were living at Albany during the early years of European settlement, and it is difficult to account for this other than as the combined result of deaths and low birth rates caused by introduced disease.

The absence of direct evidence from contemporary Aboriginal and European sources means that it is also not possible to fully assess the extent to which Aboriginal–European relations in the Albany region were affected by disease during the period covered in this chapter. There is evidence that in eastern Australia outbreaks of smallpox, a disease that was well controlled by inoculation in south-west Western Australia, led to a closer relationship with Europeans in affected areas since the newcomers were able to provide some medical assistance and care. This pattern was not repeated at Albany, where many of the town's surviving Aboriginal inhabitants began to move *away* from the town following the 1860 measles epidemic.

A visitor to Albany in 1835 wrote that the settlement was languishing, as the region's few settlers became despondent about their economic prospects.[128] The few good patches of soil suited to agriculture tended to be widely scattered, and located tens of miles inland at locations such as the Hay River near Mount Barker and at Kendenup. Poor communications, and the presence of numerous Aboriginal people, discouraged settlers considering taking their families into the interior to develop these areas for farming purposes. The few tentative early attempts at pastoralism failed as unacceptable stock losses due to the widespread prevalence of poisonous native plants made such ventures impracticable. Sir Richard Spencer lost 300 fine-wooled sheep and all of their lambs in one incident, almost certainly due to poison.[129] It was not until 1841 that government botanist James Drummond ended the controversy as to why sheep and cattle were dying by identifying these plants as the cause, thereby allowing pastoralists to instruct shepherds to herd the flocks away from infested areas.

Although the presence of poisonous plants and poor soil, and the absence of good roads combined to prevent rapid economic exploitation of Albany's hinterland, there were a few settlers who began to move away from the town, determined to succeed in their ambition to become significant owners of property. The extreme slowness with which they proceeded with development allowed Aboriginal people and Europeans time to adjust to each other's ongoing presence in what had virtually been the former's sole domain up to the end of the 1830s. The British had declared the hinterland at Albany open for settler ownership in early 1831, but although thirty-three men had bought a total of 120,000 acres by 1837, according to Spencer only one or two had even bothered to inspect their purchases.[130] Spencer's area of cultivation comprised almost all of the 30 acres under cultivation in the region as late as 1840.[131]

With the approach of the 1840s, the unique inter-racial harmony at Albany and its hinterland was beginning to unravel. Settlers such as Sir Richard Spencer and George Egerton-Warburton at the Hay River and John Hassell based at Kendenup had begun to stock their properties with sheep and cattle, and some holdings were as far as 80 kilometres from any military assistance.[132] Spencer wrote to the Colonial Secretary at Perth claiming that if the military detachment at the Hay River was withdrawn, the sheep and farmers would also have to be withdrawn as the Aborigines had become 'numerous and daring' and had repeatedly threatened his employees' lives.[133] In June 1839, a shepherd working for Mr McDonald, a squatter on crown land on the Hay River, was wounded in a spearing incident. Despite the swift despatch of a party sent to bring in the Aboriginal man or men responsible, no arrests were made. I have not been able to ascertain the shepherd's name. He was speared in the head, but it is unclear how serious the wound was and what were the circumstances of the attack. The Aboriginal man responsible for the attack, Minnan, was arrested by soldiers at Mount Barker nearly a year later but he was released on the suggestion of the acting Government Resident at Albany, who believed that isolated settlers were simply too vulnerable to reprisals should he be punished so long after the affair.[134]

In January 1840, a large group of Aborigines stole a substantial quantity of potatoes and onions from Spencer's Hay River farm. Two Europeans, presumably the Spencer property's employees, fired small shot at their legs as the Aborigines ran away so that they could later be identified.[135] This period of actual and threatened violence towards settlers at the Hay River appears to have been short-lived, and the threat may have been exaggerated in order to prevent the proposed removal of the military detachment from the area where the Spencer and Egerton–Warburton properties were located.

This brief period of heightened tension is discussed in more detail in a section of the following chapter that deals with the overall subject of whether Albany ever truly saw what could be called violent Aboriginal resistance. However, it should be noted here that contemporary observers blamed 'outsiders' visiting from east of Albany for the problems, and did not see the increase in incidents as constituting evidence that the local Aboriginal people were abandoning their policy of accommodation with the settlers.[136] Government Resident J. R. Phillips evidently thought outsiders to be the problem, and in 1841 he sent four Aborigines from Albany to Kendenup for ten days to 'convince the other Natives while there that we are not hostile to them'.[137]

Well aware that problems in the Avon Valley initially had been far worse, Albany-based settlers seem generally to have been realistic in accepting, however reluctantly, that the difficulties they faced in 1840 and 1841 were manageable without violent retaliation and could be solved in a relatively peaceful way. Phillips' experiences as a settler at the Canning River during the 1830s must have made any problems at Albany seem relatively trivial.

The idea the Aboriginal people from places other than Albany began to move into the area around 1840 tallies with Green's observation that:

> it is reasonably clear from the available evidence that up to about 1842, the Aboriginal population of King George Sound exercised territorial authority over the local area and their names and activities dominate the sources. As the port of Albany grew in significance, Aborigines from regions beyond the Sound were attracted to the European centre.[138]

After this period it therefore becomes less appropriate to use terms such as Kincannup and Menang to describe the Aboriginal people living in and around Albany.

The few farmers and pastoralists in Albany's hinterland presented a potential threat to the harmony so carefully nurtured by both traditional occupants and newcomers in the early years of the King George Sound settlement as they (and occasionally their wives and families) began to establish camps, homes and stock on land previously the exclusive domain of the Menang. The era when the British had kept themselves to the shores of the Southern Ocean was coming to an end.

The pastoralists had not erected fences, and the ancient paths and hunting grounds remained available for traditional use, but a line had been unmistakably crossed. By 1840, 2,210 sheep, 148 cattle and forty-three horses were competing with native grazing animals in the Albany hinterland, with the promise of much larger numbers to follow. It is unfortunate that the reaction of Aboriginal people to this fundamental change in their relationship with the invaders of their economic, social and cultural heartland was not recorded at the time. Reynolds has stated that we may assume that Aboriginal people throughout the continent would have extensively discussed appropriate tactics to meet the problem of permanent settler incursion upon their land. He described the outcome of such deliberations as 'practically universal', involving either large pitched battles or small and secret revenge expeditions.[139] He suggests that an uneasy peace usually grew up following this initial period of virtually open warfare, quoting a Queensland squatter:

> when they understand our superior power, and at the same time their predatory habits are still in existence – they will carry on small depredations and will no doubt take life at times, but their object is not to take life – it is not war.[140]

If such discussions took place within the Menang community, the initial outcome differed markedly from Reynolds' observations of other frontier regions. The evidence from Albany would appear to support the proposition that the early period of amicability, together with the slow rate of pastoral and agricultural expansion, allowed the Aboriginal–European relationship during this era to bypass Reynolds' first stage of conflict and move directly to the second. Rather than choosing to treat chronologically what was clearly a single story of pastoral expansion and the resulting response from the Aboriginal people affected by it, I have elected to examine the story over an extended number of years in more detail in the following chapter.

Approximately 428 Europeans were living at Albany by 1850.[141] No accurate numbers are available of the Aboriginal population who had opted to live in the town of Albany by that time. That some had made the choice to do so is shown by a report in the *Perth Gazette* of 10 May, 1850:

> The natives of Albany are frequently insufferable nuisances. They erect their huts in the *very* town, importune the inhabitants with their begging in the streets, and frequently disturb the

congregation at church with their fighting and squabbling. However, the inhabitants have themselves entirely to thank for their encroachments.[142]

The paper's Bunbury correspondent wrote the article from information received from 'A gentleman recently arrived from King George's Sound'. The disapproving tone displayed in its last sentence is an indication that a degree of harmony remained at Albany that was found surprising (and somewhat unwelcome) by a correspondent used to conditions elsewhere. Clearly, his informant had observed problems in the relationship between Europeans and Aborigines at Albany by 1850, but the newspaper article reinforces the fact that there existed a certain tolerance between the two groups that was notably absent in some other parts of the colony. Phillips' 1850 correspondence shows that eighteen Aborigines were 'constantly employed' in the town of Albany while many others had organised themselves into small groups to sell firewood and to carry water for Albany's European residents.[143]

However, Phillips' letter fails to note whether the eighteen Aborigines were in voluntary employment or were in fact in the Albany gaol and working as part of their sentence. The *Inquirer's* Albany correspondent's report in the edition of 7 May 1851 noted that Aboriginal prisoners were working at a rate he considered exemplary. The report inserts a jarring note into this discussion by pointing out that while the prisoners now looked healthy and keen, 'formerly they were nothing but skin and bone, dirty and filthy beyond conception; they walked around the town once a day, tied together with a chain or rope around their necks, and the remainder of their time confined in close, dirty cells'. The unnamed correspondent gave the credit for the radical improvement in the prisoners' lot to an also unnamed person newly in charge of the gaol. The article gives a rare insight into the actuality of life for those Aboriginal people who found themselves incarcerated under a prison system that was clearly both arbitrary and primitive in the extreme.

Labour was exceedingly short at Albany, and American whalers began to employ Aboriginal men as crew members. Martin Gibbs gave 1848 as the date of the beginning of consistent Aboriginal employment aboard whaling vessels, and noted that by 1850 they comprised at least 30 per cent of the workforce with at least nine men being employed.[144] Certainly, the taking up of such employment represents another instance of Aboriginal agency in the face of changing circumstances. Their wages were equivalent to those paid to non-Aboriginal members of crews, and those who earned them distributed the money (or the alcohol and tobacco that was sometimes paid to crews in lieu of wages) among the Aboriginal community.[145]

Although probably written partly in jest, a report in the *Inquirer* suggested that: 'The black ladies now declare they will accept no husbands except they will go whaling'.[146] If this statement at all reflected reality, it is an early example of the disruptive influence of individual wealth on a society built totally upon co-operation and shared resources. Phillips recorded how the annual whaling seasons ended with those with large amounts of wages holding sway over other local Aborigines until the drinking bouts ended with 'a good fight or spearing match'. Albany policeman Samuel Piggott baked two sacks of flour in 1850 to help persuade some Aboriginal whalers to spend their wages on something other than spirits. He had some success. Lindal used his wage of £13 to buy a whole sheep, a bag of potatoes, twenty pounds of butter and a box of raisins, all of which he distributed to 'much mirth and hilarity' to his friends during a night of traditional dancing.[147] Aboriginal culture was being maintained, but clearly European pressures and influences were beginning to bring about some modifications.

This was a time when the future relationship was being actively discussed by Albany's residents – both Aboriginal and

European – and at least one innovative idea was trialled. In 1850 a number of Aboriginal men from King George Sound who had worked in the whaling industry convened a meeting at Kendenup with men from the Cockatoo group. Lindal explained to Phillips that he would tell 'the Bush Black Fellows' that the Albany men were now 'like white men', and would govern themselves according to British law. Aboriginal offenders would in future be brought before 'Governor Lindal' to be sentenced, with Phillips to act as an advisor as to the appropriate scale of punishment for each offence – which he did on at least two occasions.[148] Phillips must have had some confidence in Lindal, for he wrote to the Colonial Secretary urging his appointment as a mounted constable at one shilling per day.[149] So confident were the town's Aboriginal law enforcers that they took an unnamed settler into custody before bringing him before the Albany Magistrate for breaching an employment contract entered into with his Aboriginal employee.[150] This parallel system of justice was apparently short-lived, for there are no subsequent references to it in official reports.

By the early 1840s it had become obvious that the initial harmony at King George Sound was coming under strain. Food resource depletion caused by settlers generated periods when Aboriginal people faced starvation, and their numbers were further significantly reduced by introduced diseases. Employment in the whaling industry caused a partial breakdown of the old patterns of annual migration. Numbers of Aboriginal people from areas distant from Albany caused disruption as they moved to the district in order to access European food, and these people sometimes brought with them attitudes based upon resistance rather than accommodation. For a short period around 1840, settlers had reason to fear for their physical safety when distant from the settlement of Albany. However, by 1850 relative peace had been restored, a process facilitated by the extraordinarily slow growth of the European population and economic expansion in the town and its hinterland.

Chapter Five

The Pastoral Era, and European Attempts to Christianise and Civilise Albany's Aboriginal Population, 1851–1877

Aboriginal–European interaction at Albany and its hinterland as the dispossession of Aboriginal land begins to gather pace

By the end of the 1840s Albany had become a small port settlement that owed its continued existence to its capacity to supply and support passing ships and the declining whaling industry.[1] The 1838 census showed the European population of the town had only risen to 170 with another 138 scattered throughout Plantagenet County, the official designation for Albany's hinterland. The boundaries of Plantagenet shifted considerably during the nineteenth century, but in the 1850s they encompassed the area outside the town of Albany extending from slightly west of the mouth of the Hay River, north-east to a point near Cranbrook, east to a point near Jerramungup and south-west to the coast west of Bremer Bay.[2] Development of this very extensive area was so glacially slow that the census of 1848 identified only eleven occupiers of agricultural and pastoral properties throughout the region. Agriculture was virtually non-existent, and the pastoral industry had not expanded beyond a few isolated and widely separated holdings struggling to cope with the presence of poisonous native plants and an acute shortage of labour. Progress in European terms had been minimal, and the hinterland of Albany had scarcely altered since the arrival of the *Amity*.

By 1850, Europeans had lived at King George Sound for twenty-three years, but the lack of any significant European settlement in the hinterland during this time enabled Aboriginal people who had survived the toll taken by European diseases to continue living traditionally to an extent that was not possible in most other settled areas of Australia. As a degree of economic growth began to occur in the town and region between 1851 and 1877, the relationship between Aboriginal and European people slowly altered. The population of Europeans increased significantly while Aboriginal numbers fell, principally because of increased exposure to disease.

However, by 1877 the earlier picture had fundamentally altered. The town of Albany had become a significant port and had enjoyed a consequent slow but steady population growth. For most of the period 1850–77, the town's European population numbered between 700 and 850. Statistical boundary alterations during this time make it impossible to present accurate population growth figures for Albany's hinterland, although there was certainly a considerable increase in the number of Europeans living in the region.[3] There was now a significant European presence in the Menang heartland, a presence that increasingly affected the day-to-day lives of its Aboriginal population. It was during the period between 1850 and 1877 that many Aboriginal people who had previously spent much of their time in Albany moved their families to areas north and east of the town. There are few documentary sources that specifically address this exodus, but it appears to have occurred as a response to official pressure, the resistance of Aboriginal people to repeated attempts to integrate them into

European society by a process of civilising and Christianising, and the increasing employment opportunities in the developing pastoral industry. Phillips also observed that a shortage of flour in the town during 1851 'has been the means of driving them from the Settlement to the country'.[4] However, it was the devastating measles epidemic of 1860 that played a major, even decisive, role in the Aboriginal exodus.

Australian mid-nineteenth-century colonial urban space was both shared and contested, and saw the gradual emergence of surveillance, regulation and legislation to control the Aboriginal presence.[5] It was felt in official circles that Aborigines ought to be excluded from towns for two principal reasons: fears that the vices of settlers would be transferred to Aboriginal people; and that Aborigines had criminal or malign intentions such as stealing, or would create a nuisance by begging, fighting and drinking.[6]

It is difficult to estimate the number of Aboriginal people living in the town and hinterland of Albany during the period covered by this chapter. The 1848 Western Australian census estimated Plantagenet's Aboriginal population to be 450, although the preamble described any attempt at accuracy as impracticable, due to 'their roving habits in search of subsistence'.[7] Police officers gathering information for the census were instructed to count the number of Aboriginal people in casual or permanent employment, and their lists gave a total of fifty-three males and seven females employed in all of Plantagenet.[8] The figure of 450 represented a compilation of the officers' presumably reasonably well-informed guesses about the overall total.

The next census took place in 1854, four years after the arrival from England of the first batch of convicts sent to the colony. This census showed that there were ninety-seven occupiers of agricultural and pastoral land in the Plantagenet region employing 136 labourers and thirty-two shepherds.[9] The region, together with the town of Albany, had a European population numbering 977.

Astoundingly, only 165 of these were men aged twenty-one years or older who either had been born in the colony or had arrived as free settlers, while the much greater number of 348 were convicts holding conditional pardons or tickets of leave. Of this latter group, 158 were in private employ, with the remainder employed on public works.[10] The convict presence in the region around Albany at this time was dominant to an extent that is difficult to overstate.

Beyond noting that twenty-eight Aborigines in Plantagenet County were in European employment (less than half the number recorded six years earlier), the 1854 census did not mention Aboriginal people. In his role as Sub-Guardian of Natives, Trimmer estimated that in 1856 there were 300 Aborigines at Kojonup and Eticup, 150 between the Gordon River and the west coast, and 120 around the Salt [Pallinup] River.[11] Eticup settler W. H. Graham estimated there were 500 Aboriginal inhabitants of the Kojonup–Eticup area in 1859.[12] On the other hand, it is possible to be considerably more precise about the number living in Albany itself. When an epidemic struck the region in 1860, Trimmer wrote that 'in and about the town [Albany] every native to the amount of sixty four have suffered'.[13] His official position made him well qualified to make such an exact statement regarding the number then living in the town.

The previous chapter discussed the devastating effects of disease upon the region's Aboriginal people, and there can be little doubt that disease continued to be far the greatest cause of population decline in the Aboriginal community during the period between 1850 and 1877.

The Western Australian census of 1870 gave official police estimates of total Aboriginal numbers in many south-western districts but for some unspecified reason the Albany District was not included, although a speculative figure of 400 was offered. The census noted that there were seventy-three Aboriginal males and forty-two Aboriginal females employed in the geographically undefined Albany region, although officials believed that the actual number in work may have been higher because of the irregular nature of rural employment.[14] Although he gave no indication where his information came from, the Registrar General estimated that disease, inter-se violence (violence occurring within Aboriginal communities), drunkenness, and cohabitation of European men (especially convicts) with Aboriginal women, had caused the population of full-descent Aborigines in the south-west to decline by 50 per cent since the beginning of settlement.[15]

The overall picture of the years between 1851 and 1877 in the Albany region is one of an Aboriginal population whose numbers were in decline, and whose members were increasingly fitting into the European economy as labourers in the pastoral industry while retaining significant aspects of their traditional way of life.

No detailed records remain from the Albany region that specify exactly where or how Aboriginal people lived, although an assiduous scrutiny of voluminous handwritten, at times almost illegible, police and court records provides some useful information. Firstly, it would appear that in 1864 there was only one camp where Aboriginal people lived in or near the Albany townsite, for in that year an Aboriginal man was arrested for being drunk at '*the* native camp'[16] (emphasis added). Shortly before his death in December 1852, Sub-Guardian Phillips recorded that he had frequently given orders 'to drive the blacks away', but found that this was inconvenient for those settlers who were offering them employment.[17] His letter failed to state why he considered these orders necessary. His successor as Sub-Guardian of Natives, Arthur Trimmer, wrote in 1853 that 'all natives except indentured servants' were to sleep 'an appointed distance from the town, and not to be seen prowling around after dark'.[18] It appears that both men were bluffing, since their decrees were not supported by legislation (it would be 1905 before authorities had this legal power).

Phillips had written to the Governor in October 1852 asking him to issue an order to remove Aboriginal huts from the townsite of Albany. Phillips stated that he had frequently issued orders to this effect, but 'there are [unspecified] parties who find it inconvenient to have them driven from the town'. The context of this reference appears to imply that European men (particularly convicts holding their ticket of leave) were consorting with Aboriginal women.

This instruction was either not enforced or had lapsed, since an 1866 entry in the Albany Police Daily Occurrence Book noted:

> The Resident Magistrate gives instructions to the police that no natives are to be allowed to camp in the townsite unless those in employ and camping on their master's allotment.[19]

Certainly there was a consistent official desire from at least 1852 to discourage Aboriginal people from living in the town. Apparently the earlier tolerant coexistence had become a thing of the past.

Presumably, police enforced the decree and closed the town camp. However, it is clear that by January 1876 at least one campsite was again in use on the outskirts of Albany. Photographs taken in that month show an Aboriginal shelter located in the vicinity of where Albany's Centennial Recreation Ground now stands, approximately 2 kilometres north of the site of the original settlement. Police records give further information. When an Aboriginal girl escaped police custody in 1876, 'An immediate search was instituted and all the Native Camps, huts, and suspected places were visited by the police within a radius of two miles of the town without success'.[20] This implies that more than one camp was in operation, but when the girl escaped again in July, the entry read: 'Immediate search instituted of all the Native Camp [singular] huts'.[21] Police did not write with future historians in mind, and it is not possible to ascertain from their records the precise number of campsites that existed in the town of Albany, nor the number of those who lived in them. Similarly, no record remains of the number, if any, of Aborigines living on their masters' allotments.

When the Victorian merchant and historian William Westgarth called briefly at Albany in 1857, he was told that settlers employed Albany Aboriginal residents as messengers and as drovers of sheep and cattle to and from the interior. He noted that many were of part descent, and that about half of these were living 'in civilised fashion', being looked after by their father or by others from within the European community.[22]

By the end of the 1870s the pastoral industry had developed to the point where individual leaseholders owned considerable flocks of sheep, with the extensive Hassell property based at Kendenup running as many as 20,000. The 1870 census stated that 299 men were then engaged in pastoralism and agriculture in the Plantagenet District, eighty-eight of whom were either farmers or lease holders. Ninety-nine of their employees were living isolated lives as shepherds or hut-keepers, and were therefore likely to have had significant contact with Aboriginal people living in the bush.[23]

The development of the pastoral industry brought an alteration in the composition of the region's European population, especially of that section living in the hinterland of Albany. Significantly, it is very likely that the large number of convicts who moved there only a few years after the introduction of the system in 1850 brought about a hardening in attitude towards Aboriginal people. These were predominantly young men who were either single or thousands of miles away from their families. The normal strictures placed on sexual attitudes and behaviour by their home communities were unenforceable and, for many, no longer relevant. The few European women they met were unlikely to marry men 'tainted by the convict stain', and Aboriginal women presented the sole opportunity for any form of female relationship. It is significant that in 1854, 348 convicts were living in an area where there were only nine single adult European women.[24] The Registrar General noted in his preamble to the 1870 census:

> Since the arrival of Convicts, and their dispersion around the Country, the immorality of the [Aboriginal] women has become a constant custom, and the early age at which the young native girls are debauched by shepherds and labourers at outstations is attended by lamentable consequences.[25]

Whatever justification the Registrar General had for his comments, they do not tell the whole story. Lois Tilbrook's genealogies of south-west Aboriginal families show that numerous marriages and long-term relationships were formed between Aboriginal women and convicts during this period, and many Aboriginal people living at Albany today trace their descent to these consensual unions.[26] The Western Australian Government wished to encourage convicts to marry Aboriginal women legally, and established a scheme whereby a grant of 10 acres would be given to such couples (the actual title being granted to the woman). At least four such grants were made at Albany.[27]

Between the writings of Alexander Collie in the 1830s, and Paul Hasluck's 1938 MA thesis published in 1942 as *Black Australians*, more than one hundred years passed when historians wrote very little about Aboriginal–European relations in the south-west of Western Australia. Albany was no exception to this general pattern. This silence was an Australia-wide phenomenon connected with the widespread perception that the topic held little interest for either academics or the general community. During the mid nineteenth century, Aboriginal people in south-western Australia were no longer considered a novelty to be commented upon at length, except insofar as they were felt to be transgressing the standards of behaviour considered desirable by British settlers. Unfortunately, partly because of this attitude, very little was written at the time that described how the relationship at Albany altered as development took place. Until well into the twentieth century it was almost universally accepted that Western Australia's Noongar population was inevitably doomed to disappear, and this attitude tended to divert many people's attention away from the topic of Aboriginal–European relations. In the early twentieth century, Daisy Bates' assertion that it was only those Aboriginal people who were of full descent that deserved attention and respect played a part in fostering this neglect.[28] By the time historians began to take a serious interest, most of the people who had been directly involved in the events of the decades covered in this chapter were no longer living.

Unfortunately there is no known account of events in the Albany region between 1850 and 1877 written by an Aboriginal person living at that time. This absence of a contemporary indigenous voice is an example of what has been referred to as 'the deafening silence historians have to work with' when writing about this era in Aboriginal–European relations in south-west Western Australia.[29] It is fortunate that local Noongar authors Kim Scott, Hazel Brown and Eric Hayward have recently made extensive use of oral history to produce books that, although their principal focus is on other decades, give some Aboriginal perspective on events that occurred in the Albany hinterland during and after the years discussed in this chapter.[30]

There is, however, much relevant information available about the period. A wealth of official documentation is filed at the Perth State Records Office and other archives that, together with letters, diaries, photographs and observations written by settlers and visitors to the region, gives a researcher a considerable amount of primary source material to work with. The journals of the Anglican clergyman John Wollaston are valuable in this respect, even if one suspects that his views on Aboriginal–European relations were far from widely held in the settler community of Albany.

With the pastoral, and to a much lesser extent agricultural, expansion into the hinterland of Albany that took place during this twenty-six-year period, the history of Aboriginal–European interaction began to divide into two stories: one about the town itself; and the other concerning the vast surrounding area that looked to Albany as its economic, administrative and social centre. At times the two stories merge, while on other occasions they have little in common. The circumstances and experiences of towns-people going about their daily business in an urban community that was moving ever further from its frontier origins increasingly began to diverge from those of their countrymen and -women who chose to live in the isolation of the virgin Australian bush.

When the 1850s began, Albany's future as an economically and socially viable town appeared uncertain. However, her selection as the delivery and despatch port for all of Western Australia's mail, together with the decision to make Albany the port where the new steam-powered vessels carrying passengers and cargo to and from the ports of eastern Australia would take on coal, allowed for three decades of quiet stability and slow but steady economic growth.[31] Apart from activity connected with shipping, there was little else to keep the settlement functioning, as the vast majority of the colony's exports and imports passed through the port of Fremantle. Although the pastoral industry grew steadily, it was situated well inland from Albany and was not sufficiently large to generate a significant economic support sector in the southern town.

It is important to appreciate how isolated Albany was at this time from the remainder of the colony of Western Australia. Before extensive work in the 1850s and 1860s was undertaken on the road linking Albany with Perth (principally to speed the transport of mail to and from the capital), the overland journey commonly took up to eight days. An article in the *Perth Gazette & W.A. Times* makes it abundantly clear that even by 1870, it was not something to undertake lightly. The would-be traveller had two choices:

> [As a P & O mail steamer arrived at Albany] Her Majesty's mails are deposited in a cart, and immediately packed off at a jog-trot; which pace being kept up night and day – only stopping to bait [feed] the horses – they arrive at the capital on the evening of the fourth day. The mail cart takes passengers when it can get them, but I find it my duty to warn the unsuspecting traveller against availing himself of this means of conveyance…four days and nights of consecutive joltings, tossings and bumpings, without sleep, with hasty meals snatched somehow or anywhere, a rushing through space at the rate of four miles an hour…
>
> There is also a passenger wagon that travels the road every month; it makes easy stages, resting at night and performs the journey in a week or eight days. Police stations have been erected for the whole length of the road at intervals of 30 miles or thereabouts, and respectable persons applying to the authorities at Albany or at Perth, will, as a rule, get a pass enabling them to obtain the accommodation of these stations which have spare rooms for that purpose…In the present state of things, however, the number of passengers is so small – averaging I believe, about four a month…the fare by the passenger wagon is £6, travellers finding themselves in everything…[32]

Albany was geographically isolated from the rest of the colony, and its inhabitants were almost as likely to look to Adelaide as their city as they were to Perth.

There was one major point on which those who had come to settle at Albany agreed with the prevailing philosophy of their Perth counterparts – the rate at which Aboriginal people were being transformed into 'civilised' and tractable Christians was frustratingly and unacceptably slow. Following the House of

Commons Select Committee of Inquiry (1835–37), the policy of the British Colonial Office was to gradually amalgamate indigenous people into the societies of the newly established settlements of the Empire.[33] All Aboriginal children in contact with the settlements at or near Perth in the 1840s had been enrolled at one or other of the local 'Native schools', as had some of the indigenous children at Albany.[34] However, none of these schools proved satisfactory from either a European or an Aboriginal perspective and by 1855 all of the schools in the Perth area had closed; at Albany, the experiment was considered to have proven even less successful, and as we have seen McKail's school closed in 1846 after three difficult years.

From the middle of the nineteenth century, official concern diminished about how to wean Aborigines from a lifestyle that was still seen as fundamentally inappropriate in a Christian and civilised outpost of the Empire. The concern lessened, not because Europeans had become reconciled to the existence of a culture at complete variance with their own, but because they found themselves at a loss as to how to achieve their desired outcome.

In 1850, two independent events occurred that together altered many of the dynamics of Aboriginal–European relations at Albany and the rest of Western Australia. The first and more subtle change arose out of events in the United Kingdom. By 1850, the humanitarian movement in Britain was becoming less influential at a time when all of the other Australian colonies were preparing for self-government, and the assumption of local control of Aboriginal policy.[35] The influence of Exeter Hall on the British Colonial Office was lessening, although its supporters continued to take an interest in Australian colonial policy and practice.[36] In the mid 1850s, the 'Manchester men' in the British Colonial Office began to overshadow the influence of the humanitarians. They were men who believed that economy in British expenditure should take precedence over any of the more 'sentimental' aims of their predecessors, and modified official policy accordingly.[37]

During the 1850s these new policies began to affect the administration of the colony of Western Australia, although they did not result in changes to the colony's legislation. Effectively, the official aim of amalgamating Aboriginal people into colonial British society ended. It failed because of Aboriginal resistance to both the aims and methods used to bring it about – principally the policy and practice of boarding and educating Aboriginal children in schools run by Europeans. Settler co-operation in the policy had been limited, with most showing a reluctance to play their assigned part by employing graduating children and granting at least some measure of social acceptance to them. As it became apparent that the policy was seen as unrealistic by both Aboriginal people and settlers it was abandoned in favour of one less idealistic, based on protection, segregation and control. This policy in various forms remained in place for the ensuing one hundred years, leading Aboriginal people increasingly to rely upon philanthropic and church groups for support. At Albany, the change in priorities resulted in a downgrading of the role of Protector and the removal of the Native Police officer previously assigned to assist him in his duties.

Concurrent with this was the second change – the arrival of the first group of convicts shipped from England to Western Australia as the forerunners of almost 10,000 others, all male, who arrived in the colony over the next eighteen years.[38] Given the very small European population of Western Australia during that period, these men necessarily exerted a marked influence on virtually every aspect of its society, although the shame felt by many settlers and their descendants meant that this was seldom acknowledged until the latter part of the twentieth century. Most of the convicts were eligible for their ticket of leave soon after arrival and were able to find employment in the private sector. A holder of one of these 'tickets' was entitled to move around the colony seeking work with private employers. Naturally, this caused a lessening of demand for Aboriginal labour. As long as these convicts were able to report to local police that they were in work, they could avoid being assigned to a gang working for the government on public works such as roads. This, together with the fact that not all convicts held tickets of leave, explains why there were convicts at Albany working on building roads and bridges, while many of their fellows were in various forms of private employment, especially in the rural areas. By 1857, approximately one in four of the town's total population were convicts.[39]

The weakening of the British humanitarian and Evangelical movements, together with the changes that transportation of convicts brought to the composition of Albany's European population, ensured an inevitable lessening of the influence of those earlier settlers who had always been aware of the moral obligation that was owed by them towards the people whose land they had appropriated.

One prominent figure who certainly felt this obligation keenly was the Anglican priest John Wollaston. He had been appointed Archdeacon for the colony and in 1849 moved to Albany where he served in a dual role as local priest of the newly consecrated St John's church and travelling clergyman throughout the south-west region until his death in 1856. Wollaston held a strong and consistent belief that colonists had failed in their Christian and civil duty to take responsibility for the welfare of the Aboriginal people who were being increasingly displaced and disrupted by their presence. He had no doubt that God had entrusted the British Government with encouraging settlers to occupy the land and bring Christian civilisation to the Noongar people.

Where Wollaston differed from so many of his fellow settlers was in his insistence that this task carried with it an inescapable moral obligation to bring what he considered to be the blessings of the Christian religion and British civilisation to indigenous people in a benevolent Christian manner.[40] There is an undated (presumably unsent) letter addressed to 'Dear Mr Editor' in Wollaston's handwriting among his papers at the Battye Library. The letter is signed 'I am, Sir your humble black servant, Kyan Gadac', and makes very clear his views on European obligation.

I am an Aboriginal black fellow and not having the learning of you white fellows I have no other way of conveying my thoughts to you and the public, except by the assistance of a white friend. That friend has explained to me in my own language the meaning of this paper talk and I say it is all 'GEBALRALICH' – very good.

There is a certain tract of land in this colony which time out of mind belonged to me. They all find I can point out its marks and boundaries and no blackfellow ever disputed my right. I have used it only as a hunting ground. It is true I have no title deeds but undisputed occupation, when continued for a long series of years, you white men, I believe, consider a just title. This land some of your tribe who have come hither over the great sea have taken away from me without paying... [missing?]

I do not want to quarrel with them about it – besides it is no purpose for I am weak and powerless and they are strong and invincible – but I wish to know whether it be just and reasonable even according to talking to you white men that some return worth having should be made for the turnover of my native soil.

I have several piccaninnies, my relations here have lots more. Let the white man take these and make them 'all same' as themselves. I do not mean in drinking and swearing and other things that are DJIRL, HINDO, DADIM, DJULGO, MENDANG, MANKIM and WARRA. But all same as gwabba white men.

Let them and others in earnest do this by giving to me and my tribe now and then a blanket or two, a few pounds of flour in return for the kangaroo skins they have sold and the flesh they have given to their dogs, and I shall be careful and let them do what they like, please with the inheritance of my forefathers.[41]

Presumably Wollaston wrote the letter to gain support for his work with Aboriginal people at Albany. It is possible that he later filed it, reflecting that the subterfuge of writing a letter to a newspaper using a false name was simply too unethical.

In 1851, Wollaston wrote to the Society for the Propagation of the Gospel, an Anglican missionary organisation prominent in overseeing the spiritual welfare of indigenous peoples throughout the Empire, claiming:

> a very strong feeling prevails among the right thinking portion of the white population that a greater effort than ever should now be made to promote the civilisation and Christian education of native children.[42]

Wollaston gave no indication of just how many of his Albany flock were 'right thinkers'. Three years earlier, Wollaston's bishop had visited Albany from his diocesan headquarters in Adelaide in order to consecrate the new Anglican Church. During this visit, Bishop Augustus Short stated that the aim of Christians in the new congregation should be to 'rescue them [Aboriginal people] from barbarism and heathenism', but regretted that 'all persons have not the faith and love' to treat them as they ought.[43] Wollaston, finding his bishop's views conformed to his own, decided to set up a school for Aboriginal children where these ideals would be put into practice.

Certainly, Wollaston would have included Henry and Anne Camfield in any list of right thinkers. Henry, who met and married Anne after arriving in the colony years earlier, had seen slavery at first hand during a brief stopover in South America when en route to Australia, and had been appalled at the spectacle. In July 1848, Camfield took up the position of Government Resident at Albany. Anne had come to the colony as a missionary, and never lost her interest in this task.[44] It appears that the Camfields took several part-Aboriginal children into their home shortly after arrival; certainly two were baptised during Bishop Short's visit in late October 1848, and it is possible that they were brought up in the Camfield household.[45] Wollaston remarked in his journal that these baptisms had achieved 'a world of good in removing prejudices'.[46] Given his subsequent experiences at Albany, he may well have looked back on this entry as prematurely optimistic.

Wollaston saw the Camfields as a solution to a problem that had been vexing him for some time. The matter became urgent when in 1848 Governor Fitzgerald resolved to carry out any death sentences imposed by the Supreme Court on Aboriginal people convicted of murdering fellow Aborigines. Unless Wollaston could convince them of the errors inherent in their custom of payback killings, Albany's Aboriginal population could very well find some of their members coming under the extreme sanction of British law. Although he considered the matter urgent, Wollaston despaired of being able to persuade Aboriginal adults of the necessity to modify their traditional practice. It appeared to him that the best approach was to establish a school to implant this message into the minds of young Aboriginal people who would abolish the custom upon their achieving adulthood. In 1851, Fitzgerald had granted 68 acres at Middleton Bay as the site of a school for Aboriginal children, but Wollaston was unable to find anyone suitable and willing to run his proposed venture.[47] He then conferred with Anne Camfield, who agreed in August 1852 to take a number of Aboriginal children into her home as students.[48] The previous year Anne had shown her concern by supporting the children of several Aboriginal women who had died in the town.[49]

It was not only Wollaston's request that led to the Camfields taking Aboriginal children into their personal care. Philip Chauncy, a government surveyor who had lived near the Camfields for several years, later wrote that an Aboriginal girl aged about three-and-a-half years had been left behind when her people left the settlement on an excursion into the bush. She had wandered about hungry and naked for several days, coming each morning to the Chauncy household's gate to ask for food. The *Perth Gazette* reported in April 1852 that the settlement at Albany was out of provisions, and this presumably had an impact upon private acts of generosity towards Aboriginal people in the town. [50] Chauncy mentioned the matter to Mrs Camfield, 'who took the child in, and soon afterwards obtained the consent of her mother to keep her'.[51] Many years later Anne wrote:

> It was from an irresistible feeling that something ought to be attempted, though the result might be ever so small, that it was begun privately with one child for six months, when a favourable answer was received to an application to the Government to support six children...the one child in question having been received into the House June 21st, 1852.[52]

Wollaston would have fully supported Anne's act of compassion, and her explanation for her concern:

> The overruling hand of God directed us to the occupying of this land, here we 'live and get gain,' and He places these objects of compassion before our eyes as trials of our faith in Him and in the salvation which He has obtained for our race, surely we will do what we can among this people, though what we individually do may be but as the offering of the widow's mite.[53]

The European population of mid-nineteenth-century Albany interacted with the local Aboriginal people in differing ways, according to a range of motives. Anne Camfield's own statement made in an official report to the Western Australian Legislative Council presents a clear picture of her own reasons for acting as she did. These reasons accorded with those of Wollaston, and were probably seen as laudable by a considerable number of Albany's more genteel settlers, even if they had no intentions of offering any practical support. In August 1852, Wollaston wrote to the Colonial Secretary:

> Mrs Camfield has volunteered to receive six native girls for a limited time, provided there is no interference from any one at Albany except myself, if it is likely to be the means of leading to a permanent establishment...the most difficult point of all [would be] the consignment of Children to our care...[54]

Wollaston suggested that the school should commence by formally signing children from another district for a period of at least ten years, agreeing with Anne Camfield that the children selected should be girls aged between two and five years.[55]

The school was partly official in nature, partly a venture of the Church of England and partly a personal work of Christian compassion by Anne and Henry Camfield. Its official nature is shown by a letter from J. R. Phillips, who had resigned his position of Government Resident in July 1847 and was writing to the Colonial Secretary in his new capacity as Sub-Guardian of Natives:

> I have been requested by the Resident to procure six Native Girls under four years of age for a school as yet I have only been able to procure three the Natives do not like parting with their children.[56]

The school had encountered its first and predictable hurdle. However, Wollaston and the Camfields persisted with their efforts to find suitable children and by November 1852 had seven girls and two boys enrolled, five of whom were over the specified age. They were also caring for a nine-month-old Aboriginal baby. It is not clear exactly how each of these (and subsequent) children passed into the Camfields' care; Wollaston noted in a letter to the Colonial Secretary that the enrolment of the five had involved 'great difficulty' but, either forgetfully or deliberately, failed to detail the nature or extent of the problems and methods involved.[57]

Phillips had 'procured' three, and Wollaston noted in his journal that another three were taken in after having been orphaned by an outbreak of influenza which also carried off Phillips. Two others were babes in arms.[58] It is now not possible to assess accurately the degree of coercion involved in gathering children for Annesfield, the name given by the Camfields to the school set up in their home. Certainly by 1852 Wollaston was not in favour of simply taking Aboriginal children without first gaining some form of parental permission; he noted that such a course had been tried at Albany, and found to be unsuccessful. In 1851, he had written from Albany to the Colonial Secretary advocating that:

A formal appeal to the Natives shd be made in the name of the Governor by the Magistracy & Guardian: the object in view shd be carefully & clearly explained to them; and those willing to have their children admitted into the School, shd be required to bind themselves not to interfere with, or interrupt their education in any way or to causelessly remove them – I wd submit that there is no hardship in this, nor any disruption of natural ties – nothing more stringent than what is required in the indentures of every white apprentice. – It wd be in vain for any individual to attempt to secure the attendance of Native Children without such formal & authoritative proceeding. – Indeed the attempt has been made at Albany without success – whereas the very nature of such proceeding wd gradually inspire the Natives with confidence.[59]

Since Henry Camfield in his role as Resident Magistrate formally indentured the first children admitted to the school for a period of ten years, there may have been at least some degree of parental co-operation with Wollaston's plan. Even if this were the case, the inequality of power involved in the whole process is obvious.

Unfortunately, no record remains either of the exact means by which such co-operation was achieved, or of the attitude of Albany's Aboriginal people to the transfer of their children to the school. Not surprisingly, problems still existed at Annesfield, leading Wollaston to write: 'An inclosed play ground for the effectual exclusion of Bush Natives, who are already exceedingly troublesome' would be required for the new school that he still hoped to have built at Middleton Bay.[60] What relationship these 'Bush Natives' had to the children living with the Camfields is not mentioned in the letter.

Eventually, the Middleton Bay idea was abandoned, and Annesfield continued to take in and educate significant numbers of Albany's Aboriginal children until the Camfields' ill health and advancing years made it necessary to close the school and transfer the children to Perth in March 1871.

It is not difficult to recognise the flaws inherent in the enterprise. Although motivated by selfless compassion, Bishop Short, Archdeacon Wollaston and the Camfields all demonstrated their agreement with the prevailing views of educated people from their era – views which revealed a lack of any real understanding of, or appreciation for, Aboriginal culture. They regarded it as a form of barbarism that should be supplanted as soon as possible by what they believed to be the vastly superior British form of Christian civilisation, and to achieve this end they were prepared to take extreme measures. As some of the older girls at the school reached a marriageable age, they were sent to a Moravian Church mission in Victoria to be married to 'suitable' Aboriginal Christian converts.[61] The first two girls chosen contracted typhoid on the ship and died soon after arriving at Melbourne, but this did not deter the Camfields who soon sent five others, all of whom were permanently separated from their relatives at Albany. Anne made it clear in her report that it would be too disruptive to the other children to have allowed any of the exiles to ever return home.[62] The two who died at Melbourne were far from the only deaths associated with Annesfield; of the fifty-five children admitted over the life of the school, seventeen died while in the Camfields' care.[63]

In an era when Albany's settlers were often either antagonistic or apathetic towards the region's Aboriginal people, Anne Camfield gave of herself wholeheartedly in what she believed to be their best long-term interests. She justified the policy of sending older children to the eastern colonies by pointing out that these colonies had set up farming establishments where 'adult natives and half-castes' were able to find profitable employment. If the older girls had remained at Albany and been sent to service in settler households, the Camfields believed that they would have been exposed to 'almost certain ruin, as we found in more than one instance to our cost'.[64] Anne and Henry had long advocated the setting up of an institution in Western Australia to provide employment for Aboriginal boys and girls 'where they can marry [within the Aboriginal community] and live happily and usefully'.[65] Until the colony's government provided this facility, they believed past experience justified their policy of transferring older children to what they considered to be more enlightened parts of Australia.

Some settlers levelled criticism at the policy of sending children to Victoria, not because of any real concern for the welfare of Annesfield's Aboriginal inmates, but simply because they resented their removal when there was a severe shortage of female labour throughout the colony. Bishop Hale responded strongly to such self-serving critics:

What! Are there not enough of these people, old and young, in all parts of the Colony without laying hands on these? Are there not enough part Europeans, roaming around uncared for and neglected? Will these not serve the purpose of would be employers? ...If would be employers do not care for the souls of these poor little outcasts, who have been rescued and brought home and watched over for their Saviour's sake?[66]

Anne responded vigorously to her critics, using the opportunity presented by an 1871 Legislative Council enquiry into Aboriginal affairs.[67] She quoted the contemporary education policy in Great Britain advocating the removal of British children from their parents, should that prove a necessary step in ensuring that the children received an education.[68] She also pointed out that criticism of the number of deaths associated with Annesfield was ill founded. Of the seventeen who died, eleven had been very near death when admitted. The other six contracted one or other of the diseases that entered Albany as a consequence of the large number of ships entering the port.[69]

Certainly, some at least of the children at Annesfield received an education comparable to contemporary British standards. Bessie Flower played the organ at St John's Church at Albany, and later wrote letters to Anne displaying a high degree of literacy. She also played chess at a competitive level with Victoria's champion player. Bessie wrote to Anne in 1867: 'I cannot tell you how I love you for taking us out of the bush and making us what we are'.[70] In 2013 a plaque commemorating Bessie's service to the church was placed on the wall near where the organ was situated. A number of her Victorian descendants made the journey to Albany, and took part in deeply moving ceremonies held at St John's to welcome them back to the land of their Menang ancestors.

Anne Camfield acted from her own highest motives, and gave love and diligent attention to her young Aboriginal charges. She was faced with a most difficult situation, given the harsh attitudes of many at Albany who saw Aboriginal girls only in the light of a potentially useful underclass whose role was to perform menial tasks in domestic service. When Wollaston set up a fund to aid in the education of Aboriginal children, he sadly noted:

> On enquiring at the Bank found (but not to my surprise well knowing the Colonial prejudices to be overcome) that, as yet, the result of my appeal for the Aborigines was (as we used to say at Cambridge) = 0.[71]

In 1871, the year that the children from Annesfield were sent to Perth to continue their education, a further attempt was made to Christianise the Aborigines living at Albany. The Irish Conference of the Methodist Missionary Society sent the Reverend J. B. Atkins to take charge of the newly established Albany Methodist Church. He was 'much depressed by the depravity of the local Aborigines', and erected a mission chapel on a block of land near Grey Street. Although details of what followed are not available, the venture quickly failed and the mission closed.[72]

Albany's Aboriginal people showed little interest in becoming second-grade members of any of the town's Christian congregations, and followed the general trend of those around Perth in rejecting the idea that becoming Christianised was in their best interests. It is not surprising that Aboriginal co-operation was difficult to obtain once it became clear to them that they were expected to give up their children and abandon their own spirituality. Certainly some, such as Bessie Flower, were grateful for the efforts of people like the Camfields, but there was no widespread adoption at Albany of either the European religion or the underlying cultural assumptions that so plainly accompanied it.

There is evidence that the majority of the town's European population were never wholeheartedly behind the efforts of Wollaston and the Camfields. Total contributions by private citizens from all parts of the colony towards the Albany school amounted to only £5 in 1852.[73] Contemporary newspaper articles, such as one that appeared in the *Perth Gazette* in 1853 claiming that 70,000 Fijians had been converted, must have added to the sense of frustration with the apparent incorrigibility of the local Aborigines.

To the majority of settlers religion was synonymous with Christianity, and civilisation with British lifestyle and values. They would have found the concept of Aboriginal people having their own distinctive religious beliefs to be alien, even incomprehensible. When Aboriginal people resisted this Eurocentric point of view, they placed themselves outside the settler agenda and resentment began to grow on both sides. Neither the government nor the churches at Albany made any further significant attempts to Christianise or civilise the region's Aboriginal people during the remainder of the century.

As noted earlier, a significant amount of written material is available to assist in the research of Aboriginal–European relations at Albany between 1850 and 1877. However, the topic was almost always incidental to the purposes of those who composed the various documents. For example, although a number of visitors wrote of their experiences as they walked the streets of Albany for a few hours while their ship was briefly in port, their observations of Aboriginal people form only a small part of these writings and tend to be both superficial and condescending. These letters and articles commonly focus upon the perceived dullness of Albany and the supposed failings of the Aboriginal people at the jetty and in the town. Typical of the genre is an article written by 'P&O Passenger' and published in 1858 by both the Melbourne *Argus* and the Perth-based *Inquirer and Commercial News*:

> King George's Sound is not a lively place. Were the colonists properly awake, the fact of the steamers stopping here would lead to provision of their supplies at a much cheaper rate than they could possibly be procured at Melbourne...But nothing of

this sort obtrudes itself upon the thoughts of the King George Soundians. They vegetate according to a plan of their own...The township is beset with great numbers of the blacks. They are tolerably fine specimens of the native, and do not appear to be quite so degraded by contact with the superior race as is, alas, too usually the case. They smear themselves profusely with a mixture of red earth and oil, which gives them a singular appearance, and a most horribly rancid smell. They amused us by throwing the spear and boomerang, were ready with any little offer of services, and highly appreciate the little 'likpence'.[74]

The Wesleyan Methodist minister Reverend Frederick Jobson wrote of his visit two years later:

> A company of aborigines, scantily covered with kangaroo skins, clotted with red grease, and bedaubed on forehead with white pipeclay, followed us – jabbered their semi-English jargon in our ears, – and, to obtain our white money, gathered for us profuse bunches of flowers, and exhibited their surprising feats of throwing the boomerang and the spear.[75]

The article, which went on to describe the Aborigines as 'disgusting', says more about the Reverend Jobson than it does about the actual situation at Albany.

Another unnamed P&O passenger saw the Aboriginal people in a very different light during his or her short stay in 1869:

> Here at Albany, we had the first sight of the aborigines, and I was not at all prepared for the amount of intelligence displayed by the few about the town some of them dressed in semi-European style. Their countenances and appearance too do not at all bespeak the low standard at which their capacity and brains have been rated. The rugged, protruding, and angular features, muscular frames,...

associated as they were with the hairy, unkept, dirty state of savagedom – did not at all support the view that I had before me one of the lowest types of the human family.[76]

These are the observations of visitors who spent a very limited time at Albany, perhaps only a few hours, and need to be treated with the caution appropriate to first impressions. They are, however, valuable since they provide some of the very few eyewitness descriptions of Aboriginal people living in the town of Albany at this time. They certainly point to the presence of a significant number of Aboriginal people who must have been camped close enough to the town jetty to take advantage of the economic opportunities presented by the numerous passenger ships that called at the port en route to or from the ports of eastern Australia. The 1858 and 1869 articles are also interesting for their descriptions of the numbers of Aboriginal people encountered in Albany. From 'beset with great numbers' in 1858, their numbers appear to have dropped considerably to 'the few about the town' by 1869. This strongly supports the evidence that there was a movement, significant but not complete, away from the town during the early 1860s.

One can only speculate about what the writers saw at Albany. Do their descriptions depict how the Aborigines involved normally behaved and dressed, or do they show the enterprise of a group of people engaged in a practice that continues to the present day whereby indigenous people from around the world 'dress up' to provide tourists with what they believe they wish to see? It is common in the USA to see Native Americans dressed in clothing and accoutrements that traditionally belong to groups from another part of the country, but which tourists feel represent 'the real Indian'. This triumph of market forces over historical accuracy is sometimes described as 'chiefing'.[77]

Certainly, when Henry Lawson visited Albany in 1890 (see Chapter Six), he claimed to have detected such enterprising behaviour. Did the Aboriginal people involved believe that the rancid-smelling oil would add to the tourists' fascination with their 'savagedom', or were they too unsophisticated in European terms to realise that this may have worked to their economic disadvantage by driving tourists away? Did they pre-date today's Aboriginal artistic performers in their enjoyment of the opportunity to display aspects of their traditional life? If anyone living at Albany at this time considered these questions, they left no record of their reflections or conclusions. Certainly, some of Albany's Aboriginal people saw the practice as an acceptable form of work suited to their talents and lifestyle, and incorporated it into their work economy.

The descriptions that visitors gave of the appearance of the Aborigines are interesting, if short on detail. Fortunately, John Dowson's recent research at the Mitchell Library uncovered three excellent photographs taken by Lieutenant Arthur Onslow during a visit to Albany in 1858, and these comprise some of the earliest images of Western Australian Aboriginal people.[78]

The first depicts a man, the second a woman, while the third shows a woman seated in the opening of a traditional shelter. These photographs provide proof that some at least of the Aboriginal people living in or near the town at that time retained and wore traditional clothing, although it is not clear whether this occurred only for special occasions. It is significant that the earlier reluctance to allow women to appear before Europeans had evidently lessened by this time. Clearly familiarity with settlers, or more broadly the process of accommodation, meant that Aboriginal men were no longer fearful of the consequences of Aboriginal women being placed in proximity to European men. Equally clearly, as one of the photographs shows, Aboriginal women also took part in displays of culture for European visitors.

Photograph taken at Albany in 1858 by Lieutenant Arthur Onslow

Mitchell Library MLMSS A 4335 item 1

Photograph taken at Albany in 1858 by Lieutenant Arthur Onslow

Mitchell Library MLMSS A 4335 item 2

Photograph taken at Albany in 1858 by Lieutenant Arthur Onslow

Mitchell Library MLMSS A 4335 item 3

Onslow noted that he had encountered some difficulty in obtaining his photographs:

> At first I had great trouble getting them to sit, as they were afraid it wd cause their death. But on seeing me take some of the McKails and by giving them 6d. they plucked up courage enough to let me bring the lens to bear on them but they are bad sitters.[79]

The German photographer Gustav Riemer, whose vessel called at Albany in 1877, took a further series of six photographs. They show Aboriginal men, women and children dressed in traditional kangaroo skin *bukas*, with several of the powerfully built men carrying spears and boomerangs. Some of the men have light-coloured markings painted onto their chests and faces, while several men and women have what appear to be white masks painted around their eyes. The photographs illustrate that the Aboriginal people living in the town of Albany retained access to their traditional clothing and weapons at least as late as 1877, but cannot answer the question as to how often they actually used them. They also demonstrate that Aboriginal people retained a sense of pride in their culture, and a willingness to display aspects of it to interested Europeans.

The six volumes of the Albany Police Daily Occurrence Books for the period between 1863 and 1877 provide another insight into Aboriginal–European relations during that period. A close reading of these journals detailing daily police activity reveals that law enforcement in the town of Albany was overwhelmingly a matter of attempting to control public drunkenness, obscene language and petty theft, with the great majority of offenders coming from the non-Aboriginal section of the community. Police officers responsible for recording the details of each offence were apparently under instruction to note if the offender was Aboriginal by writing 'Aboriginal native' or 'Ab. Nat.' after his or her name.

Photograph taken by Gustav Riemer at Albany in 1877
Mitchell Library, Photo Album F910-45/1A1

Photograph taken by Gustav Riemer at Albany in 1877
Mitchell Library, Photo Album F910-45/1A1

This method of identification is useful because at least as early as 1866, some Aboriginal people from the region of Albany were using a European name as well as what police referred to as their Aboriginal 'alias'.[80]

Although care is needed in interpreting the evidence, the vast amount of information in these journals allows a picture to be drawn of some aspects of Albany town life during the 1860s and 1870s. Firstly, serious crime investigated by the police was rare and seldom involved Aboriginal people as either perpetrators or victims. By far the majority of offences related to public order, with public drunkenness and obscene language being particularly common – for police to make eight such arrests during one day was not unusual. Many of those who came to the attention of the police were identified as convicts holding tickets of leave, and it is probable that many others were seamen out on the town while their vessel was in port. It is quite noticeable that large numbers of individuals were involved, rather than the few repeat problem drinkers that might be expected in a small town. The records make it obvious that excessive consumption of alcohol was a dominant feature of Albany's European society, although probably no more so than at other comparable port towns of the time.

On the relatively few occasions Aboriginal people were charged, the sentences imposed matched those handed down to non-Aboriginal offenders who had committed similar misdemeanours. The fact that many of the Aborigines who passed through the Albany court were from areas as far away as Eucla or were from unspecified locations, coupled with the illegibility of some records, makes it impractical to be specific about the number of those arrested who were from the Albany region.

Appendix Five is a list of the records from the Albany Daily Occurrence Books for the year 1863 that refer to Aboriginal people in the region, and is included to show the range of activities that brought them into contact with police. From this source it is apparent that in 1863 Aboriginal people were still practising firestick farming, that Aboriginal men were being employed in assisting police to capture fugitives (both Aboriginal and non-Aboriginal), that Aboriginal men were breaching master and servant legislation, presumably by engaging in traditional patterns of movement, that Aboriginal people were still engaging in forms of tribal punishment, and that they were being charged with theft and supplying other Aboriginal people with alcohol, both of which were likely to be through sharing practices and the obligations of kinship networks. Taken together, these cases show that in 1863 many traditional practices remained, and that many were being criminalised by the British justice system.

Virtually all of the formal efforts to Christianise and 'civilise' the region's Aboriginal population took place in the town of Albany. Away from the restraining influences of church, police and the numerous visitors who frequented the port and witnessed events, the relationship between Europeans and Aborigines in Albany's hinterland took on a more basic form. It was economic self-interest that predominantly determined how the growing numbers of station owners treated the numerous Aboriginal people who were still living in a more or less traditional way upon what was now officially leasehold pastoral land. The very detailed financial records entered into the Hassell Station's accounts and record book for the years 1870–72 clearly show that the owners saw it as being in their own interests to pay Aboriginal employees wages comparable to those of European workers on the station.[81] The diary of twenty-year-old pioneer farmer W. H. Graham at Eticup in 1860 and 1861 gives a picture of the few local farmers from the area very frequently using Aboriginal men to find straying horses as well as for other work such as reaping and hay making, and being paid in cash for their efforts.[82]

Pastoralism with its vast areas of unfenced and uncleared bush in its natural state was a much less intrusive form of European land use than agriculture, which later replaced it throughout the region. From 1844, annual leases with payment based upon flock size and acres occupied were available to pastoralists in the south-west of the colony. The land did not belong to the leaseholder and was liable to resumption if conditions were not met; the sense of exclusive ownership felt by a leaseholder was therefore likely to be less than that felt by a farmer holding freehold title. Crucially, the right of Aboriginal people to use pastoral land was specifically delineated in the enabling regulations of 1860:

> The aboriginal natives shall have a right to enter upon any unenclosed land comprised within the limits of any pastoral or tillage lease, or upon any part of a Class A license for the purpose of subsistence therefrom in their customary manner...[83]

Aborigines therefore held a clear legal right to continue their activities until such time as the land was enclosed by fences – and the exorbitant cost of fencing using post and rail construction ensured that virtually no land was enclosed until the 1890s.[84] Fencing wire was available from the 1850s, but was very expensive and difficult to transport because of its large (about 6 mm) diameter and consequent heavy weight. In the 1870s, cheaper and lighter steel wire could be purchased, but it was still considered too expensive for large-scale use, especially on non-freehold land that was liable to resumption by the government.

The story of pastoralism in Albany's hinterland during the period covered in this chapter is largely, although not exclusively, the story of John Hassell and his family. Hassell bought land at Kendenup in 1839 and continued to accumulate both freehold and leasehold properties during the 1840s. By 1850 he controlled 63,000 acres, mostly at Kendenup, Hay River, Kojonup and Jerramungup.[85] The enterprise prospered and by 1863, Hassell was employing fourteen shepherds, three hut-keepers, five farm labourers, and several tradesmen and cooks. In 1864, his sheep were running on 350,000 acres.[86] Six years later he was employing about forty men on a full-time basis with many more hired for busy periods.[87]

Cleve Hassell's book based on Hassell family records states that an unspecified number of Aborigines were employed on a permanent basis, and a number of others helped at lambing, shearing and with horse work. They were considered skilful at stock handling and horse riding and were an important source of labour. After 1850, convicts provided the majority of Hassell's employees until this source dried up following the end of transportation in 1868, when many convicts left the region and were replaced by Chinese labourers.[88] Presumably, both of these groups gained employment at least partly at the expense of Aboriginal workers, for the station's 1872 list of shepherds does not appear to contain any names of Aboriginal people.[89] Most of these records are concerned with business and family details. Only rarely are Aboriginal people mentioned, usually in a peripheral manner that precludes the making of a detailed assessment of the exact nature of the relationship that existed between these pastoralists and their Aboriginal employees and neighbours.

Although pastoralism was certainly less intrusive than agriculture, its extension into the Menang heartland had profound implications for those Aboriginal people living away from the town of Albany and seeking to maintain their traditional way of life. Stock ate the native grasses in the relatively few areas that favoured their growth, causing a decline in the number of native animals available for traditional hunting. When grass was scarce or unavailable, stock grazed upon other native species of vegetation, further adversely affecting Aboriginal food sources. Water had always been scarce throughout much of the region, but it was only by making the maximum use of this limited resource that pastoralists and their flocks could hope to survive. This effectively denied access for Aboriginal people during the dry summer period when the few small water sources traditionally utilised became depleted and muddied by stock.

Pastoralism also had serious implications for Aboriginal spirituality. The arrival of Europeans and their flocks on traditional land frequently involved the deliberate or unwitting interference with, or destruction of, sites and objects that had held deep spiritual significance since time immemorial. The trauma caused by such desecration, and the dislocation it caused to traditional ceremonial life, is undocumented but must have been considerable.

There were multiple reasons why Europeans began to move into the hinterland. For a few, the opportunity to own a pastoral lease appeared to present a very real prospect of economic and social advancement in a colony where the holding of land was respected and regarded as the most secure way to establish a family dynasty. For others with less capital and more moderate social ambitions, the bush represented a place where it was possible to make a relatively large sum of money from taking sandalwood or selling kangaroo skins. Others, especially convicts holding tickets of leave, chose to take the secure employment offered by pastoralists. For some of these men, this may well have been the only employment available. Presumably, they accepted the privations of their remote and often lonely existence as being preferable to the social ignominy and police harassment that could be involved with town life as a convict.

Pastoralism, and the related pursuits of sandalwooding and kangaroo shooting, grew from small beginnings to become significant industries. These activities resulted in an invasion of the hinterland by European men (relatively few women were involved) whose behaviour often caused problems when they came into close contact with those Aboriginal people still living traditionally away from the town of Albany. Not all Europeans who lived in Albany's hinterland at this time were in this category, but there is much contemporary evidence to support the claim that very many were.

The degree of disruption to traditional Aboriginal food resources caused by the activities of kangaroo shooters was clearly very significant. The Sub-Guardian of Natives at Albany, Arthur Trimmer, wrote in an official report:

> ...one man, a kangaroo hunter surrounded by 300 natives with whom he was living on the best of terms, they assisting him with his occupation and bringing him the skins of the kangaroos they themselves had taken for a small cup of flour. This man has already this season sent to the settlement 3000 skins.[90]

This is one of two references from the period that imply Aboriginal people in the hinterland were in the habit of associating in very large numbers. The other is found in a letter written to Trimmer by R. Bell, a shepherd from Eticup, who complained about Aborigines' dogs attacking his sheep:

> There is a party of natives just gone from the place. There was at least a hundred natives and at least five hundred dogs and there have been many such parties...[91]

These references indirectly indicate that the traditional practice of assembling for ceremonial purposes was still in evidence in the 1850s.

One year later, Trimmer wrote:

> ...some steps should be taken to root out the kangaroo hunters either by compelling them to take out a licence at a heavy cost or otherwise for generally they are the worst of characters and do entail so much misery amongst the natives by being the means of spreading the venereal disease.[92]

Camfield also held strong views:

> This class of man are very obnoxious in various ways. They not
> only destroy the kangaroo for the skin only, which affords food
> and clothing for the native, but they are likewise the frequent
> cause of deadly feuds among them from the circumstances of
> taking their women away.[93]

He saw the grave injustice involved in the unsustainable destruction
of kangaroos, and marvelled that the Aboriginal people did
not retaliate:

> From the country I have not received any complaints or heard
> of any outrages by them which is highly praiseworthy on the
> part of the natives, when it is taken into consideration how their
> property, if I might be allowed the expression, is destroyed by
> the skinners…no less than 7000 skins have been exported which
> shows of itself the destruction of the food and natural clothing
> of the Aborigines and while they see the animal on which they
> have all depended for food and clothing destroyed and driven
> beyond their reach they are severely punished if they only kill a
> stray sheep or calf to satisfy the cravings of hunger…[94]

Phillips expressed a similar sentiment in an 1852 report to the
Colonial Secretary in which he stated that the few sheep actually
taken were quite justifiably killed by Aborigines who were hungry.

In 1853, the Legislative Council imposed an export tax of one
shilling per kangaroo skin, and no person (except Aboriginal
hunters, and settlers taking kangaroos for their own use) was to take
kangaroos without written authority from a Justice of the Peace.[95]
Even this belated action was not taken with Aboriginal interests
primarily in mind. The records of Legislative Council debate
make it quite clear that the Governor's motive in introducing the

new tax was to lessen costs involved in policing those areas where kangaroo hunters were continually involved in acts of violence. The emphasis was on the cost of policing violence, rather than on the violence per se.

Two years later almost every householder and settler in the District of Albany petitioned the Governor to lift the tax.[96] This petition provides a rare and illuminating window into the thoughts and priorities of Albany's European settlers when faced with a conflict between their own economic interests and the economic and social well-being of the district's original inhabitants. It must have been plain to settlers that pastoral expansion would impose severe stresses upon Aboriginal traditional life. A few such as Camfield saw the problems developing and sought to do something about the situation. One might presume that the last thing the growing pastoral industry and its supporters at Albany would wish to see was the violence and social disruption known to be associated with kangaroo shooters, yet the petition, which the government ignored, showed that few settlers at Albany shared Trimmer and Camfield's perceptions or anxieties.

Phillips certainly did. In 1850 he had written to the Colonial Secretary at Perth stating that isolated Europeans were killing Aborigines in the Beaufort River area just to the north of the region defined as Albany's hinterland, and that 'application should be made to his Excellency the Governor for an increased Police Force or the Natives will be annihilated'.[97] However, economic progress at Albany had proved painfully difficult and the majority of settlers, although not prepared to take the extreme measures used at the Beaufort River, had no intention of allowing Aboriginal interests to stand in the way of an industry that was actually bringing money to the local economy. The collateral damage kangaroo shooters were causing to Aboriginal–European harmony was certainly recognised, but was obviously generally accepted as inevitable.

Many Aboriginal people at this time incorporated the sale of possum skins into their traditional hunter-gatherer economy, and travellers on the road between Perth and Albany in 1855 reported having been offered skins for sale.[98] The trade continued for decades, and together with kangaroo shooting, whaling and the staged cultural displays for tourists at Albany, gave Aboriginal people an opportunity to remain living in a partly traditional fashion while also having some entry into the European cash economy.

Men seeking sandalwood also headed into the bush, often employing Aboriginal guides to lead them to the scattered stands of suitable trees. Pastoralists commonly employed sandalwooders because they were able to use their knowledge of the country to select favoured areas where water and native grasses were available. Camfield visited a sandalwood camp at Pootenup, between Cranbrook and Tambellup, in 1849, and reported that the men involved were ill-treating Aboriginal people and infecting them with venereal disease.[99]

The arrival of pastoralists and their stock in a district presented its Aboriginal owners with a variety of choices. These ranged between outright opposition and violent resistance at one end of the scale, and an almost complete co-operation at the other. The evidence shows that most Aboriginal people living in the hinterland of Albany chose a path somewhere between these extremes. Some official efforts were made to prevent trouble arising: in 1853, Trimmer received instructions from the Governor to issue provisions to the value of £10 to Aboriginal people on Hassell's property if they desisted from their old and evidently continuing practice of burning grassland in summer. Trimmer's 1855 reply noted that this idea had been successful, although he was being optimistic if he thought at the time that the practice would cease on a long-term basis.[100]

The topic of Aboriginal resistance to settlement is central to any study of Aboriginal–European interaction on the Australian frontier, and I have chosen to discuss its importance in the Albany region in this chapter, rather than treating each instance chrono-logically. The first case of stock spearing occurred in 1838, when Spencer lost a bull and two oxen from his Hay River property.[101] There was a gradual escalation following this incident leading inevitably to bloodshed on both sides. In 1839, Minnan wounded a shepherd at Moorelup (later known as Kendenup), and was arrested by soldiers stationed at Mount Barker for the protection of local settlers. The Albany court did not consider itself authorised to deal with the case and postponed it for a year. During that time Minnan associated openly with settlers and 'performed acts of kindness to parties who were well aware of his crime'.[102] When brought to Albany, he escaped from the gaol. Peter Belches, the acting Resident Magistrate, wrote that the extended period between the spearing and any subsequent punishment made it likely that the Aborigines would feel resentment and attack vulnerable isolated settlers.[103] The police declined to pursue Minnan actively because of their inability to patrol the outlying areas effectively.

The lack of detail in official reports from Albany by men such as Trimmer make it impossible to state definitively whether some events constituted resistance or were simply a continuation of traditional practices. For example, Trimmer wrote in 1861 that Aborigines had burnt the 'runs' of two settlers on the Hay River, destroying buildings, grass, corn hay and potatoes.[104] He failed to note whether he considered the fires to have been deliberately lit, so as to cause damage to the pastoralists involved.

Sporadic spearing of livestock continued throughout the 1850s, 1860s and 1870s. The Colonial Secretary's Office records of official correspondence from Albany during the 1850s show that incidents of stock stealing were reported to Perth on average about 2.5 times per year. Unsurprisingly the practice of stock theft was deeply resented by European landholders, but was never totally eliminated in the region until the 1890s. However, there are several reasons why the taking of stock proved difficult to control. Firstly, the personal security of the few pastoralists living in Albany's hinterland depended upon the maintenance of a certain level of goodwill from the local Aboriginal people since the small detachment of troops stationed at Mount Barker or nearby might have taken days to hear of any attack upon Europeans, and could never effectively guarantee their individual security. The courts could perhaps reduce the incidence of stock theft, but they were never a completely effective deterrent and stock owners knew that the only remedy likely to have proved successful would have involved illegal punitive attacks on those Aboriginal people believed to be involved. There is no evidence to show that this was ever seriously considered. Apart from the inevitability of revenge attacks on the pastoralists involved, a too aggressive offensive – legally or extra-legally – against those taking livestock would have proved economically counterproductive since co-operative Aboriginal labour was essential to the running of pastoral holdings.

Police officers relied upon Aboriginal co-operation in tracking and apprehending offenders, and this would not have been forth-coming in the case of a too vigorous policing of the laws against stock theft.[105] I have not been able to find how many Aboriginal trackers were employed. However, Trimmer noted in 1861 that he had previously obtained a pardon for an Aboriginal man on the condition that he assist with naming and apprehending Aboriginal stock stealers. He was now suggesting that another be pardoned on the same conditions, since he had achieved such success under the scheme.[106]

In addition, the lack of fences, the carelessness of some shepherds and the cover afforded by the bush made it relatively easy to take sheep and cattle. Witnesses prepared to testify were few. Evidence could quickly be disposed of, making convictions in the courts difficult to achieve, while the porous nature of the Albany gaol ensured that many of those convicted soon returned to the interior where they continued their depredations.

Shepherds sometimes blamed Aborigines for spearing sheep when their own negligence had resulted in losses from other causes. Pastoralists were entitled to sue shepherds for negligence leading to stock loss, and a case before the Perth Civil Court in 1850 led to a shepherd having a fine imposed equal to his entire annual wage.[107] Following this case there was an obvious economic incentive for shepherds to blame Aborigines for all future stock losses, and the *Perth Gazette* of 4 January 1850 recorded in detail a case in which one of Hassell's shepherds alleged that a group of Aboriginal men and women had stolen twenty-two sheep.[108] Subsequently this proved to be a fabrication by the shepherd intended to cover up his own incompetence.

Stock spearing and attacks upon Europeans (usually isolated shepherds and hut-keepers) occurred spasmodically, but were never concerted or sufficiently serious to have led to either open warfare or the cessation of settlement in areas remote from military protection. Neville Green has listed the recorded deaths and woundings resulting from Aboriginal–settler conflict in Western Australia between 1826 and 1852.[109] The figures provided by his research indicate that Europeans in the Albany region were not at high risk of becoming victims of violent attacks during this period, and that settler violence towards Aboriginal people was also lower than that recorded in most other settled areas of the colony.[110] Green documented that Aborigines killed one European and wounded two others in the region during that twenty-six-year period, while two Aboriginal people were killed and four wounded by Europeans. These figures should be contrasted with the 121 Aboriginal and the thirty European deaths recorded as resulting from violence between Europeans and Aborigines in the colony as a whole between 1826 and 1852.[111]

Green's research has shown that between 1852 and 1877, inter-se violence caused more Aboriginal deaths and woundings in the Albany region than occurred because of conflict between

Aborigines and Europeans.[112] Albany was not alone in this. In a paper delivered to the Australian History conference in 2010, Western Australian historian Bob Reece stated that one-third of all the known Aboriginal deaths in the Swan River area between 1829 and 1840 were due to inter-se violence. It also played an ongoing role in helping to perpetuate commonly held settler assumptions about the innate superiority of their own culture, as well as reinforcing the view that Aboriginal people were simply too 'different' to ever fully integrate into European society.

An examination of court records reveals that cases from districts well away from Albany where only Aboriginal people were involved were seldom brought before the courts, although Governor Fitzgerald had introduced a policy in 1848 that this should occur. Trimmer noted in 1859 that in cases involving inter-se violence 'in Albany or anywhere in the neighbourhood the natives always apply to the Court'.[113] One cryptic record indicates that some inter-se violence occurred because of European interference in Aboriginal matters. In 1859, three Aboriginal men fatally speared an Aboriginal woman north of Cranbrook because a European employee of Hassell 'obliged a native to cohabit with her which on account of the close relationship was contrary to the native laws. Therefore she was speared'.[114]

The majority of the Aboriginal population living in the hinterland generally responded to gradual settler invasion by seeking to continue their traditional way of life, while accommodating the inevitable changes caused by the ever-increasing European incursions. It is perhaps possible to see some instances of sheep and cattle spearing as constituting isolated political acts of resistance, but the evidence does not support any contention that this formed part of a general guerrilla war against European occupation, although this was not necessarily the case in other parts of the colony. The letters of pastoralists such as John Hassell and George Egerton-Warburton give no indication that they feared for their personal safety, or that they considered the sporadic acts of stock theft as part of a concerted campaign of Aboriginal resistance. W. H. Graham's expansive diary detailing his activities on his Eticup farm gives no indication that he had any fears about living a very isolated existence in 1860 and 1861.[115] An editorial writer in the *West Australian Times* of 19 October 1863 noted that problems arose in the colony when: 'Natives begin to appreciate the flavour of mutton, and shepherds the wives of the aborigines'.[116] My reading of all of the court transcripts of cases at Albany dealing with stock spearing by Aborigines in the Albany region overwhelmingly supports this point of view, rather than supporting guerrilla war as the cause. No cases are on record where more sheep were taken than would be able to be consumed by a small group of people. Where a form of guerrilla warfare did exist, such as in the Manning Valley of New South Wales in the late 1840s, livestock was slaughtered by Aborigines on a systematic basis that had no counterpart at Albany.[117]

Even when extreme isolation made them very vulnerable, Europeans were rarely the subject of attack unless they sought to take Aboriginal women. Evidence provided by Aborigines brought before the courts on stock stealing charges showed that they killed the animals for food, rather than for motives that might indicate political resistance. It is not necessary to invoke resistance as the only possible motive: as native animals declined in number due to habitat destruction caused by sheep and cattle, and as the indiscriminate slaughter of kangaroos by Europeans reduced their availability, it was inevitable that some Aboriginal people would seek to supplement their diet with the new and readily available food source.

Although the evidence does not support the existence of organised violent resistance to European settlement in the Albany region, isolated incidents of extreme violence nevertheless occurred. In 1839, a shepherd working at the Hay River whose name and details I have been unable to ascertain became the first recorded European to be injured by Aboriginal attack since the beginning of free settlement at Albany. Two years later Charles Newell, a young shepherd of Hassell's at Kendenup, became the first European to be fatally speared when he remonstrated with a group of forty Aboriginal men who had taken some items from the Hassell homestead. A messenger rode post-haste to Mount Barker approximately 16 kilometres away to alert the small group of soldiers stationed there of what had occurred. They rushed to the scene and arrested a young man identified as the spear thrower, but immediately found themselves surrounded by a crowd of Aborigines that they later told the court numbered between 500 and 600. Fortunately for the soldiers, as well as the subsequent history of Aboriginal–European relations in the region, some of the crowd assisted them in making the arrest, although the scene was still out of control until a shot fired into the air dispersed those present.[118] The young man was escorted to Albany to face trial, but later managed to escape his guard of two soldiers. I have been unable to find any record of his name or whether he was subsequently recaptured.

Writing one hundred years after this event, local historian Robert Stephens claimed that after this affray 'the natives bowed to the inevitable and accepted the occupation of their tribal hunting grounds by the white settler'.[119] Unfortunately, he gave no references for the statement, although there may have been a local story still current to this effect. It is possible to see from documentary evidence that there was a spike in settler concern around 1840 at the Hay River and at Kendenup.[120] Government Resident Phillips indicated that Aborigines from some unspecified other areas were coming into Kendenup to receive flour rations distributed at every second full moon, and he decided to cease the handout because of the problems this caused. Probably the very large crowd that gathered after Newell's spearing comprised many people who had come in for this purpose (the full moon occurred a few days later) and their potentially threatening presence convinced Phillips that something needed to be done. The cancelling of the flour ration led to some or all of the 'outsiders' returning home, which could explain why the upsurge in violence and thefts largely ceased after 1841.

In 1861 Charles Storey, another of John Hassell's shepherds, was speared to death at Jacup, well to the east of the area covered by this book. The evidence given in court indicated that this murder resulted from an argument that developed when Storey sought to barter flour for some tobacco belonging to a group of Aboriginal men, and had little to do with Aboriginal resistance.[121] Two Aboriginal men were found guilty of the murder and were hanged.[122]

In the same year, Coban, a Noongar man, was charged with murdering Joseph Hesketh at a sheep station 50 kilometres from Albany. The government wished to encourage convicts to marry Aboriginal women, and had, as discussed earlier in this chapter, established a scheme whereby a grant of 10 acres would be made to such couples, the actual title being granted to the woman. At Albany, Hesketh and at least three other convicts, John Maher, James Egan and Ezra Moore, took advantage of the opportunity.[123] Hesketh had legally married Mary, an Aboriginal woman, before the Registrar at Albany. Coban, Mary's tribal husband, was understandably angered by what had occurred and decided to spear her while the couple slept. In the confusion caused by darkness, he speared Hesketh by mistake. Brought before the Perth Supreme Court two years later, Coban was released by a jury at the direction of the Chief Justice because of a lack of evidence caused by 'want of formality'. Surprisingly, the brief Perth newspaper report of the case made no comment about the fact that a clear case of murder could be simply dismissed in this way.[124]

Hassell reacted to these deaths by writing a letter to Sir Alexander Cockburn-Campbell, who had replaced Henry Camfield as Government Resident in January 1861:

If something is not done, we shall have a few more tragedies like Storie's… the natives are commencing here the same as they did last year robbing the huts if they can get the men out for a minute or two…natives soon forget such things as hanging etc but they do not forget to steal, spear etc…I feel that peremptory steps should be taken to put down such offences and to prevent my servants coming into collision with such delinquents.[125]

The next part of Hassell's letter is a veiled plea for (unspecified) strong police action, and makes it very clear that he did not consider Arthur Trimmer to be the man for the job:

I cannot coincide with your sending Mr Trimmer on such an occasion. I am of the opinion it requires a strong minded Policeman of Stability, a man well knowing the ways of and habits of the Natives, and a thorough bushman with two Native Police to perform the duty it seems so much required.

Probably Hassell was well aware of the punitive use of Native Police in the eastern colonies. Cockburn-Campbell, however, had come to Western Australia as Superintendant of Police three years earlier and was too experienced an administrator to comply with Hassell's demands for reprisals.[126] He requested further information from Hassell, pointing out that Constable Chester was already stationed in the Kent area to the north to handle just such problems and that Hassell should have contacted *him*. When Chester visited Jerramungup, he found only a few inconclusive reports about Aborigines stealing clothes and damper from shepherds – none of whom were prepared to identify individuals involved.[127]

Henry Reynolds has shown how decent people on the Australian frontier could become hardened by their experiences, and Hassell's letter appears to be an example of this process at work.[128] Given that two of his employees were murdered by Aborigines within a four-month period, one can understand Hassell's concern. However, the fact that he waited nine months after the second death before writing his letter appears to indicate that he was not seriously alarmed that the two deaths represented a new and violent phase in Aboriginal–European relations in Albany's hinterland.

The few Europeans killed or injured at Albany came from the lower echelons of society. This was not always the case at York or the Vasse, and helps explain why there were few settler calls for reprisals recorded at Albany. The story may well have been very different had someone with the status of Camfield or Hassell been killed. The settler acceptance of the Magistrate's lenient treatment of Coban may constitute evidence that the early good relations established at Albany still carried over to some extent, for when a shepherd was killed at the Flinders Ranges in South Australia in the 1860s, and his murderer was released after serving a prison term, the owner of the station wrote that he soon received the 'punishment so richly deserved'.[129] I have been unable to find a record of anyone from Albany expressing similar sentiments in the Hesketh case, even though the Aboriginal murderer was set free and returned to the area unpunished. It is inconceivable that settlers would have let this act of judicial mercy pass unchallenged had they held any fears for their own safety in the bush.

There were cases from the Albany region where Europeans inflicted violence upon Aboriginal people, and faced the courts as a result. In 1848, the Supreme Court at Perth convicted two of Hassell's shepherds who had tortured an Aboriginal man they accused of sheep stealing. The Perth Gazette described the case as 'one of the most horrible and brutal cases ever perhaps brought before a court of Justice', and declined to publish all of the graphic evidence, although the paper did see fit to print that the Aboriginal man named Bandit had received:

more than ten dozen lashes, on different and most tender parts of
his body, with a cat made of raw hide with several knots in each
lash, and not contented with this, when the poor fellow fainted
he was stabbed in the groin with a table fork.[130]

John Gale and James Egan each received a sentence of eight
years' imprisonment with hard labour. The newspaper report of
the next case tried that day recorded how three Aboriginal men
received sentences only one year less for the theft of a sheep.[131]
The previous year, an Albany jury had declined to convict a settler
in another case involving severe cruelty towards an Aboriginal
person. Phillips, in his role as Resident Magistrate, was unhappy
with their decision, stating:

> The inhabitants of this District are much opposed to native
> evidence and although in this case the Native evidence appeared
> so clear to the court the jury did not give much credit to it.[132]

Court records provide an indication that violent acts between
Europeans and Aboriginal people in the Albany region were not
common during the period covered by this chapter. Of course,
there always remains the possibility that such acts – even massacres –
took place but were hushed up and kept out of the court system
and never documented in any form. This was not unknown in the
eastern colonies of Australia, but there are good reasons to believe
that this did not occur at Albany. Firstly, those Noongar people
who now live at Albany and are part of Aboriginal families who
were present in the region throughout the nineteenth century
make no such claims. Secondly, although there is a persistent
rumour among the non-Aboriginal residents of Albany that
a massacre took place at or near Denmark at some unspecified
time in the past, it appears to be groundless. Local historian Bob
Howard extensively researched this idea and concluded that it had

no basis in fact.[133] He had very close ties to the Albany Noongar community and it is inconceivable that he would not have been made aware of any major incidents at Denmark, or at any other site in the town and hinterland of Albany. However, the old established patterns of retribution continued within the Aboriginal community, causing major difficulties for the colony's legal system and adversely affecting Aboriginal–European relations.

It is fortunate that Hazel Brown, an Aboriginal elder from Albany, has chosen to share some of her family's oral traditions about nineteenth-century life in the region around Ravensthorpe, as well as in the Gnowangerup and Borden districts. Her story is told in *Kayang & Me*, published in 2005. Although most of her story refers to events in areas to the east of the geographical scope of this book, it is an important guide to Aboriginal attitudes that would also have been held in the Albany hinterland. She makes clear that both resistance and accommodation occurred. For example, she disputes the common claim that European sandalwooders showed Hassell where the best land was situated, pointing out that it was actually Bobby Roberts, her great grandfather, who was responsible – a clear instance of Aboriginal accommodation.[134] Others of her ancestors took a differing approach and adopted a policy of passive resistance. As previously mentioned, virtually all of the violent resistance occurred in the region well to the east of that covered in this book. When Bob Howard claimed in his study *Noongar Resistance on the South Coast* that violent resistance was the major paradigm along the south coast, all of the examples used to support his assertion came from this eastern area stretching as far as the South Australian border.[135]

In the light of the violence that amounted at times to a form of guerrilla warfare in many other areas of Australia at the time, it is interesting to examine again the Albany and Mount Barker Police Stations' Daily Occurrence Books.[136] The Albany books commence in 1859, while those from Mount Barker begin in 1872. At no point do these records address the topic of Aboriginal–European conflict directly, but it is possible to read them across the grain to gain a significant insight into what was occurring. Firstly, they provide no evidence to suggest that police saw Aborigines as posing any type of physical threat to Europeans. Police officers undertook regular horseback patrols to check on settlers, invariably reporting that no problems were brought to their attention. Police attended many advertised public meetings, but did not report that any were related to settler concern about security. All correspondence to and from the Police Commissioner at Perth appears in the books, yet nothing suggests that direction was sought or given as to how to deal with any threat or actuality of inter-group violence. This is in sharp contrast to South Australia, where Police Commissioner Peter Egerton-Warburton (brother of George at Mount Barker) wrote in 1863:

> These savages cannot be made to understand our Laws...From 15 to 20 Troopers at hand would be required to protect our frontier stations – they should be well armed and (in my opinion) directed to use their arms.[137]

It is surely significant that the Mount Barker Police at this time usually went unarmed when out singly on long patrols in bush country where Aborigines were likely to be encountered at any time. On the very few occasions that they took the Police Station's revolver, they noted the fact in their report.

Of course it is theoretically possible that police records covered up what was really taking place, but if this were so there must have been a conspiracy carried out consistently by every police officer at both stations over an extended period, and one that could easily have been exposed by any settler sympathetic to Aboriginal people. However, to suggest that such a conspiracy probably existed ignores one basic fact – throughout Australia at this time people on the frontier tended to see very little reason to conceal the violence that was occurring in their area. Although there was often a wide discrepancy between the *details* of frontier violence and its reporting, a certain code was routinely employed that enabled its users to inform their readers of what took place, while managing to protect themselves from any possible legal consequences.[138] Words and phrases such as 'dispersal', 'chastised', 'driven off', 'taught a lesson', 'given a sense of dread' and 'used forceful methods to establish authority' were commonly used, and these euphemisms were well understood by the readers. For the few who may not have been aware of the convention, newspaper editors, such as that of *The Queenslander* in 1880, were sometimes prepared to translate:

> What disperse means is well enough known. The word has been adopted into bush slang as a convenient euphemism for a wholesale massacre.[139]

I have not found any contemporary evidence that such a code was in use in the Albany region. Apart from one instance, no phrases or words of this type appear in any of the wide range of official or unofficial records that I have accessed, and their absence is a strong indication that the local police journal entries generally reflected the reality that the Aboriginal and European sections of the population of the town and the immediate surrounds of Albany were coexisting in a mostly peaceable, if unequal, relationship. The only instance where I have found 'move on' used is in a letter written in October 1850 to the Colonial Secretary at Perth by John Phillips, who had resigned his position of Government Resident in July 1847 and was writing in his capacity as Sub-Guardian of Natives. Phillips heard that a large group of Aborigines were assembling near Kendenup for a fight among themselves and sent two policemen who 'moved them on'. In the same letter he described how relations were good, with some Aboriginal people assisting following a shipwreck.[140]

There is no local equivalent of the letter written by a South Australian pastoralist and published in the *South Australian Register* of 9 December 1865:

> The blacks have been playing up with the cattle since I left the station. They have been killing them by wholesale. I am going at them in a day or two, just to let them know that I am home again.

Historians, especially Henry Reynolds, have definitively shown that a form of guerrilla warfare occurred in many regions of Australia during the nineteenth century, and there is the temptation to assume that the resistance paradigm is universally applicable across the continent. Reece has argued that Reynolds and some other historians have tended to focus on the bloodiness of colonisation, and have failed to give sufficient prominence to accommodation, the other major characteristic of Aboriginal–European interaction.[141] The relationship in the hinterland of Albany during the period of this chapter is certainly too complex to be described exclusively in terms of either resistance or accommodation. However, there can be no doubt that accommodation represented by far the more common Aboriginal response to the creeping invasion brought by the growth of the pastoral, agricultural and sandalwood industries. As Hayward has stated when writing about his Noongar ancestors from the area near Broomehill, they 'quickly saw the futility of any physical challenge to the ever increasing...white invaders'.[142]

As the first fifty years of settlement at Albany drew to a close, the relationship between the region's Aboriginal and European inhabitants had passed from the initial stage of first contact and developed into an uneasy, if relatively peaceable, coexistence. Some Aboriginal people chose to live on the outskirts of Albany, where they lived partly in a traditional fashion and partly by selling their labour on a casual basis. Some members of this group took advantage of the economic opportunities presented by the large numbers of short-term visitors who came ashore while their vessels were re-coaled. They presented exhibitions of traditional dress and weaponry for a fee, and it is also clear that begging was sometimes a feature of such visits.

In the hinterland, the Aboriginal people who had chosen to continue their traditional pattern of life away from European influence found this to be increasingly difficult as pastoralists, shepherds, hut-keepers, kangaroo shooters and sandalwooders moved onto their lands. All of these Europeans exploited Aboriginal resources, and some also directly exploited Aboriginal people. In 1859, Trimmer wrote: 'Almost every shepherd in the district encourages the natives for the sake of obtaining their women…'[143] He also alleged that shepherds were giving Aboriginal women corrosive sublimate (mercuric chloride) as a treatment for venereal disease, thereby causing several deaths.[144] The vast area for which Trimmer was responsible meant that it was difficult to detect and punish those involved, although there is some evidence that his position at least acted as a deterrent to some extent. He informed the Colonial Secretary at Perth that he was 'constantly visiting' settlers, and was well aware of shepherds inventing complaints against Aborigines in order to cover up their own illegal activities.[145] Water and many native food resources became increasingly scarce, and a number of the sacred and significant sites that formed part of the intricate web of Aboriginal spirituality were desecrated.

Some Aboriginal people chose to take casual or semi-permanent employment with the newcomers. Court records detail several cases where some of these employees fell foul of the Masters and Servants Act by absconding from their place of employment, and were sent to Rottnest Island prison to serve a term of three months' hard labour. These convictions have at times been interpreted as a form of persecution applied solely to Aboriginal employees, but the records from the Albany courts show that the great majority of employees sentenced were European; it was a master–servant problem, rather than a European–Aboriginal problem, and the law appears to have been enforced equally in cases pursued through the courts. However, a circular issued to police by the Western Australian Colonial Secretary in 1878 reminded justices that some masters had been too assiduous in prosecuting their Aboriginal employees.[146]

Others chose to take opportunities presented by the easy availability of sheep and cattle, thereby risking bringing themselves into destructive contact with the British system of justice. Even those who respected settler property could find themselves coming into conflict because of their continuing reliance upon firing the bush when hunting. Settlers brought numerous dogs to Albany, and the descendants of these became highly prized by Aboriginal people for their ability to aid in the hunt for native animals. As the numbers of dogs increased, the damage they caused to flocks grew, causing anger and resentment on the part of pastoralists and shepherds. When in 1855 R. Bell and three other shepherds sent letters to Trimmer complaining about Aborigines' dogs, he visited the area and reported that although some damage to stock had occurred, the shepherds had greatly exaggerated its extent and were badly treating Aboriginal people. Interestingly, the comments an official placed in the margin of Trimmer's letter referred only to the dog problem – the allegations of Aboriginal mistreatment appear to have been overlooked.[147]

Overall, the relationship in the hinterland was an uneasy one. Aborigines were valued for their services as labourers and guides, but were sometimes exploited by convicts and other unscrupulous Europeans living away from the effective reach of British law. Aboriginal people learned through necessity which settlers were amenable to co-operation and as far as possible tried to avoid the rest.[148]

Until 2009, there was little challenge to the common theme of much of Western Australian historiography – that Noongar tradition, law and culture had almost disappeared because of the triple onslaught of disease, settler dispossession and repressive governmental policies. Since the publication in that year of Host with Owen's book, *It's Still in My Heart, This Is My Country*, historians have been forced to reassess this paradigm and search for evidence that will either lend it support or show that it had always been fundamentally flawed. The evidence from the Albany region indicates that Aboriginal culture and custom in the Albany region during this critical period of adjustment to European settlement were neither completely destroyed, nor remained unaffected. Aboriginal people continued to carry out some traditional practices, but through circumstances or choice began to adopt some aspects of the settler economy, culture and lifestyle. As agricultural settlement expanded in the decades ahead, this balance would become ever more difficult for the region's Noongar people to maintain.

Chapter Six

The Coming of the Great Southern Railway, 1878–1904

The beginning of a profound change in Aboriginal–European relations as the pastoral era begins to give way to the establishment of small farms by a new and very different generation of settlers

Three events dominate the history of Aboriginal–European relations at Albany and its surrounding region: the establishment of the British garrison in late 1826; the increase in close agricultural settlement brought about by the opening of the Great Southern Railway linking Albany and Perth in mid 1889; and the draconian control over Aboriginal people's lives the Western Australian Government achieved with the passing of the Aborigines Act of 1905. A major focus of this chapter is on the effects of the second of these events. During the period between 1878 and 1905, the overwhelming majority of the Aboriginal people of the Albany region lived in the rural areas opened up by the railway, and the history of their interaction with the European population was deeply affected by the expansion of settlement brought about by its construction and operation.

The new railway, together with the extraordinary population growth in the colony as a whole due to the discovery of numerous payable deposits of gold, brought a considerable increase in the number of people living in Albany and its hinterland. This progress, which was greatly welcomed by the European population who considered it long overdue, came at the cost of a hardening of attitudes towards local Aboriginal people as greater numbers of them moved out of the bush and into camps on the fringes of the growing farming towns and sidings to the north of Albany.

In his history of Albany, Donald Garden described the period between 1880 and 1900 as one of sustained growth and expansion for Albany, stating that these years were to see her achieve many of her long-held dreams. His unwritten assumption is clear: Albany's dreams were now the dreams of its *British* inhabitants. Apart from one paragraph, Garden ignored the Aboriginal population of the town and district, leaving the impression that they simply faded away – 'Gradually the old personalities of the tribes were dying out'.[1] He was correct in his assertion that the number of Aboriginal people living in the town and its immediate surrounds had declined markedly, but it is unfortunate that his book ignores the fact that this was largely because they had *moved* out, as well as *died* out. From this point forward Garden's focus shifts away from Albany's hinterland, leaving untold the story of the numerous Aboriginal people living outside the town's boundaries.

The town of Albany enjoyed considerable growth between 1878 and 1905, although there were dramatic fluctuations in its fortunes over that time. The European population grew from around 850 in 1878, to reach 2,655 in the official census of 1891. By 1901 Aboriginal people were being counted in the Western Australian census, even though the figures were published in a separate section from those of the town's European population which reached 3,594,[2] only to decline to 1,922 four years later.[3] There was also strong population growth in the region to Albany's north following the construction of the railway linking the southern port to the colony's capital. By 1901 this region's

European population had reached 2,522, spread very unevenly over the 80,000 square kilometres comprising the division then officially known as the Statistical Division of Plantagenet County.[4]

The discovery of gold in the late 1880s caused a dramatic increase in Western Australia's population and provided a major stimulus to the colony's agricultural production. Disillusioned miners swelled the ranks of those seeking to take up the newly released farming blocks along the Great Southern line, and these new arrivals frequently had a much less tolerant attitude towards Aboriginal people than did many of the pastoralists who had grown up in the region, some of whom by 1890 were third-generation residents. This coincided with a growth in the late-nineteenth-century of 'scientific racism' in Europe and the USA. Unfortunately the small Western Australian colonial society of the time was carried along with this new and powerful intellectual current, to the great detriment of Aboriginal–European relations.

New towns sprang up along the line and, for the first time since European settlement, extensive land clearing commenced in Albany's hinterland. These changes disrupted those Aboriginal people who were still living a more or less traditional lifestyle. Local Aboriginal historian Eric Hayward has written of this period: 'Noongars…began to see their country rapidly removed from their ownership, management and control, and transferred into the hands of the white invaders'.[5] At the same time, the increasing availability of European labour brought about by gold rush–inspired migration from the eastern colonies meant that farmers and pastoralists were no longer as dependent upon Aboriginal labour. Western Australia's settler population surged from less than 30,000 in 1881, to more than 180,000 in 1901. It was still possible for Aboriginal workers to continue in regular or casual employment, but they moved from being economically necessary to the settler economy to a position where many became increasingly marginalised.

For a variety of reasons detailed later, it is not possible to give a completely accurate number of Aboriginal people living in the south-west of Western Australia or in the town and region of Albany during the latter part of the nineteenth and early twentieth centuries. However, it is certain that during this period they became a very much smaller proportion of the total population. This shift in the relative sizes of the Aboriginal and European populations had profound implications for the future relationship between the two peoples, making it easier for settlers to ignore the plain fact that they were usurpers of another people's land. Virtually all of the numerous recorded statements made by Western Australian settlers during the nineteenth century acknowledging the moral dilemma inherent in dispossession predate this era. It became increasingly easier for Europeans in Albany and the region to lose any sense that they were living on Aboriginal land, or even that they were living *with* the original inhabitants in some form of symbiosis. Aboriginal people had become barely tolerated reminders of an often embarrassingly unsuccessful past, before gold and the railway had brought the promise of a new and prosperous future.

When the P&O Company closed its Albany coaling depot in 1880, a pall of gloom descended upon the town. Ships continued to call at the port to take on and deliver the colony's mail, but steam-powered vessels had increased in range to the point where it was no longer necessary to maintain a refuelling depot between Melbourne and Ceylon. A major source of employment was lost, and Albany's future appeared bleak. However, the problems caused by the closure of the coaling station proved to be short-lived. Having failed to persuade P&O to make Fremantle the colony's coaling station and mail port, the Western Australian Government reluctantly concluded that it was necessary to construct a rail line between Perth and Albany in order to allow the speedy receipt and despatch of the capital's mail. The successful completion of railways in Canada and the United States built under the land grant system led Albany's member of the Legislative Council, Thomas Cockburn-Campbell, to suggest that a similar scheme be set up in Western Australia. When the British Government gave its in-principle support in 1881, confidence in the future immediately returned to Albany.

Initially, entrepreneurs showed little interest in building a railway, but in 1883 leading Sydney businessman Anthony Hordern offered to build and operate a rail line between Albany and York that would connect with the existing line to Perth. In return he would receive 12,000 acres for each mile constructed, as well as 120 acres for each adult and 50 acres for each child brought into the colony. Fremantle remained unsatisfactory as a major port because of a rocky bar across the mouth of the Swan River, and it appeared that the railway was destined to make Albany the long-term principal gateway to Western Australia. After many difficulties, work began in late 1888 (by which time the government line extended south to Beverley) and the line opened for business in June the following year.

Albany began to benefit economically before the railway was completed, with the arrival of the first land-company migrants in 1886, and the establishment of a sleeper-cutting industry in the karri forest west of the town at Torbay (now Elleker) where 200 people were living at a bush camp by April 1887. Work began on a major new hospital at Albany, many new businesses were established, and a 656-yard-long jetty was constructed to handle the predicted increase in shipping. Growth and confidence further increased with the opening of the railway. A grand town hall was built, the Methodist and Presbyterian congregations constructed substantial new churches, and the price of land in the town increased to the point where blocks a mile from the centre of town sold for £150. Gas was reticulated to business and domestic premises, the telephone line was extended to cater for

112 subscribers, and Albany took on a more substantial appearance.[6] The town's European population increased dramatically from an estimated 1,500 in 1888, to reach 2,665 in 1891.[7]

The discovery of gold in the Yilgarn in 1888, and later at Coolgardie and Kalgoorlie, provided a further boost to the Albany economy as diggers arrived from eastern Australia to either take the train to Perth or walk to the goldfields along the track from Broomehill opened up by John Holland in 1893. For the first time, tourism became a significant industry. By the end of 1895, twenty ships per week were calling at the port and by 1901 Albany's European population had risen to 3,594, representing the high point in the fortunes of the town during its first hundred years of existence.[8]

With the removal of the rocky bar at the entrance to the Swan River and the creation of Fremantle Harbour in 1895, Albany ceased to be the colony's principal point of entry for goldminers and other new arrivals. In 1901, on the eve of Federation, Albany's residents were stunned and dismayed to find that the state's mail port would be moved to Fremantle. By 1905, the number of residents had fallen to only 1,922 as Albany entered a long economic decline that persisted until the Australia-wide post-war economic boom fifty years later finally brought a return to prosperity.

By 1878, there remained only a few Aboriginal people who still chose to live in or immediately adjacent to the town of Albany. Settlers living in the isolation of the vast and almost completely uncleared area of Albany's hinterland continued to be vulnerable to sporadic incidents of petty theft and stock spearing, but by this time Europeans in both the town and hinterland of Albany had become unquestionably the economically, socially and numerically dominant group.

There is a surprising amount of information contained in the official Western Australian censuses of 1881, 1891 and 1901. For example, the 1901 report was published in three volumes totalling

818 pages of data on topics that ranged from the religious affiliation and educational level of settlers, to the number of people (perhaps surprisingly, more than 20 per cent of the total population of the state) who were living in dwellings made from calico or canvas. The information gathered, generally by police officers visiting settlers in their homes, is very useful in identifying the demographics of Aboriginal people and European settlers who lived in the town and hinterland of Albany at three equally spaced points in time during the period covered by this chapter.

The history of European–Aboriginal relations during this period is divided into two quite separate stories: that of the town of Albany; and that of the surrounding hinterland that looked to Albany as its economic and social centre. A wide range of sources makes it clear that almost all of the Aboriginal people had moved away from the town by this time, and it is to the relationship that developed between these rural-dwelling Aboriginal people and the settlers who also made their homes in the bush that this history now turns.

Western Australia was divided into a number of districts and municipalities for census purposes. Under this system the Albany region was split into the Municipality of Albany and the Magisterial District of Plantagenet. The boundary of the latter division used for each of the three censuses stretched approximately 400 kilometres along the south coast, from D'Entrecasteaux Point west of Albany to Red Island (near Hopetoun), and extended inland for about 200 kilometres.[9] This vast area comprised approximately 80,000 square kilometres (8,000,000 hectares, or 20,000,000 acres).

A considerable amount of information about the region's Aboriginal population can be gained from the census reports. The 1881 preamble stated:

> To determine the number of Aborigines in the settled portions
> of the Colony, householders were required to state on their

schedules full particulars as to each aboriginal in their employ. By this means correct data are at hand as to the black population in the service of the white. In addition to this, each Resident or Police Magistrate was desired to obtain, if possible, information as to the number of Aborigines who, in his district, were not depending on the settlers for their subsistence; but the particulars on this point do not appear to be sufficiently reliable to be made use of in this report.[10]

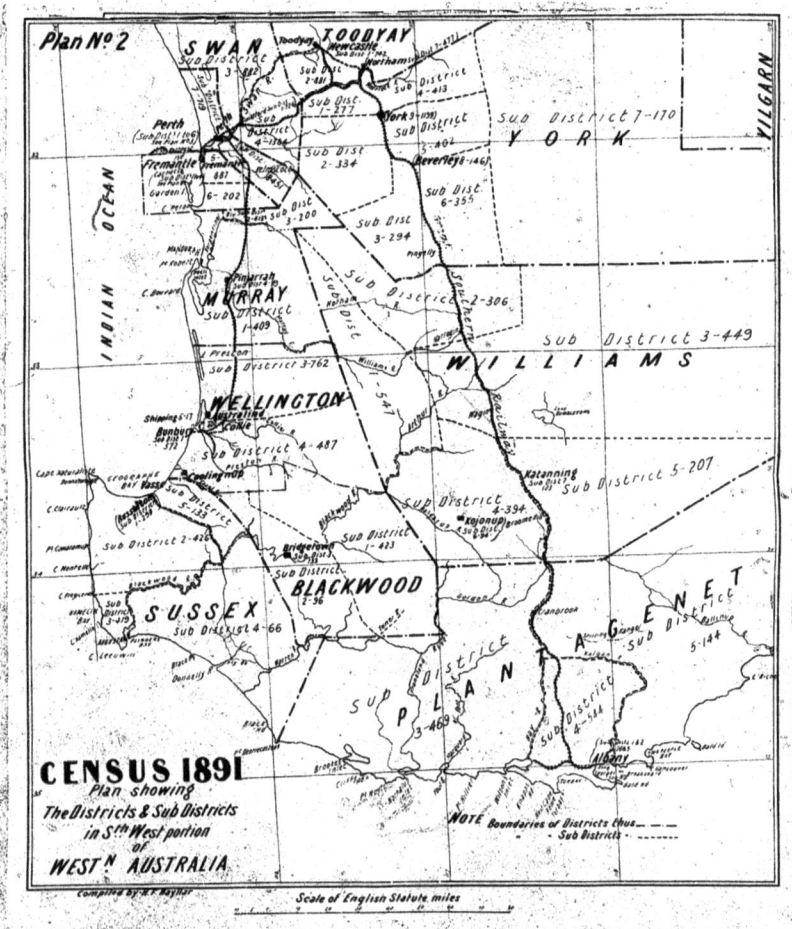

Western Australian census map of 1891 showing the District of Plantagenet

These guidelines divided Aboriginal people into the two distinct groups of those employed and therefore considered both useful and identifiable, and the remainder whose lifestyle placed them outside of the settler economy and whose numbers could only be estimated by a process that was found to be too unreliable to allow the information to be tabulated in an official report. W. H. Graham's 1880 estimate of 200 from Kojonup and Eticup provides a very rare indication from this period (and is also valuable because it shows that he believed Aboriginal numbers had fallen dramatically from his 1859 estimate of 500 from the same area).[11]

The 1881 census indicated that there were 180 Aboriginal people employed by Europeans in Albany's hinterland in 1881, 108 of whom were men.[12] The town of Albany's European population numbered 1,024, while the rural European population numbered 619 of whom 293 were adult men (the number of adult women was not recorded).[13] There was still only a very limited amount of agricultural activity in the Plantagenet District – incredibly the census shows that only 886 acres were cleared of native vegetation. A total of 257 European men were employed in 'Agricultural, Horticultural, and Pastoral pursuits', and it is safe to assume that the great majority of these were involved with the pastoral industry.[14]

A notable and surprising statistic is that only two convicts holding tickets of leave, together with another two with conditional pardons, resided in the rural area of Plantagenet in 1881.[15] Evidently, a major exodus of transported men from the region had taken place since the mid 1850s, when official figures showed that 348 were living in the Plantagenet District. It is difficult to accept the accuracy of the 1881 figures showing only four transported men in an adult male population of 293, since the Mount Barker Police frequently reported finding expirees who had died in the bush between 1879 and 1894.[16]

This was a time when many European men were living solitary and unsettled lives, poignantly illustrated by the fact that the overwhelming majority of letters written by Mount Barker police officers during the period were concerned with enquiries about the whereabouts of a missing family member or friend. Quite possibly there were more transported men in the district than the four counted in the census, but their lonely and isolated lifestyle meant that their presence went officially unnoticed. The old Williams cemetery just off the Albany Highway bears striking testimony to the harshness of the lives of some ex-convicts years after receiving their freedom. A small corner of the graveyard holds the graves of ten men identified by a nearby plaque as convicts – three are listed as having been murdered (the killer of one of these men is reported to be one of the ten) while a fourth man is recorded as a suicide.

Although Tilbrook's detailed genealogical tables published in her 1983 book *Nyungar Tradition* show that several transported men lived with Aboriginal women in the Albany hinterland, the frequently asserted claim that Western Australian rural areas long remained havens for large numbers of convicts following the end of transportation in 1868 is not supported by the 1881 figures for the Plantagenet District.[17] Many had spent time in the district, but few stayed in the long term. It is also noteworthy, and very relevant to European–Aboriginal relations that the overwhelming majority of the rural-dwelling European male population were unmarried: of the 293 adult men living and working in the bush in 1881, 230 were single.[18]

Ten years later, the census of 1891 – the first conducted following the granting of responsible government in the previous year – pointed out that although Aboriginal people were excluded from the general tables:

Nevertheless, it appears to be manifestly unfair not to recognise our civilised natives as a portion of our population. A few of them, as a glance at the portion of the Report devoted to them will show, are able to read and write, and profess the religion of the country; many are producers of our exports, and contributors to our revenue and expenditure, and all of them are, to a greater or less extent, consumers of our imports. However, as the Constitution Act of 1889 makes distinct reference to the population of Western Australia, 'exclusive of aborigines', it would not have been possible to add them to our numbers on the present occasion.[19]

Fortunately, the 1889 Act had not been interpreted as totally precluding the gathering of information about Aboriginal people in future censuses, but as a requirement that any such information be separated from statistics pertaining to the settler population:

> The sub-enumerators were instructed to return upon the schedules, as completely as possible, particulars concerning the black population actually in the employ of the white; those found in the immediate vicinity of the chief towns; and those met with roaming from one station to another.[20]

The particulars of the colony's 'full blood' Aboriginal population selected for the census included the numbers, ages, colony of birth, religion and occupation of those that fitted these criteria. For the first time information was listed separately about the colony's 'half-caste' population, even though the 575 Western Australian people counted in this category were treated as Europeans for census purposes. The official reason for publishing this extracted information was that statisticians from other countries might have considered it desirable.[21] Although the terms 'full blood' and 'half-caste' have long been superseded, I have not altered the descriptions when directly quoting documents from the period.

The figures showed that of the 5,670 'civilised natives' living in the colony in 1891, 189 lived in the Magisterial District of Plantagenet, but there is no separate information about the number of these who were residing in the town of Albany.[22] Sixty-five male and 124 female Aboriginal people in total were listed (excluding those enumerated under the 'half-caste' category) of whom thirty-one males and seventeen females were described as 'rovers' – people 'roaming from one station to another' – whose employment status is not made clear. Only four infants were listed. Of the ninety-three male 'Wage Earners', twenty-five worked as shepherds, fifty-six as 'Station and Farm Servants', six as police assistants and six as kangaroo hunters. Forty-four women were employed as 'Wage Earners': thirty-one worked as shepherds, seven as house servants, four as 'Station and Farm Servants' and two as kangaroo hunters.[23]

All were categorised as unable either to read or write, scarcely surprising when one notes that only seventeen people were literate of a colony-wide Aboriginal population listed as comprising 5,670 people.[24] The long-term failure of earlier European attempts to Christianise Plantagenet's Aboriginal population is graphically illustrated by the statistic that all but one of the 189 inhabitants were given the designation 'Pagan' as their religion – a fact the statistician regarded as 'disappointing'. Clearly, Aboriginal spirituality was granted no official recognition by those who framed the questions.

An official comment in the Census Report of 1891 pointed out that the colony-wide proportion of Aboriginal children younger than one year was less than one quarter of the figure regarded as necessary for long-term population stability:

...despite the kindness exercised towards them as regards food and clothing, and the laws which prevent the sale of intoxicants to them, [the colony's Aboriginal population] are dying out as the march of civilisation advances.[25]

The situation in Plantagenet was even worse than that of the colony as a whole – in 1891 only one Aboriginal child was recorded as being younger than one year old although the proportion of the local Noongar population under ten years of age matched that of the larger group.[26]

Forty-five of Plantagenet's inhabitants were described as 'half-castes'. None was categorised as being over fifty years of age although this may be misleading since seven were placed in the 'Not Stated' age category. Assuming few or none of the people in this category were over fifty years old in 1891, the figures show that an average of between one and two surviving children had been born per year since 1860. This would indicate that by 1881 the original children of mixed descent noted in the very early years of the settlement at Albany had either died or moved away from the region. It appears from the census report that very few children of mixed descent were born in the region in the period between the departure of the sealers and the arrival of convicts in the 1850s. However, the problems associated with data collection, and the very significant losses due to disease, make this uncertain.

The churches proved more successful with this group of part-descent Aboriginal people: fourteen described themselves as belonging to one or other of the Christian denominations, while the remaining thirty-one were listed as pagans. It is very likely that this connection with Christianity reflected a degree of identification with European society by those who claimed a denominational affiliation.

The European and mixed-descent population of Western Australia reached 49,782 in 1891.[27] The town population of Albany had grown to 2,655, while a further 1,498 lived in the remainder of the Plantagenet District, more than double the number of the previous census.[28] The percentage of adult males in the rural population had remained almost constant since the 1881 census – 700 from a total of 1,498. This census took place during a time of economic transition in the region to Albany's north: the railway had opened for business two years earlier, yet the promised agricultural boom was still in the future. The area of cleared land still remained almost negligible – a total of 2,420 acres, which represented only 0.012 per cent of the entire Plantagenet area of around 20,000,000 acres.[29]

In 1901, Western Australia conducted its first census since Federation. The Federal Attorney General gave advice to the effect that the initial intention to exclude Aboriginal people completely was unconstitutional, and that 'half-castes are not Aboriginal natives within the meaning of Section 127 of the Commonwealth Act, and should therefore be included'.[30] This directive was followed, but a decision was taken not to ignore the state's full-descent Aboriginal population entirely. Instead, the report published separate statistics for those Aboriginal people of full descent who either were employed by settlers or were living 'in close proximity to the settlements of the whites'.[31] Information gathered from and about people of mixed descent was included with the European figures, but was also used to create separate tables which allow us to gain an insight into the numbers of Aboriginal people living in Albany and its hinterland at the dawn of the new century.

The town of Albany's population in 1901 included 3,591 non-Aboriginal people, together with only three people of mixed descent and ten who were listed as 'Aborigines'.[32] A police report from Albany dated 1899 listed the following Aboriginal people who were living at Albany and given blankets during that year: Polly Pulkett, Tommy King, Bonaparte, Dicky Bumblefoot, Jackbone alias Polly, and Billy.[33] By 1905 Tommy King was in a feeble state, and a concerned citizen wrote to the Government Resident at Albany pointing out that he needed nourishing food such as eggs and milk, but would not go into hospital where these would be available. The letter was forwarded to the Aborigines Department, and the extra rations were approved.[34]

There is very little information in unofficial sources from this period about the number of Aboriginal people living in the town of Albany, apart from a newspaper report of the celebration of Queen Victoria's Jubilee in 1897 noting that twenty local Aborigines, including children, had each received a gift of food valued at ten shillings.[35]

Effectively, the rapidly growing port had become an almost completely European town. The initial intention that Albany's settlers should train Aboriginal people to work in their homes as domestic servants had come to naught – although 123 people were listed as working in that capacity it is evident from the census figures that all or nearly all of these were of non-Aboriginal descent.[36]

Only sixty-seven 'full-blooded' Aboriginal people were listed as either employed or living in the immediate vicinity of European settlements in the rural portion of the Magisterial District of Plantagenet in 1901.[37] This figure is significantly less than the 1891 count of 189 and supports Hayward's contention that Noongars found themselves less in demand as employees with the advent of the railway and the resultant large increase in the number and availability of European rural workers. A letter from the Government Resident at Albany points to another growing problem for Aboriginal workers. On his Mount Barker property, Andrew Muir had for fourteen years employed as shepherds an ex-convict named Reuben Wheeler, together with his Aboriginal wife and four children. By 1905 Muir had fenced his holding, and had no further need to employ shepherds. This action, typical of what was now occurring, left the family destitute and on government rations.

By this time disease was no longer the dramatic killer of Aboriginal people that it had been in the early and mid decades of European settlement, and the major decline in the number of those in close contact with settlers implies that many had withdrawn into the still vast area of uncleared bush to return to a more traditional way of life. Similarly, the number of people of mixed descent living in Plantagenet fell from forty-five in 1891 to only twenty-three in the 1901 census.[38] It is reasonable to assume that many of the people present in 1891 had accompanied the group who had moved away from close contact with the growing number of settlers coming into the area to take up their new farms. In her history of Cranbrook, Maxine Laurie stated that this movement had begun in the 1870s, as a change in Aboriginal attitudes led to a retreat into the almost untouched areas west of the Gordon and Frankland Rivers.[39]

None of the three censuses should be regarded as providing definitive figures for the total number of Aboriginal people living in either the colony as a whole or in Albany's hinterland. In 1896 the Governor, Sir Gerard Smith, noted that there were '15,000 or more natives still left among us...'[40] Three years later the Chief Protector of Aborigines, Henry Prinsep, estimated a figure of 30,000 – it is obvious from these wildly differing estimates that no one had any real idea. Prinsep believed that there were 4,749 Aboriginal people employed in the south-west of the colony, 743 receiving government rations, and a further 6,690 who were living independently of Europeans. However, he made clear that his estimates did:

> *not include* [emphasis in original document] what may be called wild natives, that is those who are not generally in contact with the Europeans, or inhabiting those parts which are settled or held under pastoral lease.[41]

Prinsep did not specify whether he included the more remote areas of Albany's hinterland in this category. He reported:

> The natives of the South-Western districts are widely & sparsely scattered about among the farms and small stations, but a

great many still wander about the bush in small families, only occasionally, and perhaps never, doing any work for the whites.[42]

This departmental report is the earliest available for the period. We can be reasonably certain of the numbers of those in close contact with settlers in the Albany region. The number of those who were not will always be open to conjecture.

Undoubtedly, the coming of the Great Southern Railway brought significant changes to the relationship between the Aboriginal and European people living in the areas through which it passed. Six local governments in the region have commissioned professionally written histories, all of which devote some space to the story of Aboriginal–European relations in this period, although in every case their primary focus is on agricultural development and the creation of new towns in the midst of the virgin bush. With the exception of Laurie's 1994 history of the Shire of Cranbrook, all were written in the 1970s or 1980s when the story of Aboriginal dispossession was not necessarily considered by local government figures to be an important part of their town and district's past. Consequently, the authors fail to address the major issue of why a significant number of Aboriginal families chose the years around the turn of the century to move to camps in or around the still tiny towns along the Great Southern rail line. Given that there were still Aboriginal people alive at the time when these books were written who would have been able to remember the reasons their parents had given them for moving out of the bush, this consistent omission is tragic.

These local histories do, however, provide valuable information about some of the effects of the transition from leasehold sheep stations to freehold farmlands that took place following the building of the railway. For example, the town of Mount Barker began to take shape following the opening of the first store in 1890. At this time it consisted of only a police station, a blacksmith's, a hotel and the new store, but the die was cast and by 1903 the town and district had a settler population of 741, rising to 930 three years later. Numerous farmers began apple orchards and by 1903 fruit was being exported to England.[43] Other small settlements grew up around the sidings on the Great Southern line, and several of these soon boasted a hotel, one or more stores, a football team, and the limited range of other buildings and services that was to become typical of small south-western towns.

In 1886, the Western Australian Parliament passed the Aborigines Protection Act, setting up the Aborigines Protection Board.[44] This Act marked the first time that Aboriginal employees in south-west Western Australia were afforded special protection in their conditions of employment. Previously, they had the same protection as other employees, but experience had shown that many had lacked the legal sophistication to make use of the law's provisions.[45] The new Act provided for the appointment of police officers as protectors in relatively remote areas such as Mount Barker, with responsibilities including the provision of blankets (ironically boldly striped in the red, white and blue colours of the imperial dispossessing power) and rations, the supervision of employment contracts, and the protection of the legal rights of Aboriginal people in their area. Police were also required to supervise the distribution of limited relief and medical care to destitute Aborigines. When responsible government was granted in 1890, the responsibility for Aboriginal affairs was retained by a British Government concerned about Western Australia's poor treatment of its Aboriginal inhabitants, and the Board remained in place.[46] The Act excluded 'half-castes' from its provisions unless they habitually associated with full-descent Aboriginal people.

The Mount Barker Police Daily Occurrence Books for the period give limited detail about police involvement with Aboriginal people during this time of transition. As in the earlier years discussed in the previous chapter, Aboriginal affairs were not the prime focus of the officers stationed in the town, and the Occurrence Books for the 1880s show that very little police work was associated with crimes committed by or against Aborigines. The 1890s volumes tell a similar story, with those covering the period 17 June 1893 to 25 April 1896 containing no reference at all to any involvement with Aboriginal people in the carrying out of duties throughout the vast territory for which the Mount Barker Police were responsible.

The Correspondence and Report Books from the Mount Barker Police Station are more useful, although their value to a study of the period is limited by the fact that the two volumes held by the State Records Office cover only the years between 1893 and 1910. Most of the official correspondence to and from the police at Mount Barker during the 1890s concerning Aboriginal people dealt with the rationing of the few Aboriginal people who were either not employed and were unable to care for themselves, or women and children considered at serious risk of hunger because of the death of one or more of their menfolk. These records show that it was not only the police who were supplying government rations. At Jerramungup in 1896, A. Y. Hassell requested compensation for the expenses incurred in provisioning four Aboriginal women and five children following the death of the men who had been taking care of them.[47] In this and other cases, it was obviously either observed or assumed that the Aboriginal social network had broken down to the degree that such unfortunate people would not be provided for without rationing. Constable Wall, who had by this time spent years stationed at Mount Barker, certainly believed this to be so and stated that without rationing 'they will be completely destitute and starved'.[48] The report of the Police Department for 1889 included:

> Numbers of the farms and stations have two or three elderly natives working about, and probably as many old ones past work. The cost of relief in the South-Western Districts does not exceed

6d. a head, and is often lower; but when we consider 6d. will generally provide each individual with 14 lbs flour, 2 lbs sugar, and ¼ lb tea per week, it seems enough. Natives do not always require meat, but when they do, they can take it instead of flour.[49]

Some Aborigines approached the Police Station for assistance during periods of temporary difficulty:

Ab native Peter Chillinget made his way here last night he is suffering from a bad left foot which prevents him from being able to get his living he also has a woman name Maudy they require rations until he recovers which I am giving them & will you please obtain for me the authority to Supply this man & woman with rations until he recovers he has not been in anyones employ so that he has no master to Supply him with rations.[50]

Rations were given only to those who were either infirm or in temporary difficulties, with the great majority of Aboriginal people in the district maintaining themselves by various strategies which involved working for Europeans on a casual basis while living in a more or less traditional way in the bush.

Apart from some complaints by Hassell about petty thefts, the Mount Barker Police reports from the 1890s show that there were few instances when problems between settlers and Aborigines came to the attention of police. None indicated that settlers felt in any way threatened physically by the Aboriginal people with whom they shared their lives in the bush. Although when Ethel Hassell arrived at the family property at Jerramungup in 1878, she found a building like a fort capable of withstanding a siege, with walls 'slotted for rifle fire',[51] she wrote that there never was an actual problem with the family's security.[52]

Despite the remoteness and isolation of the European properties and camps, only one violent incident involving Europeans and

Aborigines was recorded during the decade. In 1892, Mindam was arrested on a charge of absconding from Hassell's employ, but escaped custody and kept out of the way of police until mid 1897 when he was challenged by Constable Wall and two Aboriginal police assistants.[53] It was common for Aboriginal people to own a rifle for the purpose of hunting kangaroos, and Mindam used his to fire several shots at Wall who returned fire, slightly wounding the Aboriginal man.[54] Subsequently Mindam escaped from Albany hospital only to be recaptured and sentenced to a total of two years and three months on Rottnest Island.[55] Had the escapee been European, this incident could have played out in a similar way and so tells us very little about the Aboriginal–European relationship at that time. One other report was received from a settler at Bremer Bay in 1899 stating that there had been an outbreak of spearing within the local Aboriginal community, and requesting police action before someone was killed. Police replied that they would attend to the matter urgently, but no record exists of any action they may have taken.[56] The spearing outbreak presents a very clear indication that some quite foundational aspects of Aboriginal culture were still in evidence around the turn of the century – including those that had always been at complete variance with British law and cultural norms.

The employment of 'native' police assistants at Mount Barker was a continuation of a Western Australian practice that reached back as far as 1842, when Governor Hutt had provided for each Protector to employ one or two Aboriginal men in this capacity.[57] It is important to make a clear distinction between the ways these police assistants were employed in the Albany region and the very different experience in eastern Australia where Reynolds estimates that one in four Aboriginal deaths due to frontier skirmishing was caused by Aboriginal police.[58] My research has not identified any deaths in the Albany region due to actions by Aboriginal police assistants, but a degree of resentment towards them remains among some in the local Aboriginal community. Hazel Brown, an Elder with extensive links to the Great Southern region, describes them as traitors: 'I hate the white man who put the guns in my grandfather's hands, so they could get control over Noongars, and gave him the chains, so he could chain them up'.[59]

Two items in the Mount Barker Police records from the 1890s refer to the practice of placing Aboriginal offenders on neck chains when they were being brought in to the station from outlying areas after having been arrested by police on mounted patrol. The first mentions the capture of two offenders at Jerramungup in 1892. Because one of the men was ill, and because both of 'the two escapees are civilised, and not such that one would consider it necessary to chain [them] by the neck', the two were given a degree of freedom which they turned to their advantage by escaping police custody.[60] The only other reference to the practice concerned a group of Aboriginal prisoners who were neck-chained at night while their police escorts slept. When the police awoke they found that their charges had slipped out of the chains and handcuffs and escaped into the bush.[61] The 1892 letter implies that neck-chaining was more widespread and routine than the records show. Circular Order 6/558 issued by the Superintendent of Police in 1878 instructed police to desist from chaining Aboriginal prisoners by the neck unless they were 'of a desperate character', or were being brought in from a considerable distance. The latter certainly was often the case at Mount Barker, where police found neck-chaining the only practical method of allowing Aboriginal prisoners some freedom of movement while ensuring they did not escape custody during journeys that might take several days.

It also represents evidence that the police at Mount Barker were categorising Aborigines according to their degree of 'civilisation', and were not afraid to note officially the fact that their treatment varied as a result. Obviously, by the 1890s there was a diversity of Aboriginal experience in the region to Albany's north, with some Aboriginal people still living a lifestyle that was regarded (by the police at least) as far removed from that of Europeans in the district. The records do not make clear whether this was because of individual or family choice, or because of the remoteness of some areas from European influence.

The records from the Mount Barker Police Station reflect some of the important changes in the settler–Aboriginal relationship that were occurring in the hinterland of Albany as the twentieth century began; regrettably, they only partially explain *why* the changes happened. As previously mentioned, the major change that took place was that for reasons not fully accounted for by the published histories or the available Aboriginal or settler oral traditions, some Aboriginal families and individuals began to congregate in and around some of the new towns and sidings along the rail line. This change involved a move away from the modified yet still very traditional lifestyle that had evolved as the region's Noongar people adapted to the scattered but significant Europeans who had intruded upon their land since the early 1830s. It would be wrong to suggest that this 'coming in' marked the end of Aboriginal tradition and culture, but there can be no doubt that it brought far-reaching change to the Aboriginal people involved and to the relationship they shared with the rapidly growing European population.[62]

There is a widespread belief that Aboriginal reserves were established almost immediately following the opening of the railway, and that police moved people onto them with no consultation or choice being involved. This erroneous view is supported by the *Kinjarling* Aboriginal heritage report prepared for the City of Albany and the Department of Indigenous Affairs in 2005:

> During the latter part of the 19th century Aboriginal people had little choice about where they could reside. Authorities strictly

controlled people's lives restricting their movements and forcing them onto reserves and town fringe camps.[63]

Certainly, Henry Prinsep, Chief Protector of Aborigines in W.A. between 1898 and 1907, *wanted* to have this power, but he was constrained by the fact that no legislation existed that would have permitted such actions (see Prinsep's letter written in 1904, p. 272). The *Aborigines Protection Act 1886* allowed a Justice of the Peace to ask any Aboriginal person who was not decently clothed to leave a town forthwith, but this was the extent of official authority in enforcing where Aboriginal people lived. Under the *Waste Lands Act 1842 (Imperial)*, the Governor had the power to set aside land for reserves (the first Aboriginal reserve was created in 1874 at New Norcia) but Aboriginal people could not legally be compelled to live on them.[64] Prinsep drew up a Bill in 1900 that would have allowed the gazetting of town-sites as areas where Aborigines were to be prevented by law from entering, while reserves were to be established to which they could be removed and indefinitely detained. Premier John Forrest refused to place such a repressive Bill before Parliament, stating that the reserves would 'make Prisoners of the poor people in their own country. For their own good it would be said'.[65]

Forrest saw himself as a friend of Aboriginal people, having grown up at Bunbury in an era when they were still numerous, and having appreciated the essential part Aboriginal guides played in his explorations in the colony's interior. However, Forrest was a strong believer in Social Darwinism and held very paternalistic opinions about how Aboriginal policy should proceed. His principal aim was to reduce expenditure, having reached the conclusion that over-generous ration scales were encouraging dependence rather than self-reliance. In 1898, he halved the amount of meat, flour and tea, a harsh policy which was not altered until the late 1920s. Forrest's role in the treatment of Aboriginal people is somewhat enigmatic; Anna Haebich presents a picture of a man who had a genuine sympathy for their position as the original owners of the land, and who was prepared to meet Aboriginal people at the rear of his own home to discuss their grievances. He was also prepared to abandon these sympathies if it suited his own political ends.[66]

The fact that Forrest prevented Prinsep's Bill from going before Parliament meant that removal and relocation of Aboriginal people in the nineteenth century would have been illegal, and there is no evidence that it took place until the passage of the repressive 1905 Act allowed for the setting up of 'small isolated camping reserves where the Aborigines could be kept together, away from the white community and under the eyes of the local police'.[67] Aborigines certainly *were* removed to reserves, but this took place decades after the railway was built.

There was no single reason why a significant number of Aboriginal families moved closer to the new settlements prior to 1905. It would appear that those who chose to do so acted in response to a mix of pressures caused by increasing land allocation and clearing, and the perceived social and economic benefits that living near the newly established settlements would provide. Aboriginal people had a degree of choice about where they lived at this time that was not always available to them in later years.

Pressures built up on Aboriginal families towards the end of the 1890s, not all of which were due to the opening of the railway. In 1899, the government became concerned that kangaroos in the south-west were being hunted in numbers that could lead to extinction, and imposed strict controls on commercial hunting. Numbers of Aborigines, including those who worked from time to time for pastoralists, had supported their families by using their hunting skills to trap or shoot kangaroos and selling the skins – a practice that was now illegal. Haebich has described how many Aboriginal people camped for extended periods in the bush along the Tone, Gordon and Frankland rivers, and in the heavily forested areas to the west, allowing either complete or partial economic independence from employment.[68] The 1891 census identified only eight Aboriginal kangaroo hunters, but these would have been employees of European shooters. The number of those living with their families and working on their own account is unknown, but was probably quite significant. Lilly Hayward has described how her family from around Kojonup hunted kangaroos using guns and dogs and sold the skins.[69] Although the new regulation against commercial hunting of kangaroos did not apply to the widespread practice of taking possums for their valuable skins, it did make it more difficult to support a family continuing to live in the bush. The hunting of possums was a very significant economic enterprise around the turn of the century – in 1906, for example, Western Australia exported over four million skins which were sold on the world market as skunk, beaver or Adelaide chinchilla.[70]

The other obvious factor which contributed to Aboriginal families being pushed off their traditional land at this time was the allocation and clearing of blocks for farming. The granting of land to large numbers of new settlers, each of whom aspired to gaining freehold title to his relatively small farm once the conditions of the government had been met, radically altered the way Europeans viewed the land and its Aboriginal inhabitants. As mentioned earlier, by 1890 some of the pastoralists were the third generation on their properties, having grown up with a degree of familiarity with the region's Aboriginal families.[71] New settlers, few of whom were from the Albany region,[72] tended to look less sympathetically at the unfamiliar lifestyle of a group of people that the prevalent philosophy of Social Darwinism condemned to the inevitable fate of extinction. This idea of imminent extinction comes through clearly in an article in the *Albany Advertiser* published in the edition of 9 August 1898 recording the death of 'Blind Bobby': 'The natives are dying out fast in this district, and in a few years they must become extinct'.

A prominent theme running through all of the local shire histories is the understandable desire of new settlers to establish a degree of pride in their new town and district, a desire especially keenly felt by those who had come from established prosperous and socially conservative farming districts in South Australia and the eastern states. To settlers intent upon moving as quickly as possible from a frontier situation to one of middle-class landed respectability, there was a sense that Aboriginal people represented a somewhat embarrassing past and should speedily adapt to the new reality by conforming in actions and appearance to the lower socioeconomic section of rural settler society. This pressure, and the unwillingness of Noongar people to conform to such unrealistic expectations, proved counterproductive to the maintenance of good relations between the two groups.

The region's pastoralists had always been well aware that they or their forebears had moved their families and flocks onto land that had been owned by Aboriginal people for millennia, and frequently felt some resulting sense of obligation. New settlers, if they thought about it at all, were able to soothe their consciences with the convenient belief that the farms they now owned had no legal or moral attachment to Aboriginal people since the land had been purchased from the government in a normal business transaction. If there was any responsibility towards the original owners, it should be borne by the pastoralists who had pioneered the land and by those in authority who had decided to open the region for closer settlement. For the first time, there was a distinct lack of connection between those occupying land and any real sense of responsibility for their role in the continuing dispossession of its original owners.

It was not only a change of attitude that the new settlers brought to the ongoing Aboriginal–European relationship. Pastoral land use had certainly adversely affected Aboriginal traditional food sources, but to nowhere near the extent that quickly occurred as agriculture and the grazing of stock on large areas of cleared or semi-cleared land became significant forms of land use. It was frequently in the same areas, such as the numerous pockets of jam tree country that were favoured by both Aboriginal food gatherers and European farmers. The early and strong focus upon the selection and clearing of these vital and productive areas of land meant that Aboriginal people were affected much more fundamentally than a simple assessment of the proportion of the total area represented by annual clearing statistics would appear to indicate. Aboriginal access to water sources, never numerous throughout much of the region, also came under increasing pressure as the European population grew, and as fences and the new settlers' sense of exclusive land ownership caused Noongars increasingly to be regarded as intruders upon private property.[73] Shifts in European attitudes coincided with changes to the landscape itself, and together these fundamentally altered how the region's Aboriginal and European residents interacted with each other.

In making an assessment of the effects closer settlement had upon the lifestyle of Aborigines, and upon the choices they made in response, it is essential to address some of the complexities involved in what actually took place regarding the various forms of European land use in the areas opened up in Albany's hinterland. Once allocated, the land did not pass overnight from virgin bush to the fully cleared, fenced and developed farmland that one sees today. An examination of the comprehensive information published annually in the Western Australian *Blue Book* Statistical Registers of the period provides an informed appreciation of the changes in vegetation that took place during the years following the allocation of much of the land to Albany's north. Some of the statistics are quite surprising, and contradict any simplistic assumption that land clearing was the only factor that caused Aboriginal people to move out of the bush and into camps in close proximity to the new towns along the rail line.

By 1901, twelve years after the Great Southern line opened, only about 15,000 acres had been cleared in the vast Magisterial District of Plantagenet.[74] Taking the 30,000 acres designated as the Tenterden District as an example, sixty-one lots of between 100 and 368 acres were surveyed, but only 296 acres had been purchased. This snail's pace of development is explicable by further statistics from the *Blue Book* of 1895. At a time when the cost of clearing land at Tenterden was estimated to be £4 per acre – twice the amount Justice Higgins in 1907 set as the minimum weekly wage for an unskilled worker – the average wheat yield for Plantagenet in 1894 was an abysmal 4.8 bushels per acre, approximately one-tenth of the yields commonly achieved by farmers in that district today.[75] These figures illustrate that it was simply uneconomical to proceed at a quicker pace, given the poor nature of the soil and the cost of clearing the natural vegetation. The *Blue Book* of 1910 showed that the revised and by then considerably smaller District of Plantagenet, an area of approximately 3,500,000 acres south of Cranbrook and parallel to the south coast as far east as Hopetoun, was still overwhelmingly virgin bush. Only 12,797 acres had been cleared.[76] Most of the early agricultural development made possible by the railway took place in the more fertile and less densely forested area to the north of the town of Cranbrook, newly designated for statistical purposes as the District of Tambellup and comprising an area of about 3,000,000 acres. Even in this more favoured region, farmers had cleared only 44,835 acres by 1910.[77]

At first glance these figures would appear to suggest that by 1905 there was only minimal pressure from agricultural development upon the virgin bush that the region's Noongar population required to maintain many elements of their traditional way of life. Considerably less than 1 per cent of Albany's hinterland was described as 'cleared'. However, one other very significant statistic from the 1901 *Blue Book* gives a clue why this was actually far from being the case. By that year, 130,324 acres in the old District of Plantagenet were listed by their new owners as having been ringbarked, a practice that slowly killed the trees although it left them standing as bare, grey trunks. By 1910, almost 500,000 acres in the revised districts of Tambellup and Plantagenet were in this condition.[78] Ringbarking dramatically promoted the growth of grasses among the natural understorey which was soon destroyed by grazing pressure from the increased numbers of sheep and cattle.[79] Once the stock-carrying capacity of the land increased, farmers built fences to prevent neighbours' stock utilising the grass.[80] Not only did these fences have the psychological effect of clearly and authoritatively marking the enclosed area as private property, they also eliminated the need for shepherds.

Some of these shepherds were Aboriginal or were supporting an Aboriginal family. When Andrew Muir fenced his Mount Barker property in 1905 he put off an ex-convict named Reuben Wheeler who had worked for him for fourteen years while looking after his Aboriginal wife and four children. The Government Resident at Albany described how the family had consequently become destitute and dependent on meat, flour and grocery rations.[81]

Albany's hinterland might not have had large areas completely cleared by the turn of the century, but much of the land along the Great Southern line was in a condition greatly altered from its natural state. This had a very significant and devastating effect upon a wide variety of Aboriginal food resources. Pastoralism had certainly adversely affected the supply of Aboriginal food, but the changes wrought by clearing and ringbarking were far reaching and permanent. Also, farmers understandably built their homes near reliable sources of fresh water, and the areas around the house were then commonly cleared and fenced for horses and the family cow. This restricted Aboriginal people's access to water, making a traditional lifestyle increasingly difficult.

Apart from these pressures there were several factors that led some Aboriginal families to *wish* to live closer to the new settlements such as Tambellup and Cranbrook. Mount Barker Police Station records make it clear that significant numbers of European labourers arrived in the new towns looking for employment, lessening the demand for Aboriginal labour on the pastoral properties that were still in existence. However, the new settlers still required some Aboriginal workers and the towns provided a base where employment could conveniently be arranged. The coming of the railway provided relatively easy access to the Albany Hospital (or to the major hospital at Perth in more serious cases), and the Daily Occurrence books show that local police believed some Aboriginal people moved close to town in order to make use of the train for this purpose. This provides a strong indication that for some Aboriginal people at least, the era of reliance solely upon traditional medicine was passing. The new towns also became attractive because of the access they provided to food and other supplies that could be purchased with the proceeds from employment and the sale of possum skins. Sport may also have played a role. Eric Hayward notes that football teams were formed in towns such as Mount Barker and Broomehill in the years around the turn of the century and, although he states that few Aboriginal men were encouraged to join these teams during their first decade or so, his research indicates that several were playing as early as 1904.[82]

Another powerful reason why a number of Aboriginal people chose to set up camps near the towns was to access rations distributed to the aged and infirm by police acting as agents of the Aborigines Department. Until halved by the Forrest administration in 1898 (because Forrest believed that the Aborigines Protection Board ration system had made Aborigines 'lazy') the weekly ration comprised twenty pounds of flour or its equivalent monetary value in meat, three pounds of sugar and half a pound of tea. This had cost the government one shilling per head per day.[83] As hotels and stores opened, alcohol and tobacco became easier to obtain, providing another reason for families to move their camps closer to town. 'Half-castes' were permitted to buy alcohol prior to 1902, under the provisions of the *Wines, Beer and Spirit Sale Act (1880)*, and Prinsep agreed with the police that they were illegally supplying other Aboriginal people in the south-west.[84]

It is not possible to state with certainty the role alcohol played in the lives of Aborigines living in Albany's hinterland at this time. There is little in the police and court records, or the very numerous Albany newspaper reports of the strong local temperance movement, to indicate that excess drinking by Aborigines was considered a problem. It would appear that tobacco and alcohol were simply two more significant items in a list of goods and services whose ready availability in the new towns proved attractive to Aboriginal people, as well as to settlers.

Historian Tim Rowse has described this attraction as 'a colonialism not of guns and disease but of goods and desires, yet the results seemed just as devastating'.[85] Rowse was referring to Central Australia in the 1930s, where Stanner noted:

> They [the Aboriginal people of the area] are tending to drift away from their traditional tribal lands to live near white settlements where they can secure more readily the tobacco, tea, sugar, new foods, clothing and manufactured articles they have learned to value and crave.[86]

Central Australia in the 1930s is a long way from the Albany region of thirty or forty years earlier, yet it is possible to see strong similarities in the forces at work in both times and places. Reynolds notes that this movement to the outskirts of towns occurred in many parts of Australia, and represented a seeking after 'a satisfactory synthesis between the old ways and the new'.[87]

The setting up of a camp at Torbay about 15 kilometres west of Albany in 1890 appears to be an example of this attraction. About twenty Aboriginal people moved to a site near the newly opened railway line where a European woman was accused by 'Gentile' in a letter to the *Australian Advertiser* of openly supplying sly grog.[88] This is virtually the only late-nineteenth-century reference to Aborigines living west of the town of Albany that I have been able to locate, apart from an 1888 report in the *Albany Mail* stating, 'There are but few natives in the western part of the district'.[89]

The movement into towns, or to camps in close proximity to towns, was not complete at this time – indeed, Haebich's research led her to conclude that the 'marked movement of Aboriginal families out of the bush and into the permanent camps in the wheat-belt towns' took place from 1911.[90] While this is undoubtedly true with respect to the large-scale movement in south-western Australia to which she referred, the records show that in towns along the Great Southern line the process began much earlier. In 1905, P. C. McNamara ordered 'a large number of Aboriginal Natives from the Country districts' to move their camp (situated in the town of Mount Barker) to a new camp a mile north of the town on the Perth Road. McNamara appears to have anticipated the powers that would become available to police under the new Aborigines Act which was reserved on 23 December 1905 but did not receive royal assent until 4 April the following year.[91]

We can see from this report that a significant number of Aborigines at Mount Barker had made their choice to move out of the bush and into much closer proximity with their new neighbours at some time prior to the report being made. That such a profound and publicly visible shift in the lifestyle of the region's Noongar people could be well underway by 1905, yet be virtually ignored by those writing official reports at the time at every level of government, is strong evidence for the absence of European interest in their fate.

Around the turn of the century some Aboriginal people chose to work on a more or less permanent basis for pastoralists such as Ednie Hassell at Warriup Station about 65 kilometres east of Albany. The property's diaries from the early 1900s show that Dicky Bumblefoot and his wife worked regularly for extended periods, while others such as Cudgel and Charley Bullfrog worked occasionally.[92]

It is evident from contemporary sources that very few Aboriginal people lived in the town of Albany during the period between 1878 and 1905. Those who chose to remain in the town's increasingly urban setting continued to make a living by giving demonstrations of spear and boomerang throwing and by selling Aboriginal curios to the many visitors who came to see what the town's new tourist industry had to offer. For the first time since settlement began, Albany's urban European population largely lost interest in their relationship with the Noongar people. Confident that the town's progress was assured, and believing that the Aborigines of the south-west were quickly dying out, the town's European inhabitants gradually adopted a more tolerant attitude towards the few remaining Aboriginal people in their midst. When Bobby Gardiner died in 1887, his passing was noted with respect and a degree of nostalgia. The *Albany Mail* carried the following obituary:

> On Wednesday morning last, at 8 a.m., passed away to the majority, one of the best-known inhabitants of Albany. 'Old Bobby Gardiner' had for a number of years sold opossum rugs, boomerangs, and other native weapons and curios to 'new chums', and P&O passengers generally, and many persons will miss the old man's well-known figure standing near Mr Hassell's store or the Freemasons' Hotel, a position he took up with his wares in all weathers on the signalling of the arrival of a mail boat. Bobby was a kindly but somewhat eccentric old man, and was very popular in the town of which he was one of the old links, now fast breaking away, that joined its present to its past.[93]

Only three Aboriginal people were recorded as employed in the town of Albany in 1881, while 180 were in employment in the rural portion of the Plantagenet District, and it is reasonable to assume that these figures reflect the pattern of location of the region's Aboriginal people at that time.[94] The census of 1891 provides no information about Aborigines within the town precincts. Only thirteen people of Aboriginal descent were listed as residents of the town of Albany in the 1901 census – by then they were not even the largest non-European group, being significantly outnumbered by the Chinese with a population of forty-one.[95] An article about celebrations held at Albany to celebrate Queen Victoria's Jubilee in 1897 provides another indication that the town's Aboriginal population was very small; 'eight natives, the last of their race in this district' assembled to receive blankets and other gifts.[96] Since the same newspaper only nine days earlier had mentioned the presence of twenty Aboriginal people, including children, at the same event it would appear that the eight mentioned in the later report were all adults.

As we have seen, at least as early as 1857, numbers of Aboriginal people had made a practice of meeting new arrivals at the town's jetty dressed in kangaroo skins and heavily bedaubed with ochre and pipeclay. Displays of spear and boomerang throwing were given in return for money but tourists, impressed though they were by the skills shown, tended to see the enterprise as destructive of Aboriginal dignity. Thirty years later, for example, Lady Anna Brassey, wife of a wealthy English parliamentarian, called at Albany and wrote: 'It was a cold showery morning when we landed to photograph a party of natives, and to see them throw boomerangs and spears. They were the most miserable-looking objects I ever beheld'.[97]

In 1890, the poet Henry Lawson described in amused detail a performance staged at the jetty by an Aboriginal man, 'William Rex' (almost certainly Tommy King, whose Aboriginal name was Wandinyilmernong).[98] The terms and tone used by Lawson are far from flattering to 'William' and his female companions, although he believed he could detect a wink, 'momentarily closing down the whitewashed lid of the awful bloodshot optic', that indicated the performer was far more sophisticated than Lawson's fellow tourists gave him credit for.[99] The standard tour evidently included a visit to the camp on the town's northern outskirts, where tourists could observe 'where they live in a most primitive fashion', and where they could hear the nearest neighbour tell how 'they come daily to her house for water and scraps, but they never attempt to steal anything'.[100]

Lawson's tone throughout his article is one of amused supercili-ousness, verging on contempt for all things connected with Albany. Obviously, he expected his readers to take his observations with a generous pinch of salt. However, one of his statements points to a practice not mentioned in police records or other writings of the time from Albany:

> Things are arranged, out at the ends of the roads from King George's Sound, and in connection with native women, in various ways, which could not, very well, be set down here. Contracting parties take, or used to take, out parcels of old clothes and damaged tobacco as 'presents' to natives' roosters.[101]

It is difficult to assess the degree of importance that should be attached to Lawson's information on this point. The first part of his statement implies that the events described were still occurring, and that he personally had knowledge of them. However, the second sentence indicates that he was only repeating hearsay evidence. The light-heartedness of his tone further complicates the matter.

Lawson's description of 'William Rex' is of a man evidently enjoying his work, and this opens up the possibility that 'chiefing' was more than simply a way of making money when all other options ran out. An article written in 1927 by N. W. McKail, who claimed to have witnessed the Aboriginal entrepreneurs who met passengers disembarking at the P&O jetty, lends support to this idea. Bobby Gardiner, 'the bird man', was the first to greet the passengers with 'his cages of birds, his native weapons and all his stock in trade'. He 'harangued' them:

> Ladies and gentlemen, stop and see my wonderful collection of birds, the laughing hoopoes and the wonderful cockatoos. There is nothing in the world to beat them. It is worth your while to listen to the preaching cockatoos, the singing cockatoos and the dancing cockatoos are good to look at – the ladies, the parsons and the sailors. Now this here one is a ladies' bird; she is rather shy of men. I will stand her on her box and you can judge for yourselves. The cockatoo, a well trained bird, put her head under her wing, and shrieked out 'go away men, don't kiss me or I'll tell mother.' The parson's bird is then exhibited, and after singing part of a hymn and repeating the Lord's Prayer, is put away. The sailor's bird is then brought out. As soon as he was put on his feet he said: 'Damn, Hoist my breeches, belay there and see me dance a sailor's hornpipe.'[102]

McKail recalled Tommy King waiting until Gardiner's performance concluded before inviting the passengers to an area of vacant land where a mock fight with spears was staged. As soon as darkness fell, King lit one end of each of several boomerangs and threw them in spectacular fashion, with several in the air at once describing 'a spiral of fire'. A target was then set up and the audience rewarded those men who managed to hit it with their spears. A corroboree was next on the agenda featuring almost naked Aboriginal men with emu feather headdresses, 'fantastic designs painted on their legs and bodies with pipeclay and red ochre', and bones through their noses.[103]

Since the P&O coaling station had closed in 1880 and Bobby Gardiner died in 1887, McKail was writing about events he had witnessed more than forty years earlier, but his recollections certainly do not give the impression that the performers were lacking in enthusiasm for their work. On the contrary, they appear to have taken pride in showing some of their skill in dancing and in the use of traditional weapons to an appreciative audience.

The first Albany newspaper commenced publication in January 1883, and between then and the end of 1905, the town's newspapers carried numerous articles relating to Aboriginal people and issues, but only a relatively small number of items referred to events or people with connections to Albany.[104] Most of the reports concerning Aborigines from the region were brief accounts of local court cases written in the same style and format used for cases involving European miscreants. One of the few actual news items referred to the opening of an Aboriginal ward at the Albany Hospital in 1897.[105]

In some of the other items one is able to discern the beginning of a degree of Aboriginal participation in a range of mainstream sporting events at Albany and in the new towns along the Great Southern line. One hundred Aborigines attended a sports day at Katanning to celebrate Queen Victoria's Jubilee in 1897, although the newspaper report gives no indication about the extent to which they participated in events.[106] Bicycle and foot races were held in the same town in 1900 when at least two Aboriginal boys participated. A boys' cycle race for 'Aboriginals' was contested by Henry and Jack.[107] Two similar sporting days took place at Albany in 1902, again with Aboriginal people taking part. Jack, identified as an 'ab.nat.', won his heat of the Sheffield sprint, but was beaten in the final.[108] At a race meeting held at Kojonup in 1899, the last race was restricted to Aboriginal-owned horses ridden by Aboriginal jockeys.[109] A report of a race meeting at Mount Barker in 1902 gives strong evidence that at least one of the jockeys was Aboriginal, while 'Dick' (whose name was in inverted commas throughout the report) took three Albany wickets in a cricket match played at Mount Barker in the same year.[110] These newspaper references indicate that a degree of social integration was beginning to occur, led by Aboriginal participation in European sport – a theme explored in depth by Hayward in *No Free Kicks* with reference to a much later period in the region's history.

Rationing provided a consistent point of interaction between the town's small Aboriginal population and the local police officers whose duty it was to distribute food and blankets on behalf of the Aborigines Department. The other recorded points of interaction involved the enforcement of the law prohibiting the supply of alcohol to Aboriginal people of full descent and the policing of laws prohibiting drunkenness in public places. Albany's courts dealt with both offences on a reasonably regular basis, but the court transcripts and the small fines imposed reflect the fact that the breaches were considered to be relatively trivial.

George Olivey became one of only three employees of the Western Australian Aborigines Department when he took up his position as Travelling Inspector in 1899. He was given a number of horses and a bicycle, and set off on a series of epic journeys covering the length and breadth of the colony with the aim of ensuring that the Department's policies on Aboriginal employment were being complied with. During 1902, he travelled from Esperance to Perth via Ravensthorpe, Jerramungup, Broomehill, Katanning, Kojonup, Arthur River and Williams, making out brief reports about each place for Prinsep. His reports were broken up into a series of brief statements outlining the numbers of Aboriginal people who were either on government rations or employed on wages as shearers or station hands, or self-employed as sellers of kangaroo skins. Olivey was either unconcerned with those Aboriginal people not in close contact with Europeans, or was unable to discover any details of their whereabouts or lifestyle, for he ignored them in his reports from this region. His report on

Katanning is of particular interest since it is more comprehensive than those from other places. From the Resident Magistrate Dr Black and the local police constable, Olivey ascertained 'a good deal of information…on native matters'.[111] There were about eighty Aborigines in the district, of whom fifty or sixty were 'half-castes'. Four were on relief. His report gives a picture of a town where Aborigines were beginning to congregate:

> About ten half-caste men are employed on farms in the district clearing and shepherding, opossum hunting etc. Some of the half-castes have bought blocks of land. There are some large families – 4, 5, 6 children in some. About Christmas time 200 natives congregate at Katanning to play hockey. [A Noongar form of the game using a wooden ball and native timber sticks.] Some of the natives are also employed by the settlers, occasionally burning, etc, but only at odd times; they prefer to earn a living by hunting generally. The present law allows the half-caste to obtain liquor at hotels; often this finds its way into their camps and amongst the natives, and a disturbance is the result.[112]

The overall picture presented by Olivey is one of increasing Aboriginal involvement in the settler economy. Some, such as Jannuc, his wife and six or seven children from the Broomehill area, still lived 'away many miles in the bush' and were beyond Olivey's direct observation even though the family was in receipt of irregularly obtained rations.[113] He was satisfied that employers were meeting their obligations under the 1886 Aborigines Protection Act, but was concerned that some Aboriginal employees were also on the ration list. A. Y. Hassell at Jerramungup was singled out as an employer with the right attitude towards this practice:

> Mr Hassell said he did not recognise the claim of working women having relief blankets. Their men were paid and should

be able to find their women in clothes, etc. It is quite refreshing to meet a gentleman with these views. In many cases employers of native labour endeavour to obtain all the assistance possible from the department.[114]

Departmental policy was straightforward – Aboriginal people were expected to earn their own living, with rations only available to those who for reasons of age or infirmity were unable to work.

During this period a number of Aboriginal children were voluntarily placed in institutions by one or both of their parents, although unfortunately the records do not address why they took this action, or the pressures they may have been under to do so. Between 1868 and 1895, at least sixteen children from the Albany region were sent to the Benedictine Mission at New Norcia, 132 kilometres north of Perth. The mission's records of these admissions are not detailed (only eight children had their ages recorded) but note that the parents and guardians had 'surrendered' the children.[115] For example, Thomas Egan and Mary Mederan sent four of their children aged between three and seventeen years to New Norcia in 1876, having sent an older child in 1870. The records for the younger children state that Egan surrendered them to the Mission for a period of seven years to receive an education. Three subsequently died, but the remaining siblings were still living at the Mission twenty-three years later.[116] Thomas and Mary moved permanently to New Norcia to be close by their children. Some family members eventually returned to Albany where a number of their descendants are living today.[117]

As the nineteenth century drew to a close, Aboriginal culture retained a significant number of features from its pre-European past. Although many Aboriginal people were in employment, the frequently casual nature of farm work and the still large areas of bush allowed a continuation of hunting and foraging for food. Their way of life differed in many ways from that of their ancestors, but was nevertheless distinctively and unmistakably Noongar – their culture had adapted and changed, but the underlying principles that had always guided Aboriginal culture remained in place.

In October 1890, the Governor of Western Australia, Sir William Robinson, arrived by train at Albany to lead celebrations associated with the granting of self-government to the colony. Both of Albany's newspapers devoted a great deal of space to the official visit, and both published an account of a group of local Aborigines' approach to the Governor at a levee held at the Residency building, which still stands where Lockyer landed in 1826. During the afternoon, some of Albany's leading citizens paid their respects. Then:

> Shortly before the Governor left the Residency for the railway station, Tommy King, the boss aboriginal, who was accompanied by several of his tribe in their war paint, presented a petition, which read as follows:- 'to His Excellency Sir WILLIAM FRANCIS CLEAVER ROBINSON, KCMG., etc.
>
> 'May it please Your Excellency,-
>
> I, Tommy King, on behalf of the few remaining aboriginals of Albany, approach Your Excellency with submission and profound respect, welcoming you to our native shores. We would humbly remind Your Excellency that in the year 1829 all this country belonged to my tribe, of which I, at this date, would have been the Chief, but that Her Most Gracious Majesty the Queen was pleased to take it from us. Since that time we have been gradually deprived of our hunting grounds and nearly all of our kangaroos have been killed by the white men, and we are now in extreme poverty and a deplorable condition. Therefore, on this occasion when all the whitemen are rejoicing at Her most Gracious Majesty having given over our land to a Constitution, we would humbly ask Your Excellency to give us something that we may rejoice. A bag of flour, a box of tea, a bag of sugar, and some tobacco would

make us all very happy, and if Your Excellency will issue an order
to Sergeant Cunningham to procures us these, we shall be very
pleased and remain Your Excellency's most obedient servants.
'signed on behalf of the aboriginals of Albany,

'TOMMY KING'

It was taken as read...Tommy addressed a remonstrance to His
Excellency in somewhat the following terms: - 'Blackfellow have
land, whitefellow come take it away; blackfellow hear about
Sponsible cantonment, ought have something give blackfellow
buy flour, tea, sugar, plenty bacca'. His Excellency promised
that the matter should be seen into, and referred him to the
Government Resident.[118]

Several days later, the Resident, Rowley Loftie, met with about
twenty Aborigines, including several who were temporarily in
Albany as the accused and witnesses in a murder trial for an offence
committed at Fraser Range, and:

distributed to each aboriginal Proclamation gifts consisting of
10lbs. flour, a fair sized cake, ½ lb tea, 1 lb sugar, tobacco and
matches. Mrs and Miss Loftie supplemented these gifts with a
present of a quantity of lollies. Tommy King (boss aboriginal)
then proposed three cheers for Mr., Mrs. and Miss Loftie,
which were lustily given, and the ceremonies terminated with a
promenade of the dusky visitors through the Residency.[119]

Tommy King, whose Aboriginal name was recorded by Daisy
Bates as Wandinyilmernong, was a small boy when Lockyer
arrived in 1826, and was one of the few Aborigines who continued
to live in the Albany township for much of his life. Bates wrote
on the back of the postcard reproduced on the next page that he
was 'The last Albany native', but gave no reason to have made
such a definitive claim. It appears probable that Albany's European

Daisy Bates' copy of a postcard showing Wandinyilmernong (Tommy King)
Image courtesy of The University of Adelaide

settlers, cognisant of his claim to be the rightful owner of the area, gave him the (possibly ironical) name 'King'.

Tommy King's petition is an important document. Thirty or forty years before the civil rights agitation of the 1920s and 1930s which is commonly believed to mark the beginning of Aboriginal assertion of sovereignty in Western Australia, King was quite specifically claiming Albany as rightly belonging to his 'tribe', stating in unequivocal terms that it had been stolen by agents of the British Crown. Not only had the land been taken, the Aboriginal people had been deprived of their means of living in dignity. Given the tone of the language of the written petition, and assuming that the reporter was at least reasonably accurate in his description of the considerably less formal language used by Tommy King in his verbal address to the Governor, it appears unlikely that the petition was actually worded by King. This does not lessen the impact of the document, since there can be no doubt that he fully understood and endorsed the sentiments it expressed.[120]

Those Aboriginal leaders in Western Australia who expressed similar opinions decades later were following in the footsteps of their earlier compatriots who had personally witnessed the first British settlement in Western Australia from its beginning, and were painfully aware of the devastation it had brought to their people.

The years between 1878 and 1904 saw an unprecedented period of growth in the town and hinterland of Albany, due to the discovery of gold in the colony and the construction of a rail link between Albany and Perth. New towns sprang up along the line, and the first significant clearing of land for agriculture began. Although this brought increasing disruption to traditional Aboriginal practices, the relatively slow pace of agricultural expansion allowed these practices to continue, if in modified form. A number of Aboriginal people, for a range of reasons, chose to move to the outskirts of the new settlements as they became a minority group in their own heartland. Some stock spearing persisted and some isolated Europeans were subjected to petty theft of their property, but there were very few, if any, acts of violence that could be construed as constituting Aboriginal resistance to the increasing European presence.

The dawn of the new century saw an almost complete absence of Aboriginal people from the town of Albany and the beginning of a flood of new settlers to the growing new towns and agricultural regions to its north. Almost all of the ex-convicts had departed, and the European population in contact with the Aboriginal people increasingly became comprised of a very different type of person than many of those who had lived in the hinterland in the earlier decades. This was a period when racism grew significantly throughout the Western world, including Australia, and this led to the divisive and repressive measures that form the basis of much of the next chapter.

Chapter Seven

'To make provision for the better protection and care of the Aboriginal inhabitants of Western Australia', 1905–1926

The tragic consequences of the implementation of the 1905 Aborigines Act

The 1905 Aborigines Act proved to be one of the most socially divisive and devastating pieces of legislation ever passed by any Western Australian Parliament.[1] It remained in force until 1963, and its effects have been so pervasive and far reaching that it is practically impossible to envisage what might have been the future of Aboriginal–European relations had a different path been followed by the state's civil servants and legislators. It would be difficult to overstate the enduring effects of the 1905 Act upon the relationship between Aboriginal and non-Aboriginal people at Albany and its hinterland. Virtually every aspect of the relationship came under one or other of its sections, and the Western Australian Government, through the agency of the Aborigines Department, used it to gain almost total control over the lives of Aboriginal people in the region and throughout the state.

During the early years of the twentieth century white animosity of the most horrendous kind intensified in the south-west of the state.[2] Europeans almost universally believed that they were in the vanguard of progress, while Australian Aborigines were 'in the depths of primitivity'.[3] The belief that extinction was the inevitable outcome of the innate nature of 'primitive' people had the imprimatur of scientists from around the world, with Charles Darwin himself asserting that Australian Aborigines were an example of those doomed by their inability to change their habits. Respected Australians such as Daisy Bates and the prominent anthropologist Walter Baldwin Spencer added their voices to those proclaiming the scientific inevitability of an imminent extinction.[4] None of these advocated that this justified ill-treatment of Aboriginal people, but the arguments they espoused, together with the emphasis placed by the new Australian Federal Government on constructing and implementing the White Australia Policy, played into the hands of those whose attitude was racist at a fundamental level.

Because only a very few Aboriginal people lived in the town of Albany between 1905 and 1927, the story of Aboriginal–European interaction during the period almost entirely involves the life experiences of those living in the inland towns and districts that comprised the port town's hinterland.[5] The 1905 Act, the belated but very significant increase in the area of land clearing for farming, and the increasing intolerance of settlers towards those Noongars who chose to move in or near to the small regional towns all played crucial roles in the development of Aboriginal–European relations at this time. Official policy, based at least partly on this intolerance, led to the establishment of Carrolup Native Settlement near Katanning and the forced removal there of the town's Aboriginal inhabitants, where many remained until the settlement was closed in June 1922 and a large proportion of the region's Noongar people moved to the new United Aborigines Mission station at Gnowangerup.[6]

By the beginning of the twentieth century, European settlement had led many Noongar people to move from their original homelands. Daisy Bates found during her government-sponsored tour of the south-west in 1908 that 'there was not one group in any district whose members belonged to that area'.[7] She spent several weeks at the Katanning camp compiling genealogies from information supplied by Aborigines who were living in the district, and these extraordinarily detailed family trees illustrate the extent of the disruption. Bates noted the birthplace of sixty-eight old people, but only twenty-five of these had been born in Albany or its hinterland, while others came from places as far away as Eucla, Esperance and Bruce Rock. Even the twenty-five originally from the Albany region were from areas as far apart as Jerramungup, Frankland River and Denmark, with only three who gave Albany as their place of birth.[8] One of these was Nebinyan, whom Bates believed to be over eighty years of age. His father had witnessed the Marines drilling during Flinders' visit to Albany in 1801, and had passed on the dance based on their actions. A newspaper report from 1925 remarked on the almost total disappearance of Aboriginal people from the south coast east of Albany. Mr J. W. Kirwan, MLC, found this most perplexing since 'The unoccupied areas are so vast that there was ample room for the tribes of Aborigines to live as freely as before the coming of the white man to Australia'.[9]

Robert Reynolds, Senior Heritage Officer with the Albany office of the Department of Indigenous Affairs, has noted that the Bates genealogies collected at the Katanning camp cover all of the Albany Aboriginal families who claim descent from people originally from the Menang region.[10] The Knapp family's story is told in Appendix 2, and the Colbung family history provides another example. They claim ties to Albany through descent from Coolbun, an Aboriginal man who was noted in Barker's journal as owning the land around Bald Head.[11]

No records remain that would allow a historian to definitively state the exact numbers or identities of all the Aboriginal people who were living in or immediately adjacent to the town of Albany in the late 1850s before the exodus occurred, and this makes it impossible to trace the subsequent history of all who were involved. Those who left Albany at that time moved to places such as Katanning, Kendenup and Gnowangerup, where they joined Aboriginal people who either had traditional links to these areas or had come in from other regions of the state. Age-old boundaries between Noongar groups had begun to collapse in the mid nineteenth century as people moved out of their own area in search of employment. Certainly, a large number of the Aboriginal people who took part in the events recounted in this chapter were descended from those whose ancestral home was the area close to Albany, but to attempt to trace the origins of each individual or family is beyond the scope of this book.

The 1905 Act, and the methods by which its provisions were implemented, so dominated Aboriginal–European relations in Western Australia for the next half-century that it is necessary to examine its major sections in some detail. All full-descent Aboriginal people, and those with one Aboriginal parent who lived with Aboriginal people, came under the provisions of the Act. Any 'half-caste' persons 'living with an aboriginal as wife or husband', or 'who, otherwise than as wife and husband, habitually lives or associates with aborigines', and any 'half-caste child whose age apparently does not exceed sixteen years' were also included. Section 2 of the Act specifically excluded those described in the Act as 'quadroons' – those with one part-Aboriginal parent and one who was European. However, an apparent legislative oversight included these people, and others of less than half-descent, under the Act by including them in its definition of 'Aboriginal natives'. This confusion allowed administrators and police to apply the provisions of the Act to anyone of Aboriginal appearance.[12]

The Act, proclaimed in April 1906, was drawn up without any consultation with those whose lives were to be so profoundly affected by its clauses and implementation. Many Noongar people who had been exempt from the 1886 Act found themselves under the control of the Chief Protector, with all of the loss of freedom this entailed. Officers (usually local police) appointed by Prinsep as honorary protectors were given all the powers specified in the Act, as well as any others defined by regulations made for any purpose under the Act. Employment was controlled by a system of permits, and no Aboriginal person, or a male 'half-caste' under the age of fourteen years, or any female 'half-caste', could be offered work unless a permit had been obtained.[13] Protectors, acting with police support, were given the power to:

> cause any aboriginal to be removed to and kept within the boundaries of a reserve, or to be removed from one reserve or district, and kept therein. Any aboriginal who shall refuse to be so removed to or kept within each reserve or district shall be guilty of an offence against this Act.[14]

Under Section 8, the Chief Protector became the legal guardian of all Aboriginal children under the age of sixteen, and could remove those orphaned or in need to a church-run mission or other institution. A 1911 amendment to the Act increased the Chief Protector's power by giving him the authority to over-ride the wishes of the child's mother.

Section 37 gave protectors the power to move Aborigines camped in or near a town to a place: 'at such distance from such town or municipality as he may direct; and all police officers shall assist the protector in carrying out the provisions of this section'.

Section 33 effectively took away an Aboriginal person's right to manage his or her own private property and, in a breathtakingly broad clause, allowed the Chief Protector to: 'Exercise in the name of an aboriginal or half-caste any power which the aboriginal or half-caste might exercise for his own benefit'.

The Act was intended to achieve four broad aims: the legal position of Aborigines was to be clarified; legislation pertaining to Aborigines was to be consolidated; a legislative framework to enable education, welfare and medical service to be delivered was to be set up; and the extinction of the Aboriginal race was to be averted.[15] Its powers were draconian, but Prinsep believed them to be fully justified by the twin requirements of protecting a vulnerable people from the unscrupulous actions of unsympathetic Europeans, and ensuring the state was able to manage its Aboriginal population with as little expenditure as possible.

The Act and the way that it was administered denied Aboriginal people the civil rights enjoyed by the wider community, and forced upon them and the rest of the community the sense that they were different and inferior; Neville Green goes further than this, claiming that it was responsible for the creation of a pariah group within Western Australian society.[16]

The years between 1905 and 1927 saw a continuation of the situation that had developed in the latter part of the previous century – overwhelmingly the region's Aboriginal population lived in the rural areas to the north of the town of Albany, with only a few residing permanently within its limits. Some others camped as family units for extended periods at their regular places around the outskirts of the town – in a report of a court trial in 1922, several Aboriginal witnesses stated they were visiting Albany for a holiday from Carrolup and Gnowangerup.[17] A letter written by Ivan Bird to Albany historian Robert Stephens in 1945 makes it clear that this behaviour was not unusual, and shows that many Aboriginal people with ancestral ties to Albany came to the town for short but regular visits in the early twentieth century. Bird was born at Strawberry Hill Farm around 1890, and remembered how 'natives visited Strawberry Hill each winter. Thirty or forty used to camp about 200 yards north-west of the old stables across Beauchamp Street for a week or so'.[18]

Lynette Knapp of Albany recalls her father recounting how he camped as a child with his own parents, grandfather and siblings near the site of the Albany golf links at Middleton Beach. He was born in 1914. The family regularly moved between this camp, a campsite at Lower King (where Cumberland Road now passes) and the farming land to the north where they worked as shearers. Her father also told his children that there was another campsite near Hanrahan Road in Albany where other Aboriginal people visiting the town would make their temporary camp. It is fascinating to note that recent archaeological evidence shows that the Lower King site has been in use as a campsite for many thousands of years.[19]

Although it is not possible to ascertain with confidence the exact number living permanently or irregularly in the townsite, there are official and semi-official documentary sources which, together with oral records, allow a reasonably accurate estimate to be made. The most detailed information available comes from the obligatory annual reports made to the Aborigines Department in Perth by the sergeant in charge of the Albany Police Station in his role as local Protector. There is no consistent pattern followed in these reports – in some years only the number of those receiving rations was noted, in other years the only figures given relate to those in employment, and in one instance only – that for 1912 – the annual return gave figures for the number of 'full bloods' and 'half-castes'. This report also included short statements about their behaviour, and whether the officer believed Aboriginal numbers to be increasing or decreasing.[20] It appears that special Aboriginal censuses were taken in Western Australia in 1919 and 1923, but the results were unfortunately either lost or disposed of.[21] The Commonwealth census of 1921, as usual, did not count Aborigines of full descent, while other Aboriginal people were included in the general population.[22] Neither the Albany Court records nor the Albany Police Daily Occurrence Books give much useful information about the town's Aboriginal residents after 1905 and prior to 1927.

The numbers living more or less permanently within the townsite of Albany in the early twentieth century seldom exceeded ten. By 1914, the approximate mid year of the period discussed in this chapter, the town's total population numbered 4,201, so it is not surprising to find that this small number of Aboriginal people living in Albany attracted so little attention.[23] Police officers submitted irregular annual reports to the Aborigines Department providing accurate details of the number of 'sick and indigent' Aborigines supplied with the standard weekly ration of ten pounds of flour, one-and-a-half pounds of sugar and a quarter pound of tea by the Albany merchant Drew Robinson and Co. acting as contract suppliers.[24] In 1906, four were rationed, and in 1907 the number had risen to seven. Of course, the number being rationed is not a clear indication of the total Aboriginal population in the town, but the return for 1908 stated that there were only a few Aboriginal persons living in Albany, and no further figures were given until the 1912 report, which specified that there were 'no aboriginal natives in the district'.[25] Numbers had increased by 1914, when five were reported as being in employment, rising to six the following year.[26] In 1917, the number in employment had risen sharply to sixteen,[27] and it is possible that the pressure placed upon Aboriginal people living around Katanning to move to the Aboriginal settlement established in 1915 at Carrolup, 25 kilometres west of the town, caused some with historic ties to Albany to return to their old home area.[28] It is also possible that the war caused a labour shortage at Albany, and this allowed some Aboriginal people to return to their home town to take up employment opportunities. Whatever had induced them to come back to Albany, many evidently found the move home less than satisfactory, for the 1918 return showed only five Aboriginal people employed at Albany by that time.[29]

The report for 1919 is the only documentary evidence I have been able to locate from this period that specifically divides the Aboriginal people living in the town of Albany into the categories of full or part descent, and gives exact numbers for each. The police stated that there were four 'full bloods', and no 'half-castes', and this division would appear to be conclusive proof that police at Albany had been including both groups as 'Aborigines' in their previous annual reports. This is interesting because if this document did not exist, it would be possible to speculate that all of the other reports referred only to Aboriginal people of full descent, and that there may well have been considerable numbers of others living in the town whose presence the police ignored in their annual returns. During the 1920s, the annual police reports indicated that there were up to four Aborigines employed in the town, but gave no further information that would shed light on the total numbers present.

The lack of local newspaper reports about Aboriginal people in the town of Albany is strong indirect evidence that numbers were indeed low. Certainly, at Katanning – the only other town in the region to have a local press at the time – the newspapers carried a considerable number of articles and reports about the Noongar people living in and around their town. Tommy King had described himself as 'one of the few remaining aboriginals of Albany' in 1890,[30] and the evidence does not support any significant migration back into the town between then and the late 1920s.[31]

Relations between the Aboriginal and non-Aboriginal sections of the town's population appear to have been relatively good. When the town council asked nearby residents if they had any objections to a site on the Perth Road being designated a campsite for Aborigines, none were received by the deadline, although the vestry of neighbouring St Oswald's Anglican Church entered a late objection for 'various [unspecified] reasons' which the Council ignored.[32] The vestry then wrote to the Aborigines Department, but were not successful in preventing the establishment of the campsite.[33]

During the period covered by this chapter, the more naturally fertile areas of the Great Southern changed from a patchwork of isolated and partly cleared farms surrounded by large tracts of virgin bush into the extensive, rolling, highly productive areas of grain and pasture that one sees today. Towns such as Katanning, Mount Barker and Tambellup grew from a few makeshift buildings set up next to the local railway station into prosperous communities with extensive commercial and government buildings that are still in use today, in many cases under heritage listing because of their architectural merit and historical significance.[34] During this period of dramatic growth and dawning prosperity for much of the region, a large proportion of farming families were able to improve their living conditions, which had often been extremely basic by contemporary metropolitan standards, and build comfortable homes that in a few cases rivalled any in the better suburbs of Perth.[35] The period before World War I saw the peak of this building boom on farming properties and in the rural towns along the Great Southern line.

The Taylor family of Tambellup provides an excellent example of the changes in living conditions that took place within the settler community. Brian Taylor has written a family history in which he relates how his grandfather left the family farm in Victoria to take up the opportunity presented by the liberal land laws in Western Australia. After some time making bricks at Albany while assessing where to buy land, in 1898 Samuel Taylor became only the second farmer to take up residence in the Tambellup area. He and his family spent seven years living in a large canvas tent, with kangaroos, wallabies, possums and ducks providing a significant proportion of their diet. The farm steadily prospered and he was able to construct a brick and wattle and daub house on his property in 1905. He continued to add to his holding and built a second and even more substantial brick home in 1925, an elegant building that remains in use by the family today.[36]

Such social and material progress was confined almost entirely to the European population. The gulf between Aboriginal and non-Aboriginal people – always significant – widened much further as some of the things previously common to both, such as living under canvas or in rough bush shelters, poor or non-existent education, and a diet consisting largely of kangaroo, possum and flour gradually became almost entirely the lived experience of one group only.

The Katanning District forms the northern extremity of the area I have considered as forming Albany's hinterland. However, the fact that so many of the region's Aboriginal people chose to live there during the first three decades of the century makes Katanning the natural area of focus in any research dealing with Aboriginal–European relations during that period. After the Great Southern Railway opened for business, Katanning quickly became the largest inland town in the region, and the great majority of documentary evidence for this period centres on events that occurred either in the town or in the surrounding district. The hinterland's only newspapers were published in Katanning, it was the centre where Daisy Bates chose to spend an extended period seeking information from her Aboriginal informants, and it was at Carrolup that the Western Australian Aborigines Department established the state's first official Aboriginal settlement. Katanning was a natural choice for Aboriginal people to make their home because it was built on the site of a traditional Aboriginal meeting ground at the junction of three tribal areas where Aboriginal people had always congregated at certain times of the year.[37]

Eric Hayward has drawn on oral sources to write an interesting and informative account of the lifestyle of his Aboriginal grandparents, William and Minnie Hayward (nee Knapp), who were based at Broomehill but also worked around Katanning and Gnowangerup. William was the son a convict of the same name who had two families – one with an Aboriginal woman from Albany named Jackbam, and the other with a European woman whom he married, Mary Piggott, also from Albany.[38] Hayward's book provides a rare insight into how the Great Southern's Aboriginal people, by then increasingly a marginalised minority group, lived and interacted with the settlers who had moved uninvited into their midst.[39]

Around the turn of the century William and Minnie based their family camp at Broomehill where William worked as a clearer, drover, dam sinker and general farm labourer. Sometimes his work took the family by horse and cart to Katanning and Gnowangerup where he made a good living working for farmers on contract rates of pay. After work, the family would hunt for food. Occasionally William would take his mother Jackbam back to Albany where she would meet with her old friends and family. He spoke the Noongar language, and his mother passed on to him the stories associated with his traditional lands as well as the other hunter-gatherer skills of his Menang ancestors.[40] It is likely these experiences were typical of those of Aboriginal families at that time.

The first documented indication that problems were developing between European residents of the newly established town of Katanning and Aboriginal people is found in an official letter written in August 1903 by local Police Constable Hardy to the town's Resident Magistrate advising that:

> As several complaints have been made of late to me concerning the camping places of natives when in Katanning, near private dwelling houses, I would respectfully ask that a reserve may be granted for that special purpose in accordance with 61 vic.

No. 5 section of S.8.5, so that then they will not be a source
of annoyance to anyone, and further it will place a check over
the supplying of liquor to them to a great extent by the whites
who would have to give an explanation of their presence on
the grant.[41]

So began a long series of attempts by the police and the
Aborigines Department to accommodate the evident difficulty
that some at least of Katanning's European residents had with the
experience of living in close proximity to Aboriginal campsites.
A close examination of the files of these two state government
departments, together with the minutes of the Katanning Road
Board (incorporating the Katanning Local Board of Health) and
the pages of the local *Great Southern Herald*,[42] shows a steady and
inexorable increase in official control over where Aboriginal
people lived. In 1915, this culminated in their removal on foot
to Carrolup.[43]

It was not only officialdom that took an interest in the lives of
Aborigines; in 1896, the Katanning Baptist Church was formed
with a large following that included members from some of the
district's prominent farming families. The efforts of the successive
pastors and members of the congregation to ameliorate the living
conditions of the town's Aborigines, and to ensure that they
had at least some voice in their future, shines through what is
otherwise a most unedifying story. The Baptist Union appointed
Mrs Kennedy, wife of the Katanning pastor, as overseer for the
'work of civilising and Christianising the children of the natives in
the Katanning District', and she was soon visiting and instructing
'the children at the "blacks" camp'.[44] This camp was probably
on the first reserve gazetted at Katanning: following a typhoid
outbreak in the district, a 2-acre location on town lots 398 and
399 was designated as a 'hospital for Aboriginals'.[45] This was one
of the first actions of a church that was certainly focused upon

evangelisation of Aboriginal people, but which also saw justice and common humanity as concepts that should not only be applicable to European settlers.

On the recommendation of the Resident Magistrate, Prinsep pressed the Under Secretary of Lands to gazette Katanning town lot 420 as a camping ground for Aborigines. He wrote asking:

> Can you arrange for the temporary reservation of the block alluded to in the R. M.'s letter of 27/8/03, p. 11, until I may be able to get the law passed by which natives can be compelled to stop in certain localities. At present they wander where they like and there is no law to prevent it.[46]

Prinsep felt that the complaints alluded to by P. C. Hardy a fortnight earlier were justified and that something needed to be done. The Katanning Local Board of Health objected to the site as being too close to existing housing, and suggested a 5-acre alternative site within the town's boundaries but in a more isolated position.[47] In mid 1905, the reserve was gazetted as Reserve no. 9622 with its purpose listed as 'Aboriginals'.[48] The Aborigines Department files held at the State Records Office in Perth do not list any further correspondence about this reserve until 1910, making it difficult to ascertain the extent to which it was used as a campsite; Haebich concluded that it probably was used, and may have been the camp visited by Daisy Bates in 1908.[49]

When a severe outbreak of measles struck at Katanning during the winter of 1907, Daisy Bates soon discovered that some of the camp-dwellers were suffering serious effects from the disease. She contacted the town's doctor, only to find that the hospital was already over-crowded and could accept no more patients. Dr House visited the camp daily, and instructed Bates in basic patient care. She readily acknowledged his compassionate manner, but it remained a source of lasting pride that while he lost some of his patients in the hospital, none of hers died. She later had a photograph taken outside one of Katanning's principal stores showing almost all of her now recovered patients dressed in their best clothes (with several wrapped in the red, white and blue striped government-issue blankets) with Daisy standing at one end casting a motherly eye over them. On the back of the photograph, she wrote:

> Natives all recovered from measles, 40 patients at camp & no help from Katanning as measles was raging there. Dr & nurses all required [?] lost adults and children daily at Katanning. I did not lose one of my 40 patients!!! And so am giving them a feast at the Katanning Show – everything they ask for!

Daisy Bates' photograph of her measles patients in 1907
Image courtesy of the University of Adelaide

Bates is a controversial figure, due to her insistence on the existence of cannibalism within Aboriginal communities across Australia, her belief in the inevitability of Aboriginal extinction, and her absolute disdain for any Aboriginal person who had some European ancestry. Her reputation as 'Saviour of the Aborigines' has suffered considerably in recent decades as these attitudes have become widely unacceptable in Australian society, and as her integrity has come into question following research that has shown she fabricated accounts of her early background in Ireland. Reece argues that this fabrication calls into question the reliability of much else that she wrote, notably about Aboriginal matters.[50] Susanna de Vries, author of *The Many Lives and Loves of Daisy Bates*, described her as 'neither saint nor sinner, but a nuanced blend of both'.[51]

Katanning had become the major town of the inland Great Southern by 1911 and proved the natural place for Aboriginal people from outlying districts to move to in search of work.[52] It is not therefore surprising to find that the town campsite became once more a focus for local concern. This concern intensified until Carrolup was opened, and was expressed in the pages of the local newspapers, especially the *Great Southern Herald*, until the news of the Great War and the heavy losses of local soldiers pushed Aboriginal matters into the background.[53] An extract from a letter written by Corporal Purkiss of the Katanning Police to his superior officer at Bunbury gives some idea of the situation:

> During the month of March I issued ration orders £45, Aboriginal Natives blanket, clothing etc. and in looking after matters such as sick Natives takes up a lot of my time, at present there are approx. 70 camped about their Reserve which adjoins the townsite within half a mile of the Post Office, there are a number of half-castes who go out and work as white men burning off etc. and when they have a cheque earned they come into town and are supplied

with liquor and this causes trouble with the full bloods. I wrote
a report some months ago pointing out the Native Reserve was
too close to the town and asked that another Reserve be found,
but so far no action has been taken.[54]

This letter raised several issues that had the potential to worsen
Aboriginal–European relations. Police officers were feeling over-
worked and ignored by their superiors, and probably resented
having to deal with sick Aborigines (at this time the local hospital
was receiving Aboriginal patients, so police work involved
escorting more seriously ill patients to and from the train to
Albany or Perth). Perhaps the police realised that their lack of
medical knowledge would be the cause of serious problems – if so
they were perceptive, for three residents died at the camp in the
coming winter. Numbers at the camp were growing and the lack of
water there meant that residents had to rely upon non-Aboriginal
neighbours for this scarce but very necessary resource. The lack
of sanitation exacerbated the difficulties inherent in the camp's
closeness to other housing, while the perennial problems caused
by alcohol illegally supplied and consumed simply compounded
the problem.[55]

It is impossible to determine the real extent of the problems
alcohol caused during this period. Haebich accused the Western
Australian police of having a near obsession in their control of
Aborigines' consumption of alcohol at this time, and claimed that
actual consumption was not high with the exception of some
individuals. She quoted an Aboriginal man, Cliff Humphries
from Kellerberrin, in support of this claim, but he was born in
1910 and would have had no firsthand knowledge of the Great
Southern situation around that time.[56] Bill Hassell, who grew up
on the family sheep property at Warriup about 60 kilometres east
of Albany in the 1930s, remembers his parents stating that almost
no alcohol was consumed by the Aboriginal people who lived and

worked on the property except for a mug of watered rum at the end of each day's shearing.[57] Police and court records, however, show that alcohol did cause significant problems for some individuals, and the effects of this spilled over into the Aboriginal community as a whole.

In 1912, the Australian Aborigines Mission (AAM) proposed setting up a station on the Katanning town reserve and their representative, Annie Lock, met with members of the Baptist Church who organised a public meeting in Katanning where she could present her ideas. The plan involved a 25-acre addition to the reserve so that Aboriginal men could be instructed in useful agricultural skills as well as providing their families with food grown onsite. Women and girls were to be taught dressmaking, and all would learn hygiene. Fortunately, a reporter from the *Herald* attended and provided a description of the only meeting my research has uncovered in Albany or its hinterland where both Aboriginal and European people sat down together and discussed where at least some aspects of their relationship might be heading. The report is not a verbatim transcript, making it impossible to know the extent to which the local Aborigines had a developed vision, or whether they simply acquiesced in what they may have seen as another example of Europeans seeking further control over their lives. We do know that the meeting was 'a large gathering' from which a council was appointed to carry the idea forward. We also know that Charlie Hansen spoke as a representative of the Aboriginal people involved, stating that they had raised £3/3/0 towards a fund to build a new mission church and hoped Miss Lock would stay.[58]

A fortnight earlier the local Baptist pastor had written to the District Surveyor at Albany seeking to get things underway, and pointing out that there were about 120 Aborigines in the Katanning District.[59] A week later, the secretary of the W.A. branch of the AAM wrote to the Chief Protector for his suggestions about how the mission should proceed in the matter.[60] The proposed venture appeared to be on track until it came under discussion at the Road Board meeting held on the twenty-first of the month, when several members opposed the extension of the town's reserve: Mr Thomson was recorded as saying 'the further away from the town the Aborigines were placed the better it would be for all concerned'.[61] The Road Board suggested placing each family on a 2-acre lot on a site of 100 acres near the Police Pools a few kilometres from town, but this proposal appears to have gone no further.

Chief Protector Gale had earlier drafted a letter to the AAM in Perth stating his intention to visit Katanning to 'go more fully into the question with those people who take an interest in the subject', but a handwritten note scrawled across the letter reveals that Annie Lock had subsequently written to him claiming:

> there is a strong objection on the part of the Katanning people to the granting of further reserves near Katanning – that a scheme is now afoot to form a mission some distance from Katanning with the object of removing the natives out of the town of Katanning altogether.[62]

The non-Aboriginal residents of the town obviously felt strongly that something needed to be done, but were divided as to whether this should involve assisting Aboriginal people or simply removing them as far away as possible.

No one raised the topic of the reserve at the annual ratepayers' meeting in mid January 1913, but discontent continued to simmer and a petition 'numerously signed' was presented to the June meeting of the Road Board demanding that the Aborigines be removed from the town and placed on the Carrolup River Reserve 25 kilometres west of Katanning. The Board decided they would do everything within their power to see that this was done.[63] It is easy to conclude that racism was the only force that drove residents to sign the petition, and the Road Board to accede to their demand, but it is entirely possible that fear was also at work – at the time of the Board meeting, Katanning was in the grip of a severe epidemic of diphtheria with forty children ill and two deaths from the disease.[64] The local paper also reported cases of smallpox at Sydney and expressed fears that it could spread to W.A. Annie Lock must have believed that this fear was influential, for she contacted the *Herald* almost immediately and was quoted as stating 'Disinfectants and soap have been freely used and so far the camp has had no case of diphtheria or typhoid'.[65]

Events now moved swiftly. On 19 July, a meeting took place chaired by the Rev. Gilmour from the Baptist Church and attended by local police officers and a Mr A. S. Gillam, who claimed to speak on behalf of the Aboriginal people of the town.[66] The idea of a self-supporting farm at Carrolup using Aboriginal labour was floated. Gillam said that the move was 'necessary from the sanitary and moral standpoints', and that he was satisfied it would best serve the interests of local Aborigines.[67]

The Road Board pressed for a decision and arranged for Gale to visit Katanning to see for himself what was occurring at the camp. He arrived in late November and found 150 people at the camp including thirty-three children. Ninety-two were receiving government assistance. He informed his minister that families were living there so that their children could attend school while the men were seeking employment with local farmers.[68] Gale was distressed to find able-bodied Aborigines 'hanging about' the town, a problem he promised would be eradicated by an instruction to the police to rigidly enforce existing vagrancy laws. He met with the Road Board and sympathised with their request that the camp be removed from town, but pointed out that the Police Pools site had one fundamental problem – the police had the power to confine Aboriginal residents to reserves at night, but they had no such power over their whereabouts during daylight hours.[69] This site was within walking distance of Katanning and there can be little doubt that this was a crucial factor in the final choice of the more distant Carrolup as the site of the proposed settlement.

The presence of a newspaper reporter at a meeting can inhibit free discussion on sensitive topics, and it is evident that at least one Road Board member felt there was more that the meeting wanted to tell Gale, but only once the *Herald* was out of earshot. The reporter noted that the member promised that the Board 'would speak plainly to him in the [next] morning'.[70] Whether such a discussion took place or not is unknown, but there are several clues in surviving documents that lead to the conclusion that the real problem with the reserve was that European men were supplying alcohol to Aboriginal women in return for sexual favours, and it is likely that this was the problem considered too sensitive for the reporter's ears. The *Herald* editorialised that the camp's situation was leading to 'further degradation to many of the aborigines'.[71] A Road Board member noted that 'serious allegations are frequently made of happenings at the native camp', and when the Rev. Gilmour met with the Board he suggested that a nurse be appointed to the proposed Carrolup settlement so that the girls would be under her supervision.[72] A deputation of Katanning residents to Gale in November 1913 claimed that the Aborigines constituted 'a nuisance, and a menace to the morals of the youths of Katanning'.[73] It seemed clear that the only way this apparently embarrassing blot on the town's reputation could be eradicated was to take drastic action.

Inter-racial trouble in the town reached a peak in 1914 when parents of white children at the Katanning State School agitated to have the Aboriginal School that had been set up on the school's grounds in 1912 closed down. The government failed to act, and the parents at a public meeting decided unanimously to force its hand by threatening to withdraw their children unless all Aboriginal children were removed. Finally the police bowed to community pressure early in 1914 and dispersed the people from the town reserve, only to find that they soon drifted back from the reserves at Gnowangerup, Tambellup and Mount Barker where they had temporarily camped.[74] In June, the teacher at the Katanning Aboriginal School resigned and the school closed. Out of desperation with their situation, the same month Aborigines from Wagin, Narrogin and Bunbury met with the residents of the Katanning camp and drew up a set of rules governing residents' behaviour. Individuals were appointed as 'magistrates' and 'policemen' to make sure the rules were enforced, but the system soon collapsed.[75] This breakdown of self-policing appears to have been the final straw for both town residents and authorities. Following public meetings in January 1915 the police forced all of the camp residents to take up their belongings and walk the 25 kilometres to the Carrolup River.

From early 1914, when the *Southern Districts Advocate* commenced publication, two newspapers were published in the town and the very different ways in which each reported Aboriginal issues gives some insight into the range of attitudes held by people living in their catchment, which was virtually all of the area under discussion in this book. The *Great Southern Herald* frequently included stories about the problems Katanning in particular was facing, and generally did so from a non-racist perspective. The same could not be said for the paper's rival, the *Southern Districts Advocate*. From the paper's earliest issues, its editor pursued a policy of racist 'humour' that was relentless in its denigration of Aboriginal people. Headlines such as 'Amongst the Niggers' and 'Our Black Brudder', announced court reports that were written with a view to entertain what was evidently a considerably less enlightened readership than that of its older rival.[76] Not surprisingly in an era when the White Australia Policy was at its peak, the paper's racism was not restricted to the Aboriginal section of the community, with a Chinese man before the court described as 'a shrivelled up, slant-eyed Mongolian chinkee'.[77] Of the surviving issues of this newspaper, none mentions the establishment of Carrolup.

The *Advocate* reached a nadir in 1916 when reporting the near death from illness of Private K. Farmer, and the fact that he was one of four local brothers then on active service with the AIF. On the same page, the paper printed a letter that included:

> Some time ago through your valuable columns, you did much towards having the black fraternity removed from the town [Katanning]. I shall be glad if you can now explain how it was that a small army of them were outside Messrs F. & C. Piesse's office on Saturday last.[78]

The editor promised that he would investigate the matter. He evidently felt no responsibility to note for his readers that the four Farmer brothers (one of whom won the Military Medal, and two of whom subsequently lost their lives in the fighting) were members of the same Aboriginal community he had taken pride in hounding out of the town. Perhaps more than any other contemporary document I have read during my research, this newspaper page shows that there were sections of the community in the Great Southern, as in the rest of Australia in the early 1900s, who were openly racist at a fundamental level and wanted the Aboriginal people permanently removed from in and around their town. As Gale noted (see quote below) numbers of part-descent Aborigines were not declining as had been expected but were actually noticeably *increasing*, and it was dawning on the white community that the 'Aboriginal problem' was not one that time alone would solve.

The police did not choose the Carrolup site at random. In late 1912, the AAM had proposed a self-supporting settlement at Carrolup as the best solution to what had become a clearly unsatisfactory situation at Katanning for all concerned:

> It is also anticipated that many, if not the majority of Natives in the South-Western districts will, in time, be induced to make their homes at the mission, and thus as it were, form one central depot to which young, able bodied natives could come when out of work and put in their time while waiting for future employment, thus obviating the necessity of their stopping in towns. The children would have schooling, the girls taught sewing and housework and the boys rough carpentry and such other things as will tend to make them useful at farm work.[79]

Gale placed the situation squarely before Parliament in his departmental report for the year ending June 1914:

> Among the many problems facing individual states over the native question, the greatest of all is the intermingling of the white and black races. Gradually but surely the full-blood aboriginal is disappearing...Quite the opposite is the result of mating of half-castes, and throughout the Commonwealth their numbers are steadily increasing. Socially outcast from European races, their presence cannot be absorbed by the community, and they must stand alone to work out their own salvation. Inheriting the nomadic instincts of the native race, they, under present conditions, roam about the country making a precarious living, and, speaking generally, fall upon the Government's shoulders for support in their old age. Serious consideration must, in the near future, be given to this question, and while there is yet time other suitable unoccupied portions of this State, beside the settlement mentioned above [Carrolup] should be reserved for their future use.[80]

Gale had Carrolup Reserve inspected and was keen to go ahead with the scheme, but proved unable to persuade his Minister, John Drew, of its practicality or desirability. Drew then moved portfolios, a move that allowed Gale's new Minister to place the proposal before Cabinet in June 1914 only to have it rejected. Gale then went on long service leave and was replaced by A. O. Neville in March 1915. It is probably significant that the Katanning Police chose to make their move when there was effectively no Chief Protector in office. The new Minister, Rufous Underwood, was strongly in favour of the 'native settlement scheme', although opposed to mission involvement on the grounds that missionaries had failed in the past to achieve results satisfactory to the government. He wanted more stringent economies in the administration of Aboriginal affairs and believed that Neville would be more suited than Gale to administer a new policy of stricter implementation of the 1905 Act.[81]

Auber Octavius Neville held the position of Chief Protector of Aborigines until his retirement in 1940 and during this long period in office his strong views dominated both government policy and the lives of the Aboriginal people in the state. He largely ignored Aborigines of full descent on the ground that they could not be effectively assimilated into white society and would eventually die out – in the meantime they should be protected from exploitation by unscrupulous Europeans. His real interest was in integrating Aboriginal people of part descent into the wider Western Australian society and he became single-minded in his determination to bring those with any degree of Aboriginal ancestry under the control of his Department. Backed by the extensive power available to him under the 1905 Act, Neville established an unprecedented degree of control over virtually every aspect of these people's lives. Certainly, he believed himself to be acting in the best interests of Aboriginal people:

> The native must be helped in spite of himself! Even if a measure
> of discipline is necessary it must be applied, but it can be applied
> in such a way as to appear to be gentle persuasion...the end in
> view will justify the means employed.[82]

Neville became the symbol of official interference in Aboriginal
people's lives and became deeply unpopular with them.

Carrolup was the first settlement that Neville and Underwood
set up in accordance with the policy they had developed together –
a policy built on reducing both government expenditure and the
influence of Christian missions. Children were to receive training
as farm workers or domestic servants so that they would be readily
employable and not be a financial drain on the Department by
requiring to be rationed as adults. Those adults who were unable
to work because of age or infirmity would remain at the settlement
permanently, while those employed in the general community
were to live on the outside although their families were to remain

Soup kitchen at Carrolup Government Settlement, c. 1915
Courtesy State Library of Western Australia

at the settlement. If they became unemployed, they too would move into the settlement. Able-bodied adults would form a ready workforce to construct the dwellings and other buildings that would be required, and would eventually work as farm labourers on the settlement so that self-sufficiency in food would be achieved.

Neville and Underwood hoped their scheme would solve many of the problems facing their department. It would bring an economy of expenditure, provide Aborigines with employable skills, make the work of police easier by centralising the distribution of rations, and remove unemployed and highly visible Aborigines from townsites. However, their plan was fundamentally flawed – it may have met the requirements of the Aborigines Department, the police, and those town residents who had so vehemently demanded that their towns be free from Aboriginal camps, but it failed to take into account the wishes of Noongar people. It also ignored the inconvenient truth that white people had frequently shown a reluctance to play their part by employing partly trained Aborigines.

The June 1916 Chief Protector's Report to Parliament covered the first full year of both Neville's tenure in the position and the operation of Carrolup Settlement. He saw that the area was too small for there to be any realistic prospect of self-sufficiency and had the extent of the reserve enlarged to 10,000 acres. A manager's permanent residence had been erected, but the structures housing Aborigines were built with canvas walls built on frames of bush timber with roofs of galvanised iron. A total of 25 acres were cleared and the settlement was already growing sufficient vegetables to feed its inmates. Neville reported:

> When the settlement was first established, critics of the proposal were wont to say that the natives would not go to Carrolup. The contrary has been our experience, and the difficulty if any has been to keep the able-bodied natives away from the settlement...[83]

His report quoted Carrolup's Manager, Mr C. J. Fryer:

> There has been a fairly good number of natives on the settlement since same commenced, although they come and go. The able-bodied natives are expected to do what is asked of them, the women give help at the buildings in the way of washing, sewing etc. Several of the men are handy and fairly reliable. Some have worked the whole 12 months. A good many men go away shearing in the season, others do clearing and other jobs.
>
> The children have schooling half-a-day only. The accommodation for the school has not been of the best, but an up-to-date school will be built within this year. There has been an average of 15 to 20 children so far… There has been an average of about 60 natives monthly [at the settlement]…It seems only a pity that such a place was not commenced twenty years ago.[84]

Annie Lock lived at Carrolup and continued her missionary work, conducting weekly church services and assisting with the children, while local churches and other 'kindly disposed people' provided clothing and other goods, as well as picnics for the Aboriginal residents.[85] Annie Lock was unusual for her time in believing that Aborigines had a *right* to expect some compensation for having had both their land and their livelihood taken from them by settlers. Her chosen role in this responsibility was to offer them a degree of companionship and the opportunity to become 'useful' citizens.[86]

The picture painted by Neville and Fryer is so positive that it comes as no surprise to find that a second settlement was set up in 1918 at Moore River to take in Aborigines from north of Perth as far as Northampton. In order to achieve his aim of reducing expenditure Neville closed the great majority of the ration stations in the south-west and allowed Aboriginal children to be refused enrolment at most state schools – both actions that left families in the Great Southern with children or infirm members little option but to become inmates of Carrolup. As the Great War ended and men returned to work their farms, or in other jobs where they were given preference, Aboriginal people found work increasingly difficult to find. In 1919, Neville persuaded Parliament to introduce regulations to the 1905 Act allowing police to send Aborigines to the settlements without due process of the law. Whatever the original intent and practice, Carrolup had become a virtual prison, with some inmates placed there with no limitation on their length of stay and no right to leave without the Minister's permission.[87]

In December 1920 the administration of Aboriginal affairs altered. The state was divided into two zones. Neville was given responsibility for the region north of the 25th parallel while the southern portion became the responsibility of the Department of Aborigines and Fisheries. The Deputy Chief Protector, Fred Aldrich, showed little real interest in his role of providing leadership to those working with Aboriginal people in the south-west and left most of his responsibilities to his deputy, Ernest Copping.[88] The southern region received very little of the overall budget for Aboriginal affairs, and Carrolup was closed in 1922 as an economy measure.

No one in authority consulted with Carrolup's Noongar people, Neville (who was out of Australia at the time), the AAM missionaries or the residents of Katanning. The AAM was incensed over the closure and the lack of consultation. Its President wrote to the *West Australian*:

Now as a bolt from the blue has come the notification from the Colonial Secretary's department that the settlement at Carrolup is to be closed at the end of the month and the natives there assembled to be removed from their home…it will not be an easy matter to migrate natives of one tribe and district into new surroundings and the result will be a recurrence of the old trouble, for the natives will gravitate back to Katanning to become a nuisance to themselves and to the residents and an expense to the Government.[89]

A resident missionary, later to open a new mission at Gnowangerup, wrote:

> It seems like a horrible nightmare, and sometimes I wonder how I shall live through it all...My poor, poor people – torn apart from home and all their connections. Poor, dear, helpless souls.[90]

The Katanning Road Board also unsuccessfully opposed the closure, fearing that the town reserve would once more become a major problem for the town's European residents.[91] Haebich described how the decision was greeted with dismay and apprehension by the Aboriginal people directly involved.[92]

Green described Carrolup as similar to the worst of nineteenth-century English work-houses, yet some families *chose* to live there despite the regimentation and the poor standard of accommodation – surely a powerful indictment of the living conditions of some Aboriginal families residing outside of the settlement. With Carrolup's closure, town reserves became the centre of Aboriginal life in the towns to Albany's north. This was the beginning of an era when a large increase in the state's Noongar population (between 1920 and 1930 numbers rose by almost 50 per cent) meant that families were becoming larger at the same time as economic opportunities shrank with the return of men from the war. Some of Haebich's elderly informants referred to this period as the 'hard times'.[93] Significant agricultural expansion occurred in the northern parts of the region during the 1920s, further reducing the opportunities for Aboriginal families to supplement their diet by hunting native animals.

More from neglect than design, departmental policy became one of setting up even more town reserves in the state's south-west, with new reserves gazetted at Gnowangerup and Albany.[94] Non-Aboriginal residents grudgingly acknowledged their necessity as a means of concentrating workers should they be required for casual work by local farmers. The Gnowangerup Reserve was typically poorly situated just out of town between the town rubbish dump and the sanitary depot where toilet pans were emptied. As drinking water from the adjacent dam became polluted, clean water had to be taken to the reserve. Housing consisted of shelters made from old corrugated iron, hessian bags and flattened kerosene tins fastened to bush timber frames, with living conditions, especially in winter and summer, equivalent to some of the worst in the slums of today's third world countries.[95] Yet the local paper, the *Gnowangerup Star*, almost completely ignored the presence of Aboriginal people in the district apart from a brief news item in 1925 that noted two Aborigines had died in the week from 'pneumonic influenza', and that 'dry and decent accommodation' should be provided for the winter months for Aboriginal people since they were living in tents on 'the wet earth with a covering of leaves and rags'.[96] During the years of 1925 and 1926, the newspaper's reports of Gnowangerup Road Board meetings and annual ratepayers' meetings contain no mention of Aborigines – the status quo appears to have been simply accepted by the settler community as a whole.

Following Carrolup's closure, many Aboriginal families from the Great Southern moved to the new reserve at Gnowangerup and almost all of the Noongar residents of Albany today trace their roots to this town reserve and the mission that was established by Brother and Sister Wright of the AAM in 1926.[97] Police enforced a sunset curfew in the town, and Aborigines were not allowed in the town's cinema and cafes. The Gnowangerup Hospital, in common with most others in the south-west at this time, had a strict ruling that Aboriginal patients were to be treated in a tent provided for the purpose or sent to Katanning Hospital.[98] The early days of uneasy integration when small numbers of Aboriginal families were scattered throughout the region had come to an end at Gnowangerup, where the sheer numbers of Aborigines overwhelmed the always fragile capacity of settlers to coexist with them without various forms of segregation being imposed.

The mission filled a need expressed by some of the former inhabitants of Carrolup who remembered the respectful way they had been treated by AAM missionary Hope Malcolm while at the settlement. However unsatisfactory, they felt that Carrolup had been their home and they approached Malcolm to 'find them another home'. She decided upon the Gnowangerup reserve in 1922, but illness necessitated her return to Melbourne where she remained until returning to Western Australia in July 1926 with her new husband, Hedley Wright. As 'Brother and Sister Wright' the couple began the mission which they ran until 1948, when Hedley became pastor of the local Baptist Church.[99] The work began with the building of a school, and forty children were attending in 1927. A tent for Aboriginal patients at Gnowangerup Hospital was shifted to the mission and a store set up for residents to use.

The AAM missions throughout Australia had a very different philosophy from earlier Christian missions and the government settlement at Moore River. They were based on the lifestyle that Aboriginal people had established for themselves in the town camps, and acted as bases from which they could move freely as work became available for men on the surrounding farms and for women wishing to do domestic work in the town. Crucially, families lived in their own areas of the mission and children always remained with their parents and siblings. The Wrights saw themselves as assisting Aborigines rather than controlling their lives, and allowed some traditional practices such as the use of Aboriginal names and Aboriginal healers. The fact that conditions were better on the mission than in the remaining town camps in the Great Southern resulted in an influx of Aboriginal families. Gnowangerup Police, and some European residents of the town and district, resented this increase in numbers.[100]

That Aboriginal healers were still being consulted in the late 1920s is another indication that some elements of traditional Aboriginal society remained. Emmett Abraham remembered 'old people singing old songs, corroborees and one thing and another' at Narrogin (north of Katanning) in the late 1920s, and although he believed that much of the organising was done by Aboriginal people who had moved into the area from north-west Western Australia, his recollection of local stories from that period about *janarks* (devils), *bulyets* and *mummaries* (differing types of little men) shows that the old religion was still in evidence.[101] Lilly Hayward (born 1914–15) also recalled stories about *janarks*, but was very clear that she had never seen a corroboree, 'I think that was cut out before my time'.[102]

Although Katanning and Gnowangerup had the largest numbers of Aboriginal people in the region to Albany's north, there was also a resident Noongar population in other towns and districts such as Mount Barker, Cranbrook and Tambellup. Denmark, for reasons that are not entirely clear, had very few (if any) Aboriginal residents after the town's timber mill closed in 1905, although two women visited the area trapping possums in the 1920s.[103] Aboriginal employees continued to work on farms and pastoral properties. For example, Johnny Knapp, Dan McEvoy and Dave Coyne worked fairly regularly on the Hassell pastoral station at Warriup (very little of the property was cleared before the 1940s). They supplemented their wages and rations by selling wallaby, kangaroo and brush kangaroo skins, as well as wool plucked from dead sheep.[104]

The Mount Barker Police Station Report and Correspondence Book for the years 1905–10 shows that the local police felt the relationship between themselves and the Noongar population

Shearing team at Hassell's Warriup station, 1920. There are two Aboriginal shearers, Dan McEvoy, front left of picture, and Jack Kit, front right.
Photo courtesy of Bill Hassell, Albany

gave no cause for concern, with only one report that mentioned Aboriginal people during the five-year period:

> There are no natives under [employment] agreement in this district. They voluntarily work a few weeks with the settlers and move to another district. They always appear to have a sufficiency of food and clothing, game is plentiful outside the settler localities, two natives have been charged with drunkenness.[105]

By 1913, problems had begun to arise. Aboriginal numbers had increased at Mount Barker to the point where thirty-six were living in the district.[106] Parents at Mount Barker were aware of the establishment of an Aboriginal school at Katanning in 1912, and when their local school enrolled Aboriginal children the following year, they agitated to have a similar school set up in their own town. The members of the Plantagenet Road Board (the local government authority based in Mount Barker) took up the fight with a unanimous decision:

> That the Minister be written to regarding the undesirability of aboriginal children being allowed to attend the same school as the whites, and the Board would press the point of separate accommodation being provided for the black children.[107]

One month later a further letter urged haste, as 'the weather is now getting warmer'.[108] This letter suggests a concern that the hygiene standards of Aboriginal children at the school were unacceptable, although it was almost certainly an attempt to hide more racially based concerns since a subsequent medical examination of the students revealed that the children were clean and healthy.

Agitation continued, but Cabinet initially refused to bar Aboriginal children from the school. The Mount Barker correspondent for the *Albany Advertiser* (at this time the paper served Mount Barker as well as Albany) was particularly critical of this inaction, but denied that racism was involved:

> Unkindliness of feeling towards the blacks is not a factor in this matter of black and white, but on the contrary, if the townspeople were not as indiscriminately kind to them, the present trouble would not exist. As it is the place is getting far too good a name among the aboriginals, for every week sees some fresh arrival... The number of the local tribe is very small. It is the coming in of all and sundry that is the disquieting feature.[109]

Perhaps surprisingly, given the *Advertiser*'s general lack of interest in Aboriginal matters at Albany in the years before and after 1913, the editor picked up the story at Mount Barker and wrote an editorial stingingly critical of Education Department inaction:

It seems hardly credible, but it is nevertheless true, that blacks were received from the bush at the Mount Barker School and given equal treatment with white children...nothing more damaging to youthful morals than such a condition of affairs could be imagined. The public mind must revolt at the bare idea... The citizens of this state approve the expenditure of a certain amount of each year's revenue on the care of the aborigines. Public solicitude for the welfare of the blacks, however, hardly extends to their education and treatment on an equal footing with the white population. That youngsters of varying degrees of duskiness should be admitted from the bush to a country school is an outrage on decency.[110]

Eventually, in response to the withdrawal of one hundred children from the school until Aboriginal children were removed from the roll, Cabinet and the Education Department bowed to pressure. Haebich saw this as a political action taken by an unpopular government in an election year.[111] The Mount Barker correspondent wrote only one week after the printing of the *Advertiser* editorial that 'the struggles of the parents for an all white school have at last succeeded' and thanked the local member of Parliament for his efforts.[112]

The *Advertiser* carried few letters from its readers at this time, although it is now impossible to state with certainty whether this was because of policy or a lack of letters received. Certainly, no letter was printed from anyone opposed to the racism displayed during the affair by both the Mount Barker correspondent and the paper's editorial writer.

In December 1922, an area of 134 acres about 2 kilometres north-west of Mount Barker was set aside as an Aboriginal reserve under a new Department of Aborigines policy for the south-west designed to both placate European concerns about town-dwelling Noongars and to achieve savings by encouraging families to use the reserves as a less expensive alternative to Moore River.[113] Although it was not compulsory for Aborigines to move to the reserve, they were strongly encouraged to do so.

Cranbrook developed less rapidly than Katanning, and large areas of virgin bush remained well into the twentieth century. Local historian Maxine Laurie asserted that the 1910 government ban on hunting possums for their skins caused much hardship among those Aboriginal families throughout the Great Southern who had long relied upon the trade to earn a living. Some of these moved into the Cranbrook District because clearing work was available, and because the large areas of virtually untouched native bushland and forest provided reasonably assured supplies of native food during the often long periods of unemployment when the farming season was poor. Families were necessarily mobile, travelling their specific 'runs' as seasonal work such as shearing became available. Sometimes the women were able to work as domestics on the properties where the men were shearing. The main camp was situated about 40 kilometres north-west of Cranbrook at the Unanup Brook, and Aborigines would arrive there from districts to the north and south for corroborees and sporting occasions.[114] Gatherings also occurred in the townsite prior to 1910, with between seventy and eighty adults taking part in corroborees.[115]

During the first decade of the century a small number of Aboriginal men took advantage of the state government's desire to settle small farmers on the land, and were granted conditional purchase blocks in the Great Southern region. Most failed before the end of the Great War because of a combination of factors including difficulties experienced in gaining bank credit, the system of land tenure that was unsympathetic to the owners' long absences from the farm while earning money as shearers or farm labourers, the droughts of 1911 and 1914, and the pressures imposed by cultural obligations to their extended family. The post-war need to find land for soldier settlement meant that any land seen to be only intermittently occupied and farmed was resumed for returned men, and this ended the farming aspirations of the few who had overcome the earlier problems.[116]

When war broke out in 1914, several Aboriginal men from the region enlisted in the Australian Army despite an official policy that excluded them on racial grounds. It appears that some medical officers turned a blind eye to the policy, writing 'dark' in the section of the recruiting form that referred to the applicant's complexion.[117] The fact that recruiting officials were unable to note 'Aboriginal' on enlistment documents (until a change of policy in late 1917 allowed Aborigines to enlist)[118] prevents the exact number being ascertained, although assiduous work by members of Honouring Indigenous War Graves Inc. and the Local History Section staff of the Albany Public Library will continue to add to knowledge on this point. I have been unable to find evidence about the reception of local returned Aboriginal soldiers back in their home towns, but it is almost certain that the Australia-wide experience of Aboriginal soldiers was repeated in the Albany region – an acceptance while in the AIF, but a continuation of official discrimination when they returned home. At least in death they were treated as equals. Both Augustus Farmer and his brother Lawrence have their names inscribed on the District Roll of Honour at Katanning[119] alongside the other men from the district who lost their lives, and their mother was granted a pension at the standard rate of forty shillings a fortnight that was paid to dependants of all deceased soldiers.[120]

In the late 1970s, when the Shire of Katanning commissioned Merle Bignell to write a history of the town and district, some residents who had been children in the early years of the century were still alive and there were many others who had clear memories of what their pioneering parents had told them of this era.[121] The following quote from her book refers to Katanning, but it could equally be applied to other districts in the region:

In the main the average settler of the 1900s had one overriding desire – to advance materially. There was no clear-sighted ambition for social advancement, although to be thought respectable was a popular intent. Fundamentally their aim was middle-class solvency, a prosperous farm with stock and machinery, and a solid house filled with essential furniture. The puritanical virtues of thrift, hard work and sober living were followed scrupulously by a strong core who believed in six days of labour and the seventh spent in church – in some cases three times a day. Few determined settlers touched alcohol; a glass of sherry at Christmas was considered quite daring. Ex South Australians brought with them the seeds of wowserism which was strongly entrenched in that state.[122]

Published local histories of districts such as Gnowangerup and Katanning emphasise the go-ahead nature of many of the newly arriving farmers, and make it very clear that there was a great sense of pride in the progress they and their communities were making.[123]

The attitudes and experiences of the newly arrived settlers worked together to exacerbate pre-existing problems in the Aboriginal–European relationship. Just as the sons and grandsons of the original pastoral lessees had felt less of a sense of responsibility to the Noongars who had once been the sole possessors of the land, so the men and women who had come from all over Australia to make their homes in Albany and its rural hinterland frequently were not prepared to acknowledge that they owed a great debt of obligation to the Aboriginal people on whose land they were now living, and on whose labour many then depended.

Following Federation in 1901, the Australian Government's policy of restricting migration to 'white' Europeans played an important and profoundly negative role in shaping settlers' attitudes towards the region's Aboriginal people. The White

Australia Policy was based partly upon racist notions of white superiority, and partly upon the determination of working-class Australians to protect their hard-won gains by denying employers the opportunity to lower wages and conditions through the importation of cheap 'coloured' labour. Both of these policy foundations impacted upon Aboriginal–European relationships in the Albany region. Andrew Markus states that the sense of racial superiority manifested in Social Darwinist thought defined Western culture at the turn of the century, and that Aborigines were seen in Australia as inhibiting the racial homogeneity believed to be essential.[124] When Chris Watson, the Federal leader of the Australian Labor Party stated in Parliament:

> We object to them [Asian immigrants] not alone on the ground of competition with our own workmen – though I admit that this is one of the grounds – but also and more particularly on the grounds of racial contamination.[125]

and many other members of Federal Parliament made equally racist speeches, it is not surprising to find that ordinary Australians tended to take their lead. Calls by trade union leaders to preserve jobs for white Australians compounded the already hardening attitudes towards Aboriginal people.[126]

The period between 1905 and 1926 was a time when European notions of cultural and social superiority, together with a growing realisation that the south-western population of mixed-descent Aborigines was growing to an extent that many settlers found disconcerting, if not alarming, led the Western Australian Government to institute a harsh regime of bureaucratic domination and institutionalisation of its Aboriginal people. Those families with historic ties to Albany and its Menang people found themselves living as unwelcome groups in and around the quickly growing Great Southern towns, forced to integrate at a basic level with a society that denied them full economic participation or social equality.

Disruption to Aboriginal life caused by the arrival of Europeans in late 1826 had at first been relatively minimal. One hundred years later, Albany's Aboriginal people found themselves spread throughout the region known by then as the Great Southern, as their pre-European boundaries, never forgotten, became no longer practical as markers defining families' places of residence.

Despite all that they had endured, the Aboriginal people from the Albany region kept many aspects of their culture and traditions alive. The *Albany Advertiser* of 12 December 1930 carried the following advertisement.

Natives Corroboree

Natives **YORKSHIRE BOB** and **MOSES WYBUNG**
wish to notify their friends that a Native Corroboree will be held on
PARADE STREET RESERVE
AT 7 P.M. TO-NIGHT.

Work with natives, like our white brethren, has been scarce, and we much appreciate the kindness of the "Albany Advertiser" in publishing this brief note for us free of cost.
ROLL UP!   ROLL UP!
And bring your spare coppers and sixpences to help us.

The two men listed in the advertisement had close ties to Albany and obviously had retained the cultural knowledge necessary to hold a corroboree (both later met with linguist Gerhardt Laves at Albany to inform him about cultural matters).[127] This was not the first public performance for Albany's non-Aboriginal population. Eight years earlier 'a contingent of natives from the back country' performed a corroboree at the Aboriginal camp on the Perth road for 'a privileged few', before the main performance in York Street on New Year's Eve the following night. Although several of the star performers had left on the evening train, an appreciative audience of 1500 watched:

> the fantastic movements of the different native dances, to the accompaniment of the beating together of sticks, the crooning of the gins and the harsh guttural expressions of the males.[128]

One wonders what Mokare and Barker would have thought about this meeting of Aboriginal people and Europeans on the exact spot where they had exchanged cultural information one hundred years earlier. Trains, newspapers, advertising, a culturally unaware audience, and the taking up of money after the performance would all have been completely outside Mokare's experience, but the songs and dance movements may well have been very familiar to him. Despite all that they had endured, the Aboriginal people of the Albany region had kept alive their culture, however modified by their relationship with those who had moved into their land and their lives.

Epilogue

Friday 21 January 1927 marked the beginning of a week of official functions planned to celebrate the Centenary of Albany with due pomp and civic pride. The previous week's edition of the *Albany Advertiser* had informed residents that the first event would be the unveiling of the memorial stone at the Town Hall, followed by a civic reception for the Governor, Sir William Campion, KCMG, DSO. During the afternoon there would be a 'Procession of Children and Military Contingent, etc., to Residency Point.', and the 'Official Hoisting of the British Flag' near where Lockyer's flag-raising ceremony had formally established British rule at King George Sound one hundred years earlier.

The photograph taken at the assembly point near the Post Office building in Stirling Terrace shows some of the participants milling around just prior to the procession moving off. Bandsmen are making last-minute adjustments to their instruments while two young Aboriginal men, identities lost to time, prepare to take their place at the procession's head. A reporter from the *Albany Advertiser* noted that hundreds of cameras were trained on these two men as they waited, resplendent in white markings and carrying spears and shields.

One wonders how many of the photographs taken that day also captured the image of what appears to be a third Aboriginal man who was standing nearby dressed in cast-off clothing, his face invisible in deep shadow. To those present who reflected on any but the most superficial level, the Centennial procession must have been deeply symbolic of the profound changes that the previous one hundred years had brought to the original inhabitants of Albany. If anyone thought to ask the three Aboriginal men their views on what had occurred, their answers were not recorded.

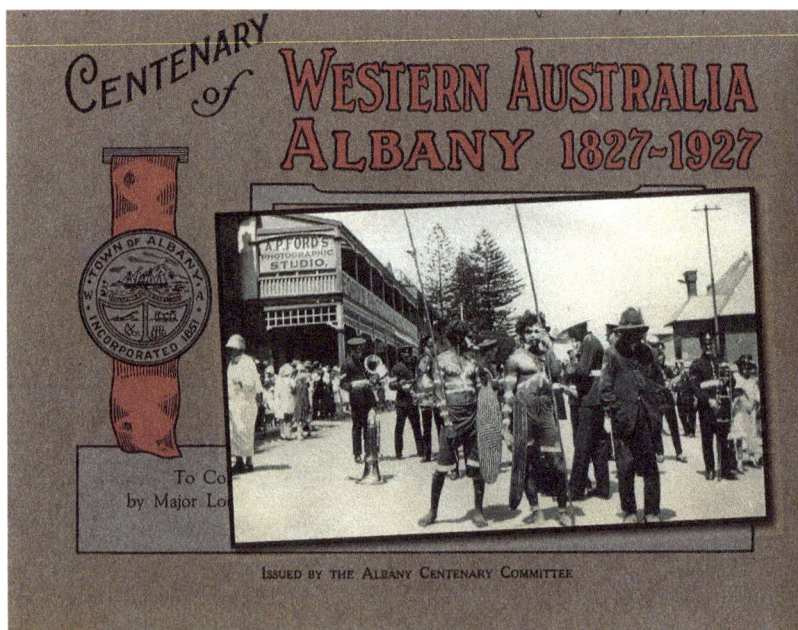

Cover page of the souvenir booklet produced by the Albany Centenary Committee to mark the Centenary of European settlement at Albany
Local History Section of the Albany Public Library

Appendices

APPENDIX 1

Seasonal Exploitation of Resources

Acknowledgement is made to Sue le Souef for her permission to use this table.

Month	Menang season	European season	Location	Food	Method
June	Mawkur	Winter	inland in small dispersed groups	large grey kangaroos, emus, rat-kangaroos and other small game, freshwater fish	pit-falls, kangaroo traps, dingoes
July					smoking game from trees
August				plants, fungi	brush and stone weirs, digging stick
September	Meerningal	Spring	start moving back to coast	young birds and birds' eggs	boomerang?
October			assembling in greater numbers	brush kangaroos, roots and grubs banksia nectar, occasional fish	surrounding and spearing, digging stick
November	—				weirs
December	Beruck	Summer	gathered in large groups on the coast	moderate quantities of fish, freshwater crayfish, tortoises, wallabies, brush kangaroos	spearing, weirs, digging stick
January					burning the bush or surrounding area
February				possums, lizards, snakes, seals	
March	Meertilluk	Autumn	start to move inland	large quantities and varieties of fish, frogs, kangaroos, wallabies	stone fish-traps, brush, weirs
April					night fishing
May	Pourner			other game if available	spearing

APPENDIX 2

Lynette Knapp traces her ancestry on both sides of her family to Aboriginal women who were born near Albany during the early colonial period and formed part of the exodus from the town to its hinterland in the mid nineteenth century. I wish to thank Lynette for providing details of their subsequent lives to serve as examples of the many other Aboriginal men and women who left their traditional country around King George Sound at this time and died far from home. A century later, some of their descendants returned to Albany, where their families now form a strong part of the town's Noongar community.

Lynette's father was born at the Albany campsite which is now the Railways football ground, and when he brought the family back in the late 1960s, he told them he wanted to return to Albany so that when he died his spirit would be released in his own country. European settlement disrupted the lives of the Menang people, but it would be a profound mistake to think that it always managed to destroy what was in their hearts.

Some of Lynette Knapp's Family History

Her mother's side

Mederan was born near the Kalgan River, probably sometime in the 1830s. She married William Egan, one of the many convicts who moved to Albany in the 1850s, and the couple moved from the town to work on the Hassell property at Kendenup. They then moved to New Norcia, where they raised a family of two boys and three girls (see Chapter Seven). One of their daughters, Catherine Egan, married William Ryder at New Norcia in 1868.

Catherine and William had a daughter, Marta. She married Herbert Binder at Northam.

Marta and Herbert had six sons and one daughter, Gertie.

Because of her Albany connection, Gertie was sent to Carrolup, where in the late 1940s she married Alf Knapp, who was head of the settlement's kitchen staff. Gertie and Alf soon moved to Toodyay, and then to Bremer Bay. They had nine children, one of whom was Lynette. Alf was a renowned tracker and took up work as a dingo trapper. He took pride in the name by which he was usually known – Dingo Alf. Alf Knapp was born at the campsite situated near the present site of the Railways football ground, and returned with his family to Albany in 1968.

Her father's side

Jakbam was born early in the colonial period at Wilson Inlet. She lived with a convict named Charles Knapp. Charles and Jakbam had a daughter, Minnie. They travelled to Cape Arid, where Charles continued on to Adelaide. Jakbam then underwent a tribal marriage with a local man named Wural. Jakbam and Wural had a son known as Johnny Knapp, before she left Wural and returned to the town of Albany to live with Wabbinyet (also known as Dicky Bumblefoot). Johnny Knapp married Annie Williams and lived mainly at Chillinup, between Albany and the Stirling Ranges. Their son, Alf Knapp, married Gertie Binder (see 'Her mother's side' above).

APPENDIX 3

Aboriginal and European Population Numbers, and Area of Land Cleared for Agriculture

Land-clearing statistics are taken from various Western Australian Annual *Blue Books*.

Date	European population		Aboriginal population		Area of cleared land
	ALBANY	**REGION**	**ALBANY**	**REGION**	
1827	c.50	none	about 40 around Albany, no accurate estimate of regional population		almost nil
1848	428	very few	estimated total of 450 (W.A. census)		almost nil
1854	total of 970		estimated total of 570 (Albany Sub-Guardian of Natives)		almost nil
1870			estimated total of 400 (police estimate for W.A. census)		1,000 acres of 20 million
1881	1,024	619	unknown, with 180 employed (police estimate for census)		886 acres of 20 million
1891	2,655	1,498	estimated total of 190 (police estimate for W.A. census)		2,421 acres of 20 million
1901	3,594	2,522	unknown, with 90 employed		15,000 acres + 138,324 ringbarked of 20 million
1910			probably less than ten permanents	unknown	12,797 acres + 500,000 acres ringbarked of 3,500,000 acres south of Cranbrook
1914	4,201		probably less than ten permanents	unknown	

APPENDIX 4

Tindale's 'Tribal Boundaries'

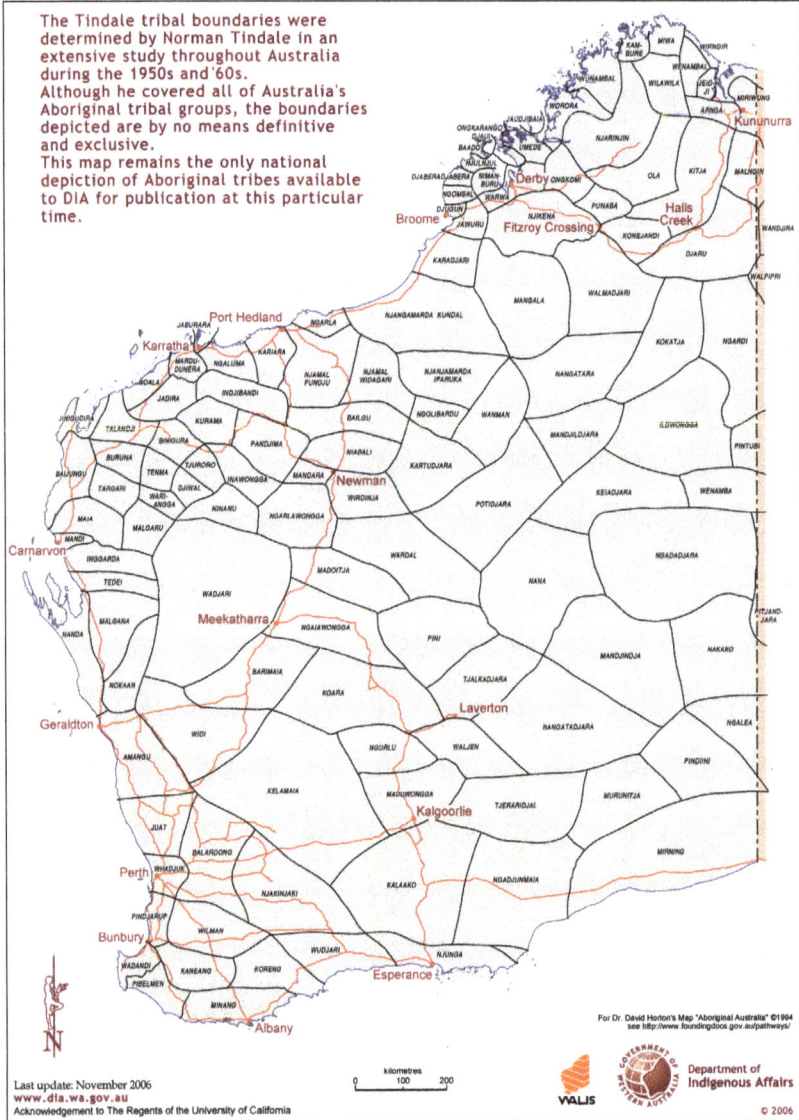

The Tindale tribal boundaries were determined by Norman Tindale in an extensive study throughout Australia during the 1950s and '60s. Although he covered all of Australia's Aboriginal tribal groups, the boundaries depicted are by no means definitive and exclusive.

This map remains the only national depiction of Aboriginal tribes available to DIA for publication at this particular time.

For Dr. David Horton's Map "Aboriginal Australia" ©1994
see http://www.foundingdocs.gov.au/pathways/

Last update: November 2006
www.dia.wa.gov.au
Acknowledgement to The Regents of the University of California

kilometres
0   100   200

Department of Indigenous Affairs

© 2006

308

APPENDIX 5

Albany Police Daily Occurrence Books for 1863

A list of occasions when Aboriginal people from the region are mentioned in the Albany Police Daily Occurrence Books for the year 1863 (SRO Cons 367, item 1, and Cons 364, item 1). I have summarised each entry. Some entries are incomplete, with no information given about the result of subsequent legal action. This year was chosen because it is the first available year, and gives a picture of police–Aboriginal interaction at the earliest stage possible, but it is somewhat atypical of later years because of the unusual number of more serious cases in 1863.

31/1/1863
P. C. Chester arrives from Jerramungup with three Aboriginal prisoners and two Aboriginal witnesses.

2/2/1863
Albert, alias Coorall sentenced to nine months at Rottnest for theft of flour and sugar. He was also charged with setting fire to the bush at Jerramungup and received three months for this offence. Kendall was charged with aiding Coorall in an attempt to escape. Woorack was charged with absconding from service with his employer.

3/2/1863
An unnamed Aboriginal man charged John Edwards (presumably a European) with 'pulling off his kangaroo skin and exposing his nakedness'. This is one of a very small number of occasions (and the earliest I have found) where an Aboriginal person brought charges against a European.

9/2/1863

Aboriginal woman (Jenny) discharged after having been charged with being drunk.

17/2/1863

Jacky Handsome charged with supplying liquor to another Aboriginal person.

27/2/1863

An Aboriginal man fell from a tree at Camballup and was seriously injured. A letter was sent to Arthur Trimmer (Sub-Guardian) at Pootenup requiring him to care for the man.

2/3/1863

An Aboriginal man sent to Rottnest prison for twelve months for having speared another in the leg.

7/3/1863

Three Aboriginal men from the Salt River cautioned and discharged for robbery of items from a shepherd's hut.

10/3/1863

An Aboriginal man sentenced to fourteen days in prison for supplying spirits to another Aboriginal man.

16/3/1863

James Hayes (presumably a European) sentenced to two months' hard labour for stealing a sheep's head and pluck belonging to an Aboriginal woman.

22/3/1863

An Aboriginal person charged with setting fire to the bush at Arthur Trimmer's property at Pootenup.

24/3/1863

Five Aboriginal men employed to catch an escaped prisoner, with a reward of £10 offered if he was brought back to Albany.

29/4/1863

Teelup charged with attempting to spear Mr Hosty, a shepherd employed by Mr Hassell at Jerramungup.

30/4/1863

Teelup charged with the fatal spearing of Charles Storey.

18/5/1863

The Magistrate at Albany refuses to hear the evidence of two Aboriginal women unless they are 'washed and cleaned'. Police employ an Aboriginal woman to wash them.

14/8/1863

Coban captured by Aboriginal men and the reward of £10 claimed.

15/8/1863

An Aboriginal person charged with setting fire to the bush. Discharged.

18/8/1863

Coban escorted to Perth for trial.

19/8/1863

Geordy charged with absconding service with Constable Chester as a Native Assistant.

27/9/1863

Police successfully employ three Aborigines to find tools stolen from a convict road gang.

12/10/1863

A police constable and a native assistant sent to the Hay River to arrest Bonaparte for stealing bread and a bottle of oil.

26/10/1863

Two Aboriginal men arrested for involvement in the murder of Chilepert at Kojonup.

12/11/1863

An Aboriginal employee charged with absconding from his place of employment.

16/11/1863

Yockolete charged with spearing Chilepert.

28/11/1863

Yockolete remanded in order to call witnesses.

26/11/1863

Another Aboriginal man arrested over the Chilepert murder.

APPENDIX 6

Period of Office of Commandants and Government Residents

A table showing the arrival and departure dates for each of the four commandants at King George Sound.

Major Edmund Lockyer	December 1826	April 1827
Captain Jos. Wakefield	April 1827	December 1828
Lt. George Sleeman	December 1828	December 1829
Captain Collet Barker	December 1829	March 1831

A table showing the period of office of the Government Residents at Albany during the nineteenth century.

Name	Commenced	Resigned or died
Alexander Collie	April 1831	November 1832
Lt. Donald Macleod (acting)	November 1832	October 1833
Sir Richard Spencer	October 1833	July 1839
Captain George Grey	August 1839	March 1840
Captain Peter Belches (acting)	March 1840	September 1840
John Randall Phillips	September 1840	July 1847
Henry Camfield	July 1847	December 1860
Sir Alexander Cockburn-Campbell	January 1861	1871

Name	Commenced	Resigned or died
Gustavus Hare	1871	1881
Rowley Loftie	1881	1899
John Wright	1899	1908

All information is taken from Donald S. Garden's *Albany, A Panorama of the Sound from 1827*

NOTES

Introduction

1 B. Reece, 'Inventing Aborigines', in V. Chapman & P. Read (eds), *Terrible Hard Biscuits*, Allen & Unwin, Sydney, 1996, p. 32.

Chapter 1: The Original Inhabitants of the Albany Region

1 J. Allen & J. F. O'Connell, 'The long and the short of it', in *Australian Archaeology*, no. 57, 2003.

2 J. Davis, 'The first 150 years', in R. M. Berndt & C. H. Berndt (eds), *Aborigines of the West*, UWA Press, Nedlands, 1979, p. 56.

3 J. Milroy, 'Aboriginal culture and society', in J. Gregory & J. Gothard (eds), *Historical Encyclopedia of Western Australia*, UWA Press, Crawley, 2009, p. 7.

4 Personal discussion with Robert Reynolds, archaeologist and Senior Regional Heritage Officer with the Department of Indigenous Affairs, Albany.

5 Ibid.

6 W. H. Douglas, 'Communication: Aboriginal languages – an overview', in R. M. Berndt & C. H. Berndt (eds), *Aborigines of the West*, UWA Press, Nedlands, 1979, p. 39.

7 N. Green, *NYUNGAR – the People*, Creative Research, Mount Lawley, 1979, p. 57.

8 D. Bell, *Daughters of the Dreaming*, Allen & Unwin, Sydney, 1983, pp. 280–1.

9 http://www.berndt.uwa.edu.au/generic.lasso?token_value=berndt (accessed 20/4/2009).

10 C. Berndt, 'Aboriginal women', in R. M. Berndt & C. H. Berndt (eds), *Aborigines of the West*, UWA Press, Nedlands, 1979, p. 37.

11 I. S. Nind, 'Description of the natives of King George's Sound (Swan River Colony) and adjoining country. Written by Mr. Scott Nind, and communicated by R. Brown, Esq., F.R.S. Read 14th Feb., 1831', *The Journal of the Royal Geographical Society of London*, vol. 1, 1832, p. 38.

12   A. Collie, 'Anecdotes and remarks relative to the Aborigines of King George's Sound', attributed to Dr A. Collie, *Perth Gazette and Western Australian Journal*, July–August 1834.

13   Ibid., p. 67.

14   Nind, p. 38.

15   Collie.

16   J. Browne, *Aborigines of the King George's Sound Region 1836–1838: the collected Works of James Browne*, compiled and annotated by K. Macintyre & B. Dobson, Hesperian Press, Carlisle, 2011, p. 13.

17   J. Mulvaney & N. Green, *Commandant of Solitude: the journals of Captain Collet Barker 1828–1831*, Melbourne University Press, Melbourne, 1992, journal entry 23/2/1831.

18   S. le Souef, *Portraits of the South West*, UWA Press, Nedlands, 1993, p. 124.

19   N. Tindale, *Aboriginal tribes of Australia*, Australian National University Press, Canberra, 1974.

20   N. Green, 'Norman Tindale's tribal territories – fact or fabrication?' conference paper.

21   B. Goode et al., *'Kinjarling', the Place of Rain*, The City of Albany and the Department of Indigenous Affairs Aboriginal Heritage Survey, a Report Prepared for the City of Albany and the Department of Indigenous Affairs, Albany, 2005, p. 42.

22   Ibid.

23   Nind, p. 43.

24   Browne, p. 7.

25   T. Shellam, *Shaking Hands on the Fringe*, UWA Press, Crawley, 2009, pp. 32–3.

26   T. B. Wilson, *Narrative of a Voyage round the World: comprehending an account of the wreck of the ship Governor Ready in Torres Straits, a description of the British settlements on the coast of new Holland, more particularly Raffles Bay, Melville Island, Swan River, and King George's Sound; also the manners and customs of the Aboriginal tribes: with an appendix containing remarks on transportation, the treatment of convicts during the voyage, and advice to persons intending to emigrate to the Australian colonies*, Gilbert and Piper, London, 1835. My copy, Dawson, London, 1968, p. 242.

27   Shellam, p. 32.

28   G. F. Moore, *A Descriptive Vocabulary of the Language in Common Use amongst the Aborigines of Western Australia*, William S. Orr, London, 1842.

29   Browne, p. 7.

30   Ibid., p. 26.

31   M. Powell & R. Hesline, 'Making tribes? Constructing Aboriginal tribal identities in Sydney and coastal New South Wales from the early colonial period to the present', *Journal of the Royal Australian Historical Society*, vol. 96, no. 2, 2010, pp. 115–48.

32   P. Crawford & I. Crawford, *Contested Country: a history of the Northcliffe area*, UWA Press, Crawley, 2003, p. 13.

33   E. J. Eyre, *Journals of Expeditions of Discovery into Central Australia and Overland from Adelaide to King George's Sound in the Years 1840–1*, vol. 1, London, 1845, p. 426.

34   Browne, p. 7.

35   Mulvaney & Green, p. 356.

36   Goode et al., p. 43.

37   Browne, p. 7.

38   Nind, p. 23.

39   J. S. C. Dumont d'Urville, *Voyage de la Corvette l'Astrolabe pendant les années 1826–29*, J. Tastu, Paris, 1833, translation from French by A. Hossen of those portions relating to King George Sound, September to October, 1826.

40   le Souef, pp. 7–8.

41   Ibid., p. 8.

42   Collie, p. 69.

43   Goode et al., p. 1.

44   Nind, p. 28.

45   Ibid., p. 23.

46   le Souef, p. 9.

47   Mulvaney & Green, p. 307.

48   Ibid.

49   Nind, p. 28.

50   http://www.environment.gov.au/biodiversity/conservation/hotspots/international-biodiversity

51   Goode et al., p. 1.

52   Ferguson, p. 134.

53   Collie, p. 96.

54   Ferguson, p. 134.

55   Ibid.

56   Browne, p. 11.

57   Collie, p. 80.

58   Crawford & Crawford, p. 26.

59   Australian Government Bureau of Meteorology, 'Climate statistics for Australian locations', monthly climate statistics, http://www.bom.gov.au/climate/averages/tables/cw_009581.shtml (accessed 17/02/2009).

60   Australian Government Bureau of Meteorology, 'About the WBGT and apparent temperature indices', at http://www.bom.gov.au/info/thermal_stress (accessed 17/02/2009).

61   Nind, p. 45.

62   Goode et al., p. 68.

63   Browne, p. 9.

64   Nind, pp. 34–5.

65   Ibid., p. 29.

66   Ibid., p. 30.

67   Ibid., p. 31.

68 Ibid., p. 36.
69 G. Grey, *Journals of Two Expeditions of Discovery in North-West and Western Australia*, vol. 2, Boone, London, 1841, p. 261.
70 R. B. Lee & R. Daly (eds), *Cambridge Encyclopedia of Hunters and Gatherers*, Cambridge University Press, Cambridge, 1999, p. 112.
71 Bell, p. 55.
72 K. Hawkes & R. Bliege Bird, 'Showing off, handicap signalling and the evolution of men's work', *Evolutionary Anthropology*, vol. 11, 2002, pp. 58–67.
73 W. E. H. Stanner's model of 'estate, range, domain' to describe the system of land ownership and use appears in 'Aboriginal territorial organisation: estate, range, domain and regime', *Oceania*, vol. 36, 1965, p. 2. 'The estate was the traditionally recognised locus ('country', 'home', 'ground', 'dreaming place')… of the territorial group…The range was the tract or orbit over which the group…ordinarily hunted and foraged to maintain life'. Stanner combined the estate and the range to form what he named the 'domain'.
74 Ferguson, p. 129.
75 Nind, p. 28.
76 Mulvaney & Green, p. 382.
77 Ferguson, p. 121.
78 Goode et al., p. 44.
79 T. B. Wilson, 'A letter to Captain Collet Barker recounting an excursion to the North West and West of King George's Sound by Dr T. B. Wilson, December 1829', in *Western Australian Exploration*, vol. 1, 1826–1835, Hesperian Press, Victoria Park, 2005, p. 117.
80 A. Collie, 'Account of four excursions in the vicinity of King George's Sound between 27th April and 15th June 1831, by Alexander Collie, Surgeon', in *Western Australian Exploration*, vol. 1, p. 245.
81 'Robert Dale's excursion from King George Sound to Koi-kyeun-u-ruff Ranges, January 1832', in *Western Australian Exploration*, vol. 1, p. 299.
82 le Souef, p. 52.
83 *The Inquirer*, 23/2/1842.
84 Nind, pp. 24–6.
85 Mulvaney & Green, p. 350.
86 Nind, pp. 26–7.
87 Ibid., p. 38.
88 Ferguson, p. 136.
89 Nind, p. 38.
90 Ibid., p. 39.
91 Ferguson, p. 136.
92 Mulvaney & Green, pp. 358–9.
93 Ibid., pp. 38–9.
94 Nind, p. 38.
95 Ibid., p. 44.
96 Ibid., p. 38.

97   Mulvaney & Green, p. 251.

98   Ibid., p. 267.

99   Collie, p. 88.

100 D. Bates, *The Passing of the Aborigines*, John Murray, London, 1966, pp. 24–5.

101 Nind, p. 38.

102 D. Bates, *The Native Tribes of Western Australia*, I. White (ed.), National Library of Australia, Canberra, 1985.

103 Bates, *The Passing of the Aborigines*, p. 25.

104 Nind, p. 38.

105 Ibid.

106 Ibid.

107 N. Green, *Broken Spears*, Focus Education Services, Cottesloe, 1984, p. 19.

108 Mulvaney & Green, p. 308.

109 Nind, p. 42.

110 Mulvaney & Green, pp. 268–9.

111 Browne, p. 20.

112 Goode et al., p. 176.

113 The use of the past tense in this chapter should not be seen as implying that these beliefs are no longer regarded as valid by Aboriginal people today.

114 Crawford & Crawford, p. 21.

115 Mulvaney & Green, p. 345.

116 Ibid., p. 283.

117 Ibid., p. 289.

118 E. Hassell, *My Dusky Friends*, C. W. Hassell, Fremantle, 1975.

119 Ibid., p. 59.

120 Ibid., p. 60.

121 Moorareet Sam Williams, *Yonker Mir*, Batchelor Press, Batchelor, 2007; C. Peterson, *Koodjal-koodjal Djook: Four sisters. The legend of the Southern Cross*, Batchelor Press, Batchelor, 2007; C. Peterson, *Yongka, Miyak: Kangaroo and Moon*, Batchelor Press, Batchelor, 2007; J. Williams & A. Dean, *Boola Miyel: the place of many faces*, Batchelor Press, Batchelor, 2007; L. Knapp, *Mirnang Waangkaniny*, Batchelor Press, Batchelor, 2012. All of these authors have strong ties to the Albany region.

In September 2011, UWA Publishing released two bilingual art books, *Mamang* and *Noongar Mambara Bakitj*, as the first in a new series inspired by old stories told to American linguist Gerhardt Laves by Noongar people at Albany around 1931.

Chapter 2: First Contact

1   D. Hunt: *Albany: First Western Settlement*, Albany Advertiser Print, Albany, undated, p. 5. Hunt gave no reference for her assertion that Monkbeelven appeared on old Dutch maps. When Robert Menli Lyon published a dictionary of Aboriginal words at Perth in 1833, he included a cryptic entry 'kai at Monkbeelven'. (*Perth Gazette and Independent Journal*, 13/4/1833.) It appears

possible that he was pointing out that *gumo* meant 'round' at Perth, while *kai* was used to mean the same at Monkbeelven. If so, historians who have used his dictionary to indicate that 'Monkbeelven' has a Noongar, rather than a Dutch, derivation, have been in error. Why Lyon would have chosen to write Monkbeelven rather than King George's Sound, is unclear. Several native-born Dutch people have informed me that 'Monkbeelven' is a not a word in the Dutch language that they are familiar with.

2   Appleyard & Manford, pp. 16–18.

3   L. Marchant, *France Australe*, Artlook Books, Perth, 1982, p. 103.

4   Ibid., p. 21.

5   D. S. Garden, *Albany: a panorama of the Sound from 1827*, Nelson, Melbourne, 1977, p. 9. Marchant has shown that Britain at that time believed (unlike France) that only effective occupation marked land as belonging to the claiming power and Britain had no plans at that stage to occupy the land claimed by Vancouver.

6   G. Vancouver, *A Voyage of Discovery to the North Pacific Ocean and Round the World 1791–1795, with an Introduction and Appendices*, vol. I. My copy, W. Kaye Lamb (ed.), The Hakluyt Society, London, 1984, p. 339.

7   Ibid., p. 336.

8   T. B. Wilson, 'Narrative of a Voyage around the World', in L. Wilson, *The Laird of Braidwood*, Wilson, Tasmania, 2006, p. 119. It is interesting to note that Wilson's statement (unattributed) was quoted in the report of the 1837 House of Commons Select Committee on Aboriginal Tribes.

9   Personal communication with Sarah Drummond, 15/6/2011.

10 C. M. H. Clark, *A History of Australia*, vol. III, 'The Beginning of an Australian Civilization 1824–1851', Melbourne University Press, Melbourne, 1973, p. 12.

11 M. Bignell, *The Fruit of the Country*, UWA Press, Nedlands, 1977, p. 9.

12 Drummond has speculated that some of this harsh treatment may have been due to the refusal of the Menang to follow the example of the Tasmanian Aborigines in trading their women (personal communication, 15/6/2011).

13 T. Shellam, *Shaking Hands on the Fringe*, UWA Press, Crawley, 2009, p. 101.

14 *Perth Gazette and Western Australian Journal*, 8/10/1842, p. 3.

15 W. F. Bynum, 'The Great Chain of Being after forty years: an appraisal', *History of Science*, vol. xiii, 1975, p. 22.

16 J. W. Gough, 'Reviews of books', *English Historical Review*, vol. lxxxi, no. cccxix, April 1966, p. 356.

17 J. Laird, 'Critical notices', *Mind*, vol. xlvi, no. 183, 1937, p. 400.

18 Ibid., p. 403.

19 Bynum, p. 10.

20 H. Carey, writing in *God's Empire*, Cambridge University Press, Cambridge, 2010, pp. 149–50, notes that the word 'evangelical' has three major meanings. Firstly, it can be used to refer to the preaching of the Christian gospel. Secondly, in Germany and some other countries it simply means 'Protestant'. Thirdly, when written with a capital E, the word refers to a group within the Church

of England who came together in the eighteenth century with the aim of rejuvenating the foundations of their church.

21   E, Dussel, 'Las Casas Bartolome, de', *Encyclopaedia Britannica*, vol. 7, 1986, pp. 168–9.

22   J. C. Beaglehole (ed.), *The Journals of Captain James Cook*, vol. 1, Cambridge University Press, Cambridge, 1955, p. 399.

23   L. Behrendt, 'In your dreams: cultural appropriation, popular culture and colonialism', *Law Text Culture*, vol. 4, no. 1, 1998, pp. 256–79.

24   J. Gascoigne & A. Curthoys, *The Enlightenment and the Origins of European Australia*, Cambridge University Press, Cambridge, 2002, p. 148.

25   Ibid., p. 149.

26   Ibid.

27   W. E. H. Stanner, *White Man Got No Dreaming: essays 1938–1973*, ANU Press, Canberra, 1979, p. 145.

28   A. Hasluck, *Thomas Peel of Swan River*, Oxford University Press, Melbourne, 1965, p. xi.

29   H. Reynolds, *The Other Side of the Frontier*, James Cook University Press, Townsville, 1981, pp. 30–1.

30   F. Armstrong, 'Manners and habits of the Aborigines of Western Australia, from information gathered by Mr F. Armstrong, Interpreter', *Perth Gazette and Western Australian Journal*, 29/11/1836.

31   Reynolds, p. 33. This belief was not restricted to Aboriginal Australians. When Captain James Cook visited the Pacific Island of Eromanga he found the same idea. F. McLynn, *Captain Cook: master of the seas*, Yale University Press, New Haven, 2011, p. 247.

32   G. Grey, *Journals of Two Expeditions of Discovery in North-West and Western Australia*, vol. 1, Boone, London, 1841, p. 302.

33   Ibid.

34   F. Armstrong, *Perth Gazette*, 29/11/1836.

35   J. Mulvaney & N. Green, *Commandant of Solitude*, Melbourne University Press, Melbourne, 1992, p. 299.

36   I. S. Nind, 'Description of the natives of King George's Sound (Swan River Colony) and adjoining country. Written by Mr. Scott Nind, and communicated by R. Brown, Esq., F. R. S. Read 14th February, 1831', *Journal of the Royal Geographical Society of London*, vol. 1, 1832, p. 47.

37   D. Bates, *Aboriginal Perth and Bibbulmun Biographies and Legends*, 1992, p. 5.

38   Reynolds, p. 36.

39   M. Flinders, *Voyage to Terra Australis: undertaken for the purpose of completing the discovery of that vast country and prosecuted in the years 1801, 1802 and 1803, in His Majesty's ship Investigator and subsequently in the armed vessel Porpoise and Cumberland schooner: with an account of the shipwreck of the Porpoise, arrival of the Cumberland at Mauritius, and imprisonment of the Commander during six years and a half in that island*, W. Bulmer and Co., 1814, facsimile edition, Libraries Board of South Australia, Adelaide, 1966, entry for Tuesday, 5/1/1802.

40 Ibid., entry for 14/12/1801.

41 Ibid.

42 Ibid., entry for 15/12/1801.

43 Ibid., entry for 30/12/1801.

44 Bates, p. 5.

45 Marchant, pp. 115–16.

46 G. Barzon, 'Pirates and wreckers of Kangaroo Island', *Evening News*, 28/9/1816.

47 P. P. King, *Narrative of a Survey of the Intertropical and Western Coasts of Australia, Performed between the Years 1818 and 1822*, vol. 2, John Murray, London, 1827, entry for 25/12/1821. My copy, http://freeread.com.au/ebooks/e00028.html (accessed 28/05/2009).

48 Ibid.

49 Ibid., entries for 24–31/12/1821.

50 Ibid., entry for 24/12/1821.

51 Marchant, pp. 249–53.

52 J. S. C. Dumont d'Urville, *An Account in Two Volumes of Two Voyages to the South Seas by Captain (later Rear Admiral) Jules S.C. Dumont d'Urville, of the French Navy to Australia, New Zealand, Oceania 1826–1828, in the Corvette l'Astrolabe and to the Straits of Magellan, Chile, Oceania, South East Asia, Australia, Antarctica, New Zealand and Torres Strait 1837–1840 in the Corvettes l'Astrolabe and Zellee*, Helen Rosenman (tr. and ed.), Melbourne University Press, Melbourne, 1987, pp. 29–30.

53 See B. Smith, *European Vision and the South Pacific*, Yale University Press, New Haven, 1985, p. 175, for a contemporary example of an illustration typical of the genre.

54 Ibid., p. 269.

55 M. M. Quoy & Gaimard, 'The natives of King George Sound', in Dumont d'Urville, p. 42.

56 de Sainson, in Dumont d'Urville, pp. 41–2.

57 These historically significant paintings were published in 1833 by J. Tastu of Paris as a series of lithographic prints. Eight of these hand-coloured prints are in the State Library of New South Wales.

58 Shellam, p. 134.

Chapter 3: From Visitors to Invaders – The Garrison Era, 1826–1831

1 L. Marchant, *France Australe*, Artlook Books, Perth, 1982, pp. 225–8.

2 Ibid., p. 231.

3 Ibid., p. 246.

4 Lord Bathurst to Governor Darling, 1/3/1826, Swan River Papers (transcripts of early Colonial Office correspondence held at the SRO), p. 3.

5 Ibid.

6 Darling to Bathurst, 10/10/1826, Historical Records of Australia, series 1, vol. 12, p. 730.

7 J. Mulvaney & N. Green, *Commandant of Solitude*, Melbourne University Press, Melbourne, 1992, p. 242.

8   Although the situation worsened after the 39th Regiment left Van Diemen's Land, the regiment was certainly involved in serious conflict in late 1826 (personal communication with Tasmanian historian Lyndall Ryan, 6/7/2011).

9   E. Lockyer, 'Report by Major Lockyer on the newly-formed settlement at King George's Sound' *Historical Records of Australia*, series III, vol. 6, p. 463.

10   Colonial Secretary Macleay, to Major Lockyer, marked No. 1, *Historical Records of Australia*, series III, vol. 6, p. 453.

11   This was not the only case from the period. When Stirling arrived at Perth in 1829, his initial instructions were hastily drafted with no information on the legal status of Aborigines. A. Hunter, 'The boundaries of colonial criminal law in relation to inter-Aboriginal conflict (inter se offences) in Western Australia in the 1830s–1840s', *Australian Journal of Legal History*, vol. 8, 2004, pp. 219–20.

12   Lockyer, p. 463.

13   T. Shellam, *Shaking Hands on the Fringe*, UWA Press, Crawley, 2009, pp. 88–91.

14   Lockyer, p. 466.

15   L. Johnson, *Major Edmund Lockyer: forgotten Australian pioneer*, Western Australian Museum Press, Albany, 2002, p. 38.

16   D. S. Garden, *Albany: a panorama of the Sound from 1827*, Nelson, Melbourne, 1977, p. 22.

17   Wakefield to Macleay, *Historical Records of Australia*, series III, vol. 6, p. 506.

18   Ibid., p. 507.

19   Ibid., p. 508.

20   Mulvaney & Green, p. 251. See also Shellam, pp. 76–7.

21   Wakefield to Colonial Secretary Macleay, *Historical Records of Australia*, series III, vol. 6, pp. 509–10.

22   Ibid., p. 515.

23   Ibid., p. 525.

24   Ibid., p. 528.

25   Ibid., p. 526.

26   N. Green, *Nyungar – the People*, Creative Research, Mount Lawley, 1979, p. 42.

27   Mulvaney & Green, p. 244.

28   Ibid.

29   W. Ferguson, 'Mokare's domain', in *Australians to 1788*, D. J. Mulvaney & J. White (eds), Fairfax, Syme & Weldon Associates, Sydney, 1987, p. 128.

30   N. Green, *Broken Spears*, Focus Education Services, Perth, 1984, p. 38.

31   Garden, pp. 24–6. Garden reproduced two early diagrammatic maps of the settlement, as well as describing the buildings.

32   Ibid., p. 30.

33   I. S. Nind, 'Description of the natives of King George's Sound (Swan River Colony) and adjoining country. Written by Mr. Scott Nind, and communicated by R. Brown, Esq., F. R. S. Read 14th February, 1831', *Journal of the Royal Geographical Society of London*, vol. 1, 1832, p. 34.

34   Ibid., p. 40.

35   Garden, p. 27.

36   Mulvaney & Green, p. 242.

37   In early 1832, Lieutenant Governor James Stirling was promoted to Governor, and the whole of the present state of Western Australia became officially the Colony of Western Australia.

38   Garden, p. 29.

39   This book uses journals and diaries written by several officials and private citizens (especially Barker's journal written while at King George Sound). Such sources have the advantage of immediacy – they give the writer's viewpoint *at that time*, rather than a later and perhaps revised version of events – and they can frequently be more revealing than official sources. There is always of course the possibility that the writer is being less than objective from a desire to appear more enlightened or prescient than was actually the case.

40   Shellam points out that Barker persuaded the explorer Thomas Bannister to publish an account of his journey across country from the Swan River to Albany in 1831 (p. 65). Barker would certainly have been aware that his own journal provided the basis for what would have been a considerably more historically valuable and interesting publication.

41   Shellam, p. 63.

42   Mulvaney & Green, p. ix. Unfortunately the original journal is now missing. Shellam, Footnote to her PhD thesis, '*Shaking hands on the fringe: negotiating the Aboriginal world at King George's Sound*', ANU, 2007, p. 44.

43   *Historical Records of Australia*, series I, vol. 14, pp. 410–11.

44   Mulvaney & Green, p. 45.

45   Ibid., p. 43.

46   Ibid., p. 32.

47   Ibid., p. 368.

48   N. Green, *Aborigines of the Albany Region 1821–1898*, UWA Press, Nedlands, 1989, p. xi.

49   Mulvaney & Green, p. 298.

50   It is interesting to find that a *taap* or knife sent by Collie back to England featured pieces of green bottle glass as part of its cutting edge. Clearly the Menang were using European gifts in ways they found useful within the context of their own culture (personal communication with Alison Wishart, National Museum, Canberra, 8/4/2011).

51   Collie, 'Report to Governor James Stirling', 1831, *Swan River Papers*, vol. 9, State Records Office, WA, pp. 110–21.

52   Mulvaney & Green, p. 293.

53   R. H. W. Reece, *Aborigines and Colonial Society in New South Wales in the 1830s and 1840s*, Sydney University Press, Sydney, 1974, p. 2.

54   Mulvaney & Green, p. 403.

55   J. Gascoigne, *The Enlightenment and European Australia*, University of Cambridge Press, Cambridge, 2002, p. 149.

56 Mulvaney & Green, p. 241.

57 Mulvaney & Green, p. 387.

58 No information appears in the journal entry (Mulvaney & Green, p. 387) that would shed light on the question of how Barker was aware of any possible misconduct by Private Quin. There are frequent examples in the journal of such cryptic statements made by Barker about other subjects.

59 *Historical records of Australia*, series III, vol. 6, p. 485. It is interesting to note Lockyer's reference to 'civilising' the Aborigines, since there was nothing in his official instructions from Colonial Secretary Macleay that would have led him to consider this as part of his job at King George Sound. It would appear that Lockyer had made an assumption that this was expected of him (or at least would be approved of) but he did not remain at King George Sound for a sufficient length of time to do very much about attempting to carry out policies that were aimed at civilising the Menang. None of his three successors appear to have seen this as an expected part of their responsibilities.

60 J. Browne, *Aborigines of the King George's Sound Region 1836–1838*, Hesperian Press, Carlisle, 2001, p. 1.

61 The colony was not officially entitled 'Western Australia' until the Colonial Office in London sent a despatch to Stirling on 4 March 1831 proclaiming him Governor of the new Colony of Western Australia.

62 As late as the 1880s, the Minute Books of the Albany Municipal Council still had on their covers 'Municipal Council of Albany (K. G. Sound)'.

63 Mulvaney & Green, pp. 393–5.

64 Ibid., p. 403.

Chapter 4: The Beginning of Free Settlement and Aboriginal Dispossession at Albany, 1831–1850

1 L. Tilbrook, *Nyungar Tradition*, UWA Press, Nedlands, 1983, p. 10.

2 Bill Hassell, who remembers when the family property at the Warriups east of Albany was a pastoral holding with almost none of its area cleared, stated that the only areas useful for grazing stock were relatively small areas of natural open grassland (personal communication, 26/9/2011).

3 J. Stirling to Colonel Irwin, 4/3/1831, CSO (Colonial Secretary's Files held at the State Records Office, Perth), file no. 1661/31.

4 J. Mulvaney & N. Green, *Commandant of Solitude*, Melbourne University Press, Melbourne, 1992, p. 405.

5 Ibid.

6 A. Collie to Colonial Secretary at Perth, 3/10/1830, 12/3/1831, CSO, 3/173.

7 A. Collie, 'Anecdotes and remarks relative to the Aborigines of King George's Sound', attributed to Dr A. Collie, *Perth Gazette and Western Australian Journal*, July–August 1834. The author of the work must have been Collie, although his name does not appear at the heads of the instalments.

8 By the end of 1830, only eighteen months after the arrival of the *Parmelia*, the population at Perth was almost 2000 (P. Statham, 'Swan River Colony

1829–1850', in C. T. Stannage (ed.), *A New History of Western Australia*, UWA Press, Nedlands, 1981, p. 181.)

9   Henry Reynolds noted the importance of the nature of the country to the history of Aboriginal–European relations in any particular area in his foreword to John Ramsland's local history of the Manning Valley of New South Wales: J. Ramsland, *Custodians of the Soil*, Greater Taree City Council, Taree, 2001, p. xiii.

10   A. Collie, 'Appendix', *Report of the Parliamentary Select Committee on Aboriginal Tribes (British Settlements)*, King George's Sound, 24/1/1832, p. 2.

11   D. S. Garden, *Albany: a panorama of the Sound from 1827*, Nelson, Melbourne, 1977, p. 38.

12   For a scientific discussion of the soils of the Albany region, see H. M. Churchward et al., *Landforms and Soils of the South Coast and Hinterland*, CSIRO Division of Water Resources, Divisional Report 81, 1988.

13   Garden, p. 40.

14   Garden, p. 39.

15   A. Collie, 'Anecdotes and remarks Relative to the Aborigines of King George's Sound', attributed to Dr A. Collie, *Perth Gazette and Western Australian Journal*, July–August, 1834, p. 61.

16   In 1839, the Government Resident at Albany, George Grey, wrote to the Colonial Secretary at Perth strongly denouncing the actions of sealers in abandoning Aboriginal women and their part-descent children at Albany, even though this was not their home area. He claimed that these people were having a very bad influence on the local Aborigines who were 'well conducted'. Sealers were perpetrating acts of 'great cruelties' upon the Aboriginal women. Grey stated that with the laws on Aboriginal evidence then in place there was nothing he was able to do about it (G. Grey, letter dated 17/11/1839). CSO 12/39. Grey noted that 'The greatest obstacle that presents itself in considering the application of British Law to these Aborigines is the fact that, from their ignorance of the nature of an oath, or the obligations it imposes, they are unable to give evidence before a Court of Justice' (http://www.austlii.edu.au/au/other/IndigLRes/1986/1/2.html#Heading2, p. 25 [accessed 4/12/2011]).

17   Garden, p. 81.

18   Collie, p. 71.

19   Ibid., pp. 73–5.

20   Garden, p. 43.

21   Report to Governor Stirling by Alexander Collie, 24/1/1832, p. 2. This extensive report was later published as an appendix to the 1837 House of Commons Select Committee's Report on Aboriginal Tribes.

22   Later, the Sub-Guardian of Aborigines at Albany used tobacco as a reward for various forms of assistance rendered to Europeans by Aborigines (A. Trimmer to Colonial Secretary at Perth, 3/4/1859. CSO 14/59).

23   Garden, pp. 46–7.

24   Ibid., p. 51.

25   N. Green, *Broken Spears*, Focus Education Services, Cottesloe, 1984, p. 73.

26   Ibid.

27   See P. Statham-Drew, *James Stirling*, UWA Press, Nedlands, 2003, pp. 261–71, for an extended treatment of the 'Battle of Pinjarra'.

28   Statham-Drew, pp. 203–4.

29   Green, p. 75.

30   Ibid., p. 76.

31   *Perth Gazette*, 2/3/1833.

32   Green, pp. 203–6.

33   Ibid.

34   Stirling to Goderich, 2/4/1832, CSO, 18/10, folio 42.

35   *Perth Gazette*, 19/1/1833, p. 10.

36   Ibid.

37   T. Shellam, *Shaking Hands on the Fringe*, UWA Press, Crawley, 2009, Chapter Eight.

38   Shellam, p. 158.

39   Moore, 25/1/1833, in J. M. R. Cameron (ed.), *The Millendon Memoirs: George Fletcher Moore's Western Australian diaries and letters, 1830–1841*, Hesperian Press, Carlisle, 2006, pp. 159–60.

40   Ibid., p. 203.

41   Ibid., p. 204.

42   D. Mossenson, 'Irwin, Chidley (1788–1860)', in *Australian Dictionary of Biography*, vol. 2, Melbourne University Press, 1967, pp. 5–6.

43   F. C. Irwin, 'Irwin to Lord Viscount Goderich, 26 January 1833', *Report of Select Committee on Aborigines*, Appendix no. 4, item no. 7, p. 132.

44   Sir R. Spencer to Robert Hay, Permanent Secretary to the Colonial Office, London, 25/3/1833.

45   R. Spencer, *Letter Book*, Local History Section, Albany Public Library, 27/12/1836.

46   G. Chessell, *Richard Spencer*, UWA Press, Crawley, 2005.

47   Green, pp. 206–14. Green used Stirling's figure of 'probably fifteen' Aboriginal deaths at the Battle of Pinjarra in October 1834 when compiling his table of casualties. However, he pointed out that the true figure may have been considerably higher. This remains the subject of considerable controversy. Many object to the word 'battle' to describe what could perhaps better be described as a massacre.

48   Spencer to the Church of England Bishop of Australia, Local History Section, Albany Public Library, 25/5/1837.

49   I. Bird, *The Story of Strawberry Hill*, Local History Section, Albany Public Library, p. 32.

50   Based on Green's figures given in his book *Broken Spears*, and the figures in the 1832 Western Australian census, there was justification for this fear. The chances of an individual male settler in the colony over the age of fifteen dying

from spearing in the years 1831–34 was approximately sixty times that faced by modern Australians from dying in a road accident.

51   W. Schooling, *The Governor and Company of Adventurers Trading into Hudson's Bay during Two Hundred and Fifty Years, 1670–1920*, The Hudson Bay Company, London, 1920. Quoted in P. Statham-Drew, 'James Stirling and Pinjarra: a battle in more ways than one', *Studies in Western Australian History*, vol. 23, 2003, p. 168.

52   Statham-Drew, 'James Stirling and Pinjarra', p. 157.

53   Spencer to Colonial Secretary Peter Brown, 19/12/1833. In *A Collection of Some of the Correspondence of Sir Richard Spencer, C.B., KCH. and Lady Spencer between the years 1833 and 1839*. Compiled by David F. Bird. Copy held by author.

54   J. Browne, *Aborigines of the King George's Sound Region, 1836–1838*, Hesperian Press, Carlisle, 2001, p. 2.

55   For detailed discussion on the topic, see T. C. Patterson, *Inventing Western Civilisation*, Monthly Review Press, New York, 1997; J. Gascoigne, *The Enlightenment and the Origins of European Australia*, Cambridge University Press, Melbourne, 2002; R. L. Meek, *Social Science and the Ignoble Savage*, Cambridge University Press, Cambridge, 2000; and P. Moloney, 'Savagery and civilisation, early Victorian notions', *New Zealand Journal of History*, vol. 35, 2001, pp. 153–76.

56   Spencer to Colonial Secretary Peter Brown, 19/12/1833.

57   Mulvaney & Green, p. 352.

58   R. Lourens, '1829–1901', in P. Firkins, (ed.), *A History of Commerce and Industry in Western Australia*, UWA Press, Nedlands, 1979, p. 11. For the Truck Act, see B. K. De Garis, 'Self-government and the evolution of party politics 1871–1911', in C. T. Stannage (ed.), *A New History of Western Australia*, UWA Press, Nedlands, 1981, p. 346.

59   P. Hasluck, *Black Australians*, Melbourne University Press, Melbourne, 1942, p. 88.

60   *W.A. Government Gazette*, 24/7/1841.

61   Ibid.

62   Ibid., 29/1/1847.

63   Ibid., 14/1/1848.

64   Hasluck, p. 88.

65   Spencer to R. W. Hay, Under Secretary of State for the Colonies, 16/6/1834.

66   Spencer to the Right Reverend the Bishop of Australia, William Broughton, 25/5/1837.

67   G. S. R. Kitson Clark, *The Making of Victorian England*, Methuen and Co, London, 1965, p. 284.

68   J. Davis, 'Longing or belonging? Responses to a 'new' land in southern Western Australia 1829–1907'. PhD thesis, UWA, 2008, pp. 45–7.

69   R. Strong, 'The Reverend John Wollaston and colonial Christianity in Western Australia, 1840–1863', *Journal of Religious History*, vol. 25, no. 3, October 2001, pp. 261–85.

70   Ibid., p. 275.

71   For a discussion on the unprecedentedly powerful position that Britain held in the economic and cultural world of the mid nineteenth century, see E. J. Hobsbawm, *The Age of Revolution*, Abacus, London, 1977, Chapter Sixteen.

72   A. Burton (ed.), *The Journals and Diaries of Revd John Ramsden Wollaston, M.A.*, The Picton Journals, (1841–44), Paterson Brokensha, Perth, 1955, p. 190.

73   Ibid., p. 221.

74   Strong, p. 284.

75   The Bible, King James Version, John 14. 6.

76   For a discussion of the place Evangelicalism played in British society, see H. Carey, *God's Empire*, Cambridge University Press, Cambridge, 2010. She points out that for Evangelicals 'Colonisation was always dubious because, as the missionary societies made plain, the arrival of British settlers was invariably accompanied by the destruction of the original inhabitants (p. 308).

77   'Sir J. Stephen, (1789–1859)', *Australian Dictionary of Biography*, online edition.

78   C. McLisky, 'Due observance of justice, and the protection of their rights: philanthropy, humanitarianism and moral purpose in the Aborigines Protection Society circa 1837 and its portrayal in Australian historiography, 1883–2003', *Limina*, vol. 11, 2005, p. 57.

79   Ibid., p. 61.

80   Hasluck, p. 54.

81   H. Reynolds, *This Whispering in Our Hearts*, Allen & Unwin, Sydney, 1996, p. xv.

82   G. Grey, *Journals of Two Expeditions of Discovery in North-west and Western Australia*, vol. 2, Boone, London, 1841, Chapter 18.

83   Ibid., pp. 381–2.

84   Garden, p. 85.

85   Ibid., p. 86.

86   Ibid.

87   M. Gibbs, 'Nebinyan's songs: an Aboriginal whaler of south-west Western Australia', *Journal of Aboriginal History*, vol. 27, 2003, p. 4.

88   Browne, p. 2.

89   Garden, pp. 65, 94.

90   R. Spencer to Murray, 9/4/1838, copy at Albany Public Library Local History Section, I.R.S./303 M27.

91   Garden, p. 65.

92   P. Taylor to the Aboriginal Protection Society, London, 1844, in R. Piggott, *Fishtraps and Floods*, Tangee, Kalamunda, 2004, p. 22.

93   Ibid.

94   J. Phillips to Colonial Secretary at Perth, 12/10/1840, CSO 15/40.

95   http://www.austlii.edu.au/au/other/IndigLRes/1986/1/2.html#Heading2, p. 25 (accessed 4/12/2011).

96   Garden, p. 68. While Phillips was a settler on the Canning River in mid 1833, he personally witnessed Yagan, Midgegooroo, Munday and Migo spear to death

two Velvick brothers who were his employees. Six years later, Phillips' boy employee was also speared fatally (*Perth Gazette and Western Australian Journal*, 4/5/1833 and 11/9/1841).

97   CSO, 149/48.

98   *Report of the Parliamentary Select Committee on Aboriginal Tribes*, House of Commons, London, 1837, pp. 126–8. This report specifically mentioned in critical terms the treatment of Aboriginal people in Western Australia and New South Wales.

99   J. Hutt to Glenelg, 3/5/1839, p. 363.

100   *Perth Gazette and Independent Journal of Politics and News*, 7/1/1853.

101   Hasluck, p. 75.

102   Ibid., p. 79.

103   Ibid., p. 74.

104   Giustiniani to Glenelg, CSO Acc.36, vol. 62/110.

105   *Bathurst Free Press and Mining Journal*, 17/4/1890, p. 4.

106   State Records Office map Plantagenet and Kent, 11A, 1876–1877, tally no. 506349.

107   For example, the *Report of the Guardians of Aborigines* for all of the colony in 1854 was printed in the *Perth Gazette and Independent Journal of Politics and News*, 27/1/1854. The report is brief, and fails even to make mention of Trimmer's work at Albany.

108   A. Trimmer to Colonial Secretary at Perth, 4/3/1859, CSO 4005.

109   A. Trimmer to Colonial Secretary at Perth, 30/8/1859, CSO 3/4049.

110   Chessell, p. 75.

111   E. Norman, *A History of Modern Ireland*, Penguin, London, 1971, p. 117.

112   Barker was the first commandant to write about Aboriginal illness, but this is probably not significant given the paucity of detail on Aboriginal matters in general in his predecessors' reports. Bowel and respiratory complaints form the great majority of his entries on the matter.

113   Browne, p. 1.

114   Interview conducted by Anna Haebich with Lilly Hayward, 1980, in Haebich, '"A Bunch of Cast-offs" Aborigines of the Southwest of Western Australia, 1900–1936', Murdoch University, 1985, p. 623.

115   J. Tebbel & K. Jennison, *The American Indian Wars*, Phoenix Press, London, 2001, p. 99.

116   L. Tilbrook, *Nyungar Tradition*, UWA Press, Nedlands, 1983, p. 8.

117   King to Hawkins, 11/6/1847, Society for the Propagation of the Gospel/ Australia/Perth 1, f. 6.

118   N. Green, 'Aborigines and white settlers', in T. Stannage (ed.), *A New History of Western Australia*, UWA Press, Nedlands, 1981, p. 120. Green is summarising Hammond's views expressed in J. E. Hammond, *Winjan's People*, Perth, 1933.

119   Ibid., p. 119.

120   G. Bolton, *Land of Vision and Mirage: Western Australia since 1826*, UWA Press, Crawley, 2008, p. 33.

121　A. Trimmer to Colonial Secretary, 6/10/1860, Local History Section, Albany Public Library, I.R.S./366M/2. Albany possessed a room at the gaol fitted out as a hospital. Neither the Albany Cemetery nor the Church of England Burial Register records any Aboriginal burials in 1860 apart from that of Margaret Guriup, aged three years.

122　A. Trimmer, 4/12/1860, SRO, 7425.

123　The 1860 epidemic spread far from Albany, and was noted as far away as New Norcia (Green's *Broken Spears*, p. 236). In 1863 it had reached the Rottnest Island Native Prison, and at least twenty-one men died from its effects (*Perth Gazette and Independent Journal of Politics and News*, 10/4/1863). For a discussion on the part disease played at the Swan River, see J. Host, with C. Owen, *It's Still in My Heart, This Is My Country*, UWA Press, Crawley, 2009, p. 26. The census of 1870 gave full details of European deaths, but merely noted that Aboriginal deaths from the epidemic were 'very numerous' throughout the colony (Western Australian census, 1870, p. 24).

124　J. Host with C. Owen, p. 99.

125　J. Campbell, *Invisible Invaders: smallpox and other diseases in Aboriginal Australia 1780–1880*, Melbourne University Press, Melbourne, 2002, p. 216.

126　Garden, p. 179.

127　D. Barwick, 'The composition and demographic impact of disease', in N. G. Butlin, *Economics and the Dreamtime: a hypothetical history*, Cambridge University Press, Cambridge, 2010, p. 215.

128　Garden, p. 58.

129　R. Spencer to Colonial Secretary, 11/2/1839, CSO 73/39.
　　　In his monograph *Noongar Resistance on the South Coast* (2008), local historian Bob Howard claimed that the sheep were driven off by Aboriginal people, but the context of the letter makes this seem unlikely. When farmers speak about 'losing' stock, it is almost always deaths that they are referring to.

130　Garden, p. 62.

131　Ibid. The State Records Office holds a digital copy of a map from this period. The date has been torn from the map, but I believe it to be from 1839 since land is shown in the name of Sir Richard Spencer (who died in that year) and J. Hassell who first bought land in 1839. It shows land alienated and the owners' names (http://aeon.sro.wa.gov.au/Investigator/Details/ImageLoad2.asp?entityId=4841621&entityType=Item_Image&imageNumber=1).

132　Ibid.

133　Spencer to Colonial Secretary, 11/2/1839, CSO 73/39.

134　P. Belches to Colonial Secretary at Perth, 2/4/1840, CSO 73/40.

135　Spencer (initial indecipherable, but not Sir Richard who was deceased by this time) to G. Grey, Government Resident at Albany, 17/1/1840, CSO 11/40.

136　J. Phillips to Colonial Secretary at Perth, 2/11/1841, CSO 196/40.

137　R. Stephens, 'Kendenup. 1840–1940', *Western Mail*, 30/5/1940.

138　N. Green, *Aborigines of the Albany Region 1821–1898*, p. xi.

139　H. Reynolds, *The Other Side of the Frontier*, Penguin, Melbourne, 1983, p. 96.

140 Ibid, p. 110.

141 Robert Stephens papers, Local History Section, Albany Public Library, I.R.S. /525M/1.

142 *Perth Gazette and Independent Journal of Politics and News*, 10/5/1850, p. 1.

143 J. Phillips to Colonial Secretary at Perth, October 1850, *Letter Book*, Rhodes House Library, Oxford University

144 Gibbs, p. 6. Gibbs states the incomplete nature of the kept and retained records preclude giving any accurate figure of those employed.

145 Ibid., p. 5.

146 *The Inquirer*, 29/11/1848.

147 J. Phillips to Colonial Secretary at Perth, November 1850, *Letter Book*.

148 Ibid., 2/12/1850.

149 Ibid., 17/12/1850.

150 Ibid., 2/12/1850.

Chapter 5: The Pastoral Era, and European Attempts to Christianise and Civilise Albany's Aboriginal Population, 1851–1877

1 D. S. Garden, *Albany: panorama of the Sound from 1827*, Nelson, Melbourne, 1977, p. 134.

2 Western Australian census, 1848, p. 10.

3 Garden, p. 135.

4 J. Phillips to Colonial Secretary at Perth, 5/7/1851, Rhodes Library, Oxford University.

5 P. Edmonds, 'The inconvenience and immorality of Aborigines in the town', in G. Worby & L. Rigney (eds), *Sharing Spaces: Indigenous and non-Indigenous responses to story, country and rights*, National Library of Australia, Canberra, 2005, p. 182.

6 Ibid., p. 192.

7 Western Australian census, 1848, p. 2.

8 Ibid., p. 12.

9 Western Australian census, 1854, p. 8.

10 Ibid., p. 6.

11 J. Parnell, *Country Cavalcade: a history of the Shire of Tambellup*, Shire of Tambellup, Subiaco, 1982, p. 35.

12 M. Bignell, *First the Spring: a history of the Shire of Kojonup, Western Australia*, UWA Press, Nedlands, 1971, p. 7.

13 A. Trimmer to Colonial Secretary at Perth, 6/12/1860, CSO 5/22.

14 Western Australian census, 1870, p. 26.

15 Ibid., p. 27.

16 Albany Police Station Daily Occurrence Book, 8/6/1864.

17 J. Phillips to Colonial Secretary at Perth, 3/12/1852.

18 A. Trimmer to Colonial Secretary at Perth, CSO 1853/36.

19 Albany Police Daily Occurrence Book, 25/8/1866.

20 Albany Police Daily Occurrence Book, 6/1/1876.

21 Ibid., 16/7/1876.
22 W. Westgarth, *Victoria and the Australian Gold Mines in 1857*, Smith Elder and Co., London, 1857, p. 390.
23 Western Australian census, 1870, p. 24.
24 The 1854 census shows that only nine single women aged twenty-one years or older lived in the Plantagenet District (p. 7).
25 Ibid., p. 28.
26 L. Tilbrook, *Nyungar Tradition*, UWA Press, Nedlands, 1983.
27 CSO 1855/vol. 317, p. 58. Held at the State Records Office, Perth.
28 Famously, she wrote in the *Sunday Times* of 2/10/1921, 'with very few exceptions, the only good half caste is a dead one'. James Harris, an Aboriginal man of part descent, angrily responded in a letter printed in the same paper on 30/10/1921: 'We say right here that Mrs Bates is no friend of ours, and we repudiate her sentiments'.
29 R. Reece, 'Our killing fields', *Eureka Street*, September 2003.
30 K. Scott & H. Brown, *Kayang & Me*, Fremantle Arts Centre Press, Fremantle, 2005; E. H. Hayward, *No Free Kicks*, Fremantle Arts Centre Press, Fremantle, 2006.
31 Garden, p. 134.
32 *Perth Gazette & W.A. Times*, 18/2/1870, p. 3.
33 N. Green, 'Access, equality and opportunity? The education of Aboriginal children in Western Australia, 1840–1978', PhD thesis, Murdoch University, 2004, p. 38.
34 Ibid.
35 Ibid., p. 41.
36 Barbara Tuchman has noted that the theological underpinnings of Evangelicalism were under increasing attack at this time from German biblical criticism, and from the High Church Oxford movement within the Church of England (*Bible and Sword*, Macmillan, New York, 1956, p. 243).
37 P. Biskup, *Not Slaves, Not Citizens*, University of Queensland Press, Brisbane, 1973, p. 13.
38 See S. Taylor, 'Who were the convicts? A statistical analysis of the convicts arriving in Western Australia in 1850/51, 1861/62, and 1866/68', *Studies in Western Australian History*, vol. 4, 'Convictism in Western Australia', pp. 19–45, for an analysis of the type of convict sent to W.A. It is instructive to note that the common belief that convicts were people who had stolen a rabbit or a loaf of bread is not supported by the evidence. In a sample of 979 transported between 1850 and 1851, only eight were convicted of poaching or of stealing food or drink (p. 35, Table 4).
39 Westgarth, p. 385.
40 For Wollaston's extensive explanation of his motives and intentions, see *Perth Gazette and Independent Journal of Politics and News*, 25/2/1853, p. 3.
41 Package of papers pertaining to St John's Church, Albany, held at the Battye Library, MN 61/119.
42 J. R. Wollaston to the Secretary, SPG, 21/6/1851.

43 J. Harris, *One Blood*, Albatross Books, Sydney, 1990, p. 263.

44 Ibid., p. 264.

45 Ibid.

46 H. W. Mann (ed.), *The Wollaston Journals*, vol. 3, 1845–1856, UWA Press, 2006, p. 122.

47 An 1857 map by surveyor Phillip Chauncy indicates the extent of the area of 68 acres set aside for the 'native institution'. This map may be accessed at http://aeon.sro.wa.gov.au/Investigator/Details/ImageLoad2.asp?entityId=2514054&entityType=Item_Image&imageNumber=1

48 J. Groves, *The Comforts of Civilisation in Early Colonial Western Australia*, Honours thesis, Edith Cowan University, 2006, p. 39.

49 J. Phillips to Colonial Secretary in Perth, 5/7/1851, Rhodes Library, Oxford University.

50 *Perth Gazette*, 23/4/1852.

51 P. Chauncy, 'Notes and anecdotes', in R. Brough Smyth, *The Aborigines of Victoria*, vol. II, (Facsimile edition, Melbourne, John Currey O'Neill, 1972), p. 259. In Groves, p. 38.

52 A. Camfield, 'The Annesfield Native Institution, Albany', in *Information Respecting the Habits and Customs of the Aboriginal Inhabitants of Western Australia, Presented to the Legislative Council by His Excellency's Command*, 1871, p. 23.

53 Ibid.

54 CSO 240/176,177. Held at the State Records Office, Perth.

55 Ibid.

56 J. Phillips to Colonial Secretary, 2/11/1852, CSO 231/123.

57 J. Wollaston to Colonial Secretary, 30/11/1852, in H. R. Mann (ed.), *The Wollaston Journals*, vol. 3, 1845–1856, UWA Press, 2006, p. 286.

58 A. Burton, *Wollaston's Albany Journal (1848–1856)*, Lamb Publications, Osborne Park, 1954, p. 197.

59 J. Wollaston to Colonial Secretary, 14/7/1852, in Burton, p. 256.

60 Ibid.

61 For the story of what followed in Victoria, see F. Jensz, 'Controlling marriages: Frederick Hagenauer and the betrothal of Indigenous Western Australian women in colonial Victoria', *Journal of Aboriginal History*, vol. 34, 2010, pp. 35–54.

62 Camfield, p. 26.

63 Ibid.

64 Ibid.

65 Ibid.

66 Paper No. 2, *Votes and Proceedings of the Legislative Council*, 1874. Hale did not identify the critics by name or location.

67 Camfield, pp. 23–6.

68 Ibid.

69 Ibid.

70 B. Flower to Anne Camfield, in B. Attwood, *The Making of the Aborigines*, Allen & Unwin, Sydney, 1989, p. 34.

71 H. W. Mann (ed.), *The Wollaston Journals*, vol. 3, 1845–1856, UWA Press, Crawley, 2006, p. 289 et seq., p. 323. The advertisement for the appeal appeared in the 16/2/1853 edition of the *Perth Gazette and Independent Journal of Politics and News*.

72 *Albany Methodist Church, Jubilee Souvenir, 1863–1913*, no author given, undated, held at the Local History Section of the Albany Public Library.

73 *Perth Gazette and Independent Journal of Politics and News*, 25/2/1853, p. 4.

74 'P&O Passenger', extract first published in the *Melbourne Argus* of 15/10/1858, and copied by the *Inquirer and Commercial News* on 10/11/1858. Reprinted in D. Sellick, *First Impressions: Albany*, Western Australian Museum, Perth, 1997, pp. 101–2.

75 The Reverend J. Jobson, *Australia: with notes by the way*, Hamilton, Adams and Co., London, 1862, in Sellick, p. 106.

76 'P&O Passenger', *Inquirer and Commercial News*, in Sellick, pp. 111–12.

77 See C. Ellis, 'Public Indians, private Cherokees', *Journal of Southern History*, vol. 77, no. 2, May 2011, p. 494(2); and R. A. Cramer, *Cash, Color and Colonialism: the politics of tribal acknowledgement*, University of Oklahoma Press, Norman, 2005.

78 J. Dowson, *Old Albany*, National Trust of Western Australia, Perth, 2008.

79 Lieutenant Arthur Onslow, Mitchell Library, MLMSS A 4335, item 1, quoted in Dowson, p. 30.

80 Albany Police Daily Occurrence Book, 25/8/1866.

81 Hassell Kendenup Station account book, 1871–72, in the possession of the Hassell family, Albany.

82 Diary of W. H. Graham, 1860–61, in the possession of the Hassell family of Albany.

83 Proposed Supplement to the Land Regulations of 1860, Chapter V, Miscellaneous Regulations, Clause 19, published in the *Perth Gazette, and Independent Journal of Politics and News*, 2/10/1863, p. 3.

84 Parnell, p. 52.

85 Garden, pp. 72–3.

86 C. Hassell, *The Hassells of Albany*, private publication, Perth, 1973, p. 33.

87 Ibid., p. 30.

88 Ibid., p. 25.

89 Hassell Kendenup Station account and record book, 1871–72.

90 CSO, vol. 187, 1859. Held at the State Records Office, Perth.

91 R. Bell to Trimmer, 27/6/1855, CSO 316/86.

92 CSO, vol. 259, 1860. Held at the State Records Office, Perth.

93 H. Camfield to Governor, CSO, vol. 218, 1848.

94 H. Camfield to Governor, CSO, 1848.

95 *Perth Gazette and Independent Journal of Politics and News*, 18/3/1853, p. 3.

96 Ibid., 14/3/1856, p. 4.

97 J. Phillips, *Letter Book*, November 1850.

98 *Perth Gazette and Independent Journal of Politics and News*, 23/2/1855.

99   Parnell, p. 22.

100   A. Trimmer to Colonial Secretary at Perth, 3/12/1855, CSO 123/55.

101   Garden, p. 84.

102   P. Belches (Acting Resident Magistrate) to Colonial Secretary, 28/4/1840, CSO, 1840, p. 73.

103   Ibid.

104   A. Trimmer to Colonial Secretary at Perth, 5/3/1861, CSO 11/61.

105   CSO, 17/6/1851, 1851, vol. 212. Held at the State Records Office, Perth.

106   CSO, 4/4/1861, 1861, vol. 19. Held at the State Records Office, Perth.

107   *Perth Gazette and Independent Journal of Politics and News*, 19/7/1850, p. 3. The account does not specify the Act under which the charges were laid.

108   *Perth Gazette and Independent Journal of Politics and News*, 4/1/1850, p. 2.

109   N. Green, *Broken Spears*, Focus Education Services, Cottesloe, 1984.

110   Green wrote: 'This is a list of most but by no means all the incidents of violence recorded in the contemporary diaries, journals, newspapers, official reports and despatches' (*Broken Spears*, p. 201).

111   Ibid., pp. 203–18.

112   Ibid.

113   A. Trimmer to Colonial Secretary at Perth, 20/9/1859, CSO 40/59.

114   A. Trimmer to Colonial Secretary at Perth, 28/9/1859, CSO 43/59.

115   W. H. Graham, Diary.

116   *West Australian Times*, 19/11/1863, p. 2.

117   J. Ramsland, *Custodians of the Soil*, Greater Taree City Council, Taree, 2011, p. 30.

118   *The Inquirer*, 20/10/1841, p. 3.

119   R. Stephens, 'Kendenup. 1840–1940', *Western Mail*, 30/5/1940.

120   See previous chapter for more details about this period.

121   *Perth Gazette and Independent Journal of Politics and News*, 15/10/1863, p. 3.

122   *Perth Gazette and Independent Journal of Politics and News*, 26/10/1863, p. 3; and N. Green, *Aborigines of the Albany Region 1821–1898*, UWA Press, Nedlands, 1989, p. 116.

123   CSO, 1855, vol. 317, p. 58. Held at the State Records Office, Perth.

124   *Perth Gazette and Independent Journal of Politics and News*, 9/10/1863, p. 3. Patrick Taylor, a prominent Kalgan farmer, had written earlier to Camfield on Hesketh's behalf in 1860: 'The accompanying application is in accordance with arrangements made last year in Perth when Mr Barlee [Colonial Secretary] told Hesketh that as soon as he selected a block of ten acres if he would send up an application he [Barlee] would see that it was formally handed over and be sent a title deed. The claim is on account of him having married a native girl...' *Fishtraps and Floods*, p. 18.

125   J. Hassell to A. Cockburn-Campbell, 5/9/1862, Local History Section, Albany Public Library, I.R.S., 530M/5.

126   Garden, p. 127.

127   Local History Section, Albany Public Library, I.R.S., 530M/5.

128   H. Reynolds, *Frontier, Aborigines, Settlers and Land*, Allen & Unwin, Sydney, 1987, p. 58.

129   J. F. Hayward, 'Reminiscences of Johnson Frederick Hayward', *Proceedings of the Royal Geographical Society of Australasia, South Australian Branch*, vol. 29, 1929.

130   *Perth Gazette and Independent Journal of Politics and News*, 8/1/1848, p. 3.

131   Ibid.

132   CSO, 149/25. Held at the State Records Office, Perth.

133   B. Howard, 'Noongar resistance on the South Coast', unpublished manuscript, 2008, http://kiangardarup.blogspot.com/2008/05/noongar-resistance-on-south-coast.html (accessed 10/03/2009).

134   Scott & Brown, pp. 43–4.

135   Howard. Howard gave a public reading of his work shortly before his death in 2009. He was well known among Albany's Aboriginal community, and his views are familiar to many of its members.

136   The Mount Barker Police District was extensive. 'Starting from Hay River Siding 28 mile GSR, Thence West about 45 miles to the Frankland River. Thence North along River East side 40 miles to Yirriminup. Thence East 35 miles along Gordon River South Side to Gordon Bridge (193 Mile Post Perth Road). Thence East 10 miles to Pootenup Siding GSR. Thence East by North East to Kyblup 35 miles. Thence North East 20 miles to Warperup. Thence East 45 miles to Jarramonup. Thence East along the Gordon River 55 miles to the Coast. Thence South along Coast 14 miles to Bremer Bay. Thence West 50 miles along Coast to Cape Riche. Thence North West 18 miles to Warriup. Thence West 30 miles to Takalarup. Thence South West 24 miles to starting point (Mount Barker Police Station Letter and Report Book, 21/5/1907, SRO ACC 427, Item 7).

137   R. Foster, '"Don't mention the war": frontier violence and the language of concealment', *History Australia*, vol. 6, no. 3, 2009, p. 8.

138   Ibid., pp. 6–7.

139   Ibid., p. 6.

140   J. Phillips, *Letter Book*, October 1850. Phillips noted in the letter: 'The natives [are] very anxious to be allowed to fight & I have no doubt they will assemble in some isolated part for their purpose'.

141   R. Reece, 'Inventing Aborigines', *Aboriginal History*, vol. 11, 1987, p. 17. For a discussion of similar criticism that arose in the 1980s, see Bain Attwood's *Telling the Truth about Aboriginal History*, Allen & Unwin, Sydney, 2005, pp. 40–2.

142   Hayward, *No Free Kicks*, p. 16.

143   A. Trimmer to Colonial Secretary, 6/3/1859. 4005.

144   A. Trimmer to Colonial Secretary, 4/3/1855. 10057/252/27

145   Ibid.

146   CSO, 1493/79. Held at the State Records Office, Perth.

147   A. Trimmer to Colonial Secretary at Perth, 3/4/1855, CSO 331/15.

148   J. Host with C. Owen, *It's Still in My Heart, This Is My Country*, UWA Press, Crawley, 2009, p. 236.

Chapter 6: The Coming of the Great Southern Railway, 1878–1904

1   D. Garden, *Albany: a panorama of the Sound from 1827*, Nelson, Melbourne, 1977, p. 239.

2   The various parts of the British Empire conducted a census every ten years. The Western Australian Census Reports from 1848 to 1901 are accessible at http://hccda.anu.edu.au/regions/WA

3   Editorial, *Albany Advertiser*, 5/1/1907, p. 3.

4   Western Australian Census Report, 1901.

5   E. H. Hayward, *No Free Kicks*, Fremantle Arts Centre Press, Fremantle, 2006, p. 16.

6   L. Johnson, *Love Thy Land*, Albany Shire Council, Albany, 1982, p. 17. A telephone line connecting Perth to Albany had been opened in 1872. A telegraph line linking Albany to the eastern colonies opened in 1877.

7   Western Australian Census Report, 1891, p. 41.

8   Western Australian Census Report, 1901, vol. 1, p. 12.

9   Western Australian Census Report, 1901, vol. 3, p. 1.

10 Western Australian Census Report, 1881, p. 3.

11 M. Bignell, *First the Spring: a history of the Shire of Kojonup*, UWA Press, Nedlands, 1971, p. 7.

12 Western Australian Census Report, 1881, p. 32.

13 Ibid., p. 26.

14 Ibid., p. 84.

15 Ibid., p. 109.

16 Mount Barker Police Station Correspondence and Report Book, 2/12/1879–2/12/1894, SRO, Accession 427, item 8.

17 L. Tilbrook, *Nyungar Tradition*, UWA Press, Nedlands, 1983.

18 Western Australian Census Report, 1881, pp. 46–8.

19 Western Australian Census Report, 1891, p. 17.

20 Ibid., p. 90.

21 Western Australian Census Report, 1891, p. 87.

22 Ibid., p. 184.

23 Ibid.

24 Ibid., p. 181.

25 Western Australian Census Report, 1891, p. 91. The Publican's Act of 1843 and the 1880 Wines, Beer and Spirits Act attempted to prevent the sale of alcoholic beverages to Aborigines. In 1902, the latter Act was amended to extend the ban on sales to 'half-castes' living with Aborigines. Such restrictions were impossible to enforce in a totally effective manner.

26 Western Australian Census Report, 1891, p. 183.

27 Ibid., p. 17.

28 Ibid., pp. 29, 99.

29 Ibid., p. 92.

30 Western Australian Census Report, 1901, vol. 2, p. 5. This section of the Australian Constitution was amended by the referendum in 1967.

31 Ibid., p. 203.

32 Ibid., pp. 12, 64.

33 Police Department files 146/1900, SRO.

34 H. F. Bailey to Resident Magistrate, Albany, 11/9/1905, Aborigines Department files, 324/05, SRO.

35 'Queen's Jubilee celebrations', *Albany Advertiser*, 15/6/1897, p. 3.

36 Western Australian Census Report, 1891, p. 50.

37 Ibid., p. 61.

38 Western Australian Census Report, 1901, vol. 2, p. 38.

39 M. Laurie, *Frankland to the Stirlings: a history of the Cranbrook Shire*, Shire of Cranbrook, Cranbrook, 1994. The Gordon and Frankland rivers (like the Swan and Avon) are actually different sections of the same watercourse).

40 Western Australian Parliament, *Votes and Proceedings*, vol. 1, no. 18, 1896.

41 Report of Aborigines Department, 1899, in *Votes and Proceedings*, vol. 2, no. 40, 1899.

42 Ibid., p. 7.

43 R. Glover, *Plantagenet, Rich and Beautiful: a history of the Shire of Plantagenet Western Australia*, UWA Press, Nedlands, 1979, p. 335.

44 *Aborigines Protection Act, 1886*, Victoria Reginae no. 25. An Act to provide for the better protection and management of the Aboriginal Natives of Western Australia, and to amend the Law relating to certain Contracts with such Aboriginal Natives, available at http://asset0.aiatsis.gov.au:1801/webclient/ StreamGate?folder_id=0&dvs=1318462665005~876 This act was commonly known as 'the Half-caste act', because it defined 'half-caste' people as Aboriginal.

45 P. Hasluck, *Black Australians*, Melbourne University Press, Melbourne, 1942, p. 152.

46 Ibid. pp. 111–12.

47 Report from Constable Wall to Sub-Inspector Lemon, Mount Barker Police Station Correspondence and Report Book, Accession 427, item 6, 22/7/1897, SRO.

48 Ibid.

49 Report of the Western Australian Police Department, 1889, p. 12.

50 Ibid., Memo from P. C. Wall to Sergeant Stokes, 27/10/1898.

51 Shire of Jerramungup Heritage Register, p. 9.

52 E. Hassell, *My Dusky Friends*, C. W. Hassell, Fremantle, 1975, p. 7.

53 Hasluck showed that the 1886 Act made the prescribed contract of service under the Masters and Servants Act no longer compulsory for Aboriginal employees, thus making many worse off. It would appear that Hassell, at least, continued to enter into legal contracts with his Aboriginal employees (Hasluck, p. 156).

54 Ibid.

55 N. Green, *Aborigines of the Albany Region 1821–1898*, UWA Press, Nedlands, 1989, p. 157.

56 Mount Barker Police Station Correspondence and Report Book, Accession 427, item 6, 11/7/1899, SRO.

57   Hasluck, p. 75.

58   H. Reynolds, *With the White People*, Penguin, Melbourne, 1990, p. 233.

59   K. Scott & H. Brown, *Kayang & Me*, Fremantle Arts Centre Press, Fremantle, 2005, p. 47.

60   Sergeant J. Farley to the Commissioner of Police, 27/8/1892, Mount Barker Police Station Correspondence and Report Book. Held at State Records Office, Perth.

61   Ibid., Report made by P. C. Wall, 14/6/1897.

62   J. Host with C. Owen, *It's Still in My Heart, This Is My Country*, UWA Press, Crawley, 2009, Chapter Eight, 'Noongar adaptation and cultural maintenance 1841–1900'.

63   Goode et al., *'Kinjarling' the Place of Rain*, The City of Albany and the Department of Indigenous Affairs Aboriginal Heritage Survey, a Report Prepared for the City of Albany and the Department of Indigenous Affairs, Albany, 2005, p. 178.

64   *Lost Lands Report*, Department of Indigenous Affairs, no authors given, 1997, p. 11.

65   A. Haebich, *For Their Own Good: Aborigines and government in the South-west of Western Australia, 1900–1940*, UWA Press, Nedlands, 1988, p. 59.

66   Ibid., pp. 53–5.

67   Ibid., p. 103. By this time, Forrest had moved to Melbourne to enter Federal Parliament.

68   Ibid., p. 20.

69   L. Hayward, interview conducted by Anna Haebich, 1980, published in A. Haebich, '"A Bunch of Cast-offs" Aborigines of the Southwest of Western Australia, 1900–1936', Murdoch University, 1985, pp. 619–20.

70   Haebich, p. 23.

71   Laurie, p. 37.

72   J. Parnell, *Country Cavalcade: a history of the Shire of Tambellup*, Shire of Tambellup, Subiaco, 1982, p. 62.

73   Henry Reynolds wrote that the concept of private property was 'perhaps the single most important element in a complex situation' on the Australian nineteenth century frontier. H. Reynolds, *Frontier*, Allen & Unwin, Sydney, 1987, p. 190.

74   Western Australian *Blue Book*, for the year 1894, compiled from official returns in the Registrar General's Office, Government Printer, 1895, p. 21.

75   Ibid., p. 293.

76   *Statistical Register of Western Australia, 1910*, Government Printer, Perth, 1912, p. 25.

77   Ibid., p. 25.

78   Ibid. This practice continued for many decades. Brian Taylor, whose family moved to Tambellup in 1897 to take up land, recalls Aboriginal contractors ringbarking trees on the family property in 1952. The trees were left standing for two years before being burnt (personal communication with the author, 28/9/2010).

79 *Blue Book*, 1901, p. 21. Bill Hassell, who farmed at Warriup east of Albany, confirmed to me that grass soon began to grow following ringbarking as sheep carried seeds into the area in their manure (personal communication with the author, 26/9/2011).

80 John Clapin, Cranbrook farmer whose family has long lived in the area (personal communication with the author, 20/10/2010).

81 Government Resident at Albany to the Chief Inspector of Aborigines, 6/6/1905, Aborigines Department files, SRO 324/05.

82 Hayward, p. 16.

83 Haebich, p. 55.

84 Ibid., p. 59.

85 T. Rowse, *White Flour, White Power: from rations to citizenship in Central Australia*, Cambridge University Press, Cambridge, 1998.

86 Ibid., p. 33.

87 Reynolds, *With the White People*, p. 130.

88 'Gentile', Letter to the editor, *Australian Advertiser*, 10/3/1890.

89 *Albany Mail*, 4/4/1888.

90 Haebich, p. 131.

91 P. C. McNamara, 16/9/1905, Mount Barker Police Station Daily Occurrence Book, Accession 427, item 5, 7/7/1905–5/12/1908. Held at State Records Office, Perth.

92 Hassell property diaries in the possession of Bill Hassell, Albany.

93 *Albany Mail*, 20/8/1887.

94 Western Australian Census Report, 1881, p. 32.

95 Western Australian Census Report, 1901, vol. 2, p. 64.

96 'Queen's Jubilee celebrations', *Albany Advertiser*, 24/6/1897, p. 3.

97 Lady A. Brassey, 'The Last Voyage To India and Australia, in the *Sunbeam*', London, 1889. In D. Sellick, *First Impressions: Albany*, Western Australian Museum, Perth, 1997, p. 184.

98 Sometimes the name is recorded as 'Wandinyil'.

99 H. Lawson, 'The golden nineties', *Australian Star* (Sydney), 1899, in Sellick, p. 193.

100 Brassey, p. 184.

101 Ibid., p. 192.

102 N. W. McKail, 'Walks with yesterday', *Western Mail*, 3/2/1927, p. 19.

103 James Browne noted that Aboriginal men had small kangaroo bones through the cartilage of their noses at a corroboree at Albany in 1836 (J. Browne, *Aborigines of the King George's Sound Region 1836–1838*, Hesperian Press, Carlisle, 2011, p. 11).

104 Five newspapers have been published at Albany: the *Albany Mail*, 1883–1889; the *Australian Advertiser*, 1888–97; the *Albany Observer*, 1890–91; the *Albany Advertiser*, 1897–present; and the *Despatch*, 1919–27. There were no other newspapers published in the Albany region in the period covered by this chapter. In the 1980s, Gordon and Gwen Norman read every edition of the various Albany

newspapers and compiled a most valuable index that has considerably assisted my research.

105   'Albany Town Council', *Albany Advertiser*, 25/9/1897, p. 3.

106   'The Queen's Jubilee', *Albany Advertiser*, 26/6 1897, p. 3.

107   'Sporting news', *Albany Advertiser*, 31/5/1900, p. 3.

108   'ANA Sports', *Albany Advertiser*, 14/1/1902, p. 3; 'Albany Week, athletic and bicycle sports', *Albany Advertiser*, 12/2/1902, p. 3.

109   'Sporting news, Kojonup Races', *Albany Advertiser*, 23/3/1899, p. 3.

110   'Mount Barker Turf Club Annual Meeting', *Albany Advertiser*, 3/1/1902, p. 4; 'Cricket, Mt Barker v Albany', *Albany Advertiser*, 4/4/1902, p. 3.

111   Aborigines Department Report for the financial year ending 30/6/1902, p. 30.

112   Ibid.

113   Ibid.

114   Ibid., p. 29.

115   Personal communication with the New Norcia Archivist, 16/3/2011. Peter Read has queried the extent to which Aboriginal people in a traumatic situation in Tennant Creek in the 1940s can truly be said to have made a free choice to send their children to an institution (P. Read, 'The Stolen Generations, the historian and the court room', *Aboriginal History*, 2002, vol. 26, p. 56). Similarly, the extent to which Egan and Mederan had a truly free choice is problematic.

116   N. Green & L. Tilbrook, *Aborigines of New Norcia 1845–1914: the Bicentennial dictionary of Western Australians*, Vol. VII, UWA Press, Nedlands, 1989.

117   Personal communication with Lynette Knapp, 17/3/2011. See Ms Knapp's family details in Appendix 1.

      For a detailed treatment of the forced removal of Aboriginal children in Australia as a whole, see A. Haebich's book *Broken Circles: fragmenting Indigenous families 1800–2000*, Fremantle Arts Centre Press, Fremantle, 2000. See also P. Read, *The Removal of Aboriginal Children in New South Wales 1833–1969*, Government Printer, Sydney, 1981.

      For the situation in Western Australia, see A. Haebich & A. Delroy, *The Stolen Generations: separation of Aboriginal children from their families*, Western Australian Museum, Perth, 1999.

118   *Australian Advertiser*, 23/10/1890.

119   *Albany Observer*, 23/10/1890.

120   Reynolds discusses a somewhat similar situation in Tasmania, when a petition to Queen Victoria was signed by eight Aboriginal people in 1846. He notes that authorship has usually been attributed to whites, but an enquiry into the matter in 1846 concluded that that the Aborigines were actually quite able to understand what they wrote – and stated so (H. Reynolds, *Fate of a Free People*, Penguin, Melbourne, 1995).

Chapter 7: 'To make provision for the better protection and care of the Aboriginal inhabitants of Western Australia', 1905–1926

1   The 1905 Act ran to eighteen pages, and can be accessed via the National Library of Australia website at http://nla.gov.au/nla.aus-vn672744-2x.

2   R. Reece, 'Aboriginals in historical writing', in R. Reece & T. Stannage (eds), *European–Aboriginal Relations in Western Australian History*, UWA Press, Nedlands, 1984, p. 138.

3   R. McGregor, *Imagined Destinies: Aboriginal Australians and the doomed race theory, 1880–1939*, Melbourne University Press, Melbourne, 1997, p. 48.

4   Ibid., pp. 51–9.

5   Several of the non-Aboriginal residents of Albany with whom I have discussed this period of their town's history have found it very difficult to accept that Aboriginal numbers were then so low. Given that the 2006 Commonwealth Census showed that 889 people from the Albany Local Government area (from a total population of 31,575) chose to identify as 'indigenous', this is scarcely surprising. I have not found any scepticism from the local Aboriginal community on this point.

6   See A. Longworth, '"Was it worthwhile?", An historical analysis of five women missionaries and their encounters with the Nyungar people of south-west Australia', PhD thesis, Murdoch University, 2005, for a discussion of the United Aborigines Mission philosophy and practices.

7   D. Bates, *Western Mail*, 11/12/1924, p. 24. This should not be taken as meaning that none were born in the Albany hinterland – rather it showed that Bates believed all were living away from the immediate vicinity of their birth site by 1908.

8   Daisy Bates Papers, National Library of Australia, Microfilm reel 5 held at the Local History Section of the Albany Public Library.

9   'Along the South Coast', *Albany Advertiser*, 29/4/1925.

10   Personal communication with Robert Reynolds, 3/12/2010.

11   Goode et al., *'Kinjarling' the Place of Rain*, The City of Albany and the Department of Indigenous Affairs Aboriginal Heritage Survey, a Report Prepared for the City of Albany and the Department of Indigenous Affairs, Albany, 2005, p. 83.

12   A. Haebich, *For Their Own Good: Aborigines and government in the South-west of Western Australia, 1900–1940*, UWA Press, Nedlands, 1988, p. 89.

13   *Aborigines Act, 1905*, Section 19.

14   Ibid., Section 12.

15   Haebich, p. 79.

16   N. Green, 'Access, equality and opportunity? The education of Aboriginal children in Western Australia 1840–1978', PhD thesis, Murdoch University, 2004, p. 20.

17   'Native child fatally burnt, coronial inquiry', *Albany Advertiser*, 18/3/1922, p. 4.

18   I. Bird to Robert Stephens, 30/6/1945, pp. 2–3, Local History Section, Albany Public Library.

19   Personal communication with Robert Reynolds, Senior Heritage Officer, Department of Indigenous Affairs, Albany, 1/1/2011.

20   *Aborigines Department Report for Financial Year ending 30th June, 1912*, Government Printer, Perth, 1912, p. 16.

21   G. Briscoe, 'Disappearance or resurgence: the Aboriginal population of Western Australia, 1900–1940', in G. Briscoe (ed.) *Counting, Health and Identity: a history of Aboriginal health and demography in Western Australia and Queensland*, Aboriginal Studies Press, Canberra, 2003, available at http://search.informit. cm.au/documentSummary;2990585907275;res=IELHEAISBN:0855754478. p. 13 (accessed 1/1/2011).

22   Ibid.

23   D. S. Garden, *Albany: a panorama of the Sound from 1827*, Nelson, Melbourne, 1977, p. 270.

24   Information about the ration scale and its distribution comes from a letter written by the Chief Protector of Aborigines to Sergeant Lean, Albany Police Station, 23/8/1909, SRO cons 566, no. 252.

25   *Aborigines Department Report for Financial Year ending 30th June, 1912*, Government Printer, Perth, 1912, p. 16.

26   *Aborigines Department Report for Financial Year ending 30th June, 1915*, Government Printer, Perth, 1915. p. 9.

27   *Aborigines Department Report for Financial Year ending 30th June, 1917*, Government Printer, Perth, 1917. p. 8.

28   Eric Hayward wrote that many Noongars elected to leave the Katanning district rather than be placed in Carrolup (E. H. Hayward, *No Free Kicks*, Fremantle Arts Centre Press, Fremantle, 2006, p. 55).

29   *Aborigines Department Report for Financial Year ending 30th June 1918*, Government Printer, Perth, 1918. p. 4.

30   See Chapter Six for King's letter.

31   When the American linguist Gerhardt Laves visited Albany over a two-month period in 1930, he spoke with thirteen Aboriginal people. Some, such as Anne Traynen, were residents of the town of Albany, while the others had close ties with the area and probably lived in the town temporally for varying periods.

32   'Albany Town Council, monthly meeting', *Albany Advertiser*, 28/6/1922 p. 3.

33   Secretary, St Oswald's Church of England, Albany to Secretary, Aborigines Department, Perth, 24/7/1922, State Records Office, Perth.

34   Katanning alone has 110 places listed under Western Australian heritage legislation (http://register.heritage.wa.gov.au/search_results.html?offset=100 [accessed 3/2/2011]).

35   This applied especially to areas such as Katanning and Tambellup. Other areas, such as Denmark and the land south and east of the Stirling Ranges where heavy timber or natural soil infertility made farming particularly difficult or impractical using the technology of the time, did not share in this growth and prosperity.

36   B. N. Taylor, *Cooperation Incorporated*, private publication, 2011.

37   M. Bignell, *A Place to Meet: a history of the Shire of Katanning Western Australia*, UWA Press, Nedlands, 1981, p. 2.

38   Daisy Bates' Noongar genealogical information uses the spelling 'Jakbam', and states that she was born near Bremer Bay. Lynette Knapp believes that she was later known as 'Polly', and lived with Dicky Bumblefoot (Wabbinyet) at the Albany campsite on the Perth Road around the turn of the century. Bates made a very brief visit to Albany in May 1908, and compiled a vocabulary with their assistance.

39   Hayward.

40   Ibid, pp. 27–51.

41   P. C. Hardy, Katanning Police to Resident Magistrate at Katanning, 14/8/1903, Department of Aborigines and Fisheries Files, SRO cons.652, item 1914/2922.

42   The *Great Southern Herald* reports of Road Board meetings commonly mention how a Road Board meeting would close, only to immediately reopen as a meeting of the Katanning Board of Health. I have attempted without success to locate the Minutes and Correspondence of the Katanning Road Board for this period.

     The *Great Southern Herald* commenced publication in October 1901. Although based at Katanning, the paper incorporated reports from other Great Southern towns such as Cranbrook, Broomehill and Tambellup, as well as from numerous smaller localities. Microfilm copies are available at the Battye Library and the Katanning Public Library. The *Mount Barker and Denmark Record* commenced publication in 1929.

43   Haebich, p. 146.

44   'News and notes', *West Australian*, 27/8/1898, p. 4.

45   http://det.wa.edu.au/aboriginaleducation/apac/detcms/aboriginal-education/apac/districts/narrogin/timeline-of-reserves.en?oid=MultiPartArticle-id-9305078

46   H. Prinsep to The Under Secretary for Lands, 9/2/1904, Aborigines and Fisheries Department files, SRO cons. 652, item 1904, 2922.

47   Ibid.

48   Ibid.

49   Haebich, p. 377.

50   B. Reece, *Daisy Bates: grand dame of the desert*, National Library of Australia, Canberra, 2007, p. 2.

51   http://susannadevries.com/desert_queen.html (accessed 22/1/2012).

52   Haebich, p. 132.

53   Two newspapers were published at Katanning during the early twentieth century: the *Great Southern Herald*, 1901–present, and the *Southern Districts Advocate*, 1914–26.

54   Corporal Purkiss, Katanning Police Station to the Officer in Charge of South Western District, Bunbury, 12/4/1911, Aborigines Department files, State Records Office, Perth, cons. 652, 2922.

55   In 1911, Gale persuaded the Western Australian Parliament to pass the Aborigines Act Amending Act. Under one of its provisions, the offence of

supplying alcohol to Aborigines increased to a fine of £100 or six months' imprisonment or both. Aborigines with alcohol in their possession could be fined a minimum of £5 or one month's imprisonment. Aboriginal convictions in the state in 1913 were four times the 1910 total of fifty-eight. Over half of these were alcohol related (Haebich, pp. 124–5).

56   Haebich, pp. 125, 19.

57   Personal communication with Bill Hassell of Albany, 26/9/2011.

58   'Australian Aborigines Mission, public meeting at Katanning', *Great Southern Herald*, 3/8/1912, p. 2.

59   Rev. W. G. Gilmore to District Surveyor, Albany, 12/7/1912, Aborigines Department files, SRO cons. 652, 2922.

60   E. V. Radford, Hon. Sec. Aus. Aborigines Mission, W.A. Branch, to Chief Protector of Aborigines Perth, 25/7/1912, Aborigines Department files, SRO cons. 652, 2922.

61   'Katanning Road Board fortnightly meeting', *Great Southern Herald*, 21/8/1912.

62   Chief Protector of Aborigines to Hon. Sec. Australian Aborigines Mission, Tennyson Street, Bellevue, Perth, 13/8/1912.

63   'Katanning Road Board fortnightly meeting', *Great Southern Herald*, 11/6/1913, p. 6.

64   Ibid.

65   'The Aborigines', *Great Southern Herald*, 14/6/1913, p. 4.

66   My enquiries with members of the Gillam family and with members of the Katanning Historical Society have failed to provide any information about Mr A. S. Gillam.

67   'The Aborigines, question of segregation', *Great Southern Herald*, 19/7/1913, p. 6.

68   Green, 'Access, equality and opportunity?', PhD thesis, Murdoch University, 2004, p. 146.

69   'Deputations to Mr Collier', *Great Southern Herald*, 1/11/1913, p. 6.

70   Ibid.

71   'Katanning Road Board fortnightly meeting', 15/8/1913, p. 6.

72   'Katanning Road Board fortnightly meeting', 8/10/1913, p. 4.

73   Haebich, p. 145.

74   Ibid.

75   Ibid., p. 146.

76   'Amongst the Niggers', *Great Southern Advocate*, 3/1/1914, and 'Our black brudders', *Great Southern Advocate*, 10/6/1914.

77   'Court reports', *Great Southern Advocate*, 17/6/1914.

78   'Letters', *Great Southern Advocate*, 11/4/1916.

79   Mr Napier, Australian Aborigines Mission Council, to Chief Protector Gale, 4/11/1912, Aborigines Department Files, SRO cons. 652, 1629/1919.

80   *Aborigines Department Report for Financial Year ending 30th June 1914*, Government Printer, Perth, 1914, p. 2.

81   Haebich, pp. 149–52.

82   Neville, 1944, pp. 80–1, in Haebich, p. 156.

83 *Aborigines Department Report for Financial Year ending 30th June 1916*, Government Printer, Perth, 1916, p. 24.

84 Ibid., p. 26.

85 Ibid., p. 27.

86 C. Bishop, 'She has the native interests too much at heart: Annie Lock's experiences as a single, white, female missionary to Aborigines, 1903–1937', in *Evangelists of Empire? Missionaries in Colonial History*, A. Barry, J. Cruickshank, A. Brown-May & P. Grimshaw (eds), University of Melbourne escholarship Research Centre, Melbourne, 2008, http://msp.esrc.unimelb.edu.au/shs/missions (accessed 19/2/2011).

87 Haebich, p. 172.

88 Ibid., p. 189.

89 C. A. Hall, Letter to the *West Australian*, 27/6/1922, p. 7.

90 *Australian Aborigines' Advocate*, June 1922, p. 6.

91 Green, 'Access, equality and opportunity?', p. 149.

92 Haebich, p. 196.

93 Ibid., p. 228.

94 In 1914, Gnowangerup town had a non-Aboriginal population of about 300. Aborigines were camped at the outskirts of the town, and at Borden, Maileeup, Pallinup and Camballup in the Gnowangerup district. Some were employed as clearers (M. Bignell, *The Fruit of the Country*, UWA Press, Nedlands, 1977, p. 215).

95 Ibid., pp. 234–5.

96 *Gnowangerup Star*, 17/10/1925.

97 I have used these titles because so many of the older Aboriginal people from Albany refer to them in this way.

98 Haebich, pp. 236, 244.

99 Longworth, p. 258.

100 Haebich, pp. 243–6.

101 Interview with Emmett Abraham (born c. 1910) recorded by Anna Haebich, 1980, for vol. 2 of her thesis, pp. 582–7.

102 L. Hayward, Haebich interview, p. 623.

103 I. Conochie, *Aborigines of Denmark*, revised 2010, essay, p. 4. Available from the Denmark Historical Society, Denmark, WA.

104 Hassell property diaries in the possession of Bill Hassell, Albany.

105 Report dated 1/8/1906, Mount Barker Police Station Correspondence and Report Book, 28/3/1905–11/10/1910.

106 *Summary of Police Reports on the Condition and Treatment of Aboriginal Natives by Employers and Others for the Twelve Months Ended June 1913*, p. 54.

107 Minutes of the Plantagenet Road Board, 27/9/1913.

108 Ibid., 20/10/1913.

109 *Albany Advertiser*, 4/4/1914. The editor at this time, Arthur Catling, had held the position for many years (although he did not own the paper) and was prominent in Albany society. Garden described him as 'a…conservative gentleman' (p. 281).

110   Ibid., 11/4/1914.

111   Haebich, p. 140.

112   *Albany Advertiser*, 18/4/1914.

113   Haebich, p. 232.

114   M. Laurie, *Frankland to the Stirlings: a history of the Cranbrook Shire*, Shire of Cranbrook, Cranbrook, 1994, p. 74.

115   Ibid.

116   For further reading on Aboriginal farmers, see A. Haebich, 'European farmers and Aboriginal farmers in South Western Australia Mid 1890s–1914', *Studies in Western Australian History*, vol. 7, 1984, pp. 59–67.

117   It is possible to view digital copies of the original enlistment documents at http://www.naa.gov.au/collection/explore/defence/service-records/index.aspx

118   http://www.awm.gov.au/encyclopedia/aborigines/indigenous.asp p. 1 (accessed 9/3/2011).

119   This roll is displayed on a wall of the Katanning Shire Hall. The Katanning School Great War Roll of Honour is kept at the Katanning Museum. Two brothers, L. and K. Farmer, have their names inscribed on the enlistment roll, and the name L. Farmer appears on the list of those killed in action.

120   Service records of Augustus and Lawrence Farmer, National Archives of Australia.

121   Bignell, *A Place to Meet*.

122   Ibid., p. 201.

123   Ibid., p. 176.

124   A. Markus, 'Of continuities and discontinuities: reflections on a century of Australian immigration control', in L. Jayasuriya, D. Walker & J. Gothard (eds), *Legacies of White Australia*, UWA Press, Crawley, 2003, pp. 176–7.

125   C. Watson, *Commonwealth Parliamentary Debates*, 6/9/1901, p. 4636.

126   Haebich, pp. 226–7.

127   See endnote on Laves on page 344. I have been unable to access his material.

128   *Albany Advertiser*, 31/12/1930.

BIBLIOGRAPHY

Abbreviations

CSO   Colonial Secretary's Office

HRA   *Historical Records of Australia*

IRS   Robert Stephens Collection, Albany Public Library.

ML   Mitchell Library, Sydney

SRO   Western Australian State Records Office

PRIMARY SOURCES

Journals written by members of the British and French naval vessels which called at King George Sound prior to the establishment of the British garrison

Cunningham, A., *Journal of the Brig Bathurst 1821–1822* (accessed from Project Gutenberg online books at http://www.gutenberg.net.au/ebooks03/0301141h.html).

Dumont d'Urville, J. S. C., *An Account in Two Volumes of Two Voyages to the South Seas by Captain (later Rear Admiral) Jules S.C. Dumont d'Urville, of the French Navy to Australia, New Zealand, Oceania 1826–1828, in the Corvette l'Astrolabe and to the Straits of Magellan, Chile, Oceania, South East Asia, Australia, Antarctica, New Zealand and Torres Strait 1837–1840 in the Corvettes l'Astrolabe and Zellee*, Helen Rosenman (tr. and ed.), Melbourne University Press, Melbourne, 1987.

Flinders, M., *A Voyage to Terra Australis*, vol. I (accessed from Project Gutenberg online books at http://gutenberg.org/files/12929/12929-h/12929-h.htm).

King, P., *A Survey of the Intertropical Coasts of Australia*, vols I and II, 1827 (accessed from Project Gutenberg online books at http://www.gutenberg.org/files/11203/11203-h/11203-h.htm).

Péron, F., *Voyage of Discovery to the Southern Lands*, Second Edition, 1824, Book 1–3, comprising Chapters I–XXI, by F. Péron, continued by Louis de Freycinet, Christine Cornell (tr. and ed.), Friends of the State Library of South Australia, Adelaide, 2006.

Vancouver, G., *Voyage of Discovery of the North Pacific Ocean and around the World*, vol. I, G. & J. Robinson, London, 1798.

Official documents

Aboriginal Affairs Department files, 1886–1926.

Aborigines Protection Board files, 1886–97. Minutes of meetings, 1891–93; Reports and Correspondence; List of agents supplying relief; Memorandum of Transactions.

Albany Court of Petty Sessions Record Books, 1884–1905.

Albany Local Court Record Books, 1875–1905.

Albany (King George Sound) Town Trust, later Albany (K. G. Sound), Municipal Council Minute Books, 1869–1926.

Albany Police Station Daily Occurrence Books, 1859–1926, SRO series 2126, consignment 1295.

Albany Police Station Correspondence Books, 1899–1901, SRO series 349, items 1–17.

Albany Quarter Sessions Record books, 1881–1902.

'Appendix', *Report by the Parliamentary Select Committee on Aboriginal Tribes (British Settlements)*, from Dr Collie, His Majesty's Resident at King George's Sound, to Governor Sir James Stirling, King George's Sound, 24 January, 1832.

Chief Protector of Aborigines, Reports to the Western Australian Parliament, 1840–1927.

Letter Book of John Randall Phillips (Sub-Guardian of Natives at Albany), October 1850 – December 1852, MSS Australia.s.1, Rhodes House Library, Oxford University.

Mount Barker Police Station Daily Occurrence Books, 1872–1910, SRO series 427.

Mount Barker Police Station Letter and Report Books, 1893–1910, SRO series 427.

Mount Barker Police Station list of settlers visited, 1882–93, SRO series 427.

Official correspondence between the Colonial Secretary at Perth and the Resident Magistrates at Albany.

Plantagenet Roads Board minutes and correspondence, 1871–1926.

Police Gazette of Western Australia, 1876–1926.

Report of the Parliamentary Committee on Aboriginal Tribes, House of Commons, London, 1837.

Van Diemen's Land, Copies of all Correspondence between Lieutenant-Governor Arthur and His Majesty's Secretary of State for the Colonies, on the Subject of the Military Operations lately Carried on against the Aboriginal Inhabitants of Van Diemen's Land, Tasmanian Historical Research Association, Hobart, 1971.

Western Australian *Blue Books*, 1834–1905.

Western Australian Statistical Register, 1896–1926.

Semi-official documents

Albany Public Cemetery Register of Burials.

Albany Roman Catholic Church Baptism List 1853–85.

Browne, J., 'Statement Respecting Natives by James Browne for the Aborigines Protection Society', 26/6/1839, pp. 1–19, ML (AK34).

St John's Church of England Burial Register.

Journals and private correspondence of residents and visitors to the Albany region

Egerton-Warburton, G., Letters from George Egerton-Warburton, his wives and children to his family in England, from 1/10/1839 to 30/7/1885. Photocopies held by the Egerton-Warburton family of St Werburghs, Mount Barker.

Graham, W. H., Daily diary of years 1860–61 while farming at Eticup. Diary in the possession of Bill Hassell, Albany.

Hassell diaries 1900–24 from their Warriup property. Hassell employee (unnamed), Daily diary while working at Warriup Station, 1905. Diaries in the possession of Bill Hassell, Albany.

Hassell Kendenup Station account and record book, 1870–72. In the possession of Bill Hassell, Albany.

Keyser, K., *Diary of Kate Keyser, 1885–1886*, Albany, 1988, Albany Public Library, Local History Section.

Spencer, Sir R. & Lady A., Correspondence, Microfilm, accession 1038 A, and typewritten copies, both at Albany Public Library, Local History Section.

Taylor, M., Diary, 1873–1875, Albany Public Library, Local History Section.

Taylor, P., Letter dated 18 April, 1844, in *Aborigines' Protection Society*, William Watts, Printer, Crown Court, Temple Bar, London, undated.

Articles written by residents of, and visitors to, the Albany region

Backhouse, J., *Extracts from the Letters of James Backhouse, When Engaged on a Religious Visit in Australia, Accompanied by George Washington Walker*, Part Five, Harvey and Darton, London, 1839.

Backhouse, J., *Narrative of a Visit to the Australian Colonies*, Hamilton Adams, London, 1843.

Bates, D., *Native Tribes of Western Australia*, White, I. (ed.), National Library of Australia, Canberra, 1985.

Browne, J., *Aborigines of the King George's Sound Region, 1836–1838: the collected works of James Browne*, compiled and annotated by Ken Macintyre & Barbara Dobson, Hesperian Press, Carlisle, 2001.

Collie, A., 'Anecdotes and remarks relative to the Aborigines of King George's Sound', attributed to Dr A. Collie, *Perth Gazette and Western Australian Journal*, July–August 1834.

Collie, A., 'Journal of an explorative excursion to the NW of King George's Sound in 1832 by A. Collie, surgeon R.N.', in Shoobert, J. (ed.), *Western Australian Expeditions*, vol. 1, 1826–1835, W.A., Hesperian Press, Carlisle, 2005.

Eyre, E. J., *Journals of Expeditions of Discovery into Central Australia and Overland from Adelaide to King George's Sound in the Years 1840–1*, vol. I, London, 1845.

Grey, G., *Journals of Two Expeditions of Discovery in North-West and Western Australia*, in two volumes, Boone, London, 1841.

Moore, G. F., 'Vocabulary of the King George's Sound Aborigines', extracted from *A Descriptive Vocabulary of the Language in Common Use Amongst the Aborigines of Western Australia*, published in *A Diary of Ten Years Eventful Life of an Early Settler in Western Australia, 1884*, Walbrook, London, 1884.

Nind, I. S., 'Description of the natives of King George's Sound (Swan River Colony) and adjoining country. Written by Mr. Scott Nind, and communicated by R. Brown, Esq., F.R.S. Read 14th Feb, 1831', *Journal of the Royal Geographical Society of London*, vol. I, 1832, pp. 21–51.

Wilson, T. B., 'Narrative of a voyage around the world', in Wilson, L., *The Laird of Braidwood*, Wilson, Tasmania, 2006.

Early Perth newspaper article series

Armstrong, F., 'Manners and habits of the Aborigines of Western Australia, from information collected by Mr F. Armstrong, interpreter, 1836', printed in the *Perth Gazette and Western Australian Journal*, October–November, 1836.

Lyon, R. M., 'A glance at the manners and language of the Aboriginal inhabitants of Western Australia; with a short vocabulary', printed in the *Perth Gazette and Western Australian Journal*, March–April, 1833.

SECONDARY SOURCES

Local histories, and other publications specifically related to the general region covered in the study, or immediately adjacent to this region

Austin, S., *Emu Point*, W.A. Museum, Perth, 2003.

Ayres, C., with Johnson, L., *The Ayres Family of Bornholm*, undated private publication, Local History Section of Albany Public Library.

Bartlett, J., *Built to Last*, Albany Advertiser, Albany, 1988.

Bartlett, J., *Journey: a history of the Anglican Diocese of Bunbury, 1904–2004*, Albany Advertiser, Albany, 2004.

Bignell, M., *A Place to Meet: a history of the Shire of Katanning*, UWA Press, Nedlands, 1981.

Bignell, M., *First the Spring: a history of the Shire of Kojonup*, UWA Press, Nedlands, 1971.

Bignell, M., *Tell Their Worth: tales of the Shire of Kojonup*, Kojonup Historical Society, Kojonup, 1997.

Bignell, M., *The Fruit of the Country: a history of the Shire of Gnowangerup*, UWA Press, Nedlands, 1977.

Brockway, M., 'The Dunns of Cocanerup', *Early Days*, vol. 11, part 4, 1970.

Cairns, D. C., *A History of Kendenup*, privately published monograph held at the Battye Archives, undated.

Chessel, G., *Richard Spencer*, UWA Press, Nedlands, 2005.

Crabb, D., *The Way to St Werburgh's*, Albany Advertiser Print, Albany, undated.

Crawford, P. & Crawford, I., *Contested Country: a history of the Northcliffe Area*, UWA Press, Crawley, 2003.

De Garis, B. K., *Portraits of the South West*, UWA Press, Nedlands, 1993.

Dickson, R., *To King George Sound for Whales*, Hesperian Press, Carlisle, 2006.

Dowson, J., *Old Albany*, National Trust of Western Australia (Inc), Fremantle, 2008.

Erickson, R., *The Dempsters*, UWA Press, Nedlands, 1978.

Ferguson, W. C., 'Mokare's Domain', in *Australians to 1788*, Mulvaney, D. J. & White, J. (eds), Fairfax, Syme & Weldon Associates, Sydney, 1987.

Forrest, R., *Kukenarup: two stories*, Department of Indigenous Affairs, Perth, 2004.

Garden, D. S., *Albany: a panorama of the Sound from 1827*, Nelson, Melbourne, 1977.

Garden, D. S., *Southern Haven: the Port of Albany*, Albany Port Authority, Albany, 1978.

Glover, R., *Plantagenet, Rich and Beautiful: history of Mount Barker Shire*, UWA Press, Nedlands, 1981.

Goode, B., Irvine, C., Harris, J. & Thomas, M., *'Kinjarling', the Place of Rain*, The City of Albany & Department of Indigenous Affairs Aboriginal Heritage Survey, A report prepared for the City of Albany and the Department of Indigenous Affairs, Albany, 2005.

Green, N., *Aborigines of the Albany Region, 1821–1898*, UWA Press, Nedlands, 1989.

Green, N., 'King George Sound: the friendly frontier', in *ANZAAS, 1983*, Smith, M. (ed.), Anthropology Department, W.A. Museum, Perth, p. 68.

Groom, S., *A Sense of Ownership: a history of the Kent River*, Kent River Conservation District Committee, Advance Press, Perth 2006.

Hassell, C. W., *The Hassells: a history of the Hassells of Albany*, C. Hassell, Private Publication, 1973.

Hassell, E., *My Dusky Friends*, C. W. Hassell, Fremantle, 1975.

Hayward, E. H., *No Free Kicks*, Fremantle Arts Centre Press, Fremantle, 2006.

Hicks, B., *Aspects of Old Albany*, Albany Printers, Albany, 1991.

Hunt, D., *Albany: first western settlement*, Town of Albany, Albany, undated.

Johnson, L., *Love Thy Land*, Albany Shire Council, Albany, 1982.

Johnson, L., *Major Edmund Lockyer: forgotten Australian pioneer*, W.A. Museum, Albany, 2002.

Knapp, L., *Mirnang Waangkaniny*, Batchelor Press, Batchelor, 2011.

Laurie, M., *Frankland to the Stirlings: a history of the Cranbrook Shire*, Shire of Cranbrook, Cranbrook, 1994.

le Souef, S., *Portraits of the South West*, UWA Press, Nedlands, 1993.

Mann, H. W. (ed.), *The Wollaston Journals*, vol. 3, 1845–1856, UWA Press, Crawley, 2006.

Muir, A., *Settler Footprints from Star: Muir Family*, Family Books, Perth, 2005.

Mulvaney, J. & Green, N., *Commandant of Solitude*, Melbourne University Press, Melbourne, 1992.

Parnell, J., *Country Cavalcade: a history of the Shire of Tambellup*, Shire of Tambellup, Subiaco, 1982.

Pettersen, C., *Koodjal-koodjal Djook: four sisters. The legend of the Southern Cross*, Batchelor Press, Batchelor, 2007.

Pettersen, C., *Yongka, miyak: kangaroo and moon*, Batchelor Press, Batchelor, 2007.

Piggott, R., *Fishtraps and Floods*, A. & B. Little, Albany, 2004.

Rourke, W. H., *My Way*, Carrolls, Perth, 1980.

Scott, K., *Kayang & Me*, Fremantle Arts Centre Press, Fremantle, 2005.

Sellick, D., *First Impressions: Albany*, Western Australian Museum, Perth, 1997.

Shellam, T., *Shaking Hands on the Fringe*, UWA Press, Crawley, 2009.

Stephens, R., *Kendenup, 1840–1940*, privately published monograph held at Battye Archives, undated.

Taylor, B. N., *Cooperation Incorporated*, private publication, 2011.

Wellstead, J. & Wellstead, P., *The Wellstead Family, 1820–1998*, Warjam, Albany, 1998.

West, D. A. P., *The Settlement on the Sound*, W.A. Museum, Perth, 1976.

Williams, J. & Dean, A., *Boola Miyel*, Batchelor Press, Batchelor, 2007.

Williams, S. *Yongker Mir*, Batchelor Press, Batchelor, 2007.

Albany and regional newspapers

Albany Advertiser, 1897–1927.

Albany Despatch, 1919–28.

Albany Mail, 1883–89.

Albany Observer, 1890–91.

Australian Advertiser, 1888–97. Albany.

Gnowangerup Star, 1925–26.

Great Southern Herald, 1901–27, (Incorporating *Tambellup Times*, 1912–24, and *Gnowangerup Times*, 1912–18), Katanning.

Southern Districts Advocate, 1914–26, Katanning, but included news from Broomehill, Tambellup, Gnowangerup, Ongerup, Cranbrook, Mount Barker and Denmark.

Colony and statewide newspapers

The Inquirer, 1840–55.

Inquirer and Commercial News, 1855–1901.

Perth Gazette & Western Australian Journal, 1833–47.

Perth Gazette and Independent Journal of Politics and News, 1848–64.

Perth Gazette & W.A. Times, 1864–74.

Sunday Times, 1902–26.

West Australian, 1879–1926.

Western Mail, 1885–1926.

Published books

Amato, J. A., *Rethinking Home: a case for writing local history*, University of California Press, Berkeley and Los Angeles, 2002.

Attwood, B., *Possession*, Miegunyah Press, University of Melbourne, Melbourne, 2009.

Attwood, B., *Telling the Truth about Aboriginal History*, Allen & Unwin, Sydney, 2005.

Attwood, B., *The Making of the Aborigines*, Allen & Unwin, Sydney, 1989.

Attwood, B., Burrage, W., Burrage A. & Stokie, E., *A Life Together, a Life Apart: a history of relations between Europeans and Aborigines*, Melbourne University Press, Melbourne, 1994.

Attwood, B. & Foster, S. G. (eds), *Frontier Conflict: the Australian experience*, National Museum of Australia, Canberra, 2003.

Atwood, B. & Griffiths, T., *Frontier, Race, Nation: Henry Reynolds and Australian History*, Australian Scholarly Publishing Company, Melbourne, 2009.

Attwood, B. & Magowan, F., *Telling Stories: Indigenous history and memory in Australia and New Zealand*, Allen & Unwin, Sydney, 2001.

Austen, T., *A Cry in the Wind: conflict in Western Australia*, Darlington Publishing Group, Darlington, WA, 1988.

Aveling, M. (ed.), *Westralian Voices*, UWA Press, Nedlands, 1979.

Banks, M., *Ethnicity: anthropological constructions*, Routledge, London, 1996.

Banner, S., *Possessing the Pacific*, Harvard University Press, Cambridge, Massachusetts, 2007.

Barwick, D., Mace, M. & Stannage, T. (eds), *Handbook for Aboriginal and Islander History*, Aboriginal History Publishers, Canberra, 1979.

Bates, D., *My Natives and I*, Hesperian Press, Carlisle, 2004, first published 1936.

Bates, D., *The Native Tribes of Western Australia*, I. White (ed.), National Library of Australia, Canberra, 1985.

Battye, J. S., *Western Australia*, facsimile edition, UWA Press, Nedlands, 1978, first published 1924.

Belich, J., *Making Peoples: a history of the New Zealanders*, North Shore, Auckland, 2007.

Belich, J., *The Victorian Interpretation of Racial Conflict*, McGill, Quebec, 1989.

Bell, D., *Daughters of the Dreaming*, Allen & Unwin, Sydney, 1983.

Bennett, M. M., *The Australian Aboriginal as a Human Being*, Chance and Bland, Gloucester, 1930.

Bentley, M., *Grandfather was a Policeman: the Western Australian Police Force 1829–1889*, Hesperian Press, Victoria Park, 1993.

Berndt, R. M. & Berndt, C. H. (eds), *Aboriginal Man in Australia*, Angus & Robertson, Sydney, 1965.

Berndt, R. M. & Berndt, C. H., *Aborigines of the West*, UWA Press, Nedlands, 1979.

Berndt, R. M. & Berndt, C. H., *Pioneers and Settlers*, Pitman, Melbourne, 1978.

Berndt, R. M. & Berndt, C. H. *The First Australians*, Ure Smith, Sydney, 1974.

Berg, M. & Wendt, S. (eds), *Racism in the Modern World: historical perspectives on cultural transfer and adaptation*, Berghahn Books, Melbourne, 2011.

Biskup, P., *Not Slaves, Not Citizens*, University of Queensland Press, Brisbane, 1973.

Blainey, G., *A Land Half Won*, Macmillan, Melbourne, 1980.

Blainey, G., *Black Kettle and Full Moon*, Penguin, Melbourne, 2003.

Blainey, G. (ed.), *Greater Britain*, Methuen Hayes, Sydney, 1985.

Blainey, G., *The Tyranny of Distance*, Sun Books, Melbourne, 1966.

Blainey, G., *Triumph of the Nomads*, Macmillan, Melbourne, 1975.

Blease, W. L., *A Short History of English Liberalism*, facsimile edition, Forgotten Books, London, 2009, first published 1913.

Bolton, G., *Land of Vision and Mirage: a history of Western Australia since 1826*, UWA Press, Crawley, 2008.

Borrie, W. D., *The European Peopling of Australia: a demographic history 1788–1988*, ANU Press, Canberra, 1992.

Bourke, D. F., *The History of the Catholic Church in Western Australia*, Vanguard, Perth, 1979.

Brandon, W., *The Rise and Fall of North American Indians*, Bowman and Littlefield, Lanham, 2003.

Bridge, C. (ed.), *New Perspectives in Australian History*, University of London, London, 1990.

Briscoe, G., 'Disappearance or resurgence: the Aboriginal population of Western Australia, 1900–1940', in Briscoe, G. (ed.), *Counting, Health and Identity: a history of Aboriginal health and demography in Western Australia and Queensland*, Aboriginal Studies Press, Canberra, 2003, available at http://search.informit.cm.au/documentSummary;2990585907275;res= IELHEAISBN:0855754478

Broome, R., *Aboriginal Australians: black responses to white dominance, 1788–2001*, Allen & Unwin, Sydney, 2002.

Broome, R., *Aboriginal Victorians: a history since 1800*, Allen & Unwin, Sydney, 2005.

Burton, A., *The Journals and Diaries of Revd John Ramsden Wollaston M.A.*, The Picton Journals (1841–1844), Paterson Brokensha, Perth, 1955.

Burton, A., *Wollaston's Albany Journal (1848–1856)*, Lamb Publications, Osborne Park, 1954.

Burton Jackson, J. L., *Frowning Fortunes: the story of Thomas Bannister and the Williams River District*, Hesperian Press, Victoria Park, 1993.

Butlin, N. G., *Economics and the Dreamtime: a hypothetical history*, Cambridge University Press, Cambridge, 2010.

Butlin, N. G., *Our Original Aggression*, Allen & Unwin, Sydney, 1983.

Campbell, J., *Invisible Invaders: smallpox and other diseases in Aboriginal Australia, 1780–1880*, Melbourne University Press, Melbourne, 2002.

Campbell, H., *KATITJIN: a guide to the Indigenous records in the Battye Library*, Battye Library, Perth, 2003.

Carey, H. M., *God's Empire: religion and colonialism in the British world, c. 1801–1908*, Cambridge University Press, Cambridge, 2010.

Carroll, J. (ed.), *Intruders in the Bush*, Oxford University Press, Melbourne, 1982.

Carter, B., *Nyungah Land: records of invasion and theft of Aboriginal land at the Swan River 1829–1850*, Advance Press, Bassendean, 2005.

Carter, D., *Dispossession, Dreams and Diversity: issues in Australian studies*, Pearson, Sydney, 2006.

Chapman, V. & Read, P. (eds), *Terrible Hard Biscuits*, Allen & Unwin, Sydney, 1996.

Christie, M. F., *Aborigines in Colonial Victoria, 1835–86*, Sydney University Press, Sydney, 1979.

Clark, C. M. H., *A New History of Australia*, vol. III, Melbourne University Press, Melbourne, 1973.

Clark, C. M. H., *Select Documents in Australian History, 1851–1900*, Angus & Robertson, Sydney, 1955.

Clement, C. (ed.), *Ethics and the Practice of History*, Studies in Western Australian History, no. 26, Centre for Western Australian History, UWA Press, Crawley, 2010.

Clendinnen, I., *True Stories*, Boyer Lectures, ABC Books, Sydney, 1999.

Clendinnen, I., *Dancing with Strangers*, Text, Melbourne, 2003.

Colebatch, H., *A Story of a Hundred Years: Western Australia 1829–1929*, W.A. Government Printer, Perth, 1929.

Collier, J., *The Pastoral Age in Australasia*, Whitcombe and Tombs, London, 1911.

Collins, D., *An Account of the English Colony in New South Wales*, Reed, Sydney, 1975, first published 1802.

Connor, J., *The Australian Frontier Wars, 1788–1838*, UNSW Press, Sydney, 2002.

Conole, P., *Protect & Serve: a history of policing in Western Australia*, Success Print, Bayswater, 2002.

Coupe, S. (ed.), *Frontier Country*, Weldon Russell, Sydney, 1989.

Cowlishaw, G., *Rednecks, Eggheads and Blackfellas*, Allen & Unwin, Sydney, 1999.

Crawford, I., *We Won the Victory*, Fremantle Arts Centre Press, Fremantle, 2001.

Critchett, J., *A 'Distant Field of Murder'*, Melbourne University Press, Melbourne, 1990.

Crowley, F. K., *Australia's Western Third*, Macmillan, London, 1960.

Crowley, F., *Colonial Australia*, Nelson, Melbourne, 1980.

Crowley, F., *Forrest*, vol. 1, 1847–91, University of Queensland Press, Brisbane, 1971.

Crowley, F. K. & de Garis, B. K., *A Short History of Western Australia*, Macmillan, Melbourne, 1959.

Curtis, E. S., *The North American Indian*, Taschen, Cologne, 1997.

Dalrymple, W., *The Last Mughal*, Bloomsbury, London, 2006.

Davison, G., *The Use and Abuse of Australian History*, Allen & Unwin, Sydney, 2000.

De Brune, A., *Fifty Years of Progress in Australia*, Halstead, Sydney, 1929.

Donaldson, I., & Donaldson, T. (eds), *Seeing the First Australians*, Allen & Unwin, Sydney, 1985.

Douglas, S. L., Roberts, A. & Thompson, R., *Oral History*, Allen & Unwin, Sydney, 1988.

Dyer, C., *The French Explorers and the Aboriginal Australians 1772–1839*, University of Queensland Press, Brisbane, 2005.

Edwards, W. W. (ed.), *Traditional Aboriginal Society*, Macmillan, Melbourne, 2003.

Elder, B., *Blood on the Wattle*, Child and Associates, Sydney, 1988.

Elkin, A. P., *The Australian Aborigines*, Angus & Robertson, Sydney, 1938.

Ewers, J. K., *Bruce Rock: the Story of a district*, Bruce Rock Roads Board, Bruce Rock, 1959.

Ferguson, N., *Empire: how Britain made the modern world*, Penguin, London, 2008.

Flood, J., *The Archaeology of the Dreamtime*, Collins, Sydney, 1983.

Flood, J., *The Original Australians*, Allen & Unwin, Sydney, 2006.

Fornasiero, J., Monteath P., & West-Sooby J., *Encountering Terra Australis: the Australian voyages of Nicolas Baudin and Matthew Flinders*, Wakefield Press, Adelaide, 2010.

Gammage, W., *The Biggest Estate on Earth*, Allen & Unwin, Sydney, 2011.

Gascoigne, J., *The Enlightenment and the Origins of European Australia*, Cambridge University Press, Cambridge, 2002.

Glynn, S., *Government Policy and Agricultural Development*, UWA Press, Nedlands, 1975.

Graburn, N. H. H. (ed.), *Ethnic and Tourist Arts*, University of California Press, Berkeley, 1976.

Graham, D., *Western Australia's Other History*, Wordstars, Midland, 1996.

Green, N. & Moon, S., *Far From Home: Aboriginal prisoners on Rottnest Island 1838–1931*, UWA Press, Nedlands, 1997.

Green, N. & Tilbrook, L. (eds), *Aborigines of New Norcia 1845–1914*, UWA Press, Nedlands, 1989.

Green, N., *Broken Spears*, Focus Education Services, Cottesloe, 1984.

Green, N., *Nyungar – the People*, Creative Research, Mount Lawley, 1979.

Greenwood, G., *Australia: a social and political history*, Angus & Robertson, Sydney, 1955.

Gregory, J. & Gothard, J. (eds), *Historical Encyclopedia of Western Australia*, UWA Press, Crawley, 2009.

Grimshaw, P., Lake, M., McGrath, A. et al., *Creating a Nation*, McPhee Gribble, Melbourne, 1994.

Hackner, B., *Busted out Laughing: Dot Collard's story (as told to Beryl Hackner)*, Magabala Books, Broome, 2003.

Haebich, A., *Broken Circles: fragmenting Indigenous families, 1800–2000*, Fremantle Arts Centre Press, Fremantle, 2000.

Haebich, A., *For Their Own Good*, UWA Press, Nedlands, 1988.

Haebich, A., *Spinning the Dream*, Fremantle Press, North Fremantle, 2008.

Haebich, A. & Delroy, A., *The Stolen Generations*, Western Australian Museum, Perth, 1999.

Hammond, J. E., *Winjan's People*, Hesperian Press, Carlisle, 1993.

Hancock, W. K., *Australia*, Benn, London, 1930.

Hannaford, I., *Race: the history of the idea in the West*, Johns Hopkins University Press, Washington DC, 1996.

Harris, J., *One Blood*, Albatross, Sydney, 1990.

Hasluck, P., *Black Australians*, Melbourne University Press, Melbourne, 1942.

Hay, D. & Craven, P. (eds), *Masters, Servants, and Magistrates in Britain and the Empire, 1562–1955*, University of North Carolina Press, Chapel Hill, 2004.

Hetherington, P., *Settlers, Servants and Slaves: Aboriginal and European children in nineteenth-century Western Australia*, UWA Press Nedlands, 2002.

Hiatt, L. R., *Arguments about Aborigines*, Cambridge University Press, Cambridge, 1996.

Horden, M., *King of the Australian Coast: the work of Phillip Parker King in the Mermaid and Bathurst, 1817–1822*, Melbourne University Press, Melbourne, 1997.

Host, J. with Owen, C., *'It's Still in My Heart, This Is My Country': the single Noongar claim history*, South West Aboriginal Land and Sea Council, UWA Press, Crawley, 2009.

Howard, M. C., *Aboriginal Politics in Southwestern Australia*, UWA Press, Nedlands, 1981.

Hunt, L. (ed.), *Westralian Portraits*, UWA Press, Nedlands, 1979.

Inglis, K., *Australian Colonists*, Melbourne University Press, Melbourne, 1993.

Isaac, R., *The Transformation of Virginia*, University of North Carolina Press, Chapel Hill, 1982.

Jacobs, P., *Mr Neville*, Fremantle Arts Centre Press, Fremantle, 1990.

Jayasuriya, L., Walker, D. & Gothard, J. (eds), *Legacies of White Australia*, UWA Press, Crawley, 2003.

Jose, A. W., *History of Australia*, Angus & Robertson, Sydney, 1913.

Katz, W. J. & Mahoney, T., *Regionalism and the Humanities: decline or revival?* Bison Books, London, 2009.

Kenny, R., *The Lamb Enters the Dreaming*, Scribe Publications, Melbourne, 2007.

Kiddle, M., *Men of Yesterday*, Melbourne University Press, Melbourne, 1961.

Kimberly, W. B., *West Australia: a narrative of her past*, F. W. Niven & Co., Melbourne and Ballarat, 1897.

Kitson Clark, G. S. R., *An Expanding Society*, Melbourne University Press, Melbourne, 1967.

Kitson Clark, G., *The Making of Victorian England*, Methuen & Co., London, 1965.

Laffer, W. H., *History of Bruce Rock and District*, reprinted by the Shire of Bruce Rock, 1976.

Lack, J., *A History of Footscray*, Hargreen, Melbourne, 2001.

Lewis, D. & Forman, W., *The Maori*, Orbis, London, 1982.

Lippmann, L., *Generations of Resistance*, Longman Cheshire, Melbourne, 1981.

Loos, N., *Invasion and Resistance*, ANU Press, Canberra, 1982.

Love, E. T. L., *Race over Empire*, University of North Carolina Press, Chapel Hill, 2004.

Macraid, D. & Taylor, A., *Social Theory and Social History*, Palgrave Macmillan, Basingstoke, Hampshire, 2004.

Marchant, L., *France Australe*, Artlook Books, Perth, 1982.

McLynn, F., *Captain Cook: master of the seas*, Yale University Press, New Haven, 2011.

McGrath, A., *Born in the Cattle*, Allen & Unwin, Sydney, 1989.

McGrath, A. (ed.), *Contested Ground: Australian Aborigines under the British Crown*, Allen & Unwin, Sydney, 1995.

McGregor, R., *Imagined Destinies: Aboriginal Australians and the doomed race theory, 1880–1939*, Melbourne University Press, Melbourne, 1997.

McKenna, M., *Looking for Blackfellas' Point*, UNSW Press, Sydney, 2002.

Meaney, N., *Under New Heavens*, Heinemann, Melbourne, 1989.

Millett, E., *An Australian Parsonage, or the Settler and the Savage in Western Australia*, facsimile edition, UWA Press, Nedlands, 1980, first published 1872.

Milroy, J., Host, J., & Stannage, T. (eds), *Wordal, Studies in Western Australian History*, no. 22, UWA Press, Crawley, 2001.

Monin, P., *This is My Place: Hauraki contested, 1769–1875*, Bridget Williams Books, Wellington, 2001.

Morton, H. & Morton Johnston, C., *The Farthest Corner: New Zealand, a twice discovered land*, Hutchinson, Auckland, 1998.

Mulvaney, J., *Encounters in Place: outsiders and Aboriginal Australians, 1606–1985*, University of Queensland Press, Brisbane, 1989.

Neville A. O., *Australia's Coloured Minority: its place in the community*, Currawong Publishing Co., Sydney, 1947.

Ogle, N., *The Colony of Western Australia: a manual for emigrants*, London, 1839.

Partington, G., *Hasluck versus Coombs: white politics and Australia's Aborigines*, Quakers Hill Press, Sydney, 1996.

Pattel-Grey, A., *The Great White Flood: racism in Australia*, Scholars Press, Atlanta, Georgia, 2000.

Patterson, A. G., *The Lost Legions*, Altimira Press, London, 2008.

Perkins, R. & Nowra, L., *First Australians*, Melbourne University Publishing, Melbourne, 2008.

Pettifer, J. & Bradley, R., *Missionaries*, BBC Books, London, 1990.

Pike, D. H., *Australia: the quiet continent*, Cambridge University Press, London, 1962.

Poad, D. et al., *Contact*, Rigby, Melbourne, 1985.

Portus, G. V., *Australia since 1606*, Oxford University Press, Melbourne, 1936.

Presland, G., *Aboriginal Melbourne: the lost land of the Kulin people*, McPhee Gribble, Melbourne, 1985.

Ramsland, J., *Custodians of the Soil*, Greater Taree City Council, Taree, 2001.

Ramsland, J., *The Rainbow Beach Man*, Brolga Publishing Co., Melbourne, 2009.

Read, P., *A Hundred Years War*, ANU Press, Sydney, 1988.

Read, P., *Belonging: Australians, place and Aboriginal ownership*, Cambridge University Press, Cambridge, 2001.

Read, P., *The Stolen Generations: the removal of Aboriginal children in New South Wales 1883–1969*, New South Wales Department of Aboriginal Affairs, Sydney, 1981.

Reece, R. & Stannage, T. (eds), *European–Aboriginal Relations in Western Australian History*, UWA Press, Nedlands, 1984.

Reece, R. H. W., *Aborigines and Colonists*, Sydney University Press, Sydney, 1974.

Reece, R. H. W., *Daisy Bates: grand dame of the desert*, National Library of Australia, Canberra, 2007.

Reilly, J. T., *Reminiscences of Fifty Years Residence in Western Australia*, Sands and McDougal, Perth, 1901.

Reynolds, H., *Aboriginal Sovereignty*, Allen & Unwin, Sydney, 1996.

Reynolds, H., *Aborigines and Settlers*, Cassell, Melbourne, 1972.

Reynolds, H., *An Indelible Stain*, Penguin, Melbourne, 2001.

Reynolds, H., *Dispossession: black Australians and white invaders*, Allen & Unwin, Sydney, 1989.

Reynolds, H., *Fate of a Free People*, Penguin, Melbourne, 1995.

Reynolds, H., *Frontier, Aborigines, Settlers and Land*, Allen & Unwin, Sydney, 1987.

Reynolds, H., *Nowhere People*, Penguin, Melbourne, 2005.

Reynolds, H. (ed.), *Race Relations in North Queensland*, James Cook University, Townsville, 1993.

Reynolds, H., *The Other Side of the Frontier*, James Cook University Press, Townsville, 1981.

Reynolds, H., *The Trevor Reese Memorial Lecture*, University of London, London, 1984.

Reynolds, H., *Why Weren't We Told?*, Penguin, Melbourne, 2000.

Reynolds, H., *With the White People*, Penguin, Melbourne, 1990.

Richards J., *The Secret War*, University of Queensland Press, Brisbane, 2008.

Richards, R., *A Guide to Sources for the History of South Western Australia*, UWA Press, Nedlands, 1993.

Roberts, S. H., *History of Australian Land Settlement*, first edition 1924, reissued by Macmillan, Melbourne, 1968.

Rowley, C. D., *Outcasts in White Australia*, vols 1–3, ANU Press, Canberra, 1971.

Rowley, C. D., *The Destruction of Aboriginal Society*, Penguin, Melbourne, 1970.

Rowse, T., *White Flour, White Power: from rations to citizenship in Central Australia*, Cambridge University Press, Cambridge, 1998.

Rusden, G. W., *History of Australia*, in 3 vols, Chapman and Hall, London, 1883.

Ryan, L., *The Aboriginal Tasmanians*, Allen & Unwin, Sydney, 1996.

Samson, J., *Race and Empire*, Pearson Longman, London, 2005.

Shaw, A. G. L., *The Story of Australia*, Faber and Faber, London, 1954.

Smith, M. A., *Peopling the Cleland Hills*, Aboriginal History Inc., Canberra, 2005.

Smith, P. M., *A Concise History of New Zealand*, Cambridge University Press, Cambridge, 2005.

Smithers, G. D., *Science, Sexuality, and Race in the United States and Australia, 1780s–1800s*, Routledge, Oxford, 2009.

Stannage, C. T. (ed.), *A New History of Western Australia*, UWA Press, Nedlands, 1981.

Stannage, C. T. (ed.), *Convictism in Western Australia, Studies in Western Australian History*, vol. 4, UWA Press, Nedlands, 1981.

Stannage, C. T., *The People of Perth*, Perth City Council, Perth, 1979.

Stannage, C. T., *Western Australia's Heritage: the pioneer myth*, University Extension, UWA Press, Nedlands, 1985.

Stannage, C. T., Saunders, K. & Nile, R., *Paul Hasluck in Australian History*, University of Queensland Press, Brisbane, 1998.

Stannard, D. E., *American Holocaust*, Oxford University Press, New York, 1992.

Stanner, W. E. H., *The 1968 Boyer Lectures: after the dreaming*, ABC, Sydney, 1969.

Stanner, W. E. H., *The Dreaming and Other Essays*, Black Inc. Agenda, Melbourne, 2009.

Statham-Drew, P., *James Stirling*, UWA Press, Nedlands, 2003.

Strong, R., *Anglicanism and the British Empire c. 1700–1850*, Oxford University Press Oxford, 2007.

Sweetman, J., *The Military Establishment and Penal Settlement*, Hesperian Press, Carlisle, 1989.

Tebbel, J. & Jennison, K., *The American Indian Wars*, Phoenix Press, London, 2001.

Tilbrook, L., *Nyungar Tradition*, UWA Press, Nedlands, 1983.

Tindale, N., *Aboriginal Family History Photographs (Tindale Collection)*, Aboriginal Affairs Department, undated.

Tindale, N., *Aboriginal Tribes of Australia*, Australian National University Press, Canberra, 1974.

Tjalaminu, M., *Ngulak Ngarnk Nidja Boodja, Our Mother, This Land*, The Centre for Indigenous History and the Arts, UWA, Nedlands, 2000.

Tosh, J., *The Pursuit of History*, Longman, Harlow, 2010.

Ward, R., *Finding Australia*, Heineman, Melbourne, 1987.

Waterhouse, R., *The Vision Splendid*, Curtin University Books, Fremantle, 2005.

Watson, D., *Caledonia Australis*, Random House, Sydney, 2009.

Westgarth, W., *Victoria and the Australian Gold Mines in 1857*, Smith, Elder and Co., London, 1857.

White, R., *Inventing Australia*, Allen & Unwin, Sydney, 1981.

Willey, K., *When the Sky Fell Down*, Collins, Sydney, 1979.

Windschuttle, K., *The White Australia Policy*, Macleay Press, Sydney, 2004.

Woolmington, J., *Aborigines in Colonial Society: 1788–1850, from 'Noble Savage' to 'Rural Pest'*, University of New England, Armidale, 1973.

Worby, G. & Rigney, L., *Sharing Spaces: Indigenous and non-Indigenous responses to story, country and rights*, National Library of Australia, Canberra, 2005.

Theses

Allbrook, M., '"Imperial family": the Prinseps, empire and colonial government in India and Australia', PhD thesis, Griffith University, 2008.

Blake, R., 'Court of Quarter Sessions and Supreme Court trials involving violent inter-racial incidents between British settlers and Aborigines in Western Australia in the 1850s and 1860s', Honours thesis, UWA, 1995.

Davis, J., 'Longing or belonging? Responses to a 'new' land in southern Western Australia 1829–1907', PhD thesis, UWA, 2008.

Green, N., 'Access, equality and opportunity? The education of Aboriginal children in Western Australia 1840–1978', PhD thesis, Murdoch University, 2004.

Groves, J., 'The comforts of civilisation in early colonial Western Australia', Honours thesis, Edith Cowan University, 2006.

Haebich, A., '"A bunch of cast-offs": Aborigines of the Southwest of Western Australia', 1900–1936, PhD thesis, Murdoch University, 1985.

Hayward, E., 'No free kicks: the experience of an Aboriginal family in Australian Rules Football', MA thesis, Curtin University, 2002.

Longworth, A., '"Was it Worthwhile?": an historical analysis of five women missionaries and their encounters with the Nyungar people of south-west Australia', PhD thesis, Murdoch University, 2005.

Shellam, T. S. B., 'Shaking hands on the fringe: negotiating the Aboriginal world at King George's Sound', PhD thesis, ANU, 2007.

Unpublished manuscripts

Bird, D. F., 'At the beginning: a close look at records of some of the earliest days and people who created much of the earliest history of King George the third Sound and who played a hand in the establishment of the first settlement in Western Australia. From the research and recollections of Augusta Maud Bird and the letters of Sir Richard and Lady Spencer as revealed in a series of articles published in the *Albany Advertiser* in 1926. Notated and updated by David F. Bird, December 2000', privately printed, 2008.

Bird, I., 'The Story of Strawberry Hill, Middleton Road, Albany, Western Australia, 1791 to 1891. Compiled from the original records by Ivan Bird', 1940. A compilation of letters, original photographs, family history and general Albany history. The work is held at the Local History section of the Albany Public Library.

Conochie, I., 'Aborigines of Denmark', revised version, dated 2010.

Crawford, I., 'Towards an ethnography of the Murrum people', draft copy, held at Albany Department of Indigenous Affairs, undated.

Garstone, R., 'Noongar Wongi', private publication, Albany, 2003.

Hicks, B., 'Henry and Anne Camfield', Albany Public Library Local History Section, 1964.

Norrish, T., 'Diary of Thomas Norrish of Broomehill', manuscript held in Local History Section of Albany Public Library, 1900.

Rowse, T., 'Quantifying the Stolen Generations', (draft version), unpublished, 2010.

Journal articles

Allen, J. & O'Connell, J. F., 'The long and short of it: archaeological approaches to determining when humans first colonised Australia and New Guinea', *Australian Archaeology*, no. 57, 2003.

Barzon, G., 'Pirates and wreckers of Kangaroo Island', *Evening News*, 28/9/1845.

Briscoe, G., 'Aboriginal Australian identity: the historiography of relations between Indigenous ethnic groups and other Australians, 1788 to 1988', *History Workshop*, no. 36, Autumn, 1993, pp. 133–61.

Brock, P., 'Mission encounters in the colonial world: British Columbia and South-West Australia', *Journal of Religious History*, vol. 24, no. 2, June 2000, pp. 159–79.

Carey, H. M., 'Introduction: colonialist representations of Indigenous religions', *Journal of Religious History*, vol. 22, no. 2, 1998, pp. 125–31.

Delmege, S., A 'Trans-generational effect of the Aborigines Act 1905 (WA): the making of the fringedwellers in the South-West of Western Australia', *Murdoch University Electronic Journal of Law*, 2005, p. 3, http://www.austlii.edu.au/au/journals/MurUEJL/2005/6.html (accessed 27/1/2011).

Drew, L. A., 'Louisiana history', *Journal of the Louisiana Historical Association*, vol. 12, no. 2, Spring, 1971, pp. 167–75.

Ellis, C., 'Public Indians, private Cherokees: tourism and tradition on tribal ground', *Journal of Southern History*, May 2011, vol. 77, no. 2, p. 494.

Foster, R., '"Don't mention the war": frontier violence and the language of concealment', *History Australia*, vol. 6, no. 3, 2010.

Gill, N., Paterson, A. & Kennedy, M. J., '"Do you want to delete this?" Hidden histories and hidden landscapes in the Murchison and Davenport Ranges, Northern Territory, Australia', in Ward, G. K. & Muckle, A. (eds), *The Power of Knowledge, the Resonance of Tradition*, papers from the AIATSIS Conference, AIATSIS, Canberra, 2001.

Hayward, J. F., 'Reminiscences of Johnson Frederick Hayward', *Proceedings of the Royal Geographical Society of Australasia, South Australian Branch*, vol. 29, 1929.

Jensz, F., 'Controlling marriages: Frederick Hagenauer and the betrothal of Indigenous Western Australian women in colonial Victoria', *Journal of Aboriginal History*, vol. 34, 2010, pp. 35–54.

Kennedy, R., 'Stolen Generations testimony: trauma, historiography, and the question of "truth"', *Aboriginal History*, vol. 25, 2001.

Merrilees, D., Dix, W. C. et al., 'Aboriginal man in southwestern Australia', *Journal of the Royal Society of Western Australia*, vol. 56, parts 1 and 2, July 1973.

Mitchell, J., 'Maypoles and electric fences: centenary celebrations in 1950s Victoria', *Journal of the Royal Historical Society*, vol. 96, no. 2, June 2010.

Nettlebeck, A. & Foster, R., 'Commemorating foundation: a study in regional historical memory', *History Australia*, vol. 2, no. 3, 2010.

Powell, M. & Hesline, R., 'Making tribes? Constructing Aboriginal tribal identities in Sydney and coastal NSW from the early colonial period to the present', *Journal of the Royal Australian Historical Society*, vol. 96, no. 2, December 2010.

Read, P., A 'rape of the soul so profound', *Journal of Aboriginal History*, vol. 7, 1983, pp. 23–33.

Read, P., 'The Stolen Generations, the historian and the court room', *Aboriginal History*, 2002, vol. 26.

Reece, R., 'Inventing Aborigines', *Aboriginal History Journal*, vol. 11, 1987, p. 17.

Rowland, M. J., 'Return of the 'noble savage': misrepresenting the past, present and future', *Australian Aboriginal Studies*, no. 2, 2004.

Strong, R., 'The Reverend John Wollaston and colonial Christianity in Western Australia', *Journal of Religious History*, vol. 25, no. 3, October 2001.

Waterhouse, R., 'Locating the new social history: transnational historiography and Australian local history', *Journal of the Royal Australian Historical Society*, vol. 95, part 1, June 2009.

Published reports

Greenfield, P., *Report on the Excavation of Windemere Road Artefact Scatter, Albany, South West Australia*, Deep Woods Surveys (W.A.) Pty Ltd, Albany, 2007.

Information Respecting the Habits and Customs of the Aboriginal Inhabitants of Western Australia, Compiled from Various Sources, published by the Legislative Council by His Excellency's Command, Perth, 1871.

Lost Lands Report, Department of Indigenous Affairs, no authors given, 1997.

Websites

The Boyer Lectures (Stanner's 1968 lecture), ABC, http://www.abc.net.au/rn/boyers/stories/s9881711.htm (accessed 1/12/2008).

INDEX

first European contacts 46–7, 50
fishing technique 26
food shortages 125, 135–6
given alcohol by visitors and settlers 67–8,
    112, 137
group disputes and killings 39–40, 90, 115
infant mortality 146
infidelity 38
initiations 36–7
intergroup obligations 28
kinship divisions 38
kinship networks 21
low birth rates 146
maintaining traditions 135
marriages 36–9
meeting with d'Urville 68–9
meeting with Flinders 53, 62–4
meetings with King 66–8
mistreated by sealers 52, 75, 97, 137
mobility 25–6
moiety divisions 38
Moore on 20
odour 35, 94
Pidgin English 95
population 34
population decline 143–7
possessions 35–6
reaction to sealers 51–3
sacred sites 42
scarification 35
sealers' children 53, 137
seasonal divisions 25, 304
seasonal habits 26–8, 31, 135–6, 304
Shellam on 20
smoking 112
spelling of name 19
spirituality 41–4
thefts by 77–8
Tindale's groupings 19–21
traditional lands 7–8, 18, 21
venereal disease 137, 146
Yallepolle incident 78–9
men's rites 32, 36–7
Menzies, Archibald 50
Mermaid 65
Methodist Church 178
Michaelmas Island 73, 75–6

Middleton Bay 108, 175
Middleton Beach 265
Midgegooroo 138
Migo 138
Milroy, Jill 12
Mindam 233
Minnan 148–9, 195
missionaries 170, 286, 290
missions see also reserves
    Benedictine Mission, New Norcia 253
    Gnowangerup 288–91
    influence on Carrolup 284
    mission chapel 178
    Moravian Church 175
    United Aborigines Mission station 260
Moenang 43
Mokare
    absences 110
    alternative spellings 81
    death 110, 113
    family estate 32–3, 82, 99
    on first contacts with Europeans 61
    on group violence 40
    guide for Collie 33
    Kincannup man 22
    life changed by British 98
    portrait by de Sainson 82
    relationship with Barker 32, 61, 81, 84,
        89, 92, 99
    relationship with Collie 105, 110–11
    relationship with Europeans 84
    relationship with Nind 81
    spirituality 43
    statue 82–3
Mongers Lake 115
Monkbeelven 48
Moore, George Fletcher 20, 118–19
Moore River settlement 286, 290, 295
Moorelup 195
Moravian Church mission 175
Morgan, John 115, 117
Morley, John 118–19
Mount Adelaide 46
Mount Barker
    Aboriginal camp 245, 292–3
    campaign to exclude Aboriginal school
        children 292–4

www.ingramcontent.com/pod-product-compliance
Lightning Source LLC
Chambersburg PA
CBHW040146270326
41929CB00025B/3386